OF WIDOWS AND MEALS

OF WIDOWS AND MEALS

Communal Meals in the Book of Acts

Reta Halteman Finger

WILLIAM B. EERDMANS PUBLISHING COMPANY
GRAND RAPIDS, MICHIGAN / CAMBRIDGE, U.K.

Published 2007 by

Wm. B. Eerdmans Publishing Co.

2140 Oak Industrial Drive N.E., Grand Rapids, Michigan 49505 /

P.O. Box 163, Cambridge CB3 9PU U.K.

www.eerdmans.com

Printed in the United States of America

11 10 09 08 07   7 6 5 4 3 2 1

Library of Congress Cataloging-in-Publication Data

Finger, Reta Halteman, 1940-
    Of widows and meals: communal meals in the book of Acts /
    Reta Halteman Finger.
        p.   cm.
    Includes bibliographical references.
    ISBN 978-0-8028-3053-1 (pbk. : alk. paper)
    1. Bible. N.T. Acts — Criticism, interpretation, etc.
    2. Dinners and dining in the Bible.   I. Title.

    BS2625.6.D56F56   2007
    226.6′067 — dc22

                                        2006039041

The map of Jerusalem that appears in Chapter 5 originally appeared in the *Illustrated Bible Dictionary*, vol. 2, by J. D. Douglas (Nottingham, U.K.: Inter-Varsity Press, 1980). It is reprinted here with permission from Inter-Varsity Press.

The quotation appearing at the beginning of Chapter 7 is from "The Gift of the Whale: Community as Steward," an unpublished master's thesis by the Rev. Dr. James E. Roghair (Garrett-Evangelical Theological Seminary, Evanston, Illinois, 2000) and is used here by permission of the author.

Unless otherwise noted, the Scripture quotations in this publication are from the New Revised Standard Version of the Bible, copyright © 1989 by the Division of Christian Education of the National Council of Churches of Christ in the U.S.A., and used by permission.

Contents

CONTENTS

Introduction

The Lukan author of Acts claims that the first Christian believers shared property and met daily for a common meal amid holy celebration. Luke sees this as a continuation of Jesus' shared life with others, including his meals with many different kinds of people. The celebration of the Lord's Supper in the context of the agape meal tradition developed along this continuum. In time, the full meal shrank to symbolic morsels of bread and sips of wine in the Eucharist.

What was the cultural and economic reality of the earliest Jerusalem community? Is commensality a necessary aspect of church life today? In this book I strive to answer these questions and affirm commensality across cultural, racial, and gender barriers as an integral part of the gospel of Jesus.

The first chapter in Part I introduces the issue of communal meals embedded in a community of goods, while recognizing resistance to economic sharing in today's modern, individualist, capitalist societies. I lay out three interpretive presuppositions: (1) a recognition of the importance of social location for scriptural interpretation; (2) a sensitivity to poor people and the understanding that the poor of the Jerusalem community were not "the other" but the majority of the community; and (3) a sensitivity to women's perspectives and women's roles in community organization, particularly in the ancient Mediterranean culture.

Chapter Two traces the history of interpretation (in the West) of the two summaries on the Jerusalem community of goods in Acts 2:42-47 and

4:32-37. Representative commentators since Augustine demonstrate that these texts have been interpreted throughout church history in ways that betray numerous cultural and ideological biases against literal property-sharing and daily commensality.

Chapters Three and Four deal with the breakdown of the seamless whole that Luke portrays, where the Jerusalem community's shared life takes its most concrete form in daily meals which are sanctified by a bread-breaking ritual and which feed everyone so that none are in need. Chapter Three asks about the relationship between the community of goods and the daily (agape) meals mentioned in Acts 2:42, 46 and 6:1. Further, can these meals be linked to the Lord's Supper? Is there one meal tradition or two? In this chapter I compare traditional, historically oriented scholarship with more current redaction and literary criticism, and then assemble social, historical, and archeological evidence to demonstrate the long and close connection of communal agape meals with the Lord's Supper/Eucharist.

Chapter Four asks, What is the relationship of the Lord's Supper with caring for the poor? Again, I compare traditional scholarship with redaction criticism. Communion services in most churches today make no direct connection, but that was not always the case. Historical evidence shows that the original association lay in the daily communal meal that fed everyone across the economic spectrum. Later, however, the meal became a time to give alms for the poor (as "the other"), thus losing the boundary-breaking unity of its original ideal.

Chapters Five through Eight in Part II make use of social history, the social sciences, and archeology to attempt a reconstruction of the actual life context of the Jerusalem community. Chapter Five lays out in more general terms the hierarchical and oppressive nature of an advanced agrarian society like that ruled by the Roman Empire in the first century. Chapter Six focuses on the city of Jerusalem itself. One criticism of the proposed historical reality of the community in Acts is that it was only a community of consumption, not of production, and thus could not long survive. What were the unique aspects of Jerusalem as a commercial city which likely would have shaped and influenced the newly organized community of Jesus-followers? This material includes Jerusalem's geography, agricultural production, population, sources of wealth, urban occupations, housing, and meal settings in peasant family life.

Chapter Seven uses insights from cultural anthropology to discuss patronage, benefactions, honor/shame values, kinship structures, and almsgiving. These ancient Mediterranean values demonstrate how a "fictive kin-group" with shared possessions and daily common meals made spiritual, social, and economic sense for the Christian community in Jerusalem. Chapter Eight introduces Essene communal life as a model for the Jerusalem believers. Essenes had been living in various communal arrangements (the Qumran Covenanters were one alternative) for about 150 years before the birth of the church and seemed to be well-regarded by many Palestinians and other Jews. Though their theology and concepts of purity differed, Essene social behavior correlates well with the descriptions in Acts of shared possessions and common meals.

Part III brings in the social context of the meals referred to in Acts 2:42, 46 and 6:1. Chapter Nine discusses the symbolic role of food and commensality in the ancient world, from earlier times as reflected in the Hebrew Bible to meal practices in the Hellenistic world, as well as those of Pharisees and Essenes in the Jewish context. Chapter Ten traces the Christian origin of communal meals back to Jesus' practice of table fellowship with all classes of ritually clean and unclean Israelites, critiquing significant recent scholarship on this topic. Jesus proclaimed the nature of his kingdom through the meals he ate with all kinds of people, just as his disciples continued the practice after his resurrection.

The universal association of women with preparing and serving meals dominates Chapter Eleven. Though overlooked by most scholars, the presence of the Hellenist widows in Acts 6:1 provides a window into women's roles in the communal meals of the Jerusalem church. Here I supplement scholarship on women eating at public meals with anthropological analysis of peasant women's central roles in meal preparation and serving. This background, coupled with a discussion on the meaning and roles of widows in Greco-Roman and Jewish culture, suggests a quite different interpretive possibility for Acts 6:1-6. Were the neglected widows missing the ancient equivalent of Meals on Wheels in their lonely little huts — or were they losing out on the honorable female role of serving at the communal meals?

Part IV draws this material together in a visual layout and detailed exegesis of Acts 2:41-47 (Chapter Twelve) and 6:1-6 (Chapter Thirteen). If "the devil is in the details," a phrase-by-phrase analysis of the Greek text can reveal nuances overlooked when the larger socio-economic context is kept in view. When the translation of even one word shifts at a crucial place in the text, the whole picture can change.

eating together come at the table

After drawing final conclusions, in the last chapter I focus on contemporary examples of commensality within committed Christian communities. Though we cannot and would not wish to return to ancient agrarian society, the physical necessity of food and the social and symbolic aspects of eating with others are as critically important today as they were in the first century. Some groups of Christians today find creative ways to express their theology of the shared meals described in the Gospels and Acts. Adapting the words of Paul in 1 Corinthians 11:27, they "eat the bread and drink the cup of the Lord in a worthy manner" by sharing their meals and their lives with each other. They can serve as contemporary models, reminding the rest of us that the wine we sip and the morsel of bread we solemnly and privately swallow at the communion table hold but a tiny piece of the true meaning of eating "a supper of the Lord."

With Whom Do You Eat — and Where and When?
Sharing Possessions and Breaking Bread

The first-century Christian training manual, the *Didache,* includes a prayer for the bread-breaking that opens the common meal. The prayer begins with these words: "Just as this broken loaf was scattered over the hills as grain, and, having been gathered together, became one; in like fashion, may your church be gathered together from the ends of the earth into your kingdom."

Although the four chapters in Part I of this book hardly signify a sacred loaf of bread, the image of scattered portions brought together — and then broken — seems apt. After an introductory chapter in which I describe my approach, the other three chapters represent both scattering and gathering. Although I am arguing for the meals described in Acts as communal, sacred, and feeding all regardless of social status, I have broken the seamless whole apart and given each of these emphases their own chapter.

The communal meals of these early believers were embedded in a community of goods. So in Chapter Two I trace the history of interpretation of the texts in Acts 2:42-47 and 4:32-37 that describe this economic sharing.

But the meal itself, encompassing rituals of bread-breaking and wine-pouring, was split apart into agape meals, funerary meals, and a separate Eucharist. In fact, arguments abound over whether "communion," "Lord's Supper," "Eucharist," and "bread-breaking" mean the same thing or represent different practices. Chapter Three discusses these intricate relationships from various angles.

In Chapter Four I return to economic and sociological issues. When everyone eats meals in common, and all eat the same food together, there are no social divisions. But as soon as shared economic life is rejected because of impracticality (or for any other reason), higher and lower classes quickly develop. When actual, daily meals are separated from a ritual bread-and-wine ceremony, the poorest members do not get enough to eat. Under the best of circumstances, then, the more affluent give charity to the less affluent or destitute, patronage develops, and superior/inferior attitudes result.

So much for scattering. Unfortunately, the history of the church too often reflects the symbolic unity of Jesus' inclusive meals refracted into many broken pieces scattered over hillsides, each carrying only part of the total meaning. In these three chapters (Two to Four) I show scholars struggling with these various meanings and how to relate them to their own cultural contexts.

On the other hand, in these same three chapters I have tried to gather together these various comments scattered throughout Western Christian scholarship (mostly since the Reformation) and from various social and political locations. Through scholars' dialogue with each other, and through advances in archeology, literary analysis, and the social sciences, it is my hope that we can get a better picture of the profound social, spiritual, and physical meaning of eating meals together in the church of Jesus Christ.

Chapter One

Stating the Question: A Middle-Class Bias against Communal Sharing?

While studying the book of James in a New Testament course at Messiah College, I asked my students to each do a service project, such as helping at a soup kitchen in the nearby city of Harrisburg, Pennsylvania. In her report, one student commented on the food she helped serve to the families and various homeless people who showed up at the meal. "The food looked pretty good," she said. "I could have eaten it myself — if it hadn't been a soup kitchen."

R. H. Finger

Just after the account of Peter's Pentecost sermon in Acts 2, after "about 3,000 persons were added" to the community of Jesus-believers, Luke summarizes the situation in this way (my translation):

> 41They [those who repented and were baptized] welcomed his [Peter's] message, were baptized, and about 3,000 persons were added in that day.
> 42They were continuing faithfully in the teachings of the apostles and in the communal sharing, in the breaking of the bread and in the prayers.
> 43Awe was coming to every soul, and many wonders and signs were happening through the apostles. 44And all the believers were together and were sharing everything 45and were selling possessions and prop-

erty and were distributing them to all according as any were having need.

46Day by day, continuing steadfastly with one mind, they were in the temple, breaking bread by households, sharing food in great gladness and generosity of heart, 47praising God, and having favor with all the people. And day by day the Lord was adding to their whole group those who were being saved.

According to this text, the believers shared possessions and ate a common meal together every day. A second reference to daily meal tables comes in Acts 6:1-6, though the setting and the literary form of the text are different. Here a problem has arisen in community organizing. There are now two ethnic groups, and the Hellenists complain against the Hebrews that their widows are being overlooked in the daily service of tables. Steps are taken in verses 2 to 6, not to discontinue the practice, but to share the workload and to bring about justice.

Personal Roots in Communal Life

I must have been in junior high when I first heard a sermon on the above text — the only sermon I can recall from my childhood. Visiting my grandparents' church one Sunday, I heard their preacher expound on the texts in Acts 2 and 4 describing how the earliest Christian community in Jerusalem shared everything in common.

My grandparents' congregation was 1950s conservative Mennonite, and by today's American middle-class standards they lived quite simply: they were hard-working farmers or small business people, with little formal education beyond grade school. Though Mennonites were accustomed to interpreting biblical texts quite literally, in this case the minister made an exception. The texts on communal sharing should *not* be applied literally. In fact, he said, they describe a brief experiment that was impractical and eventually failed. The lesson was that we should not make the same mistake.

Why did I remember that sermon from my youth and forget the others? Perhaps I was so used to hearing how we *should* obey the Bible that I was shocked to hear that we *shouldn't!*

In the coming years this admonition became the path of least resistance, as Mennonites from previously tight-knit communities sought higher education, abandoned dress regulations, and moved more and more into mainstream culture. Many now have lifestyles largely indistinguishable from the lifestyles of individualism, consumerism, and market capitalism that characterize American society today.

I say "largely" but not entirely. The Anabaptists' underground subsistence on the margins of European society for two hundred years and the struggle to carve out communities in the New World are bred too deeply in our bones for us to entirely forsake a shared life. My denomination has never practiced a strict community of goods, as do the Hutterites. Yet in our literal interpretations of the Bible there is a long tradition of sharing because of the church's calling to relate as "one body" (1 Cor. 12:13), partakers of one bread (1 Cor. 10:7), and having one God and one Lord (Eph. 4).[1] Such communal attitudes have led to very concrete actions, even today: sharing potluck meals in our churches; establishing several long-term intentional communities; traveling with the Mennonite-Your-Way Directory instead of motels; setting up alternate systems of social welfare, health care, and mental-health care (Mennonite Mutual Aid); organizing worldwide projects of relief and development (Mennonite Central Committee); sponsoring annual quilt auctions/folk festivals (MCC Relief Sales) in various areas of North America; arranging "Civilian Public Service" for conscientious objectors to war; helping victims of natural disasters (Mennonite Disaster Service); encouraging micro-economics in Third World countries (Mennonite Economic Development Association); and providing many service opportunities around the world for our youth.

My roots in a more communal lifestyle have led me back to the account in Acts of the earliest social practices of the Jesus movement in Jerusalem. Here among Luke's interpreters lies a wide diversity of views, because such intense sharing has sounded either impractical or unrealistic and utopian to most commentators within the history of Christian tradition. A literal sharing of possessions, as Luke describes, cuts across the grain of Western capitalist assumptions and the sacred notion of private property. Was this organizational structure the result of expectations of an imminent apocalypse, and thus impractical and short-lived? Did it eventually impoverish the Jerusalem church? Or was Luke using these terms to symbolize a spiritual unity among the first believers? Or was he idealizing

---

1. Menno Simons, "A Humble and Christian Justification and Replication," in *The Complete Works of Menno Simons*, vol. 2 (Elkhart, Ind.: John F. Funk & Brother, 1871), p. 309.

the origins of the church, using Greek utopian concepts and terminology to present a golden age that never actually happened? The current interest in the socio-economic setting of the New Testament documents impels me to take a new look at these texts.

I am especially interested in the believers' practice of commensality,[2] since in 2:42 they were as devoted to the breaking of bread as they were to the other aspects of their new life together. Indeed, eating together in the household appears to be one of the major ways in which they shared their common life. As long as all were welcomed to the table as members of the household, Luke could declare in 4:34, "there was not a needy person among them." Commensality is also significant because of its relationship to the Lord's Supper/Eucharist, which became a central ritual of the church. What is the connection between the two? And what is lost when "women's work" of preparing food and showing hospitality in the household morphs by the fourth century into a ritual with the bare symbols of bread and wine given only by authorized male priests in a public building?

Interpretive Presuppositions

There are three presuppositions I consciously bring to this study that provide a frame of reference for how I will approach communal meals in Acts.

Recognizing the Importance of Social Location

Elisabeth Schüssler Fiorenza challenged the concept that "the true exegete is expected to examine all the material in a truly dispassionate manner in order to study the past 'for its own sake' and to find out what actually happened."[3] Instead, we must always exercise a "hermeneutic of suspicion" about the vested interests, unconscious or otherwise, of both the interpreter and the text itself. For Schüssler Fiorenza, the locus of authority lies not in the biblical text but in women's experience. Since then, postmodernism has continued to affirm this experience-centered perspective.

---

2. I am using *commensality* in its ordinary sense of "eating at the same table."

3. Elisabeth Schüssler Fiorenza, *Bread Not Stone: The Challenge of Feminist Biblical Interpretation* (Boston: Beacon Press, 1984), p. 97.

I prefer David Scholer's adaptation of her principle. He commends her for "calling attention to the fact that we have too often denied that our own experience is tied deeply to how we interpret the text." Although he believes that the locus of authority is in the text, he also believes that "it is never experienced anywhere but in actual individuals and communities. These individuals and communities are the only interpreters. . . . All interpretation is socially located, individually skewed, and ecclesiastically and theologically conditioned." Making the same claim about the biblical texts themselves, Scholer continues, "We also come to see that the persons who wrote the biblical texts were also socially located, individually skewed, and theologically conditioned."[4]

This is an important principle, to which my following points are all related. Here I would call attention to the skepticism or even the hostility many interpreters have shown toward the possibility that early Christians did successfully share a community of goods and daily commensality in their households. I suggest that some of this reaction is due to their own social locations in a different culture, class, and time. I will, of course, approach the text from my own social location as an Anabaptist Mennonite.

Through the Eyes of the Poor

Many of my instincts in text interpretation cannot arise out of a present experience of poverty. However, income in my lower-class family of origin was always precarious, and middle-class privileges like an occasional restaurant meal or weekend trip were far beyond our reach. Yet within my extended family and larger community, I always felt rich in relationships and a sense of belonging. These experiences affect my point of view as I examine issues of wealth and poverty that lie behind these texts in Acts 2 and 6.

My own theology of wealth and poverty was strongly influenced by reading, over many years, *The Other Side* and *Sojourners* magazines, with their emphasis on "peace and justice," especially as these issues related to race relations, poverty, and communal life. These influences resulted in our family's move to an African-American neighborhood in Chicago in

4. David M. Scholer, "How Can Divine Revelation Be So Human?" *Daughters of Sarah* 15 (May/June 1989): 12.

1976, with its share of crime, unemployment, drugs, and despair. From the efforts of an intentional community with whom we related in the neighborhood, a thriving church and community center were born — Circle Urban Ministries and Rock of Our Salvation Church. One reads the Bible in a different way after living in a mixed-class black urban community.

Not long before that, Latin American liberation theology began taking concrete shape among the poor in Central and South America. The Second General Assembly of the Latin American Bishops' Council (CELAM), which was held in Medellín, Columbia, in 1968, confirmed the Roman Catholic Church's three "options" or choices: for the socioeconomically poor, for their integral liberation, and for the base church communities.[5] This meant that the starting point for understanding theology and social and historical reality was to be from the perspective of the underclasses. Rather than beginning from the top down, with its paternalistic "helping" mentality, this perspective would begin from the grass roots up to the rest of society. The base communities that developed as a result of this resolution learned how they as poor people could live in solidarity, could study the Bible together, and could take more control over their own lives than they ever previously realized.

Of course, when poor people study the Bible (and many Catholics had not previously been encouraged to use the Bible in private study), they have different ways of looking at it than do middle-class people for whom economic survival is not in question. Issues of power, faith, and money come together in different ways. Rosemary Ruether has described the impact this rediscovery of the Bible has had on those in these base communities:

> They read the Bible much as medieval and Reformation radicals read it, as a critical and subversive document. They find in it a God who sides with the poor and with others despised by society; who, at the same time, confronts the social and religious institutions that are the tools of injustice.[6]

Liberation theology thus represents a break from a more academic form of theology. The first priority must be living with and being committed to the

5. Leonardo Boff, *Faith on the Edge: Religion and Marginalized Existence* (San Francisco: Harper & Row, 1989), p. 13.
6. Rosemary Ruether, "Basic Christian Communities: Renewal at the Roots," *Christianity and Crisis* 41 (1981): 235.

poor and their struggle for liberation. But even the academic tools are different, as Teresa Whalen points out: "Whereas in the past, philosophy was used as an aid to theology (e.g., Aquinas' use of Aristotle), liberation theology is using the social sciences — more specifically, sociology and political science."[7]

The fact is, however, that most scholars who have expounded on communal life in the early chapters of Acts have not come from these underclasses but are usually immersed in middle-class or upper-middle-class Western society. So often from this perspective, the poor and lower classes are seen as "the other" — either the "deserving poor," to whom we should give alms, or the shiftless and lazy who just aren't working hard enough. Today, as the gap between rich and poor seems to grow ever wider in our country and in our world, there is as great a need as ever to challenge colonialism, paternalism, and government policies that discriminate against those with less power and wealth.

Fortunately, in the last twenty-five or thirty years, a great deal of energy has been expended in New Testament studies on understanding the cultures of the Mediterranean world where Jesus lived and where Christianity took root. The disciplines of sociology, anthropology, and archeology are brought to bear on these studies, giving us a better understanding of what it was like to be part of the large majority of people living at subsistence level in an agrarian society. For example, feminist New Testament scholar Luise Schottroff has brought an awareness of economic and political realities, especially for Palestinian women, into her work. The following represents the kind of analysis that provides insight for my own study:

> Acts 2:45; 4:34, 37; and 5:1f presuppose that money had to be raised in order to provide for all members of the original congregation in Jerusalem. The money derived from the sale of fields or houses. Had those fields been large enough that, by its own labor, the congregation could have grown sufficient food to make up for its lack, there would have been no reason to sell them. Acts 2:45 and the other verses reflect an economic situation comparable to that of Matthew 20:1-16 [Parable of the Laborers in the Vineyard] . . . ; either there are no more landholdings or the land owned is too small to supply the needs of the

7. Teresa Whalen, *The Authentic Doctrine of the Eucharist* (Kansas City, Mo.: Sheed & Ward, 1993), p. 86.

people. What land remains must be sold so that provisions can be bought. And this means that the condition of grinding poverty escalates, becoming ever more the rule.[8]

Issues of wealth and poverty have often been pushed to the margins of theology in Western scholarship. Yet economics must be a central issue as we examine the possibility of daily commensality in the context of a community of goods described in Acts 2 and 6. We must look through the eyes of the poor in order to find additional insight into the question of communal meals in the earliest church in Jerusalem.

Through the Eyes of Women

In ancient Mediterranean culture, even more than ours, women were responsible for preparing and serving meals. What does the significance of table fellowship as a central ritual in the believing community say about women and their roles in the early church? Did women's work of meal preparation and serving elevate their status in the church, since Jesus has stated in Luke 22:27 that his role was to serve at table, not to be served? What women's story lies behind the Hellenist/Hebrew conflict of Acts 6:1? How might it relate to the women disciples in Luke 8:1-3 who had already been providing these services for the Jesus community?

As a feminist, I must examine these texts with an eye for what is going on underneath them. The recognition that the biblical texts arise from a patriarchal society was first clearly articulated for me by Elisabeth Schüssler Fiorenza in her groundbreaking work *In Memory of Her.*[9] Furthermore, the New Testament writers themselves wrote generally from a male perspective. Says Schüssler Fiorenza,

> Since the early Christian communities and authors lived in a predominantly patriarchal world and participated in its mentality, it is likely that the scarcity of information about women is conditioned by the androcentric traditioning and redaction of the early Christian au-

8. Luise Schottroff, *Lydia's Impatient Sisters: A Feminist Social History of Early Christianity* (Louisville: Westminster John Knox Press, 1995), p. 97.

9. Elisabeth Schüssler Fiorenza, *In Memory of Her: A Feminist Theological Reconstruction of Christian Origins* (New York: Crossroad, 1983).

thors. This applies particularly to the Gospels and Acts, since these were written toward the end of the first century. Many of the traditions and information about the activities of women in early Christianity are probably irretrievable because the androcentric selection or redaction process saw these either as unimportant or as threatening.[10]

While I do not fully share Schüssler Fiorenza's attitude toward the Lukan writings, it is clear to me that there is an untold women's story behind the widows' complaint in Acts 6:1. Luke has given us only the public, and therefore male, perspective on it.

Related to this is male-oriented language itself, both Greek and English. Proper translations must be done to clarify in many cases that women *were* there, even when they are hidden behind masculine language. Schottroff reflects at length on how many texts, even though couched in androcentric language, are critical of patriarchy.[11]

Throughout this study I will be seeking to understand and look behind both androcentric texts and androcentric interpretations of these texts, suggesting alternate ways of reconstructing the situation as it might have happened.

But before we look for women's roles in our texts, we must first deal with a history of (mostly male) reactions to Luke's account of the Jerusalem Jesus-community, with its shared economic lifestyle.

---

10. Schüssler Fiorenza, *In Memory of Her*, p. 49.
11. Schottroff, *Lydia's Impatient Sisters*, Part III: "The Critique of Patriarchy and the Power to Become a New Being," pp. 119-223.

Chapter 2

Economic Sharing in Acts?
A History of (Mis)Interpretation

*The apostles . . . did not demand, as do our insane peasants in their rag-
ing, that the goods of others . . . should be common, but only their own
goods.*

Martin Luther

Common sharing . . . must be held in check.

John Calvin

*Where [communal sharing] is not the case it is a blemish upon the
Church and ought verily to be corrected.*

Peter Rideman, Hutterite

How have the Acts texts on a shared community of goods been interpreted
in later centuries and cultural situations? This chapter surveys representative viewpoints throughout Western church history, primarily since the
Reformation.[1] I assert that attitudes toward socioeconomic texts such as

---

1. To compare the history of Eastern Orthodox, Coptic, or African Christian interpretations with this survey would be fascinating but beyond the scope of this book. My interest
here is limited to the major interpretive influences upon North American (and, to a certain

these will be significantly more influenced by factors other than herme-
neutical principles or other objective criteria. In other words, if it is not in
the economic, political, or theological interests of an interpreter or an interpretive community to share material goods (beyond alms-giving), they
will find different ways to explain these texts.

One may further note, however, that the disciplines of biblical studies and theology have not traditionally interacted with economics (or any
of the sciences or social sciences, for that matter). Biblical commentators
who are not personally and consciously suffering under unjust economic
structures rarely express awareness of them, much less critique them or
propose creative systemic changes.

Pre-Reformation Understandings

After Christianity became a state religion, the orthodox church assumed
the relevance and practicality of the community-of-goods texts — but only
as a model for monastic life. Only celibate monks and nuns were thought to
be able to live out the "counsels of perfection"; ordinary laypeople lived in
the world and were subject to less stringent standards of moral life.[2]

By 360 c.e. groups of men and women in monasteries in Egypt and
Syria were physically separated from the life of the parish church and congregation, worshiping and living by their own rules.[3] In the West, John
Cassian founded two monasteries in Marseilles in Gaul, one for women
and one for men, around 415. His writings, the *Institutes* and *Conferences,*
give the classic expression to the understanding that monks were the successors to the original Christian community in Jerusalem.[4]

---

extent, European) churches today. A similar version of this chapter was published in the
Mennonite Weekly Review 78, no. 2 (April 2004): 235-70.

2. Justo L. González, *Faith and Wealth: A History of Early Christian Ideas on the Origin, Significance, and Use of Money* (San Francisco: HarperSanFrancisco, 1990), p. 231.

3. Owen Chadwick, *John Cassian* (Cambridge: Cambridge University Press, 1968),
p. 1; Augustine, *De Opere Monachorum* 25; *De Sancta Virginitate* 45. See also Athanasius, *De
Vita Antonii* 2; Jerome, *Epistulae* 58:4; 130:14; *Regula Magistri* 82:20-21; 87:14; Benedict, *Rule,*
chs. 33, 34, 57.

4. John Cassian, *Institutes* 2.5; *Conferences* 18.5. In Cassian's Eighteenth Conference,
he struggles with the problem that troubled the monastic movement for its first two hundred years: whether living as a hermit was a higher way than living in a celibate community.
In theory, Cassian accepted the common Egyptian view that the hermit life was superior, but

Many other monastic writings cite the summaries in Acts 2 and 4 as their legitimation for sharing the common life. Augustine, for example, assumes that it is only monks and nuns who follow the common life described in Acts 2 and 4.[5] Augustine did not imagine any other sharing of goods or common life apart from monasticism.

Throughout pre-Reformation history, various lay groups attempted to live what they called an apostolic life. Some, like the Humiliati in Italy, the Waldensians in France, the Beguines in the Low Countries, and, later, the Beghards and Brethren of the Common Life in Germany and the Netherlands, encountered resistance from the hierarchy or conservative members of the clergy.[6] Though not cloistered, they did take vows of celibacy and some kind of voluntary poverty. But within the established church no model existed for families to share a community of goods.

Reformation Attitudes toward a Community of Goods

The interpretations of Luther and Calvin must be seen in the context of a sixteenth-century European society in turmoil. Although some monasteries and convents reflected the ideals of community, morality in other male monasteries had seriously deteriorated, and some religious orders of the church had themselves become wealthy at the expense of ordinary citizens. Between 15 to 30 percent of the urban population of that period was homeless or hungry, dependent on alms for survival.[7]

At the same time, social movements emphasizing more rights for the underclasses were threatening the stability of the social order. In Germany in 1524 and 1525, Luther's early teachings had sparked a mass rebellion of

---

in practice he discouraged monks who wanted to become hermits. He thought only perfect men should go into the wilderness, and he saw himself as a beginner. See Chadwick, *John Cassian*, p. 54.

5. Augustine, *De Opere Monachorum* 25; *De Sancta Virginitate* 45. See also Athanasius, *De Vita Antonii* 2; Jerome, *Epistulae* 58:4; 130:14; *Regula Magistri* 82:20-21; 87:14-15; Benedict, *Rule*, ch. 33, 34, 57.

6. Thomas P. Rausch, S.J., *Radical Christian Communities* (Collegeville, Minn.: Liturgical Press, 1990), pp. 66-71.

7. Preserved Smith, *The Age of the Reformation* (New York: Holt, 1920), pp. 558-59, quoted in the introduction to Martin Luther's "Ordinance of a Common Chest" (1523) in *Luther's Works*, American edition, ed. Helmut T. Lehmann, vol. 53 of *The Christian in Society*, 2d ed., ed. Walther I. Brandt (Philadelphia: Muhlenberg Press, 1962), p. 161.

peasants against the ever-increasing dues and services demanded by their princes. Anabaptists, believing church and state should be separate, refused to ally themselves with either Catholics or Protestants. Their congregations developed their own systems of communal sharing, thus posing another threat to the social order.

Martin Luther

Martin Luther did not specifically address the relevant passages in Acts until a sermon he delivered in 1538. However, his "Ordinance of a Common Chest" (1523) proposed how the wealth of monasteries taken over by the government should be dispersed. After doing justice to those who chose to stay and those who chose to leave, he recommended that the government should "devote all the remaining property to the common fund of a common chest, out of which gifts and loans could be made in Christian love to all the needy in the land."[8]

In 1526 Luther's "German Mass and Order of Worship" discussed three kinds of worship, the third service representing an "evangelical order" in which serious Christians would meet in homes to pray, read, baptize, "receive the sacrament," discipline each other, and solicit gifts for the poor.[9] Though Luther does not quote Acts 2 and 4, the picture he creates is not unlike Luke's description of the early church.

But by 1538, when Luther did preach a sermon on Acts 2:44, he no longer spoke of the "third way," since he realized few people would follow him on it.[10] As Hans-Joachim Kraus puts it, "His cautious impulses induced him finally to let fall the concrete practices about worship which he had expressly stated in the 'German Mass' that serious Christians ought to do."[11] However, he believed that the early church did share a community of goods *(communio bonorum)* and that it would be impossible to live that way ex-

---

8. Luther, "Ordinance of a Common Chest," p. 172.

9. Martin Luther, "The German Mass and Order of Service," in *Luther's Works*, vol. 53, pp. 63-64.

10. Martin Luther, "Predigt am Mittwoch nach Pfingsten," June 12, 1538. *Predigten des Jahres 1538*. Martin Luthers Werke: Kritische Gesamtausgabe. Vol. 46 (Herman Böhlaus: Weimar Nachfolger, 1912, 1967), pp. 428-32.

11. Hans-Joachim Kraus, "Aktualität des 'Urchristlichen Kommunismus'?" in *Freispruch und Freiheit* (Munich: Christian Kaiser Verlag, 1973), p. 309, my translation.

cept by a "work of the Holy Spirit." But this sermon made few specific applications. Luther expressed "no requirement, no guiding model for a new order of society, no law to follow, but only the 'worship of love.'"[12]

But even if communal sharing was the "work of the Holy Spirit," Luther felt compelled to discourage movements in his own day that struggled for greater equality of rights and material wealth. He first sympathized with the demands of the peasants, but when the movement became more violent, he urged the princes to subdue it by any bloody means necessary. In "Against the Thieving and Murdering Mobs of Peasants" (1525), Luther writes, "The gospel does not make goods common, except in the case of those who, of their own free will, do what the apostles and disciples did in Acts 4:32-37. They did not demand, as do our insane peasants in their raging, that the goods of others . . . should be common, but only their own goods."[13] Luther turned increasingly to established authority to maintain the peace and order,[14] ignoring the context of Acts 4 in which the apostles were constantly challenging the authority of the religious and political leaders.

Luther did believe in an original community of goods in Jerusalem, and his early writings demonstrate a wistful longing to follow their practice. But he could not see beyond the traditional marriage of church and state and thus adjusted his theology accordingly. By aligning himself with the state and not with the peasants, Luther remained in his social class and did not exhibit solidarity with the poor. Unlike the church in Acts 4:34, in his church there were many needy persons indeed.

John Calvin

In his commentary on Acts, Calvin takes pains to interpret 2:44 properly, "on account of fanatical spirits who devise a *koinonia* of goods whereby all civil order is overturned."[15] He allows that Luke could mean that the be-

---

12. Kraus, "Aktualität des 'Urchristlichen Kommunismus'?" p. 308.

13. Martin Luther, "Against the Thieving and Murdering Mobs of Peasants," in *The Christian in Society,* vol. 46, *Luther's Works,* p. 51.

14. Harold J. Grimm, *The Reformation Era, 1500-1600* (London: Macmillan, 1965), p. 176.

15. John Calvin, *The Acts of the Apostles 1–13,* Calvin's Commentaries, trans. John W. Fraser and W. J. G. McDonald, ed. David W. Torrance and Thomas F. Torrance (London: Oliver & Boyd, 1965), p. 87.

lievers lived together in the same place, but he prefers to see it simply as their "agreement" together. Their liberality was the result of this harmony, in that the rich sold goods to help the poor.

Calvin notes two extremes concerning giving. "For many on a pretext of civil order conceal what they possess and defraud the poor, thinking that they are doubly righteous so long as they do not seize another man's goods. Others are carried away to the opposite error, desiring to have everything mingled together."[16] Here he especially criticizes the Anabaptists because "they thought there was no Church unless all men's goods were heaped up together and everyone took therefrom as they chose."[17] Because of his own fear of the breakdown of social order, Calvin recommends that "common sharing . . . must be held in check."[18]

Calvin quotes the Pythagorean proverb that says "All things are common among friends" to prove that, since surely the Pythagoreans didn't hold houses or wives in common, "this community of goods of which Luke speaks does not do away with household government." Rather, they "brought forth their goods and held them in common only with the object of relieving immediate necessity."[19] Here Calvin criticizes monks in wealthy cloisters who technically own nothing but who "have no other interest in the community of goods than seeing that they are fully and luxuriously provided for, although the whole world should starve."[20]

Calvin regards Barnabas as an exception when it came to sharing wealth in the Jerusalem community — "most likely there were many who made no inroads upon their possessions"[21] — revealing his projection of sixteenth-century European social and economic structure back into first-century Palestine. He tacitly assumes that the majority of Jerusalem believers owned land and other private property as did those in his own class.

In the *Institutes* (IV, 1, 3) Calvin makes an analogy between the inequality of material possessions and the diversity of gifts given by the Spirit. "The communion of saints," he says, promotes sharing "whatever benefits God confers upon them." He goes on to say,

16. Calvin, *The Acts of the Apostles 1–13*, p. 88.
17. Calvin, *The Acts of the Apostles 1–13*, p. 87.
18. Calvin, *The Acts of the Apostles 1–13*, p. 88.
19. Calvin, *The Acts of the Apostles 1–13*, p. 88.
20. Calvin, *The Acts of the Apostles 1–13*, p. 88.
21. Calvin, *The Acts of the Apostles 1–13*, p. 129.

> This does not, however, rule out diversity of graces, inasmuch as we know the gifts of the Spirit are variously distributed. Nor is civil order disturbed, which allows each individual to own his private possessions, since it is necessary to keep peace among men that the ownership of property should be distinct and personal among them. But a community is affirmed, such as Luke describes, in which the heart and soul of the multitude of believers are one [Acts 4:32].[22]

Calvin thus assumes that the hierarchical, oppressive socio-economic order of his day is God-given. Poor people should accept their lot as ordained by the Spirit, since this is the only way to preserve social order.

Both Luther and Calvin conformed their biblical interpretation of the early chapters of Acts to a society where everyone was nominally Christian. They wanted to reform the church while maintaining the socio-economic status quo. Giving alms to help the needy and to relieve some of the worst cases of hunger and homelessness helped to calm feelings of social unrest. The views of these reformers shaped Protestant orthodoxy for centuries to come and often adversely affected religious groups who more literally applied the economic sharing described in Acts 2:42-47 and 4:32-37 to their own communities.

The Radical Reformation and the Community of Goods

The Anabaptists

Anabaptists are considered part of the "Radical Reformation" of the sixteenth century because their way of life threatened both Catholics and Protestants alike. Not only their communal sharing but also their belief in the separation of church and state symbolized by voluntary adult baptism struck supporters of the existing social order as peculiar. Though the Anabaptists' tendency toward literal interpretation of the New Testament emphasized intentional community, persecution from both Catholics and Protestants also demanded sharing possessions and help of every sort in order to survive.

Anabaptist movements seem to have sprung up in several areas of

22. John Calvin, *Institutes of the Christian Religion*, Library of Christian Classics, vols. 20-21, ed. John T. McNeill, trans. Ford Lewis Battles (Philadelphia: Westminster Press, 1960), pp. 1014-16.

Europe around the same time: in Zurich, Switzerland; in southern Germany under Hans Hut; and in the Netherlands, where it won mass support as nowhere else.[23] Menno Simons, the former Roman Catholic priest who later became the leader of the Anabaptist movement in Holland, based the group's sense of community on being one body (1 Cor. 12:13), partakers of one bread (1 Cor. 10:17), and having one God and one Lord (Eph. 4). He did, however, explain that this oneness had very concrete results. Like Acts 4:34, Menno asserted that Anabaptists "receive the wretched" and "do not suffer a beggar among them." Though many fathers and mothers were "killed with fire, water, and sword . . . and the times are hard; nevertheless none of the pious nor the children left behind by the pious, who are willing to adapt themselves among us, have had to beg."[24] Rather than calling for or demanding a common purse, Anabaptists emphasized stewardship and the radical sharing of material goods, first with fellow believers but on many occasions with their enemies and persecutors as well.

Most Anabaptists saw the εἶχον ἅπαντα κοινά ("having all things common") of Acts 2:44 not as a special commandment of Christ, but rather as a necessary and short-lived adjustment to the needs of the situation in Jerusalem. The Swiss Conrad Grebel specifically protested the charge that he taught "that no one should be interested in his possessions."[25] Felix Manz, first Anabaptist martyr in Zurich (1525), declared that he understood "community of goods" to mean a willingness to help those in need.[26] Menno Simons vigorously denied the charge that Anabaptists practiced a community of goods:

> For although we know that the apostolic church had this practice in
> the beginning, as can be seen in the Acts of the Apostles, nevertheless
> we note from their epistles that it disappeared in their time . . . and was

23. James M. Stayer, Werner O. Packull, and Klaus Deppermann, "From Monogenesis to Polygenesis: The Historical Discussion of Anabaptist Origins," *Mennonite Quarterly Review* 46 (April 1975): 83-121.

24. Menno Simons, "A Humble and Christian Justification and Replication," in *The Complete Writings of Menno Simons*, ed. John C. Wenger, vol. 2, trans. Leonard Verduin (Scottdale, Pa.: Herald Press, 1956), p. 309.

25. Harold S. Bender, *Conrad Grebel, c. 1498-1526: The Founder of the Swiss Brethren Sometimes Called Anabaptists* (Scottdale, Pa.: Herald Press, 1950, 1971), pp. 159, 205.

26. Robert Friedman, "Community of Goods," in *The Mennonite Encyclopedia*, ed. C. Henry Smith, Harold S. Bender, Cornelius Krahn, and Melvin Gingerich (Scottdale, Pa.: Scottdale Publishing House, 1969, 1982), p. 658.

no longer practiced. Since we do not find it a permanent practice with the apostles . . . we have not taught or practiced community of goods, but we urge earnestly and zealously to practice liberal giving, love, and mercy, as the apostolic writings teach. . . . And even if we had taught and practiced community of goods, as we are falsely accused of doing, we would still not be doing otherwise than the holy apostles . . . themselves did in the former church at Jerusalem.[27]

Why this spirited denial of communalism? The major reason has political, not exegetical, roots. By the early 1530s, Anabaptists had broken apart into pacifist and militant wings, the latter represented by the Münsterite experiment of 1534-1535 in northern Germany. In Münster, an apocalyptic sect taught the right of true believers to destroy those who would not accept their message of rebirth.[28] Rather than modeling their movement on the pattern of the early church, as pacifist Anabaptists were doing, they took the Old Testament as their model and saw themselves as the Israelites in exodus from Egypt.

One of the leaders, John Mathijs, dictated a form of communalism based on his interpretation of Acts 2 and 4. Money, food, and real property were declared to be common, although householders were allowed to continue using what was theirs. To show compliance, doors of houses had to be left open day and night.[29] After Mathijs was killed in a skirmish, John Beukels took over leadership and introduced polygamy, partly to emulate Old Testament patriarchs, and partly because the male population was being decimated in the fighting.[30]

Since then, Münster has been used as a negative example of what can happen when the communal sharing described in Acts 2 and 4 is practiced literally. Luke T. Johnson, for instance, maintains that events like the Münster experiment and the 1978 massacre in Guyana under Jim Jones are the logical results of a community of goods because the practice encourages loss of individuality, greater social control, and the growth of authoritarianism.[31]

27. Menno Simons, quoted in Friedman, "Community of Goods," p. 659.

28. George Huntston Williams, *The Radical Reformation* (Philadelphia: Westminster Press, 1962), pp. 362-86.

29. Williams, *The Radical Reformation*, p. 370.

30. Williams, *The Radical Reformation*, p. 372.

31. Luke T. Johnson, *Sharing Possessions: Mandate and Symbol of Faith* (Philadelphia: Fortress Press, 1981), pp. 118-24.

The Mennonites and the Amish have never practiced a literal community of goods. Yet their attitude of sharing enabled them to survive persecution for two centuries in Europe and to assist each other in establishing close-knit communities in Pennsylvania beginning in the early eighteenth century.[32] After both World Wars, North American Mennonites and Amish helped many of their counterparts in Germany and Russia escape intolerable political situations and settle in Paraguay and Canada.

The Hutterites

The Hutterites began as part of the Anabaptist movement of the early sixteenth century. For over 450 years they have been practicing a full community of goods, family-style. They are the only example in Western history of a noncelibate group that has successfully carried on this practice for so long a time. The Hutterites (named after their first leader, Jacob Hutter) flourished during the sixteenth century in Moravia and Slovakia under the protection of the nobles. By the late sixteenth century, there were about a hundred Hutterite farm colonies, with twenty thousand to thirty thousand members.[33]

The primary statement of early Hutterite faith is Peter Rideman's *Account of Our Religion, Doctrine, and Faith,* first published in 1565.[34] Rideman argues that just as God has given all material as well as spiritual gifts to share, so these gifts are to be shared with the whole body. God's entire created order is designed for all things to be common, and only human sinfulness has led to private property.[35] Needed renewal was found in the early church. "For this reason the Holy Spirit also at the beginning of the Church began such community right gloriously again, so that none said that aught of the things that he possessed was his own, but they had all

32. See especially "Part Three: Historical Case Studies," in *Building Communities of Compassion: Mennonite Mutual Aid in Theory and Practice,* ed. Willard Swartley and Donald B. Kraybill (Scottdale, Pa.: Herald Press, 1998), pp. 103-70.

33. Robert Friedman, "Hutterian Brethren," *Mennonite Encyclopedia,* vol. 2, pp. 854-857.

34. Peter Rideman, *Confession of Faith: Account of Our Religion, Doctrine, and Faith* (Rifton, N.Y.: Plough Publishing House, 1970).

35. Rideman, *Confession of Faith,* p. 88.

things in common (Acts 2:44-45; 4:32-37)."[36] The Apostle Paul supported such communal sharing, and "where this is not the case it is a blemish upon the Church and ought verily to be corrected."[37]

For Hutterites then and now, the texts on community in Acts 2 and 4 are a scriptural witness that a literal community of goods was a historical reality in the early church and therefore should be practiced today.

Reformation and post-Reformation Europe as a whole has not shown much toleration for groups practicing communal sharing in some form on the economic and material level.[38] Consequently, groups who used Acts 2 and 4 to apply a communal lifestyle have been marginalized and have had little influence on mainstream Protestant orthodoxy. The high commitment demanded cannot be realized in state churches full of nominal Christians.

The Development of Historical Criticism in Europe

Two movements during the nineteenth century left their imprint upon the interpretation of the community of goods described in Acts: the rise of communistic socialism and the development of historical criticism of the Bible.

In 1826 Wilhelm de Wette published *Introduction to the New Testament,* in which he noted that there were many uncompleted and defective details in Acts.[39] For example, in Acts 2:44 and 4:32, 34, Luke expresses himself "too strongly." He really means to speak of a willingness to share possessions with others in the community.[40]

A few years later, in 1831, F. C. Baur introduced "tendency criticism," his theory that early Christianity was composed of two conflictual parties,

36. Rideman, *Confession of Faith,* p. 90.

37. Rideman, *Confession of Faith,* p. 90.

38. Robert Jewett says, "Many . . . utopian groups began in Europe and found they could not flourish there because of official harassment that lasted through the nineteenth century." See his *Paul the Apostle to America: Cultural Trends and Pauline Scholarship* (Louisville: Westminster/John Knox, 1994), p. 75.

39. W. Ward Gasque, *A History of the Interpretation of the Acts of the Apostles* (Peabody, Mass.: Hendrickson, 1989), p. 25.

40. Noted in Heinrich A. W. Meyer, *Handbook to the Acts of the Apostles,* translated from the 4th German edition by Paton J. Gloag (New York: Funk & Wagnalls, 1889), p. 70.

the Jewish-Christian party (founded by Peter) and the Gentile-Christian party (Pauline) — and therefore the New Testament documents are skewed by theological bias and do not necessarily represent historical events accurately. Using this theory, he hypothesized that Acts was written by a Paulinist who wanted to defend Paul's mission to the Gentiles against the criticism of the Jewish-Christian party.[41] Though Baur never wrote a commentary on Acts, his son-in-law Eduard Zeller did so, applying tendency criticism to the whole document.[42] Zeller understood Acts 1-7 to be full of contradictions — a mishmash of legends, myths, and fictitious creations of the author. The description of property-sharing in Acts 2 and 4 is so extreme that it cannot be excused as hyperbole; it is an "unhistorical account . . . founded on lofty concepts of a later period regarding the state of the original church."[43] Friedrich Spitta, more detailed and adept at cutting and pasting, says that Acts 2:44 was added by a later redactor, and the community of goods in 2:45-47 refers only to that practiced by the apostles.[44]

Ernest Renan's 1866 commentary on Acts[45] was not quite as skeptical as Zeller's, but Renan believed the writer of Acts had exaggerated and "overcolored" his description. Thus the writer's doctrine of absolute poverty had shaped the facts to fit his beliefs. From a practical point of view, a true community of goods could only work in a very small church where people live in the same neighborhood (indeed, it came to an end as the community grew and administrative difficulties arose).[46] Renan also claimed, naively, that such a community would have been easier to initiate in the East, where people didn't have many needs. In the East, people had few cares, and there was no "slavery of labor," as in the industrial European West.[47]

Other commentators were less skeptical of the historicity of the Acts' community of goods. In his 1834 commentary Heinrich A. W. Meyer in-

41. Gasque, *A History of the Interpretation of the Acts of the Apostles,* p. 30.

42. Eduard Zeller, *Die Apostelgeschichte nach ihrem Inhalt und Ursprung kritisch untersucht* (Berlin: Habel, 1854). E.T.: *The Content and Origin of the Acts of the Apostles Critically Investigated,* trans. Joseph Dare (Edinburgh: Williams & Norgate, 1875).

43. Zeller, *Die Apostelgeschichte nach ihrem Inhalt und Ursprung kritisch untersucht,* pp. 213-14.

44. Friedrich Spitta, *Die Apostelgeschichte: Ihre Quellen und deren Geschichtlicher Wert* (Halle: Verlag der Buchhandlung des Waisenhauses, 1891), pp. 71-72.

45. Ernest Renan, *The Acts of the Apostles* (*Les Apôtres,* 1866), translated from the French (New York: Carlton, Madison Square, 1866), p. 105.

46. Renan, *The Acts of the Apostles,* pp. 104-5.

47. Renan, *The Acts of the Apostles,* p. 106.

sisted that Acts describes a real community of goods where the members truly possessed everything in common.[48] Henry Alford, whose 1872 commentary on Acts was the first British commentary to interact seriously with German scholars,[49] agreed. Sharing was voluntary but gradually became a custom.[50] Its purpose was relief for the poor. Both Meyer and Alford believed that this community of goods happened only in Jerusalem, for rich and poor are both mentioned in the letters of Paul, James, and John. It was connected not with the Essenes but rather with the practice of Jesus and his disciples as described in the Gospels.[51] The communal sharing ceased because of inconveniences such as those described in Acts 6:1, and probably explains the later poverty of the Jerusalem church.[52]

The oft-reprinted commentary of Richard Rackham (1901)[53] connected more clearly than those above the sharing of goods with Jesus' practice and teaching.[54] Like Renan, Rackham regarded this as a local institution that could not survive economically as the church grew in numbers. He believed its demise was due to a lack of organized labor as well as to lost goods during persecution. Nevertheless, the common purse and shared life had provided a sense of brotherhood at a time when other ethnic and family ties had been broken. Indeed, the common life was the greatest "wonder and sign" (vv. 43-45) of all.[55] The community of goods was put into practice because the believers expected Jesus' imminent return. Later, when that didn't happen, the selling of possessions was succeeded by sending alms from one church to another.[56]

---

48. Heinrich A. W. Meyer, *Kritisch exegetisches Handbuch über die Apostelgeschichte* (Göttingen: n.p., 1835). E.T.: *Critical and Exegetical Handbook to the Acts of the Apostles,* translated from the 4th edition (1870) by Paton J. Gloag (New York: Funk & Wagnalls, 1889), p. 70.

49. Henry Alford, *The Acts of the Apostles, the Epistles to the Romans and Corinthians,* vol. 2 of *The Greek Testament,* 6th ed. (New York and Boston: Lee & Shepard, 1872).

50. Alford, *The Acts of the Apostles,* p. 30.

51. Meyer, *Kritisch exegetisches Handbuch über die Apostelgeschichte,* p. 70; Alford, *The Acts of the Apostles,* p. 30.

52. Meyer, *Kritisch exegetisches Handbuch über die Apostelgeschichte,* p. 70; Alford, *The Acts of the Apostles,* p. 30.

53. Richard Belward Rackham, *The Acts of the Apostles,* 17th printing (Grand Rapids: Baker, 1964).

54. Rackham, *The Acts of the Apostles,* p. 35.

55. Rackham, *The Acts of the Apostles,* pp. 41-42.

56. Rackham, *The Acts of the Apostles,* p. 42.

Other major nineteenth-century commentaries by G. V. Lechler, R. J. Knowling, and H. B. Hackett[57] also assume that the Jerusalem believers' communal life was rooted in historical reality, but place their emphasis on the willingness of the believers to hold their possessions *as if* they were common property rather than as a full, literal community of goods. As need arose, then, possessions would be sold. These commentaries emphasize poor relief as the major reason for communal sharing.

The development of the historical-critical method during the nineteenth century called attention to the book of Acts in a new way. Stressing rational objectivity, historicity, and source criticism, these scholars nevertheless reacted to Acts in light of their own social and political contexts. Many reflections in these nineteenth-century commentaries have been carried over into later commentaries and other theological writings of the twentieth century.

In spite of erudite learning in theology, philosophy, philology, classics, or standard history, even the best biblical commentators did little social or economic analysis. They either ignored or rejected any resemblance between the Jerusalem community of goods and the socialist communism struggling to be born. G. V. Lechler, for example, saw the Jerusalem arrangement "contending against this modern and ungodly communism and against every false leveling process."[58] These judgments reflect an all-male, all-Western European, all upper-class academy, living in a society where individualism is growing and capitalism is assumed to be the only appropriate economic system. From this perspective, the poor are "the other," those of lower classes, who are dependent on the charity of those above them. Such a mentality can hardly imagine a community of goods working on anything but a small scale, and thus it was promptly discontinued when problems arose and the money ran out.

Around the same time that Knowling's commentary in the famous Greek Expositor's Testament series appeared, an Acts commentary in the English Expositor's Bible series (with the same editor) laid bare a more

---

57. G. V. Lechler, *The Acts of the Apostles*, translated from the German (New York: C. Scribner, 1871); Richard John Knowling, *The Acts of the Apostles*, Expositor's Greek Testament, ed. W. Robertson Nicoll (Edinburgh: n.p., 1900; Grand Rapids: Eerdmans, 1951); Horatio B. Hackett, *A Commentary on the Acts of the Apostles* (Philadelphia: American Baptist Publication Society, 1882). Knowling's commentary appears equally conversant with German and British scholarship.

58. Lechler, *The Acts of the Apostles*, p. 83.

popular and naked reflection of Victorian England's sharp class divisions and paternalistic concept of the "white man's burden." G. T. Stokes viewed the Jerusalem experiment as a socio-economic disaster.[59] The community of goods in Acts was a mistake — even an evil — that should never have happened. As in Thessalonica later, so here in Jerusalem the believers' intense expectation of the return of Christ led naturally to financial irresponsibility:

> The community of goods was adopted in no other church . . . [and] no Christian sect or Church has ever tried to revive it, save the monastic orders, who adopted it for the special purpose of completely cutting their members off from any connection with the world . . . and, in later times still, the wild fanatical Anabaptists at the Reformation period, who thought, like the Christians of Jerusalem, that the kingdom of God, as they fancied it, was immediately about to appear.[60]

Stokes sees this incident recorded in Acts as "a significant warning for the mission field" that should encourage missionary churches "to strive after a healthy independence amongst their members."[61] Since another evil connected with sharing of goods was the conflict between the Hellenists and the Hebrews, Stokes saw this account as also teaching prudent poor relief and almsgiving to the church at home:

> No classes are more suspicious and more quarrelsome than those who are in receipt of such assistance. . . . Managers of almshouses, asylums, charitable funds, and workhouses know this . . . and ofttimes make a bitter acquaintance with that evil spirit which burst forth even in the mother Church of Jerusalem.[62]

For fifteen pages, Stokes continued preaching in this vein. One wonders if he ever read Dickens's *Oliver Twist*.

---

59. G. T. Stokes, *The Acts of the Apostles.* The Expositor's Bible, ed. W. Robertson Nicoll (New York: A. C. Armstrong & Son, 1903).

60. Stokes, *The Acts of the Apostles,* p. 198.

61. Stokes, *The Acts of the Apostles,* p. 200.

62. Stokes, *The Acts of the Apostles,* p. 203.

Through the Lenses of Socialist Communism and Social History

Such attitudes could hardly be farther apart in tone and content from those expressed by socialist writers of the same period. The socialist philosophy of Karl Marx and Friedrich Engels profoundly affected some interpretations of the community of goods described in Acts. With a materialist view of history that emphasized the solidarity of the working classes, some socialists or communists analyzed the Jerusalem community and consequent development of the Christian church as an important stage in the evolution of civilization toward a communistic society.

Already in 1850, Engels realized that the roots of his economic philosophy lay in biblical religion, expressed in the sixteenth-century Anabaptist movement. But he saw Anabaptism through the actions of his hero, the militant Thomas Münzer, who had led the peasants' revolt against the princes and bourgeoisie of Germany in 1525.[63] Discounting Münzer's theology as mere religious "propaganda," Engels otherwise praised him as an anti-Catholic, anti-Christian revolutionary who believed the kingdom of God should come in this life, "a society without class differences, private property, and a state authority" alienated from the people.[64]

Building on Engels' approach, Karl Kautsky provided the most detailed discussion of the earliest Christian community from a communist perspective in *Foundations of Christianity*.[65] Kautsky's materialistic view of history sees the rise of Christianity as an important stage in humankind's development. Because Kautsky assumed social progress throughout history — "a continuous evolution from lower to higher forms" (*FC*, p. 11) — he compared Christian "communism" with the proletarian movement of the nineteenth century, but also contrasted it as ultimately inferior.

Kautsky shared the extreme skepticism of the historicity of the New Testament with other radical European thinkers of his day.[66] But what the

63. Friedrich Engels, *The Peasants' War in Germany* (Moscow: Foreign Languages Publishing House, 1956).

64. Engels, *The Peasants' War*, pp. 67-78; quote from p. 72.

65. Karl Kautsky, *Foundations of Christianity: A Study in Christian Origins*, authorized translation from the 13th German edition (London and New York: Monthly Review Press, 1925). Hereafter this work will be cited parenthetically in the text.

66. Among the most extreme was German Bruno Bauer, applying his methods to Acts in the monograph *Die Apostelgeschichte. Eine Ausgleichung des Paulinismus und des Judenthums innerhalb der christlichen Kirche* (Berlin, 1850). See also Gasque's chapter, "The

early Christian writings do reveal is something about the *social conditions* of their time:

> The historical value of the Gospels and of the Acts of the Apostles is probably not of higher value than that of the Homeric poems, or of the Nibelungenlied. . . . But such poetic narrations are of incalculable value for the study of the social conditions under which they arose, and which they faithfully reflect, no matter how many liberties their authors may take in their treatment of facts and persons. (*FC*, p. 42).

Thus the description of the communal meals and the community of goods in Acts 2, 4, and 6 is authentic. In fact, Kautsky shows how logical and inevitable is this communistic development, since Christianity began among the "proletarian elements almost exclusively and was a proletarian organization . . . for a long time after its earliest beginnings" (*FC*, p. 323). A related characteristic of the movement was "a savage class hatred against the rich," which is expressed most clearly in the Gospel of Luke (*FC*, p. 327). Matthew, written several decades after Luke, revises this class hatred to attract wealthier and more cultured persons; hence "the poor" become "poor in spirit," and so on (*FC*, pp. 329-30).

Since Christianity is proletarian, "it is natural that it should aim to achieve a communistic organization" (*FC*, p. 331). But the Jerusalem church had only a communism of consumption, not of production. Communism in Kautsky's day meant concentrating wealth at one place (as in a state or a municipality) for the sake of production. But in the Greco-Roman world, the concentration of wealth in a few hands meant anything but the basis for production and therefore of the social welfare (*FC*, p. 340). The rich used their wealth to purchase luxury items and to maintain their status and political power.

As the church evolved and spread out geographically, Christian groups retained their property-sharing but remained communities of consumption only, based on private contributions by the members. The only activities that held them together were their daily common meal and their charity work (*FC*, p. 411). And by the fourth century the common meal was

---

Radical Descendants of the Tübingen School" (in *A History of the Interpretation of the Acts of the Apostles*), which includes A. Pierson, S. A. Naber, A. D. Loman, and its leading representative, Willem Christiaan van Manen.

eliminated, and the church had entirely "ceased to be a proletarian institution" (*FC*, pp. 421-22).

It is small wonder that Kautsky aroused the ire of scholars who viewed the New Testament from a middle-class capitalistic perspective, and those who saw religious motives at the heart of those writings. Yet Kautsky betrayed his own modern Enlightenment perspective by eviscerating the role of religion in the New Testament world. He seemed unaware of religious motives pervading Greco-Roman society — pagan, Jewish, and Christian — and attributed all motivation to economics and politics. Kautsky further alienated New Testament scholars by using inflammatory terms like "communism" for a community of goods and "propaganda" for the preaching of the gospel.

Yet Kautsky was well ahead of his time in grasping the value of the New Testament documents, including Acts, for what they can say about the *social conditions* of the first century in the Mediterranean world. His opponents overreacted by refusing to see early Christianity in economic or social terms at all. Indeed, most of the early Christians *were* poor, living at subsistence level. Daily communal meals did make a lot of sense, given their economic situation. A good deal of Kautsky's economic analysis regarding early Christianity is quite accurate. To ignore either the religious or the socio-economic aspects of this movement is to misunderstand the holistic nature of the Christian gospel and the day-to-day survival of believers' communities in the first centuries of the era.

Sociological Responses to Socialist Communism

Ernst Troeltsch and Johannes Weiss

Ernst Troeltsch (1865-1923) was a contemporary of Kautsky, a German philosopher-theologian who was among the first to ask questions about sociological influences on church doctrine and, conversely, to examine the sociological implications of what the church taught. Troeltsch's observations on the early church's practice of a community of goods are found in *The Social Teaching of the Christian Churches* (first published 1912).[67] His

67. Ernst Troeltsch, *The Social Teaching of the Christian Churches*, trans. Olive Wyon (London: George Allen & Unwin Ltd.; New York: Macmillan, 1931, 1949, 1950; Louisville:

interpretation reflects major sociopolitical ideas and movements in late nineteenth- and early twentieth-century Europe.

Troeltsch set out his ideas in sharp contrast to a communist philosophy of history and economics. "The message of Jesus is not a program of social reform."[68] It did not arise out of a class struggle and in no way is it connected to political-social revolutions. Rather, Jesus' message is a "summons to prepare for the coming of the Kingdom of God," which "is to take place quietly within the framework of the present world-order, in a purely religious fellowship of love, with an earnest endeavour to conquer self and cultivate the Christian virtues."[69] Though Troeltsch assumed the community of goods was historical, it was thoroughly impractical, primarily a response to the "rapture of their first love." It was a communism based solely on consumption; "its members will continue to earn their living by private enterprise, in order to practice generosity and sacrifice. . . . It has no theory of equality at all," nor was it hostile to the institution of the family.[70] It soon outgrew itself and led to the total impoverishment of the church, fading away without even a struggle for the principle. "The fundamental idea was solely that of the salvation of souls."[71]

Love is the core of communalism. Though the idea contains a revolutionary element — seen in the monastic system, medieval communistic movements, the Anabaptists, and among "modern fanatics and idealists" — it has no desire for revolution and is socially conservative.[72] The central idea of religion is based upon a monotheism that sees all humanity under a benevolent deity. Recognizing this loving God will lead us to a sense of love which sees that earthly possessions are for everyone and that we need to share with those in need. It is the religious impulse toward love that has affected society sociologically, in the form of promoting individualism (the worth of each individual) and universalism (God loves everyone).[73]

These are tenets of classical liberal theology. The tone is abstract and

---

Westminster/John Knox Press, 1992). It was first translated into English in 1931 and has been reprinted as recently as 1992, demonstrating that Troeltsch's ideas are still attracting serious attention.

68. Troeltsch, *The Social Teaching of the Christian Churches*, p. 61.

69. Troeltsch, *The Social Teaching of the Christian Churches*, p. 61.

70. Troeltsch, *The Social Teaching of the Christian Churches*, p. 62.

71. Troeltsch, *The Social Teaching of the Christian Churches*, p. 63.

72. Troeltsch, *The Social Teaching of the Christian Churches*, pp. 63-64.

73. Troeltsch, *The Social Teaching of the Christian Churches*, pp. 70-71.

intellectual, giving no evidence of understanding the practical organization involved in the growth of the early church, nor of identification or solidarity with the poor. Moving in the latter direction, Troeltsch assumed, leads back to socialist communism, which is forced and never based on love.[74]

Troeltsch's work, however, did provide a sociological basis from which others could grapple with aspects of Christian faith and religion. One such exegete of Acts was Johannes Weiss. In *Earliest Christianity: A History of the Period* A.D. *30-150*,[75] Weiss demonstrated a greater awareness of economic and sociological issues than had commentators of the previous century, even as he strongly refuted Kautsky's position. Weiss claimed that the generalized statements about property-sharing in Acts 2:44, 4:32 and 34 bear the stamp of a later redactor who idealized the beginnings of Christianity.[76] By Acts 6:1-6 we see that the needy are provided with alms, which was the usual Jewish practice of charitable relief.[77] It would have been a true example of collectivism "if Joseph Barnabas and others turned over their houses and lands as such to the group, for common or joint use. . . . But any such idea was wholly alien to the old community."[78]

Statements about the blessedness of poverty and woes pronounced on the rich in Luke's Gospel (i.e., 6:20-26) reflect not class hatred but a later period when the ruling classes of Judaism and the poor Christians were hostile toward each other.[79] The real reason for such willingness to share property in the original community was that they were expecting an imminent Parousia, a notion totally opposite from a communistic scheme of social reform, which assumes a permanent organization in the present world.[80]

---

74. H.-D. Wendland echoes similar sentiments in *Ethik des Neuen Testaments* (Göttingen: VandenHoeck & Ruprecht, 1970), p. 38; noted in Kraus, "Aktualität des 'Urchristlichen Kommunismus'?" pp. 314-15.

75. Johannes Weiss, *Earliest Christianity: A History of the Period* A.D. *30-150*, vol. 1, trans. Frederick C. Grant (Gloucester, Mass.: Peter Smith, 1970).

76. Weiss, *Earliest Christianity*, vol. 1, p. 68.

77. Weiss, *Earliest Christianity*, vol. 1, p. 72.

78. Weiss, *Earliest Christianity*, vol. 1, p. 72.

79. Weiss, *Earliest Christianity*, vol. 1, p. 74.

80. Weiss, *Earliest Christianity*, vol. 1, pp. 72-73.

Shirley Jackson Case

Troeltsch's ideas on the "social teachings of the Christian Churches" were picked up in different ways. During the 1930s in the United States, Shailer Mathews and Shirley Jackson Case asked further questions about the social history of Christianity. Case insisted that early Christianity be studied "in the full light of the conditions and processes of the actual life of real people . . . within a concrete social nexus."[81] In his Rauschenbusch lectures of 1933 — titled *The Social Triumph of the Ancient Church* — Case specifically discussed "Christianity and worldly goods."[82] He saw the ancient church's ideas about wealth and property starting out with a primitive or ignorant attitude and evolving in a positive direction. The earliest community in Jerusalem was so indifferent toward possessions that they quickly fell into poverty and had to be bailed out by the collection which Paul organized for them from the more prosperous Gentile churches.[83] Paul's ideas helped to change attitudes, because he asked the believers in the churches he founded to continue in their present vocations and callings (1 Cor. 7:17-24).

Nevertheless, the economic structure of the Roman Empire was such that a huge gap existed between the mass of the poor and the few rich, who wantonly displayed their luxury. Christians were disgusted at this pride and selfishness, and they "spurned wealth as the inevitable concomitant of wickedness."[84] By the end of the first century, however, it was gradually dawning upon Christians that "prosperity could be made to serve worthy religious ends."[85] Part of the "social triumph" of the ancient church is that it eventually practiced Christian charity on a worldwide scale and brought "the material resources of the world into the service of religion."[86]

Case showed more awareness of "the actual life of real people" than Troeltsch did. Yet his analysis derived not only from sociological research

---

81. Shirley Jackson Case, "Whither Historicism in Theology?" in *The Process of Religion*, S. Shailer Mathews Festschrift, ed. M. H. Krumbine (New York: Macmillan, 1933), p. 64.

82. Shirley Jackson Case, *The Social Triumph of the Ancient Church* (New York: Harper & Brothers, 1933).

83. Case, *The Social Triumph of the Ancient Church*, p. 41.

84. Case, *The Social Triumph of the Ancient Church*, p. 48.

85. Case, *The Social Triumph of the Ancient Church*, p. 50.

86. Case, *The Social Triumph of the Ancient Church*, p. 91.

into Greco-Roman culture, but also from assumptions he absorbed from his own culture and era. Unlike Kautsky, who saw the decline of communalism in the church as a deterioration and a sellout, Case viewed the church's use of wealth as appropriate and progressive. This is consistent with his optimistic, progressive view of history that the wars and economic depressions of the twentieth century had not yet expunged from his outlook. For Case, the poor are definitely "the other," but with capitalism's rosy future and the church's proper use of wealth, worthy poor can be taken care of.

The Interlude of Neo-Orthodoxy: Brunner, Bonhoeffer, and Barth

For the next forty-five years, little was done to push forward Case's social analysis of early Christianity. European neo-orthodoxy, with its emphasis on the revelatory word of God, spread to North America and began to displace the more optimistic social gospel.[87] Neo-orthodoxy's reaction to liberal theology in the face of destructive world wars is understandable. However, its stress on the otherness of God and God's discontinuity with human beings, as well as its separation of faith and reason, rendered this approach antihistorical and antisociological.

The Swiss theologian Emil Brunner discussed Acts 2:44, 45 and 4:32 under the heading of ecclesiology. Brunner did see that the most "immediately credible expression" of God's self-giving love was this Christian community of goods.[88] Yet he highlighted the typical neo-orthodox gap between the life of faith and actual concrete social life in this world. When love takes such a concrete form, he claimed, it is unrealistic and impractical. It led to the impoverishment of the Jerusalem community, and then disappeared. But even though it is not practical, it is the ideal of "brotherly

87. It is true that some effort was made to develop sociological methods of biblical study. Rudolf Bultmann, a great pioneer of form criticism, understood that he was dealing with popular traditions from the lower strata of society. Ironically, however, he forsook this method in favor of a "demythologizing" program in order to make Christianity palatable to the modern scientific mind. See Rudolf Bultmann, *The History of the Synoptic Tradition*, trans. John Marsh (New York: Harper & Row, 1963), pp. 3-4.

88. Emil Brunner, *The Christian Doctrine of the Church, Faith, and the Consummation*, vol. 12 of *Dogmatics*, trans. David Cairns with T. H. L. Parker (Philadelphia: Westminster Press, 1962), p. 33.

love," reminiscent of Calvin's emphasis on spiritual unity while he supported the economic and social status quo.[89]

Dietrich Bonhoeffer's ecclesiology also viewed the church as the original essence of community, but as a spiritual community, not necessarily a social organization.[90] Significantly, Bonhoeffer stressed the community of goods in Acts 2:44 as flowing from the "word and sacrament" of 2:42. The sharing of material goods is clarified by the apostles' teaching and daily communal meals, becoming, in Protestant theological terminology, "word and sacrament." Bonhoeffer did not challenge the historical actuality of the community of goods so much as ignore its concrete, social organization in order to highlight the spiritual reality it represents.

In his massive *Church Dogmatics*, Karl Barth referred only once to the community of goods in Acts 2:42-47, and this within a section on Jesus as King.[91] Barth argued that the attempt to share all material goods in the original Jerusalem community was grounded in Jesus' teaching and actions. Reacting against a theological liberalism that looked for the kingdom of God to be realized in Western society, Barth insisted that Jesus was not a reformer championing a new order against old ones. Rather, he "set all principles and programs in question because he displayed a freedom which we can only describe as royal."[92]

Barth understood Jesus' attitude as one of passive conservativism. He acknowledged existing orders, subjected himself to them, and advised his disciples to do the same — but yet was always superior to them. However, he and his disciples did call the economic order into question by not owning possessions.[93] Jesus issued an either/or call to sell everything and follow him. The earliest post-Pentecostal community boldly took up this challenge, even though it was only an attempt to live like Jesus. Indeed, Barth allowed, there have been numerous impulses toward an economic reordering of community where Jesus' gospel is proclaimed, but none has ever succeeded.

---

89. Brunner, *The Christian Doctrine of the Church, Faith, and the Consummation*, pp. 33-34. A footnote after this paragraph indicates that this "primitive Christian communism" was naive because it applied only to consumption and not to production.

90. Dietrich Bonhoeffer, *Sanctorum Communio: Eine Dogmatische Untersuchung zur Soziologie der Kirche* (Munich: C. Kaiser, 1954), p. 93.

91. Karl Barth, *Church Dogmatics: The Doctrine of Reconciliation*, vol. 4, bk. 2, trans. G. W. Bromiley (Edinburgh: T&T Clark, 1958), pp. 171-78.

92. Barth, *Church Dogmatics*, vol. 4, p. 172.

93. Barth, *Church Dogmatics*, vol. 4, p. 177.

Barth believed that Jesus' call to give no thought to material possessions (Matt. 6:25) is not workable in the present order of society: "There
can be no sound or solid economy without this laying up and taking
thought."[94] But Jesus' call is not necessarily practical and does not lead to a
better social order. It is a simple call to freedom. It is "the royal man Jesus
penetrating to the very foundations of economic life in defiance of every
reasonable and . . . honorable objection."[95]

Behind both Bonhoeffer's and Barth's reflections on the social order
lie their eschatological viewpoints. A true and lasting communal sharing
can never happen on this earth, but it is part of the final culmination of life
and history, the point where the whole world will know that Jesus Christ is
Lord.[96] That is why communism is ultimately unworkable. Although its
impulse starts from the same origins as the community of goods in Jerusalem, it diminishes and narrows the messianic ideal.[97]

As long as neo-orthodoxy dominated the interpretation of the Acts
texts on community of goods, no advances could be made toward understanding "the actual life of real people" in the early church. The neo-
orthodox theologians recall the Reformation social ethic, with its concern
to distance itself from Christian "fanaticism."

Shifting Emphases: Style and Redaction Criticism

The major question dominating Acts criticism during the nineteenth and
early twentieth centuries had been its historical accuracy, with related issues of authorship and sources. But two scholars began shifting the emphasis toward literary studies of Acts: Henry J. Cadbury, probably the most
important American in the history of Lukan research; and the German
Martin Dibelius, who pioneered "style criticism" of Acts. They were followed by Ernst Haenchen and Hans Conzelmann.

---

94. Barth, *Church Dogmatics,* vol. 4, p. 178.
95. Barth, *Church Dogmatics,* vol. 4, p. 178.
96. William Hordern, *A Layman's Guide to Protestant Theology* (New York:
Macmillan, 1955), p. 136.
97. Kraus, "Aktualität des 'Urchristlichen Kommunismus'?" pp. 324-25.

Henry J. Cadbury and Martin Dibelius

Henry Cadbury's primary contribution to scholarship on the community of goods in Acts was his identification of 2:43-47 and 4:32-37 as Lukan summaries, the "connective tissue by which memorabilia are turned into the beginnings of a continuous narrative."[98] As an editor, Luke used sources for the intervening narratives. Then he broke up these narratives by inserting generalized summaries that he wrote himself.[99] Cadbury was not necessarily skeptical of Luke's historicity; it just wasn't his primary concern.[100]

Along with Rudolf Bultmann, Martin Dibelius pioneered use of the form-critical method for the Gospels. However, in applying it to Acts, he called it "style criticism" because the structure of Acts "was dissimilar to that of the Synoptics."[101] In using this approach, he called for an end to "one-sided interpretation, which only inquired about the historical reliability of the material."[102]

Dibelius concluded that Luke did not adequately understand the early development of the church. So he interposed general summaries between various scenes and narratives that link them together. In this way individual events become examples of something mentioned in a general summary. For example, the sale of possessions in 4:32-35 leads on to the story of Ananias and Sapphira.[103] As a historian in the ancient rather than the modern sense, Luke omitted, altered, or generalized what really happened. For example, referring to the community of goods mentioned in

98. Henry J. Cadbury, "The Summaries in Acts," in *The Acts of the Apostles,* vol. 1 of *The Beginnings of Christianity,* ed. Frederick J. Foakes-Jackson and Kirsopp Lake; *Additional Notes to the Commentary,* vol. 5 of *The Beginnings of Christianity,* ed. Kirsopp Lake and Henry J. Cadbury (Grand Rapids: Baker, 1933, 1966), pp. 392-402.

99. Cadbury, "The Summaries in Acts," p. 399.

100. Richard Pervo, "On Perilous Things: A Response to Beverly R. Gaventa," in *Cadbury, Knox, and Talbert,* ed. Mikeal C. Parsons and Joseph B. Tyson (Atlanta: Scholars Press, 1992), pp. 37-43 (39).

101. Martin Dibelius, "Stilkritisches zur Apostelgeschichte," *Eucharisterion für H. Gunkel* (Göttingen, 1923); E.T.: "Style Criticism of the Book of Acts," in *Studies in the Acts of the Apostles,* ed. Heinrich Greeven (London: SCM Press Ltd., 1956, 1973), pp. 1-25.

102. Martin Dibelius, "Zur Formgeschichte des Neuen Testaments," *Theologische Rundschau,* New Series 3 (1931), pp. 207-42 (211); quoted in Ernst Haenchen, *The Acts of the Apostles: A Commentary,* translated from the 14th German ed. (1965) by Bernard Noble, Gerald Shinn, Hugh Anderson, and R. McL. Wilson (Philadelphia: Westminster Press, 1971), p. 35.

103. Dibelius, "Zur Formgeschichte des Neuen Testaments," p. 35.

the summaries, Dibelius noted that "in order to bring out the communal ideal . . . [Luke] overdoes the communism."[104] Dibelius expressed no interest in the historical or sociological possibility of a community of goods.

Ernst Haenchen

Ernst Haenchen systematically applied Dibelius's method to the whole of Acts in his massive commentary entitled *The Acts of the Apostles*. The writer of Acts, who lived toward the end of the first century and thus cannot be Paul's companion Luke, reads his own Gentile Christian theology back into the earliest days of the church.[105] Haenchen noted that 4:34 has in view the Old Testament text of Deuteronomy 15:4, about there being no needy persons in the community. But because Luke's language also reflects Greek utopian phrasing about "friends having everything in common," Haenchen concluded that the writer is suggesting that the "primitive Church also realized the *Greek* communal ideal."[106] Luke probably generalized verses 34-35 from the examples of Barnabas and Ananias and Sapphira. "In reality, no doubt, the good deed of Barnabas only survived in memory because it was something out of the ordinary, not the rule." Though he considered the possible connection between the Jerusalem community and the Essenes at Qumran, Haenchen ruled it out because only celibate monks could practice a total community of goods.[107] For him, family life and monastic life are incompatible.

Haenchen believed that the actual reality behind Luke's idealizing generality was that the Jerusalem community, always struggling in poverty from the beginning, was affected by the deteriorating economic situation of Palestine through famine and political unrest. They were driven to help each other and to depend on sharing from other congregations in order to survive. In other words, Luke looked at a bad economic situation through rose-colored glasses and made it sound like a Golden Age.

104. Dibelius in a letter to Haenchen, 10 February 1947, quoted in Haenchen, *The Acts of the Apostles*, p. 40.

105. Ernst Haenchen, "Das 'Wir' in der Apostelgeschichte und das Itinerar," *Zeitschrift für Theologie und Kirche* 58 (1961); referred to in Gasque, *A History of the Interpretation of the Acts of the Apostles*, p. 241.

106. Gasque, *A History of the Interpretation of the Acts of the Apostles*, p. 233.

107. Gasque, *A History of the Interpretation of the Acts of the Apostles*, p. 234.

Haenchen did not connect economics with the gospel, and Jesus' teachings and practice of communal sharing did not figure in his understanding of the structure of the Jerusalem church. Nor did he seem aware of ancient Palestinian family life. Haenchen apparently knew nothing of contemporary Hutterites, who have lived *as families* in just such communities, or of the many types of intentional communities in the past and present who have organized a common purse or intensive sharing. His analysis seems far removed from the world of the economically and politically oppressed.

Hans Conzelmann

In 1954 Hans Conzelmann published an influential monograph on the theology of Luke-Acts.[108] Conzelmann's historical skepticism was even greater than Haenchen's, and he attributed nearly the whole of Acts to the writer's literary and theological motives — it was essentially a historical novel.[109] Thus, the summaries in Acts should not be seen as historical but as a literary device. In Acts 2:42-47, the writer is clearly idealizing the original community and its sharing of property. This information was either handed on by tradition or deduced through knowledge about communistic groups in the contemporary world — either actual, such as the Essenes, or idealized, such as the original community of Pythagoreans. Conzelmann argued that

> Idealized communal portraits are associated with utopian dreams or accounts of primeval times. . . . Thus Luke's portrayal should not be taken as historical . . . and we cannot speak of a "failure of the experiment," nor can we draw conclusions for a primitive Christian communistic ideal. . . . Furthermore, Luke does not present this way of life as a norm for the organization of the church in his own time. It is meant as an illustration of the uniqueness of the ideal earliest days of the movement.[110]

108. Hans Conzelmann, *Die Mitte der Zeit* (Tübingen: J. C. B. Mohr, 1954); E.T.: *The Theology of St. Luke* (New York: Harper, 1961).

109. Hans Conzelmann, *Acts of the Apostles*, vol. 43 of *Hermeneia: A Critical and Historical Commentary on the Bible* (Philadelphia: Fortress Press, 1987).

110. Conzelmann, *Acts of the Apostles*, p. 24.

The same criticisms of Haenchen may be applied to Conzelmann, though the latter's dismissal of any historical reality behind the Lukan summaries seems even more presumptuous.

Reactions to Style and Redaction Criticism

Conzelmann's interpretation proved far too radical for evangelical scholars, who defended Luke as a historian. I. Howard Marshall's 1980 commentary reflects concerns similar to those of nineteenth-century exegetes.[111] Marshall argues that it is possible that in their first flush of religious enthusiasm, the early believers may have had a total community of goods, influenced by some of Jesus' sayings and the contemporary Jewish Qumran sect. But Acts 4:34–5:11 demonstrates that the community may not have been so tightly knit, since the selling of possessions was entirely voluntary, and goods were held until needed.[112]

F. F. Bruce concurs, although he does concede that Luke has idealized the scene somewhat.[113] The tone of C. S. G. Williams' commentary[114] is more negative, also reminiscent of some nineteenth-century attitudes. The "communism" described in Acts was totally different from the modern economic and political form. It was voluntary and unsuccessful, ending with the widows' complaint in 6:1. Thus the community became impoverished, and Paul felt it necessary to raise a collection.[115] Donald Guthrie also distances these texts from modern communism. The sharing of property was entirely spontaneous, because material possessions were simply not important to these believers.[116]

Generally, commentators who emphasize Luke as a historian seem concerned to explain "what actually happened" in terms that reflect something less than a total property-sharing, as something quite different from

---

111. I. Howard Marshall, *The Acts of the Apostles: An Introduction and Commentary*, Tyndale New Testament Commentaries (Grand Rapids: Eerdmans, 1980).

112. Marshall, *The Acts of the Apostles*, p. 84.

113. F. F. Bruce, *The Acts of the Apostles*, rev. ed. (Grand Rapids: Eerdmans, 1990), p. 131.

114. C. S. G. Williams, *The Acts of the Apostles*, Black's/Harper's New Testament Commentaries (New York: Harper & Row, 1957).

115. Williams, *The Acts of the Apostles*, p. 71.

116. Donald Guthrie, *The Apostles* (Grand Rapids: Zondervan, 1975).

an economic system such as modern communism, and/or to stress that whatever sharing there was did not last long.[117]

Redaction and Literary-Critical Studies on a Community of Goods

The influence of Haenchen and Conzelmann on biblical studies was considerable. By far the majority of scholars accepted the redaction-critical method and embarked upon the task of supporting, rejecting, or modifying Conzelmann's concept of Luke's theology.

Two recent commentators who accept Conzelmann's picture of Lukan idealizing of the community of goods in Acts are Luke Johnson and Gerhard Krodel. Johnson's interest in the theme of possessions dates back to his doctoral dissertation from 1977.[118] He notices that both Luke's Gospel and Acts lay a strong stress on possessions (or the lack of them), and he asks about the literary symbolic meaning of possessions for Luke. Through a detailed exegesis, he concludes that

> Luke sees possessions as a primary symbol of human existence, an immediate . . . manifestation of the self. But . . . possessions do not merely express the inner condition of [one's] heart; they are also capable of expressing relations between persons and the play of power between persons. Indeed, . . . possessions are a sign of power.[119]

117. Other commentators also say nothing about Lukan idealizing or redactional emphases. According to R. C. H. Lenski, *The Interpretation of the Acts of the Apostles* (Columbus, Oh.: Wartburg Press, 1944), this arrangement was not "communistic" but voluntary. Many Diaspora Jews were now living in Jerusalem and living off their wealth, which they shared as a revival of the old Mosaic law (pp. 118-19). G. H. C. MacGregor, *The Interpreter's Bible* (Nashville: Abingdon, 1954), claims that communalism was a continuation of Jesus' practice. But it broke down because of dissension between Hebrews and Hellenists, and the administrators were driven from the city (pp. 50, 73). William Neil, *Acts of the Apostles*, New Century Bible (Grand Rapids: Eerdmans, 1973), says that sharing was voluntary and involved practical sharing of personal possessions. The property was held in trust for whenever need arose. Even so, it was an unrepeatable standard and was only instituted in Jerusalem because of the expectation of the imminent Parousia (pp. 80-81).

118. Luke T. Johnson, *The Literary Function of Possessions in Luke-Acts*, SBL Dissertation Series, 39, ed. Howard C. Kee and Douglas A. Knight (Missoula, Mont.: Scholars Press, 1977).

119. Johnson, *The Literary Function of Possessions in Luke-Acts*, p. 221.

In a later volume, Johnson popularizes his conclusions and reflects on them theologically for the sake of the contemporary church. Possessions symbolize a person's very self and speak to the human nature of acquisitiveness. The way we respond to other people and their needs is the way we respond to God. Yet the Bible does not consistently propose one model of sharing possessions that is eternally valid.[120]

Johnson contrasts a communal lifestyle with Western society's concept of private property and helping the needy through alms. Because of the terminology Luke used to describe the communalism of the Jerusalem community ("one heart and soul," "all things common"), Johnson associates this community of goods with Greek utopian thought that looked backward to a primitive Golden Age and is unrepeatable later. Not unlike Brunner, he sees Luke's description as an idealized picture "against which later communities could measure themselves. Luke is not proposing this picture as a concrete example to be imitated."[121]

Johnson sees several problems with *all* attempts to establish a community of goods, from "benign forms" found in monasteries and the Bruderhof movement, to "malignant forms" found in Jim Jones' community in Guyana or in sixteenth-century Münster. First, a community of goods will emphasize unity at the expense of individuality and diversity. Second, it will lead to strong social control and firm boundaries concerning who is in and who is out. Third, it will tend toward authoritarian structure.

Consequently, Johnson is much more favorable toward almsgiving, which he regards as characteristic of "normative" Judaism. Here there is a sense not of "making equal" but of caring and sharing so that the needs of the poor are met. However, this solution does nothing to deal with class structure and middle-class Christians' tendency to view the poor as "the other."

In his Acts commentaries in both the 1981 Proclamation series and the 1986 Augsburg series,[122] Gerhard A. Krodel offered an argument very similar to that of Johnson. The property-sharing described in Acts is a highly

---

120. Luke T. Johnson, *Sharing Possessions: Mandate and Symbol of Faith*, Overtures to Biblical Theology, ed. Walter Brueggemann and John R. Donahue (Philadelphia: Fortress Press, 1981).

121. Johnson, *Sharing Possessions*, p. 129.

122. Gerhard Krodel, *Acts*, Proclamation Commentaries (Philadelphia: Fortress Press, 1981); *Acts*, Augsburg Commentary on the New Testament (Minneapolis: Augsburg Press, 1986).

idealized portrait that has no basis in history because of numerous inconsistencies between the summary statements and the rest of the narrative.[123] For example, if no one called anything they possessed their own, how could they give alms? Yet almsgiving is a Lukan emphasis. The real reason that Luke paints such a rosy picture can be traced to his concern about the indifference of rich Christians in his own community. He wants them to find new ways to close the gap between rich and poor, "so both can be 'one heart and one soul' (4:32). . . . In Acts this ideal picture shows the direction for social responsibility rather than constituting a timeless directive."[124]

Social-Scientific Criticism

Since the 1970s, insights from the social sciences have infused new life into biblical studies, adjusting and refining the earlier models of Kautsky and Case into "thick descriptions" of ancient cultures. The disciplines of social history, sociology, and cultural anthropology shed light on human values and behaviors and socio-economic structures in Palestine and Jerusalem during the first century. However, little has been done to propose a comprehensive model by which an actual community of goods might have reasonably existed as something more than an idealization on the writer's part.

Already in 1929, Joachim Jeremias had described social realia in *Jerusalem zur Zeit Jesu*[125] but made no attempt to analyze these facts in social-scientific fashion. Philip Esler's *Community and Gospel in Luke-Acts* contains extensive sections on table fellowship and poverty and wealth, but Esler uses a redactional approach that primarily asks what there was about economic disparities in Luke's community that would lead him to idealize "the social welfare arrangements in the early Christian community in Jerusalem."[126] A number of essays in *The Social World*

123. Krodel, *Acts* (Augsburg), p. 94.

124. Krodel, *Acts* (Proclamation), p. 25.

125. Joachim Jeremias, *Jerusalem zur Zeit Jesu* (1929); E.T.: *Jerusalem in the Time of Jesus*, trans. F. H. Cave and C. H. Cave (Philadelphia: Fortress Press, 1962).

126. Philip Esler, *Community and Gospel in Luke-Acts* (New York: Cambridge University Press, 1987). One could argue that many social realities of Luke's day would be similar to those of the thirties in Jerusalem, but Esler does not discuss this. Nor does he make any connection between communal meals and issues of wealth and poverty.

of Luke-Acts[127] deal with issues related to the Acts summaries in chapters 2 and 4, but the authors are not exegeting particular texts. The ambitious six-volume series edited by Bruce Winter, *The Book of Acts in Its First-Century Setting*, comes somewhat closer in Brian Capper's essay, "The Palestinian Cultural Context of Earliest Christian Community of Goods."[128] But Capper and the entire series lean more heavily on social history and archeology, so that the conceptual framework is predominantly historical rather than social-scientific. The essay that most directly addresses this issue is S. Scott Bartchy's "Community of Goods in Acts: Idealization or Social Reality?" in *The Future of Early Christianity*.[129] This essay does draw on the work of social scientists for its analysis of the community of goods described in Acts summaries.

Acts commentaries, however, have been slow to pick up on these insights. C. K. Barrett's 1994 International Critical Commentary on Acts includes a dense, eleven-page analysis of Acts 2:41-47 alone.[130] But his evidence is primarily linguistic, textual, historical, and archeological. Luke Johnson's 1992 commentary uses redactional and literary criticism but lacks social analysis.[131] In the Expositor's Bible Commentary series, Richard Longenecker includes one sentence on socio-economic factors, noting that the situation of famine and political unrest gave the believers many opportunities for sharing.[132] But Longenecker uses social history without benefit of social-scientific analysis. This leads him to see these acts of sharing as both voluntary and extraordinary, done only in response to special

127. Jerome H. Neyrey, ed., *The Social World of Luke-Acts: Models for Interpretation* (Peabody, Mass.: Hendrickson, 1991).

128. Brian Capper, "The Palestinian Cultural Context of Earliest Christian Community of Goods," in *The Book of Acts in Its Palestinian Setting*, ed. Richard Bauckham, vol. 4 of *The Book of Acts in Its First-Century Setting*, ed. Bruce Winter (Grand Rapids: Eerdmans, 1995), pp. 323-56.

129. S. Scott Bartchy, "Community of Goods in Acts: Idealization or Social Reality?" in *The Future of Early Christianity*, ed. Birger A. Pearson (Minneapolis: Fortress Press, 1991), pp. 309-18. Bartchy's commentary on Acts in the Word series is forthcoming and can be expected to include social-scientific analysis.

130. C. K. Barrett, *Acts 1–14*, International Critical Commentary (London and New York: T&T Clark, 1994, 2004).

131. Luke Johnson, *The Acts of the Apostles*, Sacra Pagina 5 (Collegeville, Minn.: Liturgical Press, 1992).

132. Richard Longenecker, *The Gospel of John and the Acts of the Apostles*, Expositor's Bible Commentary (Grand Rapids: Zondervan, 1981), pp. 288-92, 310-12 (310).

needs within the community at that time. They "were not meant to be normative for the church."[133]

Approaching from a different angle, the Calvinist economist Gary North sees autonomous, individualistic capitalism as the preferred economic system assumed in the New Testament.[134] Jesus affirms this in his parables of the talents and of the workers in the vineyard. The rich young man who could not part with his money merely illustrates the difficulty of being a responsible steward of wealth. North insists that "the practice of selling goods and sharing the proceeds with the brethren [sic] was limited to the Jerusalem church and was strictly voluntary."[135] He speculates that, because of the imminent destruction of Jerusalem prophesied by Jesus (Matt. 24:17-18), "there was little reason to hold on to property." But later the norm was always charity, not a "system of communist production and distribution."[136]

In their 1983 article entitled "Possessions in Luke-Acts: A Sociological Perspective," Donald B. Kraybill and Dennis M. Sweetland see possessions serving different functions at different stages in the growth and development of the early believers.[137] In the Gospel, possessions must be left behind in order to disassociate oneself from the larger society. But in the Jerusalem church, they "are now a symbol of his or her commitment to the new structure."[138] Possessions are not lost but instead are invested in the group as a whole. The original attitude toward possessions as evil shifted toward their being useful for community cohesion. Kraybill and Sweetland think sociologically but show little anthropological understanding of ancient Mediterranean culture.

The question commentators do not seem to ask is this: *What socioeconomic system would have been normative for first-century Palestinian Christians?* Against what cultural background does the Jerusalem community of goods stand? If Luke presents it as unusual, how was it so within its first-century, agrarian culture? Without some grasp of ancient economic

---

133. Longenecker, *The Gospel of John and the Acts of the Apostles*, p. 311.

134. Gary North, *An Introduction to Christian Economics* (Nutley, N.J.: Craig Press, 1976).

135. North, *An Introduction to Christian Economics*, p. 222.

136. North, *An Introduction to Christian Economics*, pp. 222-23.

137. Donald B. Kraybill and Dennis M. Sweetland, "Possessions in Luke-Acts: A Sociological Perspective," *Perspectives in Religious Studies* 10 (1983): 215-39.

138. Kraybill and Sweetland, "Possessions in Luke-Acts," p. 237.

systems and social values, the tendency is always to evaluate the descriptions of the early Jerusalem community by the standards of one's own culture.

Conclusion

This history of scholarship on the community of goods in Acts 2:42-47 and 4:32-37 has demonstrated not only a variety of views but also significant negative reaction and even hostility toward the intense communal sharing described in these texts. Few commentators, except some from Anabaptist traditions, consider that these texts describe a lifestyle that Christians ought to emulate in some way. The following brief review summarizes ways in which various social and political locations of commentators have contributed to their wary attitudes toward communal sharing.

Union of Church and State. When most citizens are only nominal Christians, a commitment to sharing wealth so that all have enough is impossible. The Reformation period provides ample evidence that, as long as biblical scholars assume a state church, they cannot realistically imagine voluntary property-sharing to emulate the practices of Jesus and the early church.

Abstraction of Spiritual Qualities. We see this tendency especially in the later Luther, Calvin, Troeltsch, the neo-orthodox theologians, and Luke Johnson. But when the message is generalized and abstracted, readers can neither try to reconstruct the original situation nor respond ethically in a concrete way.

Classism and Paternalism. Most commentators come from middle or upper-middle classes, assume capitalism's superiority to other economic systems, and have profited by it. Although classist and paternalistic attitudes are expressed most egregiously by Stokes, the majority of other commentators betray an "us-them" mentality by not recognizing their social location compared with that of the earliest Christians. Sharing goods and eating together do not sound attractive if it means giving up class privileges and relating to those of a lower class.

Reactions against Communism. Commentators in the West have been biased against *koinonia* because of strong Western emphases on capitalism and private property and because of the antipathy toward the communism practiced by the Soviet Union, Eastern Europe, and China. Robert Jewett notes that "this hostility was reinforced by twentieth-century atrocities in creating collective farms on the graves of peasant farmers and by enforcing industrial communism through Gulag Archipelagoes."[139]

Historical Skepticism in Liberal Scholarship. The rise of "higher criticism" produced doubt about the historical accuracy of many New Testament writings, especially the early chapters of Acts.

Lack of Adequate Research Tools. Until quite recently, biblical scholarship has assumed that *ideas* are the determining factor in the historical process.[140] (This helps explain why a materialist philosophy like Marxism fell on such deaf ears.) Thus, theology is the *real* historical reality, while social and cultural data are helpful background but not essential for interpreting texts.[141] A second assumption is the "big man" view of history, where individual geniuses (mostly male) shaped development, underplaying circles and groups who transmitted and produced texts.

Historical criticism was also successful in identifying facts — "that" or "what" information — but less so when it came to questions of "why" or "how."[142] How was ancient society organized? How did the natural and social environment shape attitudes and values? Questions of "how" are especially missing in the discussion of the Acts community of goods; commentators have not asked what other social and economic alternatives the Jerusalem believers might have had besides their community of goods. If it did break down, what system replaced it? Without a proper sociological imagination and adequate tools, scholars fall back on abstract theological explanations.

Inadequate Definition. Negative reactions toward communalism arise from a lack of exploring its full range of meaning. Many commentators assume an all-or-none attitude: a group shares everything in common — housing, clothing, food — and perhaps must also be celibate because of close daily contact.

Yet there are many methods of practicing communal sharing. Those who recognize the biases and limitations inherent in the above history of scholarship on communalism in Acts can begin to explore various ways in which believers have adapted Jesus' teaching and practice of community to

139. Robert Jewett, *Paul the Apostle to America*, p. 74.

140. Bengt Holmberg, *Paul and Power: The Structure of Authority in the Primitive Church as Reflected in the Pauline Epistles* (Philadelphia: Fortress Press, 1980), p. 201.

141. John Elliott, *What Is Social-Scientific Criticism?* (Minneapolis: Fortress Press, 1993), p. 12.

142. Elliott, *What Is Social-Scientific Criticism?* pp. 12-13.

many sociopolitical situations. One basic mode of sharing community, for example, is through regular communal meals. Some scholars make little or no connection between a community of goods and daily communal meals. Yet for a society with a subsistence economy, how food is obtained, shared, and eaten becomes a very high priority. Moreover, the fact that the Lord's Supper became the central rite of the Christian church needs to be linked to the early Christian practice of sharing meals together. We need to explore these connections because they will help us understand the rapid growth of the church in its first few centuries — and this in turn should help us think creatively about church growth not only in Africa but in the West as well.

Chapter Three

Naming the Meal: Agape, Eucharist, Bread-Breaking

After the United Church of Christ congregation in the Philippines re-hearsed the life-sustaining properties of the coconut for Filipino society, the liturgy came to a high point. Holding up the coconut, the presider recited, "The body of Christ which is broken for us," and then, with a couple of loud whacks with a bolo knife, cracked it open (a feat requir-ing considerable skill). After letting the juice flow into a bowl, the litur-gist raised the bowl and proclaimed, "The blood of Jesus Christ which is shed for us." The stillness was filled with an awe that was palpable each time. The gathered congregation, children and adults together, then came forward and joyfully partook of coconut dipped in coconut milk.

Gordon Zerbe, "Children and the Jesus Supper,"
in *Vision: A Journal for Church and Theology*,
Spring 2001

Luke's description is so simple in Acts 2:42-47. The believers were united spiritually and shared material possessions so that none were in need, and they ate a meal together every day with joy. But behind this text and the second summary of the growing community in 4:32-37 lies a world of or-ganizational detail and theological reflection that we can never fully re-cover. Faith, work, family relationships — Luke presents a seamless whole in the daily lives of people in a subsistence economy struggling to keep themselves and each other alive and thriving.

Unfortunately, Western biblical interpreters have tended to split apart the theological, spiritual, social, and economic implications of these and related texts. This history of interpretation has branched into subcategories with separate questions. In this and the following chapter we will examine three interconnected topics: the relationships between (1) a community of goods and the commensality of Acts 2:46 and 6:1; (2) the daily meal and a sacramental understanding of the Lord's Supper, or Eucharist; and (3) community, commensality, and care of the poor.

Guided by biblical interpretation, tradition, and cultural practices, the Christian church as a whole has not retained economic communalism, but the celebration of the Eucharist remains one of two essential rituals[1] of nearly all Christian groups around the world. Christians believe the poor should be helped, but few Western Christians assume that social communalism is the solution. How did the seamless whole break apart?

For each of these issues, I have chosen representative interpreters from three general categories: (1) commentaries or monographs from the last two or more centuries using precritical, traditional, and more historically oriented viewpoints, (2) commentaries using redaction or style criticism, and (3) special studies that more consciously integrate social history and the social sciences.

Common Life, Common Meals: The Daily Meal of Acts 2:42, 46 in a Community of Goods

Traditional and Historically Oriented Scholarship

The Latin Vulgate's translation of verse 42 would imply that there is no relationship at all between property-sharing and meals. They persevered, says the Vulgate, *in doctrina apostolorum et communicatione fractionis*

---

1. Although the terms "ritual" and "ceremony" are often interchangeable, even in Webster's Unabridged Dictionary, some scholars differentiate between the two. Rituals deal with status transformation, such as baptism and marriage, and happen to individuals at one point in time. Ceremonies confirm society's values and happen at regular intervals. In this sense, the Eucharist is a ceremony, not a ritual. See Mark McVann, "Rituals of Status Transformation in Luke-Acts: The Case of Jesus the Prophet," in *The Social World of Luke-Acts: Models for Interpretation*, ed. Jerome H. Neyrey (Peabody, Mass.: Hendrickson, 1991), pp. 333-60.

panis ("in the apostles' doctrine and communication of bread-breaking") rather than the alternate translation, *et in communione, in fractione panis* ("and in fellowship/*koinonia*, in breaking of bread"). Κοινωνία thus becomes the hierarchical "communication" of the sacrament from the apostles to the laypeople. Gone are both the communal sharing and eating together. This interpretation, though accepted and adopted in practice by traditional Roman Catholicism, is refuted in several nineteenth-century commentaries, such as those of H. A. W. Meyer and Henry Alford,[2] as well as by the contemporary Jesuit M. Manzanera.[3]

Others acknowledge that the communal meals mentioned in verses 42, 46 are part of the intense sharing of the believers and highlight the family atmosphere. The community is like a "family where joint meals, sacramental feasts, and charitable distributions run together,"[4] and the poor probably found in these meals "their chief means of sustenance."[5] Indeed, the communal meal is the primary aspect of the community of goods.[6] However, those commentators who stressed that a true community of goods existed, but only in Jerusalem, are then obliged to make some separation between property-sharing and bread-breaking, for they do see this meal as the beginning of the church-wide practice of agape meals, or love feasts.[7]

How exactly were these communal/sacramental meals carried out?

2. H. A. W. Meyer, *Handbook to the Acts of the Apostles*, 2d ed., trans. William P. Dickson (New York: Funk & Wagnalls, 1889), p. 68; Henry Alford, "The Acts of the Apostles, the Epistles to the Romans and Corinthians," in vol. 2 of *The Greek Testament* (Boston and New York: Lee & Shepard, 1872), p. 29.

3. M. Manzanera, "Koinonía en Hch 2,42. Notas sobre su interpretación y orígen histórico-doctrinal," *Estudios Eclesiasticos* 52, no. 202 (July-September 1977): 307-29. The major thesis of this article is discussed below.

4. Joseph A. Alexander, *The Acts of the Apostles* (London: n.p., 1884), p. 90.

5. G. H. C. MacGregor, *Acts*, vol. 5 of *The Interpreter's Bible* (Nashville: Abingdon Press, 1954), p. 51.

6. Laurence E. Browne, *Acts of the Apostles*, The Indian Church Commentaries (London: Society for Promoting Christian Knowledge, 1925), p. 56; Richard John Knowling, *The Acts of the Apostles*, Expositor's Greek Testament, ed. W. Robertson Nicoll (Edinburgh: n.p., 1900), p. 95; I. Howard Marshall, *The Acts of the Apostles: An Introduction and Commentary*, Tyndale New Testament Commentaries (Grand Rapids: Eerdmans, 1980), p. 83.

7. Alford, "The Acts of the Apostles," pp. 29-30; Meyer, *Handbook to the Acts of the Apostles*, p. 68; C. S. C. Williams, *The Acts of the Apostles* (New York: Harper & Row, 1957), p. 87; J. Rawson Lumby, *The Acts of the Apostles*, Cambridge Bible for Schools and Colleges (Cambridge: Cambridge University Press, 1893), p. 52.

Κατ' οἶκον (relating to house or household, v. 46) is understood in various ways. Meyer and Alford believe the meals were held in just one place, whereas Horatio Hackett and Laurence Browne prefer separate groups at different places, and J. Rawson Lumby thinks the best reading is "now at one house, now at another."[8] Seizing the opportunity to encourage family worship, G. V. Lechler stresses meals in private homes.[9] More sensitive to social realities, F. F. Bruce and Richard Longenecker use the phrase "by households," since households, not nuclear families, were the primary social unit at that time.[10]

Among this category of scholars, only Richard Rackham directly connected these meals with Jesus' practice of open table fellowship.[11] Rackham's also was the only older commentary (1901) that attempted a sociology of commensality, noting that eating together has always been a sign of fellowship, especially among Semites. "To eat bread or salt with another, even a deadly enemy, created a bond which could not be violated."[12] A common meal became a seal of fellowship. More recently, William Willimon noted that, since social boundaries are enforced most rigidly at table, eating together becomes a mark of solidarity across class lines.[13] William Neil commented on the common meal at Qumran,[14] but decided Luke was not detailed enough to make any comparisons.

8. Meyer, *Handbook to the Acts of the Apostles,* p. 71; Alford, "The Acts of the Apostles," p. 31; Horatio B. Hackett, *A Commentary on the Acts of the Apostles* (Philadelphia: American Baptist Publication Society, 1882), p. 56; Browne, *Acts of the Apostles,* p. 57; Lumby, *The Acts of the Apostles,* p. 30.

9. Gotthart Victor Lechler, *Acts,* Lange's Commentary on the Holy Scriptures, trans. Philip Schaff (Grand Rapids: Zondervan, 1886), p. 59.

10. F. F. Bruce, *The Acts of the Apostles* (Grand Rapids: Eerdmans, 1990), p. 131; Richard Longenecker, *The Gospel of John and the Acts of the Apostles,* Expositor's Bible Commentary (Grand Rapids: Zondervan, 1981), pp. 288-92, 310-12 (291).

11. Richard Belward Rackham, *The Acts of the Apostles* (1901; Grand Rapids: Baker, 1964), p. 36.

12. Rackham, *The Acts of the Apostles,* p. 36.

13. William Willimon, *Acts,* Interpretation series (Atlanta: John Knox Press, 1988), p. 41.

14. William Neil, *Acts of the Apostles,* New Century Bible (Grand Rapids: Eerdmans, 1973), p. 82.

Redaction and Literary Criticism

As stated in Chapter Two, some of the most influential commentators of the twentieth century view the summaries in Acts as Luke's creation of an idealized early church. In their view, the summaries are included to provide links and elaborations between the various scenes and narratives. Luke generalizes from the narratives and at the same time uses Greek utopian language to paint the beginnings of Christianity in the best possible light. He may either be edifying his readers and/or challenging them to deal with issues of rich and poor in their own Christian community. Some scholars in this section do not necessarily rule out any historical traditions as a matter of principle, but neither do they extend any real effort in this direction.

Thus, discussion of the relationship between the community of goods and communal meals in 2:42 and 46 is almost entirely missing from the major commentaries of redaction critics such as Ernst Haenchen, Hans Conzelmann, Gerhard Krodel, and Luke Johnson. If an actual community of goods never existed, how can it relate to communal meals — which may never have existed either?

Underneath the Redaction:
Searching for Sociohistorical Traditions

Scholars in this section, while taking Lukan redactional interests into account, also look for actual historical traditions Luke may have used.[15]

A monograph on issues of poverty, wealth, and possessions in the Lukan writings by H. J. Degenhardt[16] includes a discussion of the summaries of Acts 2:42-47 and 4:32-37. Luke's Greco-Roman audience has little concept of almsgiving; it is not a feature of pagan Greco-Roman society, where the destitute are generally ignored.[17] But Luke believes that God is

---

15. There is not necessarily a sharp distinction between some scholars here and in the first section (such as Jeremias).

16. *Lukas, Evangelist der Armen, Besitz und Besitzverzicht in den lukanischen Schriften. Eine traditions- und redaktionsgeschichtliche Untersuchung* (Stuttgart, 1965); described by François Bovon, *Luc le Théologien: Vingt-cinq ans de recherches, 1950-1975* (Neuchâtel-Paris: Delachaux & Niestlé, 1978); E.T., *Luke the Theologian: Thirty-Three Years of Research, 1950-1983*, trans. Ken McKinney (Allison Park, Pa.: Pickwick Press, 1987), pp. 392-94.

17. I will provide more detail on this in Chapter Four.

concerned about the poor and so requires alms. Luke has traditional information about the great liberality of the first Christians, who organized their charity by taking over the Jewish form of a daily basket for foreigners and a weekly bowl for the local poor. Using Greek idealistic language, Luke then transposes this into a description of a community where members voluntarily dispose of their possessions so that none are in need. The κοινωνία is the spirit of communion, which is expressed in commensality. This breaking of bread goes beyond a liturgical ritual to a common meal, which is a form of assistance to the poor. The descriptions of communal sharing in Acts, then, have nothing to do with an expectation of an imminent Parousia. Rather, they are a charge to Luke's own community to take seriously Jesus' teachings on caring for the poor and his calling Christian leaders to radical poverty.

Degenhardt's real interest is socio-redactional. If Luke is calling his community to share with the poor through a common meal in obedience to Jesus' teachings, it could be extrapolated that some tradition lies behind Luke's description of the Jerusalem community. However, Degenhardt does not draw that conclusion.

Though Degenhardt does not see a true community of goods underneath the Lukan summaries, M. Manzanera is looking for exactly that historical reality. Rejecting the interpretation that κοινωνία means primarily a "spirit of communion," Manzanera points out that Luke was writing for believers who understood this as a technical term meaning some kind of institutional property-sharing that includes "apportioning and distribution."[18] Manzanera also rejects the redaction-critical explanation that Luke is idealizing the early community by using Greek utopian language. Actual Greek Christian readers of Luke's day would never have taken this description seriously or been able to apply it, since such sharing could only happen ideally among *friends* who shared basic social and economic equality. The idea of redistributing possessions with the goal of eliminating poverty would have been unthinkable in Greco-Roman society.[19]

The only way to understand this technical term κοινωνία is through a Jewish tradition of communal goods that goes back as far as Leviticus, is reiterated in the Leviticus Targum and several New Testament references, and is currently understood to have been historically realized in the Essene

18. Manzanera, "Koinonía en Hch 2,42," p. 310.
19. Manzanera, "Koinonía en Hch 2,42," p. 318.

communities that were contemporary with Jesus and the early church.[20] Even though Josephus used Greek idealistic language to explain these communities to his Greco-Roman pagan audience, the Essenes themselves were motivated by their Jewish tradition found in the biblical writings.[21] So also were the early Christians.

Manzanera provides further literary evidence for this connection through examining the writing called "Two Ways." This document does not presently exist, but parts of it are found in the Christian writings of the *Didache* (chapters 1–6) and the Epistle of Barnabas (chapters 18–21), where both include exhortations to "share everything with your neighbor and do not claim that anything is your own." The following line clarifies that material possessions are in view: "If you are sharers in what is imperishable, how much more so in perishable things?" (*Did.* 4:8; *Barn.* 19:8).

But the origin of the "Two Ways" is not Christian but Jewish, for there are close literary and doctrinal similarities in the Manual of Discipline from Qumran (1QS 3:13-14, 26). Though the Essenes as Jews would not have differentiated between "perishable" and "imperishable," evidence for roots of material sharing among the earliest Christians (who would have used Essene structures as a model) can be seen in the document called The Apostles' Doctrine, which says the reverse: "If we are members in mortal things, how much more should we be consecrated in sacred things."[22]

The Essenes saw themselves as a true remnant of Israel through their observance of the Law, and thus practiced an actual community of goods. Manzanera does not think it would be very historical to think that the Jerusalem community began without following any previous model. This model was already present in the milieu in which John the Baptist and Jesus were educated. The fraternity that surrounded Jesus, made up of his disciples and the women "deacons" who lived in renunciation of property with a common purse, was the immediate antecedent of the κοινωνία of Jerusalem.[23]

Manzanera does not directly discuss commensality, though he implies its historicity as well, since communal meals were also a major feature of the Qumran community.

---

20. Manzanera, "Koinonía en Hch 2,42," p. 314.
21. Manzanera, "Koinonía en Hch 2,42," p. 320.
22. Manzanera, "Koinonía en Hch 2,42," p. 325.
23. Manzanera, "Koinonía en Hch 2,42" p. 329.

Food in Various Forms: The Meal in Acts 2:42, 46, Suppers, Agapes, and Eucharists

What do scholars see as the relationship between the common meal in the Acts community and later descriptions of "agape meals"? Between this common meal and the Lord's Supper, or Eucharist, as sacrament?

Traditional and Historically Oriented Scholarship

Commentary Survey

A view prevalent at least into the nineteenth century is that the breaking of bread in 2:42 means simply the celebration of the Lord's Supper.[24] Roman Catholics grounded their communion practice of not giving wine to the laity in this text.[25] Others lean toward bread-breaking as an ordinary meal, since this fits with the sense of all the other Acts passages where the breaking of bread is mentioned. If it also includes the Lord's Supper here, it cannot in 27:35, where sailors aboard Paul's ship are pagan.[26] Nevertheless, Johannes Weiss insists that bread-breaking was not an ordinary, everyday meal, which might be called an "eating of bread," but was a meal eaten with other believers and had a religious character. Although the breaking of bread was a Jewish ritual at the beginning of a meal, it now carries over to the whole meal. But it is not likely that this joyful meal was identical to the Lord's Supper, and there is no evidence it was connected with Jesus' death. Nothing in Acts shows Jesus' death as central, nor does the *Didache*.[27] Longenecker also sees the bread-breaking as an "ordinary" meal but with a sacred flavor, as were Jewish meals.[28]

---

24. Meyer, *Handbook to the Acts of the Apostles*, p. 69 (Meyer notes that Lightfoot also held this view); Alford, "The Acts of the Apostles," p. 29; Lumby, *The Acts of the Apostles*, p. 29.

25. Alford, "The Acts of the Apostles," p. 29.

26. Kirsopp Lake and Henry J. Cadbury, *The Acts of the Apostles: English Translation and Commentary*, vol. 4 of *The Beginnings of Christianity*, ed. F. J. Foakes Jackson and Kirsopp Lake (London, 1920-1933; Grand Rapids: Baker, 1965), p. 28; R. C. H. Lenski, *The Interpretation of the Acts of the Apostles* (Columbus, Oh.: Wartburg Press, 1944), p. 120.

27. Johannes Weiss, *Earliest Christianity: A History of the Period* A.D. *30-150*, vol. 1, trans. Frederick C. Grant (Gloucester, Mass.: Peter Smith, 1970), pp. 56-57.

28. Longenecker, *The Gospel of John and the Acts of the Apostles*, pp. 289-90.

By far the majority of these commentators saw these meals as ἀγάπαις, of which the Lord's Supper was a part. Even though breaking bread referred specifically to the Lord's Supper ritual, everyone at that time as well as in Luke's day would have taken for granted that it was in the context of a whole meal.[29] Some suggested that beyond Jerusalem these meals were held only on Sundays (Acts 20:7); a few thought the full meal was separated from the Lord's Supper after the abuses at Corinth. According to Rackham, agape meals later became specialized and were held in churches. They were one of the earliest subjects of church legislation, and by the fourth century there was a strong tendency to suppress them. Nevertheless, as late as 692 it was necessary for the Trullan Council to forbid holding an agape meal in church.[30]

The interpretation of breaking bread as a common meal with some religious significance, or as an agape meal that included the Lord's Supper, was a definite advance over ancient and traditional Roman Catholic practice, which emphasized ritual and hierarchy over communal table relationships. However, it is disappointing that so little connection is made with Jesus' table fellowship. Most of these commentaries also lack adequate reflection on what they mean by "the Lord's Supper," since the tone of the meals in Acts 2:42, 46 seems quite different from that in 1 Corinthians 11:23-26 and that of the Last Supper accounts in the Gospels. The following subsections discuss several studies that tackle this issue.

Special Studies on the Lord's Supper and Communal Meals in Acts

The literature on the Lord's Supper is vast, and much of it does not directly concern our Acts texts. Too often Acts 2:42-47 is slighted, for it is difficult to clarify the relationship between the earliest meals of the Jerusalem com-

---

29. These include: I. H. Marshall, *Acts of the Apostles,* Tyndale New Testament Commentaries (Grand Rapids: Eerdmans, 1980), p. 85; Alford, "The Acts of the Apostles," p. 29; Bruce, *The Acts of the Apostles,* p. 131; Neil, *Acts of the Apostles,* p. 81; Browne, *Acts of the Apostles,* p. 57; Willimon, *Acts,* p. 41; Williams, *The Acts of the Apostles,* p. 72; Lenski, *The Interpretation of the Acts of the Apostles,* p. 116; MacGregor, *Acts,* p. 51; Lechler, *Acts,* pp. 56-57; Rackham, *The Acts of the Apostles,* p. 37; Hackett, *A Commentary on the Acts of the Apostles,* p. 55; Thomas Ethelbert Page, *The Acts of the Apostles* (London and New York: Macmillan, 1895), p. 95.

30. Rackham, *The Acts of the Apostles,* pp. 37-38.

munity and the Last Supper portrayed in the Gospels and in 1 Corinthians 11. The former are joyful and daily, whereas the Lord's Supper is tied to Jesus' death and set within a Jewish Passover celebration. Several studies have attempted to reconstruct early Christian meal practices to explain this relationship.

A Double Origin for the Lord's Supper   The theory of a double origin of the Lord's Supper was first proposed by Friedrich Spitta in 1893,[31] although Hans Leitzmann's 1926 version is better known.[32] Leitzmann conjectured that the Jerusalem meal was the foundational one. It was simpler, it continued Jesus' table fellowship, and it involved the bread-breaking blessing only at the beginning of the meal. "There is no bridge leading from the Jerusalem rite to the metaphor of the bread and the body."[33] Although Leitzmann believed the account of the Last Supper in the Synoptics was historically valid, he did not think it was related to the ritual of the Lord's Supper. The latter happened first in Pauline churches, where it was derived from Hellenistic meals for the departed.[34]

The value of Lietzmann's proposal for my thesis is that it recognizes the religious character of the meals in Acts and traces them back to the practice of Jesus, even if they have no connection with the Lord's Supper ritual. However, Leitzmann's view of the Hellenistic origin of the Lord's Supper has been challenged by both Joachim Jeremias and H. G. Kuhn in favor of Palestinian origins. Let us turn now to a discussion of the work of two scholars who have written significant monographs on the Last Supper and the Lord's Supper and who relate the issues to Acts 2:42-47.

Acts 2:42 as an Early Christian Worship Service   By investigating its Semitic and Palestinian origins, Joachim Jeremias asserts the priority of the Lord's Supper formula in Mark 14:22-24 over that in Luke 22 and Paul's words in 1 Corinthians 11.[35]

---

31. Friedrich Spitta, "Die urchristlichen Traditionen über Ursprung und Sinn des Abendmahls," in *Zur Geschichte und Literatur des Urchristentums* (Göttingen: 1893), pp. 207-37.

32. Hans Leitzmann, *Messe und Herrenmahl* (Bonn: 1926); E.T., *Mass and Lord's Supper: A Study in the History of the Liturgy* (Leiden: E. J. Brill, 1979), pp. 204-8.

33. Leitzmann, *Messe und Herrenmahl*, p. 207.

34. Leitzmann, *Messe und Herrenmahl*, p. 207.

35. Joachim Jeremias, *The Eucharistic Words of Jesus,* trans. Norman Perrin (London: SCM Press Ltd., 1966).

Like Leitzmann, Jeremias believes that the earliest meals of the believers were more likely repetitions of the daily table fellowship of Jesus
with his disciples than repetitions of the Passover ceremony. There were
originally two kinds of meals in the earliest church, and only later (but still
in pre-Pauline times) did the ordinary meal celebration become "linked
with and influenced by the remembrance of the Last Supper."[36] If indeed
the meals of Acts 2:42 continued the practice of Jesus' ordinary table fellowship, it is quite plausible to think of them being held daily, or at least
quite often, rather than being merely a literary fiction.

But Jeremias thinks Luke takes the later practice of combining the
communal meal with the Eucharist and projects it back onto the earliest
church in Jerusalem. He understands the "κοινωνία" of verse 42 to refer to
the communal meal, and the "bread-breaking" to refer to the Eucharist.[37]
Against many of the commentators mentioned above, he believes that
bread-breaking cannot refer to a whole meal because it was never used that
way in Jewish custom; it only refers to the rite by which the meal began,
with the tearing of the loaf and the blessing.[38]

Can the Eucharist be celebrated with only bread and no wine?
Jeremias says yes. Ancient Jewish writings show that wine was drunk
only on festive occasions, such as during the entertaining of guests, at a
circumcision, engagement, or marriage; or in the house of the bereaved
during the seven days of mourning. Otherwise it was used only for me-
dicinal purposes. In everyday life, people drank water. Even at the main
meal of the day, bread, salt, and water were the main menu items, especially for the poor.[39] The reason Jesus and his disciples drank wine at the
Last Supper was that it was the Passover meal, and wine was required for
Passover. Even the poorest had the right to four cups of wine at this
meal.[40]

An ordinary meal at which the Eucharist was celebrated, then, would
not necessarily include wine. Two texts hint at this. In 1 Corinthians 11:25,
Paul reminds the Corinthians to remember Jesus "*as often as* you drink"
(NRSV, italics mine), implying that they may not be drinking the cup as

---

36. Jeremias, *The Eucharistic Words of Jesus,* p. 66.

37. Jeremias only deals with the bread-breaking reference in verse 42 because (following Cadbury's insight about Lukan summaries) he thinks vv. 43-46 were a later expansion.

38. Jeremias, *The Eucharistic Words of Jesus,* p. 120.

39. Jeremias, *The Eucharistic Words of Jesus,* pp. 50-51.

40. Jeremias, *The Eucharistic Words of Jesus,* p. 54.

often as eating bread. In Luke 22:19-20, Jesus says, "Do this in remembrance of me" only after breaking the bread.[41]

By comparing several early Christian writings such as the *Epistula Apostolorum* (140-70 C.E.), the *Apostolic Tradition* of Hippolytus, and the *Didache,* Jeremias concludes that the oldest ritual in the church was having the agape meal first, followed by the Eucharist. This leads Jeremias to theorize that Acts 2:42 describes the sequence of an early Christian service. Apostolic teaching comes first, followed by an agape meal, for which Luke uses the term κοινωνία. The bread-breaking refers to the Eucharist, and prayers conclude the service.

But it is not clear why the term "breaking of bread" could not also refer to the Jewish blessing at the beginning of ordinary meals like the ones Jesus had regularly with his disciples. The communal meal, then, would be implied in 2:42, since bread-breaking always preceded a meal. The action would be further explained in verse 46.

Jeremias's theory is not compelling, for it separates worship from ordinary daily living. As I see it, the text intends to show that the lifestyle of the community was integrated, with material issues inseparable from prayer and spiritual nourishment. Moreover, the κοινωνία in verse 42 seems to be further elucidated not so much by meals alone but by material sharing (vv. 44-45). Forms of κοινός (common) are used in both places.

Jeremias's theory has not been universally accepted by other New Testament scholars. On the other hand, his connecting these meals with Jesus' table fellowship in a Palestinian context advances the discussion over Lietzmann's theory of Hellenistic origins.

A Single Origin for the Lord's Supper   I. Howard Marshall's 1981 volume *Last Supper and Lord's Supper* argues (against Jeremias) for the priority of the Paul/Luke Lord's Supper tradition.[42] Luke stresses communal meals in Acts because of his general interest in meals, as is shown by the many references in his Gospel to Jesus at meals. The dramatic post-Resurrection account of bread-breaking at Emmaus in Luke 24 in particular shows that the presence of the risen Jesus was being experienced by the disciples both

---

41. Jeremias, *Eucharistic Words,* p. 115.

42. I. H. Marshall, *Last Supper and Lord's Supper* (Carlisle, England: Paternoster, 1980; Grand Rapids: Eerdmans, 1981), pp. 123-33.

in his exposition of the Scriptures and in his meal with them. "Luke intends his readers to see that these two things belong together."[43]

This paves the way for an approach to Acts 2:42, 46, where Marshall follows Jeremias in seeing the four activities in 2:42 as constituent parts of an early Christian gathering, provided "it is not interpreted too rigidly."[44] Like Jeremias, Marshall is inclined to think κοινωνία refers to the common meal itself, while "breaking of bread" refers to the Lord's Supper. Though this may reflect the practice of Luke's day, Luke's terminology appears primitive, and this practice conforms to Paul's description in 1 Corinthians 11.[45]

Marshall disagrees with Lietzmann and others who posit two kinds of meals in the early church: the solemn remembrance of Jesus' death and the joyful expectation of his return. The Testament of the Twelve Patriarchs shows, for example, that farewell meals can be celebrated with rejoicing.[46] Even though Luke does not mention the death of Jesus in his accounts of meals in Acts, he only reports that such meals *were held* rather than describing *how* they were held. Luke complements Paul's understanding of the Supper by stressing the joyous celebration of salvation in the presence of the risen Lord.[47] I would add that Luke's reference to eating with joy seems consistent with his overall theological emphasis on the risen Jesus and presence of his Spirit, whereas Paul shows greater interest in reinterpreting Jesus' death.[48] Thus they may be characterizing the same meal in different ways.

Marshall rightly emphasizes communal meals in Acts as a continuation of Jesus' previous meals with his disciples, as well as a reflection of meal practices of other groups at that time. However, in light of property sharing in 2:45, "κοινωνία" should not be restricted *only* to common meals.

---

43. Marshall, *Last Supper and Lord's Supper*, p. 125.

44. Marshall, *Last Supper and Lord's Supper*, pp. 126-27.

45. Marshall, *Last Supper and Lord's Supper*, p. 127.

46. Marshall (*Last Supper and Lord's Supper*, pp. 141-47) quotes Bo Reicke, *Diakonie, Festfreude und Zelos in Verbindung mit der Altchristlichen Agapenfeier*, Uppsala Universitets Årsskrift 5 (Uppsala: A.-B. Lundequistska Bokhandeln, 1951).

47. Marshall, *Last Supper and Lord's Supper*, pp. 130-33.

48. Suzanne Watts Henderson sees Paul's emphasis on "the death of the Lord" in 1 Corinthians 11:26 as referring not to substitutionary atonement but to Jesus' self-sacrifice that the wealthy Corinthians who do not share their meals must emulate in order to truly eat a meal like Jesus ate — a "supper of the Lord." "If Anyone Hungers . . . An Integrated Reading of 1 Cor. 11:17-34," *New Testament Studies* 48 (2002): 195-208 (202).

If meals were shared regularly in households, sharing would inevitably become more generalized in this subsistence economy.

The Tradition of Agape Meals

If the historicity of the common meals of the Jerusalem community can be posited on the basis of Jesus' meal practice, it can also be shown that the agape meals — or communal love-feasts that included the Eucharist — became a churchwide practice in the years following.

The earliest unmistakable reference to a full meal with sacramental dimensions is 1 Corinthians 11:17-34. "When you come together" (συνέρχομαι, vv. 17, 18, 20, 33, 34) implies a regular gathering; but because of their lack of unity, the believers do not eat "a supper of the Lord" but each eat their own suppers, and thus there is inequality ("one goes hungry and another becomes drunk," v. 21). "A supper of the Lord" (κυριακὸν δεῖπνον) is an inclusive meal like those Jesus ate with all kinds of people, a full meal where people bring food — but it is shared so that all have an equal amount. Only when discerning the *whole* body of believers (v. 29) can they eat bread and drink wine (the body and blood of the Lord Jesus) without bringing judgment on themselves. What Paul describes here is an agape meal.

Jude 12 is the earliest occurrence of the term ἀγάπαις (plural of ἀγάπη) clearly referring to meals in the sense of the Christian communal meal — ἐν ταῖς ἀγάπαις ὑμῶν . . . συνευωχούμενοι ("in your agapae, while feasting together").[49] False teachers had come to the meals and were apparently feasting with the other believers "without reverence." Richard Bauckham notes that the mention of ἀγάπαις here is probably not because the meals were subject to particular abuse by false teachers, but because they were the focal point of the common life of the Christian community, where the presence of false teachers would have been especially dangerous.[50]

Another probable reference to agape meals is 2 Peter 2:13, where the writer uses similar language to complain about false prophets. The phrase

---

49. Richard Bauckham argues that the provenance is Palestinian, that its attribution to James's brother Jude could be accurate, and that it may be one of the earliest writings in the New Testament. See "Jude," *HarperCollins Bible Commentary*, rev. ed., ed. James L. Mays (San Francisco: HarperSanFrancisco, 2000), p. 1184.

50. Richard J. Bauckham, *Jude, 2 Peter*, vol. 50 of Word Bible Commentary (Waco: Word Books, 1983), p. 85.

ἐν ταῖς ἀπάταις αὐτῶν συνευωχούμενοι ὑμῖν ("[reveling] in their dissipation while they feast with you") is evidently based on Jude's words about
the agape. The writer uses ἀπάταις (dissipation) as a deliberate pun, since
he uses the same word for "feasting."[51] Bruce Metzger notes that several
manuscripts do use the word ἀγάπαις, which he concludes is a scribal attempt to assimilate the text to the one in Jude.[52] The author added "with
you" to make it clear that he was talking about the common meals of the
church.[53]

Since ἀγάπη is the Greek word for self-giving love, there are other
hidden ἄγαπαις in the New Testament. Today, when "Christian love" is reduced to a good feeling toward other people or to providing "charity" for
unfortunates, it may be hard to grasp how immediate and practical ἀγάπη
was in the early church. In a letter full of admonitions to love, 1 John 3:17-
18 implies radical sharing: "How does God's love [ἀγάπη] abide in anyone
who has the world's goods and sees a brother or sister in need and yet refuses help? Little children, let us love [ἀγαπῶμεν], not in word or speech,
but in truth and action." Everett Ferguson believes that Jesus' instruction
in Luke 14:12-14 about inviting the poor and crippled and lame and blind
to banquets was taken seriously. He comments, "That *agape* came to mean
'love feast' is a testimony to the practical nature of early Christian love and
to the prominence of a meal as a way of expressing love."[54] (In later chapters I will use insights from anthropology to further demonstrate why
sharing food was a natural way of expressing love in that culture.)

Bo Reicke sees a hidden agape meal in John 13:1: "Having loved his
own who were in the world, he loved [ἠγάπησεν] them to the end." These
words set the stage for the love-act that Jesus will complete during his last
meal with his disciples: washing their feet in the context of a communal
meal. Reicke sees ἠγάπησεν (loved) as an indication of the technical term
ἀγάπη, in the sense of love-feast.[55] The name for these communal meals
may have developed from the meal the risen Jesus had with seven of his

51. Bauckham, *Jude, 2 Peter,* p. 266.

52. Bruce M. Metzger, *A Textual Commentary on the Greek New Testament* (New York:
United Bible Societies, 1975), p. 704.

53. Bauckham, *Jude, 2 Peter,* p. 266.

54. Everett Ferguson, "Agape Meal," in vol. 1 of *The Anchor Bible Dictionary,* ed. David
Noel Freedman (New York: Doubleday, 1992), p. 90.

55. Reicke, *Diakonie, Festfreude und Zelos in Verbindung mit der Altchristlichen
Agapenfeier,* p. 12.

disciples on the shore of Lake Tiberias (John 21:1-24). Although the greeting of peace (εἰρήνη) had characterized the other two meals Jesus had with the fearful disciples after his resurrection (John 20:19, 26), the last meal centers on Peter's conversation with Jesus about love.[56]

The letter of James particularly emphasizes the practical dimensions of community. From James 1:19 on, with communal worship in view, believers must be "doers of the word" (vv. 19-25), especially as it relates to caring for orphans and widows (v. 27). James 2:2 talks about an assembly (συναγωγή) with its closing benediction, "Go in peace" (2:16). But this is useless if not accompanied by an actual clothing and feeding of those who lack: "If a brother or sister is naked and lacks daily food, and one of you says to them, 'Go in peace; keep warm and eat your fill,' and yet you do not supply their bodily needs, what is the good of that?" (2:15-16).

Because ἀγάπη appears to have so many practical dimensions, because the Gospels so often highlight Jesus' meals and feedings, and because poverty and malnutrition stalked most first-century Mediterranean peoples, it is not difficult to see agape meals as implicit in numerous other New Testament texts that urge believers to "agape" each other. Robert Jewett has called attention to Romans 13:8: "Owe no one anything, except to love one another; for the one who loves another has fulfilled the law." This comes in the context of practical exhortations of how believers should live in the light of God's free grace explained in Romans 1–11. Paul has just encouraged the Romans to pay their taxes and not owe anyone anything — except for the continuing debt of loving each other. In other words, continue your agape meals so that everyone will have enough to eat.[57]

Catacomb Art

There is nonliterary evidence for agape meals as well. Meal scenes are common in catacomb paintings, often without clear distinctions between stories from the Gospels, the Last Supper, the Lord's Supper, a funerary meal, and an agape meal. In some of the pictures the words εἰρήνη (peace) and

56. R. Lee Cole, *Love Feasts: A History of the Christian Agape* (London: Charles Kelly, 1916), pp. 61-63.

57. Robert Jewett, "Are There Allusions to the Love Feast in Rom. 13:8-10?" in *Common Life in the Early Church: Essays Honoring Graydon F. Snyder*, ed. Julian V. Hills et al. (Valley Forge, Pa.: Trinity Press International, 1998), pp. 265-78.

ἀγάπη (love) are connected with a meal, but ἀγάπη is predominant. In many of the pictures there are not twelve figures (to denote the Last Supper) or ten or eleven (as in the post-resurrection meals) but seven, the number at the meal on Lake Tiberias. Furthermore, most pictures of meals portray a plate containing fish, the food eaten at agape meals.[58] In his examination of pre-Constantinian art, Graydon Snyder comments on the frequent presence of fish and loaves of bread in early Christian portrayals of a meal. "Unquestionably," he says, "the early Christians celebrated a meal together that was based on the Multiplication of the Loaves."[59] This meal with bread and fish "became the primary kinship or fellowship meal of the early Church."[60]

Literary and Redaction Criticism

Without question, redaction and other methods of literary analysis have advanced scholarship on Luke-Acts. Luke has an agenda — no doubt several agendas — and he writes artistically and persuasively. The challenge is to evaluate how much he has integrated historical sources into his narrative and how much this narrative reflects his own social location decades later. In the following paragraphs I will discuss four major Acts scholars who use redaction criticism and also tend to be skeptical of Luke's historical accuracy, especially for the Jerusalem church.

Since Ernst Haenchen believes that the summaries of the Jerusalem community in Acts 2:43-47 and 4:32-37 flow entirely from Luke's pen, he says little about any historical background to the communal meals. Since the only other reference to daily tables is in 6:1, this likely means that Luke projected his own experiences of ritual meals onto those of the Jerusalem community.[61] These Christian meals took place "at home" or in a number of houses. They are described as full meals (τροφέ). Because the Christians partook of them with simplicity and gladness (v. 46), one supposes that by Luke's time such meals were under grave suspicion in the larger pagan so-

---

58. Cole, *Love Feasts*, p. 61; Ferguson, "Agape Meal," p. 91.

59. Graydon F. Snyder, *Ante Pacem: Archaeological Evidence of Church Life before Constantine* (Macon, Ga.: Mercer University Press, 1985), p. 64.

60. Snyder, *Ante Pacem*, p. 25.

61. Ernst Haenchen, *The Acts of the Apostles: A Commentary* (Philadelphia: Westminster Press, 1971), pp. 195-96.

ciety.[62] Haenchen thinks that the phrase "breaking of bread" indicates an entire ritual meal. Thus Luke can avoid using phrases like "This is my body" and "This cup that is poured out for you is the new covenant in my blood" (as in Luke 22:19-20), which may have sounded suspicious to outsiders[63] — though why Luke does use them in his Gospel is unclear.

Hans Conzelmann asserts that the breaking of bread in 2:42, 46 is just as idealized as the sharing of property. He agrees with the majority who see bread-breaking as the entire meal. In considering the suggestion that the writer is referring to a pre-Pauline Lord's Supper, Conzelmann implies that Luke's thinking is a little fuzzy. "Luke is thinking of the ordinary daily meal here, but he does not make a distinction between it and the Eucharist. The unity of the two is part of the ideal picture of the earliest church."[64] Conzelmann speculates less than others about what the church in Luke's time may have been like, since he believes that "Luke does not present this way of life as a norm for the organization of the church in his own time."[65]

Gerhard A. Krodel's 1986 commentary popularizes redaction-critical assumptions that the summaries in Acts are generalized from specific narratives, and that Luke is reflecting his own time rather than the period of the earliest church.[66] Krodel sees two meanings in Luke's meal descriptions in verse 46. "Breaking of bread" refers to the Eucharist, and "partaking of food" refers to regular meals. Krodel does not think Luke means that the Lord's Supper was celebrated daily, but rather once a week on Sundays (cf. Acts 20:7). "Day by day" refers only to the first clause about the believers' presence in the temple. But the partaking of food did occur daily, and it was "an occasion of joyful remembrance of the meals with Jesus before and after Easter."[67] The reader is left to assume that this daily meal is not communal but, unlike the Lord's Supper, takes place in private homes like ours today.

Krodel briefly describes the evolution of the Eucharist from surrounding the regular meal to being included at the end of it. However, he is very unclear about what was occurring in Luke's time and what was occurring in the Jerusalem church. Even his separation of the regular meal from

---

62. Haenchen, *The Acts of the Apostles*, pp. 192-93.

63. Haenchen, *The Acts of the Apostles*, p. 191.

64. Hans Conzelmann, *Acts of the Apostles* (Philadelphia: Fortress Press, 1987), p. 23.

65. Conzelmann, *Acts of the Apostles*, p. 24.

66. Gerhard Krodel, *Acts*, Augsburg Commentaries (Minneapolis: Augsburg Press, 1986), p. 92.

67. Krodel, *Acts*, p. 93.

the Eucharist cannot be shown to have happened by the time Luke wrote. Krodel does not provide consistent, logical analysis of this text.

In comparison to the space he gives to sharing possessions, Luke Johnson says little about communal meals in Acts 2:42, 46, other than that they are part of Luke's idealized portrait of the community. He does think they refer to more than ordinary meals because the resurrected Jesus was recognized at the breaking of the bread.[68] Further, the "gladness" suggests eschatological joy in his presence. Johnson notes that the household is the place for these meals, and it will be increasingly mentioned throughout Acts as the location of cult activities (5:42; 8:3; 11:14; 16:15, 31-32; 18:8; 20:20).[69] But the term "household" is undefined and implies only a literary construct.

None of these scholars suggests that these meals may reflect a continuation of Jesus' practice of table fellowship,[70] nor do they see any connection to contemporaneous Essene practices of commensality, nor do they attempt to connect meals in Acts to the historical agape-meal tradition.

Underneath the Redaction:
The Search for Sociohistorical Traditions

So the search continues for historical reality behind the narrative in Acts. The research presented below, while taking account of redaction-critical issues, looks for actual traditions behind the meals of Acts 2:42, 46.

Gerd Lüdemann: κοινωνία through Shared Meals

Gerd Lüdemann has moved away from exclusive dependence on redaction criticism to search for evidences of Acts' historicity; his concern is not unlike that of the editors of *The Beginnings of Christianity.*[71] Lüdemann uses Paul's letters and other New Testament writings as a check, along with re-

---

68. Luke Johnson, *The Acts of the Apostles,* vol. 5, Sacra Pagina (Collegeville, Minn.: Michael Glazier, 1992), p. 58.

69. Johnson, *The Acts of the Apostles,* p. 59.

70. That is, unless Jesus' meals are also a literary construct by the Gospel writers. There is plenty of debate about this, some of which I will discuss in a later chapter.

71. Gerd Lüdemann, *Early Christianity According to the Traditions in Acts: A Commentary,* trans. John Bowden (Minneapolis: Fortress Press, 1989; Göttingen: Vandenhoeck & Ruprecht, 1987).

sponsibly weighing Luke's literary structure and redactional material, and the traditions that lie behind them.

According to this method, Acts 2:42-47 is a Lukan summary, primarily redactional in language. The Jerusalem community is generalized, developed timelessly through using Greek ideals, but Luke also uses them as *paranesis*.[72] Verse 42 and possibly verse 43 may go back to tradition. The information about the κοινωνία, selling possessions, and communal meals is new to Acts; the origin might be sought in Jerusalem. There is an accurate historical tradition that the Jerusalem community assembled and stayed together in κοινωνία through their shared meals. This could have been a continuation of Jesus' table fellowship with his disciples, a regular repetition of his last meal, or ordinary Jewish meals. The meals take place in homes of members of the Jesus community like Mary's house (12:12). However, all this would be groundless *if* Luke is using paranetic traditions from Paul's letters and prematurely transferring them to the Jerusalem community.[73]

Lüdemann's analysis, while not detailed, illustrates a change in attitude from Conzelmann's skeptical stance, which had proved so influential. It provides reasons why communal meals and the sharing of goods are historically plausible.

Bo Reicke: The Case for One Single Sacrament of Table Fellowship

An older but somewhat neglected study by Bo Reicke addresses the relationship between agape meals and the Lord's Supper in the early church.[74] In the New Testament and other early Christian writings, Reicke finds four different names for the community meal: bread-breaking (Acts 2:42, 46), the Lord's Supper (1 Cor. 11:20), Agape or love feast (Jude 12; Ignatius Rom. 7:3-4), and the Eucharist (*Didache* 9:15; Ignatius Phil. 4:1-2). But his evidence shows that there was one original unity that later split into different types. The different names may be attributed to different geographical regions or to emphasis of one part of the meal over another, but for some time they were fundamentally the same thing.[75]

72. Lüdemann, *Early Christianity According to the Traditions in Acts*, p. 47.

73. Lüdemann, *Early Christianity According to the Traditions in Acts*, pp. 48-49.

74. Reicke, *Diakonie, Festfreude und Zelos in Verbindung mit der Altchristlichen Agapenfeier*.

75. Reicke, *Diakonie, Festfreude und Zelos in Verbindung mit der Altchristlichen Agapenfeier*, pp. 9-10.

> According to the divinely instituted day/rule of
> the Lord, having been gathered together, break a
> loaf. And give thanks [εὐχαριστήσατε], having
> beforehand confessed your failings, so that your
> sacrifice may be pure.
>
> *Didache* 14:1, trans. Aaron Milavec

Apart from the recounting of the Last Supper and from 1 Corinthians 10 and 11, accounts of bread-breaking occur without reference to wine: the disciples at Emmaus (Luke 24:30, 35); Paul at Troas (Acts 20:7, 11); Paul before the shipwreck (Acts 27:35); *Didache* 14:1; Ignatius Ephesians 20:2. Both of the last two texts show plainly the bread-breaking indicates a sacrament, and it is clearly the Eucharist. The *Didache* text specifically includes thanks, confession of sins, and sacrifice. The Ignatius text shows the broken bread as "medicine of immortality" to eternal life through Jesus Christ. The terms "Eucharist" and "bread-breaking" must therefore not be separated.[76] (Jeremias suggests two reasons why: wine was not drunk at ordinary meals, and the poor could not have afforded it anyway.)

Reicke discusses the two places in the New Testament where ἀγάπη is used for a meal: John 13:1 and Jude 12 (see above). In both cases the meal is meant to be sacramental.[77] In Ignatius's Romans letter (7:3) he names the body and blood of Christ as a permanent, or imperishable, agape (ἀγάπη ἄφθαρτος), and in Smyrnaeans 6:2; 7:1, and 8:2 the concepts of ἀγάπη *(agape)* are synonymous with εὐχαριστία *(eucharistia)*.[78]

Didache 9:5 uses the word εὐχαριστία in a context that implies the

---

76. Reicke, *Diakonie, Festfreude und Zelos in Verbindung mit der Altchristlichen Agapenfeier*, p. 11.

77. By "sacramental" I am assuming Reicke means something like the definition used in *The Oxford Companion to the Bible*, ed. Bruce M. Metzger and Michael D. Coogan (Oxford: Oxford University Press, 1993), p. 666: Sacraments are "occasions of encounter between God and the believer, where the reality of God's gracious actions needs to be accepted in faith to effect a true meeting. . . . [They are a] means of grace insofar as they are occasions when the gracious act of God is made present to the believer (1 Cor. 11:26)."

78. Reicke, *Diakonie, Festfreude und Zelos in Verbindung mit der Altchristlichen Agapenfeier*, pp. 12-13.

presence of the traditional ἀγάπη meal. Between the first table-prayer in Chapter 9 and the second in Chapter 10, there must be a genuine meal, because 10:1 says, "After you have eaten and are satisfied, you shall in the following manner give thanks." Without ἀγάπη, the meal would not be εὐχαριστία.[79]

Even though there is only one single community meal, Reicke cautions against assuming too much uniformity. Just as there are different forms of baptism but only one single baptism in Christ, so there are different forms of the meal but only one single Christian sacrament of table fellowship. No doubt each writer chooses the form of the word he wants to stress. Using "bread-breaking" or "Lord's Supper" may emphasize the food. "Agape" stresses the loving community. And "Eucharist" refers to the

---

... break one bread which is the medicine of immortality [φάρμακον ἀθανασίας] and the antidote against death. ...

Ignatius to the Ephesians 20:2

---

thanksgiving over the food. (An analogy is "Mass," which comes from *missa*, the dismissal at the end of communion service, which now stands for the entire event.)[80]

In that case, references to breaking bread and eating with joy in Acts 2:42, 46 also refer to table fellowship. If communal meals were the central rite of the Christian communities from before Paul wrote to the Corinthians about 50 C.E. to at least through the death of Ignatius in 107 (or 116) C.E., they would have been a reality Luke was familiar with. Though he may have used language on friendship from Hellenistic philosophy to characterize the Jerusalem community, Luke was nevertheless speaking of an actual practice of communal eating.[81]

79. Reicke, *Diakonie, Festfreude und Zelos in Verbindung mit der Altchristlichen Agapenfeier*, p. 13.

80. Reicke, *Diakonie, Festfreude und Zelos in Verbindung mit der Altchristlichen Agapenfeier*, p. 14.

81. There is plenty of evidence later than Ignatius for agape meals, although their ex-

If indeed there was only one communal meal at this time, and since Paul cites a liturgy used at this meal that he claims was received tradition from Jesus and that appears to be pre-Pauline (1 Cor. 11:23-25), it is not hard to extrapolate Jerusalem believers holding communal meals after Pentecost.

Berndt Kollmann: Jesus and the Early Christian Love-Feast

More recently, Berndt Kollmann has traced the origin of the early Christian meals by constructing a trajectory of six stages for the first 150 years.[82] Most relevant for my interests are the first and second stages. In the first stage, the historical Jesus practices open table fellowship with his disciples, tax collectors, sinners, and others. In the second stage, these meals continue after Jesus' death and begin to be seen through a variety of allegorical, eschatological, and messianic lenses. The followers of Jesus in Hellenistic Judaism concentrate on the saving significance of bread, which eventually leads in some circles to identifying bread and wine with the body and blood of Christ. By the last quarter of the first century, Kollmann projects three different cultic meal traditions in different geographical areas.[83]

In Acts 2:42-47, Kollmann searches for a pre-Lukan meal tradition underneath Luke's redactional summarizing. The term "breaking bread" in verse 46 is not Lukan but a broader Christian term for an entire communal meal, a term also found in Acts 20:7, 11, Ignatius Ephesians 20:2, and *Didache* 14:1. Lukan idealizing has provided a sacramental character to the bread-breaking in Luke 22:19 and 24:30, but the historical origins of bread-breaking are not sacramental but are found in the joyful communal meals around Jesus. Acts 2:42, 46 therefore fulfills Mark 2:18-19, where the wedding guests rejoice and do not fast when the bridegroom is with them. The joy expressed in Acts 2:46 results from the presence of the risen Jesus in the

---

act connection with the Eucharist is not always clear. John F. Keating traces the history of the agape from New Testament writings to the fourth century, quoting from church fathers (besides Ignatius) such as Justin Martyr, Tertullian, and Chrysostom, and from numerous church ordinances. See *The Agape and the Eucharist in the Early Church: Studies in the History of the Christian Love-Feasts* (London, 1901; reprint: New York: AMS Press, Inc., 1969).

82. Berndt Kollmann, *Ursprung und Gestalten der frühchristlichen Mahlfeier*, GTA 43 (Göttingen: Vandenhoeck & Ruprecht, 1990).

83. Kollman's trajectory is condensed in a review by Hal Taussig in *Journal of Biblical Literature* 111, no. 4 (Winter 1992): 733-35.

midst of those gathered.[84] In this way, according to Kollmann, Luke has used the term "breaking bread" from his own day to describe the practice of table fellowship by the historical Jesus. Use of the same term in Acts 2:46 shows that the practice was continued after Jesus in the earliest church in Jerusalem.

Both Reicke and Kollmann use the term "sacramental" in a more ecclesiastical sense than does Bruce Chilton, to whom we turn next.

Bruce Chilton: A Veritable Feast of Meanings

In his monograph connecting table fellowship with purity issues, Bruce Chilton proposes a trajectory of six stages in the development of the Eucharist.[85] Using "generative exegesis," he employs both literary and linguistic analysis of texts, their contexts, and their histories of formation. The diversity of New Testament texts on the Eucharist must lead back to a variety of historical practices.

"Purity," begins Chilton, "is the means by which certain objects and gestures are privileged and paradigmatic. Unclean actions and objects are those which are proscribed or marginalized."[86] Purity concerns for secular Westerners are those that relate to health, physical cleanliness, and appearance. For Jesus, the main issue was the *direction* from which purity should proceed: it begins internally and works outward in words and actions (Matt. 15:15-20; Mark 7:17-23).

For Jesus, to eat meals in fellowship with other Jews was not to ignore purity concerns but to demonstrate the purity of all Israelites, based on forgiveness. He gave those most marginalized by the Temple system the opportunity to look forward to the coming kingdom of God. These meals were "practical parables as evocative as verbal parables."[87] In fact, Chilton argues that the statement Jesus made at the Last Supper — "I will not drink wine with you until I drink it anew in the kingdom of God" — could have been made at any of his meals, because the meaning assures the hearers that "the wine of the kingdom will soon be enjoyed."[88] The kingdom

---

84. Kollmann, *Ursprung und Gestalten der frühchristlichen Mahlfeier*, pp. 71-75.

85. Bruce Chilton, *A Feast of Meanings: Eucharistic Theologies from Jesus through Johannine Circles* (Leiden: E. J. Brill, 1994).

86. Chilton, *A Feast of Meanings*, p. 32.

87. Chilton, *A Feast of Meanings*, p. 39.

88. Chilton, *A Feast of Meanings*, pp. 44-45.

Jesus prayed for (as in the Lord's Prayer) would surely come. What made the wine "sacred" was not the wine itself but the fact that it was consumed within a pure fellowship. This is Chilton's first stage.

With this view of purity, Jesus surely would have pushed for cultic reform; hence his focus on the Temple sacrificial system. Like the Pharisees, he perceived commerce in the Temple as unclean, a violation of the law that states the sacrificial animal must be one's own. But his action to rid the Temple of commerce failed, so he saw *himself* as the sacrificial victim, with wine representing his blood and bread his body. As in Luke's account (22:17), the cup is first, following the Leviticus method of bleeding the victim before cooking its flesh.[89]

Now Jesus' meals take on new significance (the second stage). The wine and bread symbolizing Jesus' blood and body are better sacrifices than an offering in the Temple. The "sacrifice of sharings" in Leviticus 3 becomes a "festive meal in a cultic context."[90]

Chilton calls the third stage "Petrine," since, according to Acts, Peter takes the leadership in the earliest church in Jerusalem. Here Luke portrays the development of meals eaten at home, although the people also congregate and worship at the Temple. Two factors account for Temple attendance. First, the vendors were eventually removed from the Temple to another location, and in 36/37 Vitellius removed Caiaphas as high priest. In this sense, the Temple was "cleansed," and the Jesus community around Peter could worship there[91] (though Acts 3–5 does report conflict). Second, with the growth of this established community (and likely others elsewhere), the meals became domesticated, held in homes rather than in cultic or special settings. The order of wine-before-bread was reversed to conform to ordinary meals, which began by breaking bread and (if wine was served) ended with the cup. With his explicit reference to a "new covenant" (Mark 14:24 and par.), Jesus was seen as a teacher of purity comparable to Moses. Celebrating meals in households rather than sacrificing at the Temple also had the effect of widening the circle of purity to include Israelites who lived far away and non-Jews who worshipped Yahweh (e.g., Cornelius; Acts 10:2).

The fourth stage is dominated by the more conservative James, who takes over leadership of the Jerusalem church from Peter (Acts 12:17).

89. Chilton, *A Feast of Meanings,* pp. 57-67.
90. Chilton, *A Feast of Meanings,* p. 73.
91. Chilton, *A Feast of Meanings,* pp. 79-80.

James wants to limit Gentile participation by identifying the sacred meal with Passover, to be celebrated only once a year in Jerusalem by circumcised Jews. This is picked up by all the Gospels, where the twelve Jewish disciples celebrate the Passover meal.

This move was resisted by Paul (the fifth stage), who in 1 Corinthians 11:17-34 insists on the Petrine view that the meal is a sacrifice of sharings by using the terms "memorial" and "covenant" (vv. 24-25). In fact, the idea of celebrating only once a year is specifically counteracted by verse 25c — "as often as you drink" — making any festive meal an appropriate occasion of the memorial (the word "it" is not in the Greek text). Paul may have emphasized Jesus' death instead of joy because in a Greco-Roman context such meals could have become drinking and sex parties.[92]

Chilton's work makes clear where "sacramental" actually lay in the first three and the fifth stages of the "feast": in the *commensality* rather than in any separate ritual using bread and wine. By referring to Leviticus 3 and the sacrifice of sharings — literally, "peace offerings" — Chilton sees no connection of the meal to an offering for sin. It is not until John's Gospel (the sixth stage) that Jesus dies on the day that lambs are slaughtered for Passover and becomes "the Lamb of God who takes away the sin of the world" (1:29).

Robert Jewett: Evidence for Daily Communal Meals

If Chilton's "Petrine stage" is correct, it is not hard to imagine such meals held every day, for they were celebrations of unity in a purified, forgiven Israel at the same time that they provided ordinary nourishment for the community in their various households. But is there any external evidence for such *daily* meals? Most commentators point to Acts 20:7 to show that very soon "bread-breaking" was practiced only on Sundays.[93]

---

92. Chilton, *A Feast of Meanings*, p. 112. But see Henderson's comment in note 48.

93. In fact, Acts 20:7 need not imply this. Paul was returning to Jerusalem and visiting Christians at Troas along the way. Since Paul was planning to sail the next day, they met the evening before, at the end of the Sabbath (τῇ μιᾷ τῶν σαββάτων), to break bread and hold a discussion. If Paul had instead planned to sail on Wednesday or Thursday, they would no doubt have had a "last supper" with him the evening before. Further, Acts 20:11 says that after Paul's long talk and Eutychus's restoration to life, Paul again broke bread with the others (in the middle of the night) and continued talking until dawn. This text hardly proves that the reason they broke bread on Sunday was that they only ever broke bread on Sundays.

Robert Jewett's examination of the Thessalonian correspondence may speak to this question indirectly.[94] Much scholarship on early house churches assumes Christians met in homes of a patron who not only provided space but likely most of the food for the meal. However, Peter Lampe,[95] Jewett, and others have posited the existence of small groups living and meeting in tiny rented rooms of tenement buildings, without a patron.[96] References in both letters to manual labor and working with one's hands, along with the absence of any named patrons, lead Jewett to conclude that the Thessalonian Christians had to provide their own space and food.

The admonition to "work with your hands" (as Paul says he exhorted them to do when he was there) in 1 Thessalonians 4:9-12 is in the context of Paul praising them for how much they already ἀγαπᾶν (agape) each other, but saying now they should do so even more. They should work with their own hands "so that you may . . . be dependent on no one" (v. 12). The text of 2 Thessalonians 3:10 is even stronger, now a command: "Anyone unwilling to work should not eat."

The form of this command is a typical example of casuistic law, where the first half of the saying describes the offense and the second half provides the consequence. Parallels to this command can be found in Qumran scrolls, where disobeying rules of the community can result in exclusion from the common table of the "pure"; in regulations of Greco-Roman guilds, where the penalty is exclusion from the common meal or from the guild itself; and in boarding schools, where the threat of withholding food is used to get pupils to study. All of these parallels come from settings where groups are eating their meals together regularly.[97]

The command concerns those who do not want to work — they may

94. Robert Jewett, "Tenement Churches and Pauline Love Feasts," in *Paul the Apostle to America: Cultural Trends and Pauline Scholarship* (Louisville: Westminster/John Knox, 1994), pp. 73-86.

95. Peter Lampe, *Die stadtrömischen Christen in den ersten beiden Jahrhunderten: Untersuchen zur Sozialgeschichte* (Tübingen: J. C. B. Mohr, 1989); E.T.: *From Paul to Valentinus: Christians at Rome in the First Two Centuries*, trans. Michael Steinhauser, ed. Marshall D. Johnson (Minneapolis: Fortress Press, 2003); "The Roman Christians of Romans 16," in *The Romans Debate*, ed. Karl P. Donfried (Peabody, Mass.: Hendrickson, 1991), pp. 216-30.

96. In the following chapters I will deal in more detail with material informed by social history, sociology, and anthropology.

97. Jewett, "Tenement Churches and Pauline Love Feasts," p. 82.

not eat. But food can only be withheld in a community that eats meals together regularly, not just once a week. Form criticism shows that this type of casuistic law tends to arise out of many situations and becomes abstracted as common law.[98] If so, it means that the author of 2 Thessalonians did not create this rule but passed it on as wisdom received from earlier communal situations.[99]

If the Thessalonians were eating together regularly in a communal context that depended on the labor of all in order to put enough food on the table, and if the admonition about such work was made in the context of an encouragement to love each other, daily agape meals must be in view in these texts. The practicality of daily commensality in Christian communities will become clearer in Part II, which examines the social world of Acts 2 and 6.

The Dead Sea Scrolls and Meals among the Contemporary Essenes

Although I will discuss the Qumran Covenanters and other Essenes in Chapter Eight, this more general introduction serves to remind us that communal groups in Palestine existed before and throughout the life of Jesus and of the early church, until 70 C.E.

The possible connection of Essene communal meals with the Jerusalem community was already raised during the nineteenth century, though it was usually rejected or seen as very tenuous. But even after the Dead Sea Scrolls showed beyond doubt that these communities had existed, with highly structured property-sharing and communal meals, commentators who stressed Luke's idealizing tendencies and Greek utopian concepts of community underplayed the influence of Essene practices on the Jerusalem community. For example, Conzelmann allows that Luke's picture of sharing property may have been partly influenced by his "knowledge about communistic groups, whether real (Essenes and the Qumran community) . . . or ideal" (Pythagorean communities).[100] After discussing Greek ideals of friendship, he dismisses the Essene influence with a para-

98. Hans Jochen Boecker, *Law and the Administration of Justice in the Old Testament and Ancient Near East,* trans. J. Moiser (Minneapolis: Augsburg Press, 1980), pp. 150-55, cited in Jewett, *Paul the Apostle to America,* p. 151, n. 56.

99. Jewett, "Tenement Churches and Pauline Love Feasts," pp. 82-83.

100. Conzelmann, *Acts of the Apostles,* p. 24.

doxical statement: "Despite the existence of communistic groups in the vicinity of Jerusalem, Luke's portrayal should not be taken as historical (some sort of organized means of support would have been necessary, as in those groups)."[101] Luke Johnson never once refers to Qumran or the Essenes in his commentary on Acts 2:42-47.[102]

Yet scholarship that investigated analogies between communal meals at Qumran and early Palestinian Christian meal practices was available before either Conzelmann's commentary (1963) or Johnson's commentary (1992) was published. I refer here to Krister Stendahl's introduction and an essay on meals at Qumran by Karl Georg Kuhn in the 1957 edition of *The Scrolls and the New Testament,* edited by Krister Stendahl.[103]

Subsequent research and reflection on the Scrolls have tempered the enthusiasm with which Qumran Covenanters and the Essenes as a whole have been compared to the early Christian movement. There is no evidence, biblical or otherwise, that directly links the two groups. Yet they must be regarded as cousins who share the same ancestor of intertestamental Judaism.[104] The Palestinian Christians must have known of the Essenes, who had lived in the area for the past 150 to 200 years. A provocative link is John the Baptist, who also lived in the wilderness and baptized repentant Israelites, not unlike the Essenes, who purified themselves through a ritual bath before each meal (1QS 3.4, 9; 5.13; 6.16; CD 9.21, 23).

Both Essenes and Christians stressed their election as the particular people of God, where membership demanded initiation and obedience, and where eschatology was the frame of reference.[105] The Essene Manual of Discipline (1QS) contains minute regulations for group discipline, the punishment for disobedience being exclusion from the common meals. This was no arbitrary punishment, for the meals were the focal point of Essene

---

101. Conzelmann, *Acts of the Apostles,* p. 24. The parenthetical remark in this sentence seems directly contradictory to the rest of the sentence.

102. Johnson, *The Acts of the Apostles,* pp. 56-63.

103. Krister Stendahl, "The Scrolls and the New Testament: An Introduction and a Perspective" (pp. 1-17), and Karl Georg Kuhn, "The Lord's Supper and the Communal Meal" (pp. 65-93), in *The Scrolls and the New Testament* (New York: Harper, 1957; New York: Crossroad, 1992). The 1992 edition contains a "substantially revised and enlarged edition" of Kuhn's original article.

104. N. T. Wright, *The New Testament and the People of God* (Minneapolis: Fortress Press, 1992), p. 204.

105. Stendahl, "The Scrolls and the New Testament," pp. 7-16.

eschatology, the anticipation of the Messianic Banquet that was to come. Says Stendahl, "The actual meal of the Essene Community (cf. 1QS 6.4-6) is defined as an anticipation of the Messianic Banquet. In its central religious act the sect understands itself as an anticipation of the Age to Come."[106]

The Gospels also speak of the concept of the Messianic Banquet (cf. Matt. 8:11; Luke 22:30) and show theological interest in Jesus' meals and feedings of the multitudes. All four accounts of the Last Supper in the Synoptics and Paul (as well as the *Didache*) have a strong note of anticipation. "Jesus will not taste of the meal until it comes to its fulfillment in the Kingdom of God, and by the celebration of the meal Christ is proclaimed until his coming again."[107]

There are also significant differences between the meal practices of the two groups. A priest was essential for an Essene meal, but the early church had no such requirement. Women either were not present or did not count for a quorum (which had to be ten men) at an Essene meal, whereas Christian meals were held in family-style households, and women belonged to the church as a matter of course (Acts 1:14; 2:18; 5:14; 8:3; 8:12; 9:2). A definite order of rank pervades the description of Essene meals, but no evidence of hierarchy characterizes the Christian meals described in Acts.[108]

Nevertheless, in addition to Jesus' meal practices, the earliest Christians had a model of a sect, right in their homeland and Palestinian culture, which practiced daily commensality — with bread and grape juice — that had deep religious and eschatological meaning.

Conclusion

In this chapter I have dealt with two of three major questions about the social practices of the Jerusalem church: how do the Jerusalem church's daily common meals relate to its economic sharing, and what connection do these meals have with the sacrament of the Eucharist? There is overlap with the third question, which arises in Acts 6:1 concerning caring for the poor; this question I will discuss in the following chapter.

106. Stendahl, "The Scrolls and the New Testament," p. 10.
107. Stendahl, "The Scrolls and the New Testament," p. 10.
108. Kuhn, "The Lord's Supper and the Communal Meal," p. 86.

The three sections under each of the two questions represent different methodologies of interpretation. The first section discusses traditional scholarship from the nineteenth century to the present that mostly assumes Luke's historical accuracy. A major question for these commentaries was whether the meals in Acts have a sacramental dimension or are just ordinary meals. The majority believed that the meals had some sacramental significance and connected them to the later practice of celebrating the ritual of the Lord's Supper in connection with a full meal, the agape, or love feast.

Several special studies came to different conclusions. Hans Leitzmann proposes a double origin to the meals: one a solemn remembrance of Jesus' death, and the other a more joyful celebration of his resurrection and future return. I. Howard Marshall argues for one meal that could be both joyful and solemn. Joachim Jeremias sees Acts 2:42 as the description of an early Christian worship service, which includes apostles' teaching, κοινωνία as offering for the poor, bread-breaking (celebration of the Eucharist), and prayer.

These scholars discussed questions that are still relevant today, and a genuine effort was made to present a cohesive picture of the early church. The strongest gain was the emphasis on the communal meal as part of the Christian agape meal tradition. However, a major weakness was the tendency to emphasize theological issues at the expense of the social, or not integrating them (though with exceptions, such as some of Jeremias's work). The contemporary separation of Eucharistic ritual from the socioeconomic commensality that originally lay at its root has been tacitly read back into the Lukan texts. Only one commentary touched on the sociology of meals in a Semitic tradition, and the possibility that meals in the Jerusalem community were a continuation of Jesus' practice of table fellowship. Consequently, the conclusions of these writers were more or less skewed by their theological presuppositions and limited by the lack of access to or interest in our present knowledge of ancient Palestinian social and cultural conditions gained through archeology and social-scientific criticism.

Later, redaction criticism became very influential in Lukan studies. Although appreciating Luke as a skilled writer with his own interests advances our understanding, commentators discussed in this second section overemphasized Luke's theological and literary redactional concerns to the serious neglect of social and historical issues. Lukan idealizing of the early Christian community, the literary symbolism of communal meals and households, and speculation about how the text applied to Luke's own community replace reflection on what might have actually happened in the early days in Jerusalem. Theological interests also predominate in redaction criticism to the detriment of social analysis. A middle-class or upper-middle-class milieu is also assumed.

However, the group of scholars discussed in the third section has moved the discussion forward in significant ways. Though they generally recognize redactional issues, they also look for historical strands and traditions underneath Lukan summarizing. Essene and Qumran research has proved fruitful, providing parallels with early Christian practices. References to sharing of goods turn up in Christian and Qumran documents, both kinds of which have appropriated parts of a now-lost document called "Two Ways," which stresses property-sharing. Descriptions of both Essene and early Christian commensality are characterized by eschatological expectation and joy, even though strong differences exist.

Instead of believing that two kinds of meals — joyful and solemn — originated separately, Bo Reicke, Berndt Kollmann, and Bruce Chilton trace a development from Jesus' meals with his disciples to bread-breaking with many meanings, depending on geographical and social location, along with cultural, political, and theological changes in church and society. Evidence for *daily* communal meals beyond Jerusalem exists in two passages in the Thessalonian letters which show that, years later, believers in Thessalonica must have been eating together every day, for the admonition "Anyone unwilling to work should not eat" can only make sense in such a situation.

Despite the weaknesses noted above and the biases elaborated upon in Chapter Two, I maintain that the many helpful insights in this chapter are significant. They will be used to flesh out a cohesive and realistic picture of communal meals in Acts 2 and 6.

But first I must discuss a major lacuna: What would have been the economic value of communal meals in the Jerusalem church? How do the communal meals in Acts 2:42, 46 relate to the care of the poor, which some think is suggested in Acts 6:1?

Chapter Four

Meals on Wheels for the Widows?
Common Meals versus Poor Relief

Remove far from me falsehood and lying;
   give me neither poverty nor riches;
   feed me with the food that I need,
or I shall be full, and deny you, and say, "Who is the LORD*?"*
or I shall be poor, and steal, and profane the name of my God.

Proverbs 30:8-9

When and where is the communion meal still an act and example of
mutual sharing, caring, and love? . . . Often only individual salvation
[is] sought and experienced, . . . restricted to the soul or life after death
[so] that no attention is paid to the body, to the present plight and needs
of human society, especially to the people who exist in appalling pov-
erty; and to the many suffering creatures all over the world.

Markus Barth, Rediscovering the Lord's Supper

What is the connection between the communal meals described in Acts
2:42, 46 and the Hellenists' complaint concerning neglect of their widows
in 6:1-6? If the community ate together "by households," how could Hellenist widows be overlooked? Did the system break down? Did ethnic strife
or gender discrimination enter the picture? Or does this issue cover up

deeper problems in this intentional community? Experts in the field seriously differ!

Traditional and Historically Oriented Scholarship: Commentaries

Although the κοινωνία *(koinonia)* of Acts 2:42 has sometimes been interpreted as giving alms to the poor, most commentators in this category do not discuss poverty or class issues until 6:1, where Hellenist widows are being overlooked.[1] They all assume that these widows represent the most helpless or destitute persons in that culture — though there is little sociological analysis of why this might have been so.[2] G. V. Lechler (1857) reflects his class and paternalism most when he wonders if some of the needy themselves were selfish and were attracted to the church as the "provision which was made for the poor became more and more ample." The widows do not represent all of the poor, but they are a group of "lonely females" who would be more easily overlooked than other poor families who had a Hellenistic father to "support his claims with comparatively greater vigor"![3]

The interpretation of two terms were problematic — διακονία (a term with varied meanings) and τράπεζαις (tables). For most, the "daily διακονία" was a distribution by means of the tables in 6:2. Though several assumed that τράπεζαι meant money tables from which large sums of money were administered and distributed to the whole community,[4] oth-

---

1. Exceptions are Alexander and MacGregor, who suggested that the poor in the Jerusalem community were fed by means of the communal meals of Acts 2:42, 46. See Joseph A. Alexander, *The Acts of the Apostles* (New York: Scribner, Armstrong, & Co., 1875; reprint: Minneapolis: Klock & Klock Christian Publications, 1980); G. H. C. MacGregor, *Acts, Romans: The Interpreter's Bible* (New York, Nashville: Abingdon Press, 1954).

2. C. S. G. Williams does consider whether the widows might refer to an organized section of the church, but decides it is too early for a defined order of widows. See *The Acts of the Apostles*, Black's/Harper's New Testament Commentaries (New York: Harper & Row, 1957), p. 96.

3. Gotthart Victor Lechler, *Lange's Commentary on the Holy Scriptures: Acts,* trans. Philip Schaff (Grand Rapids: Zondervan, 1886), p. 103. Lechler needs to reread the parable of the persistent widow in Luke 18:1-7!

4. R. C. H. Lenski, *The Interpretation of the Acts of the Apostles* (Columbus, Oh.: Wartburg Press, 1944), p. 242; J. Rawson Lumby, *The Acts of the Apostles,* Cambridge Bible for

ers thought it meant handing out either money or food[5] to the needy. Several referred to the "Basket and Tray," the Jewish custom of almsgiving described in the rabbinic writings.[6]

R. Lee Cole rejected the interpretation of money tables: "That there was a distribution of money daily, and that it was of such amount as to require the services of seven officers of the church, and that there were so great number of Christian poor in one small city . . . is the height of improbability." Cole saw the tables for the feeding of the poor and possibly "almost all the members of the early church."[7]

Others also considered the possibility of daily public meals.[8] The "daily διακονία" is the right of admission to the common meal in various house churches[9] where rich and poor eat together.[10] The role of the Seven, then, would be to superintend daily service at literal common tables where alms were also distributed.[11]

With the exception of Henry Cadbury, all commentators surveyed believed both Hebrews and Hellenists were Jews who spoke different languages (Aramaic and Greek). Some assumed political differences existed

---

Schools and Colleges (Cambridge: Cambridge University Press, 1893), p. 73; F. F. Bruce, *The Acts of the Apostles* (Grand Rapids: Eerdmans, 1956; rev. ed., 1990), p. 182.

5. This is sometimes called "a dole for the needy." See C. S. C. Williams, *The Acts of the Apostles* (New York: Harper & Row, 1957), p. 96; Heinrich A. W. Meyer, *Handbook to the Acts of the Apostles*, trans. Paton J. Gloag (New York: Funk & Wagnalls, 1889), p. 123; G. H. C. MacGregor, *Acts*, vol. 5 of *The Interpreter's Bible* (Nashville: Abingdon Press, 1954), p. 88; Donald Guthrie, *The Apostles* (Zondervan: Grand Rapids, 1975), p. 55; Jerome Crowe, *The Acts*, New Testament Message 8 (Wilmington, Del.: Michael Glazier, 1979), p. 41.

6. William Barclay, *The Acts of the Apostles* (Louisville: Westminster/John Knox, 2003), p. 51; MacGregor, *Acts*, p. 88; Richard Longenecker, *The Gospel of John and the Acts of the Apostles*, Expositor's Bible Commentary (Grand Rapids: Zondervan, 1981), p. 330.

7. R. Lee Cole, *Love-Feasts: A History of the Christian Agape* (London: Charles H. Kelly, 1916), p. 48.

8. Henry Alford, "The Acts of the Apostles, the Epistles to the Romans and Corinthians," vol. 2 of *The Greek Testament* (Boston and New York: Lee & Shepard, 1872), p. 62.

9. William Neil, *Acts of the Apostles*, New Century Bible (Grand Rapids: Eerdmans, 1973), p. 102.

10. Laurence E. Browne, *Acts of the Apostles*, The Indian Church Commentaries (London: Society for Promoting Christian Knowledge, 1925), p. 105.

11. Richard B. Rackham, *Acts of the Apostles* (1901; Grand Rapids: Baker, 1964), p. lxxxii; Bruce, *The Acts of the Apostles*, p. 182. (He says that *if* daily allocations were made in the form of food, the task of the Seven may be to preside at communal meals.)

between Hebrews and Hellenists,[12] although there was little analysis of what issue brought about the crisis. The dominant Hebrews may have looked down on the Hellenists,[13] or their widows may not have been as well-known and thus were overlooked.[14] (For more on this, see Chapter Thirteen, pp. 253-54.)

When scholars assume (as the great majority of these do) that a true community of goods did not exist and that the poor were supplied with alms, they see Acts 6:1-6 as important because it shows a division between ministry of the word and ministry of the table (physical needs).[15] Some imply that the former is superior to the latter.[16] However, this is not over-emphasized, since the Seven are never represented as serving tables. G. H. C. MacGregor thinks it more likely that the administrative matter had brought to a head the tension between Hebrews and Hellenists, and that the function of the Seven was parallel to the apostolate.[17] Kirsopp Lake and Henry Cadbury agree: the Seven were the leaders of the Hellenistic Christians, while the Twelve were the leaders of the Hebrews.[18]

Discussions by C. S. G. Williams and Lake and Cadbury both stress that 6:1-6 intends to explain the breakdown of Christian "communism." A dole for the needy was necessary, says Williams, when this experiment ended in impoverishment[19] — though if this were true communism, it is hard to understand why some would be poorer than others, and where this dole would come from.

Though most commentators in this category tended to interpret the

---

12. See, for example, French L. Arrington, *The Acts of the Apostles: An Introduction and Commentary* (Peabody, Mass.: Hendrickson, 1988), p. 41. It is possible that the Hebrews were more entrenched in law and the Hellenists were more aggressive.

13. Alford, "The Acts of the Apostles," p. 61.

14. Arrington, *The Acts of the Apostles*, p. 65.

15. Lechler, *Lange's Commentary on the Holy Scriptures: Acts*, p. 104.

16. Alexander stresses that only males qualify even for the office of serving tables (*The Acts of the Apostles*, p. 243), and Lenski asserts that the women could not even vote on the new officers, on the grounds of Genesis 2:18-23 and 3:16 and 1 Timothy 2:12-14 (*The Interpretation of the Acts of the Apostles*, pp. 241-42). Lenski's 1944 commentary may reflect the American postwar effort to redomesticate women.

17. MacGregor, *Acts*, p. 90.

18. Kirsopp Lake and Henry J. Cadbury, *The Acts of the Apostles: English Translation and Commentary*, vol. 4 of *The Beginnings of Christianity*, ed. F. J. Foakes Jackson and Kirsopp Lake (London, 1920-1933; reprint: Grand Rapids: Baker, 1965), p. 63.

19. Williams, *The Acts of the Apostles*, p. 96.

tables as food tables at which the poor (or everyone) ate, they could not visualize how this would have been organized. If there were public communal meals, why didn't the widows come? If there were ethnic tensions between Hellenists and Hebrews, why were only the widows overlooked? Many questions are left unanswered by those who seek historical traditions in the text.

Redaction and Narrative Critics

Ernst Haenchen sees the daily διακονία in Acts 6:1 as a description of poor-relief from Luke's own time period. By then the size of the community would have created problems. Hellenist widows were numerous because many Diaspora Jews settled in Jerusalem for their final years and left wives without relatives to care for them. Because the type of poor-relief described in 6:1 is different from the Jewish weekly basket and daily tray, Haenchen concludes that Jewish Christians had by then developed their own system. This presupposes a lengthy evolution and final estrangement from the synagogue.[20] Haenchen prefers moneychangers' tables in 6:2 — not for "the general financial administration of the community, but the care of the poor."[21]

The real issue, Haenchen suspects, is deeper than poor widows. What underlying conflict would Luke prefer to cover up in order to maintain his rosy picture of the earliest church? He concludes that the Hellenists were pushing for more freedom in relation to the law.[22] The Hebrews, who had been in charge of the distribution to the poor, were opposing the Hellenists, and one way they did this was by beginning to neglect care for their widows.

Haenchen makes no connection between communal meals and care

20. Ernst Haenchen, *The Acts of the Apostles: A Commentary* (Philadelphia: Westminster Press, 1965, 1971), pp. 260-62. Martin Goodman contests Haenchen's view in *The Ruling Class of Judea* (Cambridge: Cambridge University Press, 1987), asserting that private charity was common in Jerusalem during this period (pp. 65-66). See also David Seccombe, "Was There Organized Charity in Jerusalem before the Christians?" *Journal of Theological Studies*, new series 29 (1978): 140-43. I will say more on this subject below.

21. Haenchen, *The Acts of the Apostles*, p. 262, n. 2.

22. This oversimplistic view was proposed by F. C. Baur in 1865 and has influenced many interpreters since then. See above (pp. 22-23) and the exegesis in Chapter Thirteen.

of the poor. Poor relief is clearly peripheral to what he sees as the real problems between two ethnic groups in Jerusalem Christianity. Though he seeks historical reality underneath the text, he doesn't trust Luke's version of it.

Regarding the daily διακονία, Hans Conzelmann says nothing, although his brief excursus on Acts 6:1-7 indicates that he is dismissing the issue:

> The actual events which lie behind this account of the selection of the seven can be perceived only vaguely, because Luke has radically reworked the material in order to avoid the impression of an internal crisis during the time of the apostles. The neglect of precisely this group, namely the Hellenist widows, is incomprehensible on the basis of what Luke reports. The conflict gives the impression of being artificially constructed. . . . Luke has revised his sources in line with his conception of the church.[23]

The installation of the seven men reflects the custom of the church of Luke's day and cannot be used to reconstruct the polity of the early church.[24] But Conzelmann provides no evidence for this. He notes that "local officials of the Jewish community and also ancient councils consisted of seven members,"[25] but since he does not clarify a time period for these customs, they may just as well be happening earlier. It would be more likely for early Jerusalem Christians to perpetuate Jewish customs than later Christians in Luke's presumably non-Judean provenance. Conzelmann does refer to precedents in the Septuagint about appointing helpers or successors (as in Numbers 27:16-23 and Exodus 18:14-25), precedents surely as well-known among the earliest Jewish believers as by Luke himself.

Gerhard Krodel also makes no connection between daily communal meals and neglect of the widows. The apostles were in charge of the community's funds and therefore supervised the daily distributions. The neglected widows were an internal problem that threatened the solidarity of the community, so it was solved by appointing auxiliary leaders. Krodel compares this procedure with that of Exodus 18:14-25, where Moses takes

23. Hans Conzelmann, *Acts of the Apostles* (Philadelphia: Fortress Press, 1987), p. 44.
24. Conzelmann, *Acts of the Apostles*, p. 45.
25. Conzelmann, *Acts of the Apostles*, p. 45.

the advice of his father-in-law to get help for his overwork.[26] Krodel agrees with Conzelmann and Haenchen that Luke's version of the story in Acts 6:1-6 has only the vaguest correlation with historical reality.

Widows and meals are barely mentioned in Joseph Leinhard's "Acts 6:1-6: A Redactional View."[27] The only historical kernel here is the conflict between Hebrews and Hellenists, the appointment of the Seven, and the list of their names. Even the two-step process of appointment is Luke's elaboration.

Because of Luke Johnson's general preference for almsgiving over sharing of possessions, he sees the daily διακονία of Acts 6:1 as a program of welfare for the poor, with no apparent relation to communal meals. The complaint about the widows underscores that "every welfare system has difficulties balancing need and resources, as well as fairness in distribution."[28] Unlike Haenchen, Johnson emphasizes the similarity of this program with the rabbinic description of organized charity in local Jewish communities.[29]

Johnson translates διακονία as "service" and notes that the same term is used in 6:2 for the "service of tables" and in 6:4 for "service of the word." He rightly observes that "Luke consistently joins the exercise of authority to service at table and the disposition of possessions" (Luke 9:1-17; 12:35-48; 16:1-13; 19:12-27; 22:24-30; Acts 2:42-47).[30] However, such table service or handling of possessions is more literary and symbolic than literal, having to do with actually serving tables. The twelve apostles' authority over the table service of 6:2 symbolizes their spiritual authority. When the seven Hellenists are given that authority over the distribution of food or other goods, hands are laid on them, and thus spiritual power is transferred to them.[31]

But does this say anything about who actually served the tables or distributed food? Since this is a "foundation story" similar to many in Hel-

26. Gerhard A. Krodel, *Acts*, Augsburg Commentary on the New Testament (Minneapolis: Augsburg Press, 1986), p. 132.

27. Joseph T. Lienhard, "Acts 6:1-6: A Redactional View," *Catholic Biblical Quarterly* 37 (April 1975): 228-36.

28. Luke T. Johnson, *The Acts of the Apostles*, Sacra Pagina 5 (Collegeville, Minn.: Michael Glazier, 1992), p. 106.

29. Johnson, *The Acts of the Apostles*, p. 106, n. 7.

30. Johnson, *The Acts of the Apostles*, p. 106.

31. Johnson, *The Acts of the Apostles*, p. 111.

lenistic literature, Johnson sees no need to hunt for historical strands underneath the text. Rather, he says, "Luke's description has provided a utopian vision of what the Church might be in its finest realization."[32]

A welcome exception in this category is F. Scott Spencer's "Neglected Widows in Acts 6:1-7," where he confirms commentators' repeated neglect of these widows.[33] Rejecting a redaction-historical approach, he uses narrative analysis to place this pericope in a series of six stories about widows that Luke includes, from Anna in Luke 2 through the widows at Joppa in Acts 9. Widows represent the most vulnerable and powerless class of persons in the ancient world, and Luke wants to highlight Jesus' attention to and concern for them. Thus, when the apostles want to give up their care of the widows in order to preach, Spencer sees Luke criticizing them for their "unholy alliance with unjust judges (Luke 18:1-8), hypocritical scribes (20:45-47), and an exploitative temple system (21:1-6)."[34] Though the apostles solve the immediate problem, they implicitly prioritize prayer, teaching, and preaching over care of the poor. Spencer, however, makes no connection between widows and the daily communal meal that was supposed to feed *all* members of the community. He does not explain how, in a community of shared possessions, some widows remained isolated and destitute.

Most commentators in this section are more concerned about political or ethnic conflicts hidden beneath the text, church structure, and Luke's own theological agenda or contemporary concerns; accordingly, they make no serious connection between the communal meals in 2:42, 46, the "daily διακονία," and the "διακονία of tables" in 6:1-2. Though Johnson does think διακονία means "service," he turns that into an abstraction.

Searching for Sociohistorical Traditions: Special Studies

If we consider the widespread practice of agape meals discussed in Chapter Three, the comments of Lawrence Browne, Stephen Neil, and perhaps MacGregor (see above, n. 1) make the most sense: the daily διακονία somehow takes place at a daily meal where all the believers, not just the poorest,

---

32. Johnson, *The Acts of the Apostles*, p. 62.

33. F. Scott Spencer, "Neglected Widows in Acts 6:1-7," *Catholic Biblical Quarterly* 56, no. 4 (October 1994): 715-33.

34. Spencer, "Neglected Widows in Acts 6:1-7," p. 729.

are fed. In greater detail, Bo Reicke's study of agape meals (see Chapter Three) provides additional context for the relationship of these meals to the welfare of the poor.

Bo Reicke: Agape Meals and διακονία

Bo Reicke insists that διακονία is an integral part of early Christian worship, which included an agape meal. By διακονία, he means chiefly "care of the poor," either *Armenspeisung,* a feeding of the poor, or *Armenspenden,* alms for the poor,[35] with a fluid relationship between the two (*Diakonie,* p. 37).[36]

The miraculous feedings of the five thousand and the four thousand recorded in Matthew 14:13-21 and 15:32-39 (with parallels) symbolically represent the sacramental service that was later practiced by the church. Nevertheless, because they were miracles, and because they fed not just the poor but all the people, they do not provide the concrete background of the agape meal (*Diakonie,* pp. 21-22). That background, contends Reicke, is the Last Supper.

Both Luke and John set the ideal of the practical διακονία in connection with the Last Supper (Luke 22:24-27; John 13:1-20). Jesus is among the disciples as one who serves at a meal — and so it must be with them. Reicke sees the verb διακονέω (to serve) used in the Lukan writings both as a liturgical term and as a technical term for serving at a meal. Here alms are present; the disciples interpret the departure of Judas in John 13:29-30 as if he were going out to give something to the poor (*Diakonie,* pp. 22-24).

A "Supper of the Lord" (κυριακὸν δεῖπνον) as a full meal in 1 Corinthians 11:17-34 has already been established, and the reason Paul refuses to call the Corinthians' meal a κυριακὸν δεῖπνον is that they are humiliating those who have nothing by going ahead with their *own* suppers. In other words, the διακονία is being neglected during the liturgy, and Paul is particularly concerned that they should be connected (*Diakonie,* pp. 32-33). Chrysostom's detailed commentary on this passage about inviting the

---

35. Bo Reicke, *Diakonie, Festfreude und Zelos in Verbindung mit der Altchristlichen Agapenfeier,* Uppsala Universitets Årsskrift 5 (Uppsala: A.-B. Lundequistska Bokhandeln, 1951), p. 21. Hereafter this work will be referred to parenthetically in the text.

36. This fluid relationship is quite different from the perspective of either Luke Johnson (Chapter One) or Dominic Crossan (see Chapter Ten).

poor to a common table demonstrates that even as late as the fourth century Chrysostom found it entirely natural that a feeding of the poor should happen in connection with the Christian worship service (*Diakonie*, pp. 33-35).[37]

The connection with meals and worship in James is also relevant here, since James speaks of the worthlessness of the peace benediction at the end of a service when widows and orphans are not being warmed and fed (*Diakonie*, p. 38). Reicke also sees these concepts reflected in Hebrews 13:10: "We have an altar from which those who officiate in the tent [or tabernacle] have no right to eat." The "altar" is a communion table where Jesus' sacrifice is remembered. The text continues in 13:15-16: "Through him, then, let us continually offer a sacrifice of praise to God. . . . Do not neglect to do good and to share what you have, for such sacrifices are pleasing to God."

Rather than a feeding of the poor in an agape meal, here the διακονία consists of putting alms for the poor (or church officials) on the Eucharistic table and distributing them to the poor after the worship. Comparisons can be made with Paul's statement in 1 Corinthians 9:13-14 about those preaching the gospel being supported "by the gospel" (*Diakonie*, pp. 35-36).

According to Reicke, there is only a small difference, caused by practical circumstances, between feeding of the poor and alms for the poor. His strongest case for this is Acts 2:42-47 and 6:1-6 (*Diakonie*, p. 37). The daily διακονία of 6:1 is an actual feeding, since waiting on tables is referred to in 6:2. The care for the poor through "spending of possessions" (essentially, almsgiving), however, is shown in Acts 2:42-47, though the distribution mentioned in verse 45 probably consisted mainly of food (*Diakonie*, pp. 26-28). This was done in the context of worship in verse 42. (Reicke agrees with scholars like Joachim Jeremias who see this text as a description of an entire worship service.) Κοινωνία here refers to distribution or spending because of the context. That this care for the poor was originally part of the worship life of the early community is shown in Acts 6:1-6, where it is clear that it was taken care of by the apostles themselves (*Diakonie*, p. 25).

In his discussion of the Acts texts, however, Reicke observes that his definition of *who the poor are* has changed. In Acts 2 there is not a group of needy people set apart from others by their poverty; everyone is poor,

---

37. See Chrysostom's sermon on 1 Corinthians 11:19.

for they have renounced their possessions in order to fulfill the Old Testament ideal of the poor as a holy community (in the LXX, Ps. 9:18; 12:5; 35:10; 37:14; 40:17; 69:33; 70:5; 86:1; Isa. 61:1). As such, they persist daily in the Temple and are "propertyless, freely dependent people" (*Diakonie*, pp. 27-28).

More clearly than anyone else thus far, Reicke has called attention to a vital connection between communal meals and caring for the poor. The διακονία of Acts 6:1 equals the κοινωνία *(koinonia)* plus the bread-breaking of 2:42-47. Nevertheless, Reicke could benefit from more recent insights of the social sciences, economics, and liberation theology, which could further enhance his thesis. Two interrelated issues need further unraveling.

First, Reicke's definition of the poor as including everyone in Acts 2:42-47 means that a feeding of the poor and alms for the poor are *not* the same thing. If everyone was poor in the Jerusalem community, and yet because of communal sharing none was in need, there was no separate welfare system of poor relief. *Everyone* ate from a common table. Achieving that goal meant a high level of organization and lessened class differences. This is why the awareness of inequality experienced by the Hellenist widows was so intolerable, and why the apostles had to call together *all* the people. Only when "the poor" are "the other" — the "charity cases," those "not like us" — can an organization relegate their care to a committee who hands them some alms on the side.

Another of Reicke's observations could have been much stronger with a clearer understanding of Palestinian economics. He says that Jesus' feedings of the five thousand and the four thousand do not provide the concrete background of an agape meal because they fed not just the poor but all the people. Knowing what we now do about Palestinian peasantry of the first century, and knowing the kind of people who were attracted to Jesus, it is hard to imagine that the crowds that were fed at those meals were *not* poor. With few exceptions they must have been people living at a subsistence level. Thus these meals do provide an important background for the agape meal.

Second, if the poor are not "the other," one of the definitions of διακονία changes. When διακονία is used in the context of a meal, it means serving and waiting on tables for *all* people involved in that meal, and not the care of just those identified as poor. Everyone eats because everyone is hungry, and in the physical feeding there is sacramental meaning because the risen Christ is present in this sharing of bread. It is, of course, important that the poorest are taken care of, but their basic needs are met and their dignity preserved in the διακονία of tables.[38]

Reicke's conception of διακονία as care of the poor is one that is commonly understood today, and one that too easily shades into classism and paternalism. Despite the above limitations, his particular contribution is recognizing that this caring for the poor is linked in early Christian writings with serving meals, and that these meals are an integral part of Christian worship. In this way he helps to advance my thesis that daily communal meals in Acts 2 and 6 make historical sense beyond Lukan idealism.

Widows and διακονία

All interpreters discussed so far have been male. None have observed the conjunction of women, communal meals, and service at meals in Acts 6:1 — though if they ever attended a church potluck, they would have unconsciously made that association. Scholars like Haenchen, Conzelmann, Krodel, and Gerd Lüdemann even suspect the overlooked widows are only of secondary importance, and the real conflict is ethnic and theological.

But the presence of women in an androcentric text should be carefully noted. In patriarchal societies like that of first-century Palestine or Luke's milieu, women are not mentioned unless they are a problem or are exceptional.[39] So the mention of widows in Acts 6:1 must mean not only that they are the real issue, but that the issue is related to serving meals — the daily διακονία.

Craig C. Hill and other scholars have indirectly supplied additional evidence that the text does concern women and meals and does not cover up a growing split between two groups in the Jerusalem church.[40] The ten-

---

38. One must reckon with various degrees of poverty, for there are poor people, destitute people, and starving people. I don't think the Acts texts or any others in the New Testament imply that there was total and complete economic equality among all the Christians in a church. But the level of sharing prevented the economic gaps between people from being too large. And an important aspect of subsistence culture, as we will see in Part II, is that even the most comfortable peasant was only one harvest away from dire need; and, further, that economic mobility was generally downward.

39. Elisabeth Schüssler Fiorenza, *In Memory of Her: A Feminist Theological Reconstruction of Christian Origins* (New York: Crossroad, 1983), p. 44.

40. Craig C. Hill, *Hellenists and Hebrews: Reappraising Division within the Earliest*

sion between Hebrews and Hellenists existed not because of differing ideological outlooks but because of language differences. Hebrews spoke Aramaic, probably with Greek as a second language, and the Hellenists spoke only Greek. Although language itself (with its attendant cultural differences) surely affected interactions between believers, there is no basis in the New Testament texts for theological division along Hebrew/Hellenist lines. From a historical perspective it is entirely natural that the growth in numbers of the Jerusalem church would have affected daily table service. With many people to care for, and with the selling and redistributing of possessions, it is quite likely that more administrators would be needed.[41] Hill's research (explained in more detail in Chapter Thirteen) helps focus the discussion on the logistics involved in serving daily communal meals in a community of goods.

So if the real issue does have to do with fairness in the daily διακονία, what can we know about these overlooked widows? It is universally claimed that they were poor because widows in the Bible were always poor. They did not have a male relative to support them in this highly patriarchal culture. Some, like Reicke, assume the widows were poor because διακονία means "caring for the poor through a distribution of food or other goods." And since the Christians had apparently set up a system similar to the Jewish "Basket and Tray" for caring for the poor, these widows were supposed to be taken care of by the church. For whatever reason — racial, ethnic, political, or otherwise — poor Hellenistic women were neglected in the dole that was distributed daily.

But were these widows poor? Already in 1933 Lake and Cadbury were raising a tangential issue. They do regard these widows as needy, but since they were receiving regular support, some organization must have existed within the Jerusalem community. Because of such continuing organization, "widows" came to have a double meaning: (1) all women who had lost their husbands; and (2) a selected number of this group "who were appointed to a definite position in the organization of the church as part of the 'Clerus.'"[42]

Church (Minneapolis: Fortress Press, 1992); C. F. D. Moule, "Once More, Who Were the Hellenists?" Expository Times 70 (1958-59): 100-102.

41. Hill, Hellenists and Hebrews, p. 26. There is no definite proof that all seven were Hellenists.

42. Lake and Cadbury, The Acts of the Apostles, p. 64. See especially instructions regarding widows in 1 Timothy 5:3-16.

But Turid Karlsen Seim points out that both the Luke-Acts texts and the social reality behind them are not at all uniform about the poverty of widows.[43] No doubt many widows — perhaps most — faced economic insecurity. But at the same time, to be widowed meant greater freedom for a woman than she had ever had before.[44] Perhaps the women named without husbands in Luke-Acts should be considered widows even if that term is not used.[45] It cannot be assumed that the widows of Acts 6:1 were destitute.

Elisabeth Schüssler Fiorenza notes that the text does not say the widows were poor. Instead, the conflict between the Hellenists and the Hebrews may have involved the role and participation of women at the Eucharistic meal. "The expression that they were 'overlooked' or 'passed over' in the daily διακονία could indicate either that they were not assigned their turn in the table service or that they were not properly served."[46] Schüssler Fiorenza believes this problem is similar to the problem of table-sharing among Jewish and Gentile Christians in Antioch. The Hellenists may have taken for granted the presence of women at table, while the Hebrews opposed it.[47]

It is true that the presence of women at public meals was not always taken for granted in the Greco-Roman world.[48] Schüssler Fiorenza, however, retains the traditional assumption (against Hill) that the Hellenists were the liberal group, while the Hebrews were conservative. Nevertheless, people are not always liberal or conservative in the same ways. If they had originally lived elsewhere in the Empire, Hellenists could very well have absorbed Roman cultural assumptions that women should participate in public meals, even if they did have conservative views on the Law and the Temple. These meals, however, were not public but were eaten "by households," family-style. (I will say more about this in Chapter Thirteen.)

Some years earlier, Mary L. McKenna had argued that the Hellenist widows were not in need — on the basis of Acts 4:34-35, which says that

---

43. Turid Karlsen Seim, *The Double Message: Patterns of Gender in Luke and Acts* (Nashville: Abingdon Press, 1994), p. 231.

44. Freedom to choose is presupposed, for example, in 1 Corinthians 7:8, 39-40.

45. I will say more about this in Chapter Thirteen.

46. Schüssler Fiorenza, *In Memory of Her*, pp. 165-66.

47. Schüssler Fiorenza, *In Memory of Her*, p. 166.

48. See Kathleen Corley, *Private Women, Public Meals* (Peabody, Mass.: Hendrickson, 1994).

"there was not a needy person among them."[49] She proposed that these widows were part of an official group of women who were responsible for the daily διακονία (table service). This group had begun with the Galilean women mentioned in Luke 8:1-3 as those who served and provided for Jesus and those around him — and who also had followed him to Jerusalem and were counted among the disciples in Acts 1:14. Perhaps as Hellenist women joined the group, tensions did arise. The Galilean women may have received special honor to the detriment of the Hellenists.[50]

Organizing and managing a household and its meals was one of the few administrative roles open to women, and they often valued it highly. For example, when Pomponia, the wife of Roman senator Cicero, was not given the responsibility of organizing a meal at one of their estates where they were to spend the night, she complained that she was just a guest in her own household. She was so angry that she refused to eat the meal in her husband's and brother-in-law's company. Cicero did not understand her anger because he underestimated the importance of this managerial power to his wife in her own house.[51] Given this social reality in Mediterranean culture, it would not be surprising if women competed for the honor of organizing communal meals in the early Jerusalem community, especially if they carried particular religious significance.[52]

Conclusion

This chapter continues the survey of commentators on communal meals in Acts from chapter 2, but it moves from the daily meals in Acts 2:42, 46 to the "daily *diakonia*" and the "*diakonia* of tables" in 6:1-6. Does this text talk about communal meals, or the distribution of alms to poor widows? And can we be sure the widows are poor? Again, interpreters from the nine-

---

49. Mary L. McKenna, *Women of the Church: Role and Renewal* (New York: P. J. Kennedy & Sons, 1967), pp. 39-41.

50. McKenna, *Women of the Church*, pp. 39-41.

51. Cicero, *Atticus* 5.1, 3-4; Jane F. Gardner and Thomas Wiedemann, *The Roman Household: A Sourcebook* (New York: Routledge, 1991), pp. 55-56. See also Jane F. Gardner, *Women in Roman Law and Society* (Bloomington: Indiana University Press, 1986), pp. 70-71.

52. Supportive anthropological information about women's roles in agrarian Mediterranean cultures will be picked up in Chapter Eleven, and combined with further exegetical material in Chapter Thirteen.

teenth century to the present fell into three categories: traditional, historically-oriented commentators; redaction critics; and those doing special studies on issues related to the above questions.

Scholars in the first group were divided when it came to the daily διακονία of 6:1-2. It was generally assumed that the widows were objects of charity and that διακονία referred to care of the poor. But whether food was distributed or they were fed by means of a common table was an open question. (Only a minority thought the tables were for the distribution of money.) These conclusions generally betray middle-class or upper-middle-class assumptions of the poor as "other," as unfortunates who need handouts but who are not really equal members of the group. Even those who interpreted the text as a feeding at a common table assumed only "the poor" were fed in this manner.

Redaction critics in the second group wondered how much Luke had shaped this text for theological or ideological reasons, perhaps to cover up tensions in the growing church in Jerusalem and to portray it as an ideal rather than a historical reality. Some voiced strong suspicions that the issue of poor relief was only a smokescreen for these deeper conflicts. These scholars may also reflect class and gender bias, since widows and "the poor" were not their main concerns, and they saw no significance in the relationship between communal meals and women.

In the third section, Bo Reicke's work on table fellowship and agape meals discussed in the previous chapter connected well with his interpretation of Acts 6:1. The διακονία, understood as feeding the poor or giving alms to the poor, was an intimate part of these meals for many years. But feeding the poor in the Jerusalem community was not a separate charity because everyone in this community was part of the righteous poor, who renounced possessions and redistributed them. Thus the διακονία of tables concerns everyone. Yet Reicke also evidences some of the same cultural and social limitations of those interpreters in the above two sections, especially when he assigns "the poor" to their own separate category of those who need to be fed or given alms.

More recently, research on Acts 6:1-6 has concerned the widows. Feminist scholars provide new insights by placing these women in the position of *subjects* rather than objects of charity. The issue here is probably not poor relief at all, but problems relating to administration of daily meals. Since women are intimately bound up with serving food, especially in this culture, the widows may have been responsible for organizing the daily common tables. Luke may possibly be referring to an established order of widows.

In the upcoming chapters, I will use insights from Chapter Three and this chapter to fill out a cohesive and realistic picture of communal meals in Acts 2 and 6. But to be interpreted well, these texts demand an understanding of the culture, worldview, and values of ancient Mediterranean people, of Palestinian Jews in particular, and of the early Jewish believers who both reflected and stood out against their culture and its social and religious practices. With that in mind, in Part II and Part III I will provide further insights from the social sciences about the commensality of the Jerusalem Christians. In Part II I will attempt to reconstruct important aspects of their broader social world, while Part III will deal with ancient meal practices and the role of women in preparing and serving meals.

The Social World of Acts 2:41-47 and 6:1-6

A hundred years ago, the Marxist theorist Karl Kautsky was insisting that no matter how inaccurate an ancient writing may be when it comes to facts and persons, it would always faithfully reflect the social conditions under which it arose.[1] For this reason, though Kautsky rejected the theology of the New Testament writings, he did believe Acts 2:42-47 and 4:32-37 were talking about a literal community of goods and daily commensality. But until recently New Testament studies have tended to use social and cultural data as background information rather than as an integral part of text interpretation.[2] Yet for Acts 2:41-47 and 6:1-6 such data must not be ignored, since these texts inextricably wed the economic and social organization of the Jerusalem community to its theology and spirituality. Social-scientific criticism has made us more acutely aware of the cross-cultural leap required for understanding any literature from another time and place. Whatever Luke had in mind in these texts must be seen within the cultural background of the Eastern Mediterranean region of the first century.

In the following section of four chapters I will create a scenario of this ancient world and its values and practices as they relate to our texts on commensality. In the past two decades, scholarship on social-scientific

1. Karl Kautsky, *Foundations of Christianity: A Study in Christian Origins,* translated from the 13th German ed. (London and New York: Monthly Review Press, 1925), p. 42. See Chapter 2, pp. 27-29.

2. John H. Elliott, *What Is Social-Scientific Criticism?* (Minneapolis: Fortress Press, 1993), p. 12.

criticism of the Bible has multiplied exponentially, becoming both more comprehensive and more precise. We may know more today about the Mediterranean culture of the first century than anyone since perhaps the fourth or fifth centuries, when Christianity had become the official religion of the Roman Empire.

Because of the amount of current material already published in this area, I will include only a general sociological overview, along with more specific cultural understandings that are needed to address one basic question: In what sort of community, with what sort of economic organization, would daily communal meals make sense?

Chapter Five

From the Top Down: Socio-Economic Structures of an Agrarian Society

[On PBS's News Hour with Jim Lehrer*] Mark Shields got off one of the few broadcast or printed critiques of the Reagan years, calling Reaganomics "a disaster," with its "tax cuts for the well-off and budget cuts for the not well-off."*

Washington Spectator, 1 July 2004

Rome was not the evil empire of its ancient time. Rome was not the axis of evil in its Mediterranean place. Rome was not the worst thing that had ever happened to its preindustrial world. Rome was simply the normalcy of civilization within first-century options and the inevitability of globalization within first-century limits . . . .

Who they were there and then, we are here and now. We are, at the start of the twenty-first century, what the Roman Empire was at the start of the first century.

John Dominic Crossan and Jonathan L. Reed,
In Search of Paul: How Jesus' Apostle Opposed Rome's Empire with God's Kingdom

The geographical area around the Mediterranean Sea dominated by the Romans before and after the turn of the era fits the description of an ancient agrarian society. Such agrarian societies, according to the anthropologist Gerhard Lenski, have advanced technology and production over that of previous types of cultures (such as the iron plow pulled by animal energy). They maintain order through a strong military structure and hierarchical system of government.[1] Galilee, home of the original disciples of Jesus, was ruled by the client king Herod Antipas (4 B.C.E.–39 C.E.), while Judea had been under the direct control of a series of Roman governors since 6 C.E. Pontius Pilate ruled from 26 to 36 C.E., followed by two short-lived governors, Herod Agrippa I (40-44 C.E.), and a succession of seven more Roman governors until the Jewish War of 66 C.E.[2]

Evidence of an advanced agrarian society is the presence of cities, which then dominate the countryside around them. The larger the settlement, the more it tends to center agriculture, trade, and manufacturing around itself. As Jonathan Reed explains, "The significance of any ancient city to its citizens and rural dependents [is] rooted in power relations — political rule, economic control, and social status."[3] Thus the socially dominant groups in an agrarian society live in urban areas and are comprised of officials, priests, scholars, scribes, merchants, and soldiers. Below them, craft-workers and shopkeepers ply their trades, surrounded by day laborers and beggars. The political elite depend on the priestly class to establish and maintain the legitimacy of their rule, to justify their taking from the common people most of what they produce, and to perform administrative, diplomatic, and instructional tasks.[4] At the same time, at least 90 to 95 percent of the population would have been rural peasants, engaging in "primary" industries like farming, fishing, crafts, and the extraction of raw materials.[5]

Certainly the rural Galilean believers would have been familiar with this urban structure from regional cities like Sepphoris, Tiberias, and Caesarea Maritima. Jerusalem in Judea may have seemed less obviously Hellenistic and Roman because of its prominence as the center for Jewish faith and the site of the great Second Temple. However, it was top-heavy

---

1. Gerhard Lenski, *Power and Privilege: A Theory of Social Stratification* (New York: McGraw-Hill, 1966), pp. 190-93.

2. K. C. Hanson and Douglas E. Oakman, *Palestine in the Time of Jesus: Social Structures and Social Conflicts,* 2d ed. (Minneapolis: Fortress Press, 2002), p. 68.

3. Jonathan Reed, *Archeology and the Galilean Jesus: A Re-examination of the Evidence* (Harrisburg, Pa.: Trinity Press International, 2002), p. 66.

4. Lenski, *Power and Privilege,* p. 260.

5. Gideon Sjoberg, *The Pre-Industrial City* (New York: Free Press, 1960), p. 83.

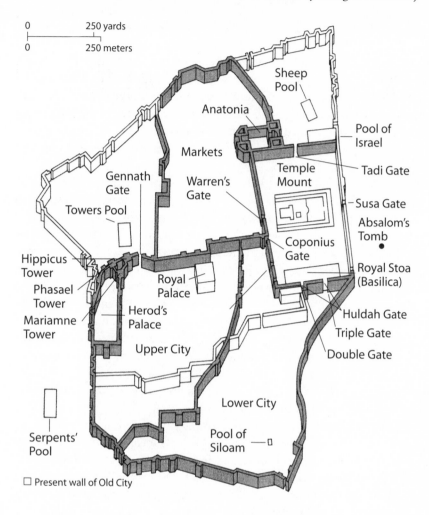

0   250 yards

0   250 meters

Sheep Pool

Anatonia

Pool of Israel

Markets

Temple Mount

Tadi Gate

Gennath Gate

Warren's Gate

Towers Pool

Susa Gate

Absalom's Tomb

Hippicus Tower

Coponius Gate

Phasael Tower

Royal Palace

Royal Stoa (Basilica)

Mariamne Tower

Herod's Palace

Huldah Gate

Triple Gate

Upper City

Double Gate

Lower City

Serpents' Pool

Pool of Siloam

☐ Present wall of Old City

with a priestly ruling class of Sadduceans and high priests, who compromised with the Romans whenever necessary in order to keep their power. Although the governor usually resided at the provincial capital of Caesarea Maritima, military or judicial responsibilities would bring him to the Antonia Fortress just north of and overlooking the Temple in Jerusalem, especially during important Jewish festivals (i.e., Passover; John 18:28 and parallels; see the map of Jerusalem above).

Land: Owned by the Rich, Worked by the Poor

An advanced agrarian society of this type could support a tiny leisure class, which derived its income from rents, taxes, or political office. The most desired form of wealth was in land, which was seen as the major method of producing goods. In such a society, about 1 to 3 percent of the population usually owned one-third to two-thirds of the arable land. Large landowners lived in the city as absentee landlords and left the management of their estates to stewards.

However, land "ownership" is more complex than that. Lenski discusses the "proprietary theory of the state,"[6] which means that a state is a piece of property that belongs to its owner(s): the king or the elite nobles (two parties often in a power struggle with each other). Peasants who live on the land in a particular state never fully own whatever land they work and may consider their patrimony, for the desires of those in power over them always trump the little people. Thus, from the perspective of the elite, taxes, tributes, rents, and services are what are owed them for leasing the land to the peasants. The balancing act is to squeeze as much as possible out of the laboring peasants, without making their subsistence impossible and thus risking violent rebellion.[7] Douglas Oakman uses the term "redistributive network," meaning that "taxes and rents flowed relentlessly away from the rural producers to the storehouses of cities (especially Rome), private estates, and temples."[8]

Throughout the first centuries of the Common Era, control of land in Palestine as well as elsewhere in the Mediterranean world was gradually passing into the hands of fewer and fewer people. Taxes were increasing because of the growing bureaucracy of the state and the ever-growing standard of living for the upper classes. Many peasants had to make do on one or two acres and were forced to earn extra income by seasonal labor on large estates.

---

6. Lenski, *Power and Privilege*, pp. 216-19.

7. Douglas Oakman, "The Countryside in Luke-Acts," in *The Social World of Luke-Acts: Models for Interpretation*, ed. Jerome H. Neyrey (Peabody, Mass.: Hendrickson, 1991), pp. 151-79 (159). It seems ironic that, as I write this, the U.S. Supreme Court has just made a 5-4 decision enabling cities and towns to exercise "eminent domain" by allowing private developers to buy out and appropriate private homes and property for new development if the area is "blighted."

8. Oakman, "The Countryside in Luke-Acts," p. 156.

Most of the elite lived in cities, where they could hire a small number of specialists to produce the luxury goods and services only they could afford. Thus it was in the interests of the powerful to keep everyone else out of the city and working in the countryside to produce food and other raw materials.[9] For this reason, and because the cost of transporting goods was so high, cities in agrarian societies were much smaller than are cities in industrial societies today — perhaps 5 to 7 percent of the population.[10] The vast majority were peasants working the land. Although some scholars have seen a more symbiotic relationship between city and countryside in ancient Palestine, others rightly stress the overall hostility which, from time to time, would erupt in open rebellion. Representatives of the latter include, among others, Oakman, Richard Horsley, Jonathan Reed, and Dominic Crossan.[11]

The people of the Mediterranean cultures did not have a term for "economics" as we understand it today. The word from which we get "economics" is οἰκονομία *(oikonomia),* which referred to the household, the unit of production. The household included all persons under the authority of one household head, all descendants from a common ancestor, all one's property, and all one's servants.

Ancient Mediterranean people believed in a "zero-sum," limited goods concept. There was only so much wealth in the world, so one household's gain had to be another's loss.[12] Although there was borrowing and lending, wealth was rarely for the sake of production — capital used to make more products to create more wealth. Rather, it was used for consumption. The wealthy and powerful used money for luxury items and for

9. Richard Rohrbaugh, "The Pre-Industrial City in Luke-Acts," in *The Social World of Luke-Acts,* ed. Neyrey, pp. 125-49 (132).

10. Lenski, *Power and Privilege,* p. 200; Rohrbaugh, "The Pre-Industrial City in Luke-Acts," p. 133.

11. Oakman, "The Countryside in Luke-Acts," pp. 151-79; Oakman, *Jesus and the Economic Questions of His Day,* vol. 8 of Studies in the Bible and Early Christianity (Lewiston/ Queenston: Edwin Mellen Press, 1986); Richard Horsley, *Archeology, History, and Society in Galilee: The Social Context of Jesus and the Rabbis* (Valley Forge, Pa.: Trinity Press International, 1998); Jonathan Reed, *Archeology and the Galilean Jesus;* John Dominic Crossan and Jonathan Reed, *Excavating Jesus: Beneath the Stones, Behind the Texts* (San Francisco: HarperSanFrancisco, 2001).

12. Hanson and Oakman, *Palestine in the Time of Jesus,* pp. 111, 199; Bruce Malina, *The New Testament World: Insights from Cultural Anthropology,* 3rd ed. (Louisville: Westminster/ John Knox Press, 2001), pp. 89-90.

political gain, to make themselves more powerful. The poor borrowed to meet their subsistence needs, which then drove them deeper into debt because high rates of interest made it impossible for them to repay their creditors. In this way, peasants were driven off their ancestral lands, and those without property were forced to sell themselves or their children into bond-slavery.

Although both Greece and Italy had become slave societies, others used different forms of dependent labor. Palestine never had a large slave population because it already had peasants as dependent labor. They farmed the land, did extra seasonal labor for daily wages, or were self-employed artisans or day laborers.[13] Little emphasis was placed on efficiency or labor-saving devices. Peasant or tenant labor was always in abundant supply, and it was generally believed that technological advancements would simply increase the perennial problem of unemployment.

Walls within Walls: The Agrarian City

The social stratification in the society was mirrored by the physical arrangement of city, village, and countryside. Each urban area in which the social elites lived was surrounded by smaller villages, places where some of the raw materials were processed before being brought into the city. The entire system was connected by centralized land control and systems of taxation.[14] Behind the supposedly placid Gospel scenes of farmers sowing seeds and fishermen plying their nets in Lake Galilee lies the iron fist of Roman occupation, with its administrators taxing and squeezing as many goods as possible from the land and its people. Peasants struggled to retain what they had, to survive at the level of subsistence. For all but a few of the most fortunate or ruthless, upward mobility was out of the question.

In general, the elite occupied the central part of a city and lived in larger homes, sometimes spacious villas or large, first-floor apartments cared for by slaves.[15] This central core was surrounded by crowded areas

13. Oakman, *Jesus and the Economic Questions of His Day*, p. 22.

14. Rohrbaugh, "The Pre-Industrial City in Luke-Acts," p. 132.

15. Rohrbaugh, "The Pre-Industrial City in Luke-Acts," p. 134; Jerome Carcopino, *Daily Life in Ancient Rome: The People and the City at the Height of the Empire* (New Haven: Yale University Press, 1940), p. 26. See also Bruce W. Frier, *Landlords and Tenants in Imperial Rome* (Princeton: Princeton University Press, 1980).

where lived the non-elite who provided services for the upper class. They did not live side by side but were physically and socially isolated from each other.[16] The non-elite population of the cities was continually replenished by the dispossessed from the villages and rural areas. Most social mobility was downward, because peasant families often had more children than they could support, and the practice of primogeniture tended to push younger sons off the land.[17] On the outer edges of the city gathered the outcasts — the prostitutes, the beggars, and those whose occupations repulsed others by their smells, such as tanners and fullers.[18] Lenski classifies the latter as "unclean and degraded classes," and the former as "expendables."[19]

Inside its walls, the city also was arranged roughly in concentric circles. In the center stood the religious symbols of temple or shrine, surrounded by the upper classes living in luxurious villas or large apartments. Sometimes inner walls blocked off their spaces from the market area, or the neighborhoods of ethnic trade groups (see diagram on p. 106).[20]

Richard Rohrbaugh continues:

The internal walls, moreover, were usually arranged so that watchmen could control traffic and communications. . . . Most streets were unpaved, narrow, badly crowded and would not have allowed passage of wheeled vehicles. Many would have been choked with refuse and frequented by scavenging dogs, pigs, birds, and other animals. Shallow depressions in the streets allowed some drainage, but also acted as open sewers. Large open spaces were few in most cities, and those that

16. Exceptions would be the slaves or servants necessary in the big houses, who may have occupied small rooms nearby. For example, excavations at Pompeii, Italy, reveal large, elegant houses with adjoining shops on the first floor and bedrooms in the mezzanine area for shopkeepers, most likely slaves or freedpersons of the elite. See John Dominic Crossan and Jonathan L. Reed, *In Search of Paul: How Jesus's Apostle Opposed Rome's Empire with God's Kingdom* (San Francisco: HarperSanFrancisco, 2004), p. 326. Any persons of humble origins, however, would have to "know their place" in order to live in proximity to the elite, just as house slaves in the American South had a code of behavior when working in the "big house" around their owners.

17. Lenski, *Power and Privilege*, pp. 290-91. A New Testament example is the story Jesus told of the Prodigal Son.

18. Rohrbaugh, "The Pre-Industrial City in Luke-Acts," p. 145.

19. Lenski, *Power and Privilege*, pp. 280-85.

20. Rohrbaugh, "The Pre-Industrial City in Luke-Acts," Figure 5-2, p. 135.

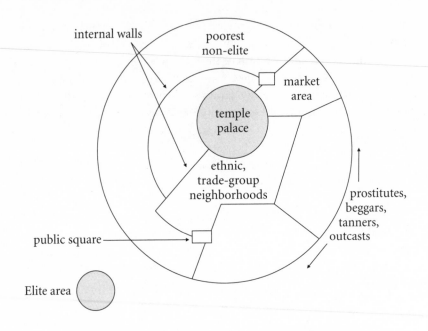

did exist were often at intersections of the few paved thoroughfares. Such open squares often served as gathering places for ceremonies or public announcements.[21]

The city of Jerusalem fit well into this pattern. However, because it was built on a hilltop and comprised of two levels, the configurations are slightly different, with Herod's palace and other elite homes on a somewhat lower level from the Temple Mount. Market areas in agrarian cities were usually close to the religious center; Jerusalem's *agora* lay in the Tyropoeon Valley next to the Temple.

Original disciples of Jesus such as Peter, James, and John were fishermen drawn from the peasant class in Galilee and, according to Acts, were headquartered in Jerusalem after Jesus' departure. Jesus' mother and his brother James, also from peasant stock (artisan class), are also mentioned as being in Jerusalem at this time. Three of the Gospels note that many women had followed Jesus from Galilee to Jerusalem for Passover, though we cannot know how many of them stayed to develop the Jesus commu-

21. Rohrbaugh, "The Pre-Industrial City in Luke-Acts," p. 135.

nity that began there. A few may have been independently wealthy patrons (i.e., Joanna in Luke 8:3), but most would have been drawn from the lower classes living at subsistence level, even the dispossessed and (to use Lenski's terminology) the "expendables." How did they survive the shift in geographical location and the loss of previous livelihood? How might the simple practice of sharing food and eating together have kept them alive?

Chapter Six

Jerusalem: Productive City on a Hill

Happy is everyone who fears the LORD, who walks in his ways.
You shall eat the fruit of the labor of your hands;
   you shall be happy, and it shall go well with you.
The LORD bless you from Zion.
   May you see the prosperity of Jerusalem all the days
      of your life.

Psalm 128:1-2, 5

I first visited Jerusalem in January 1993, on a bus trip after a week of archeological digging in the Negev. A Mediterranean storm had been brewing all week, and we wore winter coats as we hauled buckets of dirt off the Byzantine and Roman ruins at Nitzana. I will never forget the relentless uphill climb of the bus as it pushed through dropping temperatures and glowering skies to Mount Zion, with its layers and layers of rich and terrible history.

All weekend, rain pounded the city, and water ran in sheets down stone-paved streets and boulevards. Though we climbed the Via Dolorosa on wet and frozen feet, I could only imagine what such a storm would have done to the tiny, unpaved, sewage-clogged alleys of lower-class Jerusalem in Herod's day. At least festivals like Passover and Pentecost were held in warmer, drier months, when pilgrims from Galilee and all over the known world would swell the population several times over.

Besides serving as the center of Jewish faith, what was Jerusalem like in the first century? How did the inhabitants support themselves? Does it make sense to imagine Jesus people sharing possessions in a community of production as well as consumption? This chapter describes Jerusalem's geography, economics, and culture in order to provide a realistic venue for the earliest households of believers.

Jerusalem's Geography, Agriculture, and Population

As shown on the map in the previous chapter, Jerusalem fits well the description of a pre-industrial, agrarian city. Geographically, culturally, and politically, it belonged to the province of Syria, producing similar products of woolen goods and perfumed ointments.[1] However, because of its mountainous location, it was poorly situated for trade and had no large quantities of raw materials except stone. The area around the city produced wool and hides from cattle and sheep, and wood and olives from olive trees. A serious problem was lack of water, for it had only one major spring, Siloah in the south.[2]

But no ancient city in an agrarian society could have survived without nearby agriculture. Grain was heavy and bulky, so transportation costs by animal-drawn cart from a distance would have been prohibitive.[3] In between the smaller villages that ringed Jerusalem were large tracts of agricultural lands that provided the food necessary to support the city. Beginning in 1977, archeological teams have excavated and surveyed the agricultural land that at the time would have lain immediately outside ancient Jerusalem. A 1981 survey discovered hundreds of carefully planned

---

1. Joachim Jeremias, *Jerusalem in the Time of Jesus: An Investigation into Economic and Social Conditions during the New Testament Period,* translated by F. H. Cave and C. H. Cave from the 3rd edition of *Jerusalem zur Zeit Jesu* (Philadelphia: Fortress Press, 1969), p. 4.

2. Jeremias, *Jerusalem in the Time of Jesus,* p. 27.

3. See the comparative costs of moving one ton of goods in pre-industrial China in John Pilch and Bruce J. Malina, "Agrarian Society," in *Biblical Social Values and Their Meaning: A Handbook,* ed. John Pilch and Bruce J. Malina (Peabody, Mass.: Hendrickson, 1991), p. 6. See also M. I. Finley, *The Ancient Economy,* 2d ed. (Berkeley and Los Angeles: University of California Press, 1984). Compared to transport by steamboat, the cost of transport by animal-drawn cart was over five times as expensive; that by pack donkey was ten times as expensive.

farm units and related remains scattered around Jerusalem.[4] Because of steep hillsides, terraces were formed from the natural stepped limestone topography, on which crops were planted. One farm dating from the latter part of the Second Temple period (first century B.C.E. to first century C.E.) shows an elaborate water system created from a spring.[5] Around these agricultural plots were stone walls to keep out animals. Other agricultural installations have also been excavated: wine and oil presses, cisterns and towers. It is estimated that 60 percent of the hills west of Jerusalem are today covered with agricultural terraces, most of them ancient.[6] The soil around the city was well-suited for olive groves (e.g., the Mount of Olives in the Gospels).

Estimates of Jerusalem's population during the years before the Jewish War have varied widely. Recent calculations and surveys of calculations do not even agree on whether previous estimates should tend to be revised upward or downward. Jeremias's older estimate (1943) of 20,000 inside the city walls and 5,000 to 10,000 outside[7] has been used by many commentators in the decades since. Magen Broshi has since estimated 60,000.[8] Wolfgang Reinhardt, assuming urban population density much higher then than now, estimates Jerusalem's population at this time at 100,000 to 120,000 inhabitants.[9]

Both Reinhardt and Broshi conclude that estimates based on water supply are worthless, since it is impossible to calculate how many liters of water would have been used per person per day. On the other hand,

---

4. Gershon Edelstein and Shimon Gibson, "Ancient Jerusalem's Rural Food Basket," *Biblical Archeology Review* (July/August 1982): 46-54.

5. Edelstein and Gibson, "Ancient Jerusalem's Rural Food Basket," p. 52.

6. Zvi Ron, "Agricultural Terraces in the Judean Mountains," *Israel Exploration Journal* 16 (1966): 33-49 and 111-22; quoted in Edelstein and Gibson, "Ancient Jerusalem's Rural Food Basket," p. 53.

7. Jeremias, *Jerusalem in the Time of Jesus*, p. 84. The 1943 date refers to an essay that later was included in this book.

8. Magen Broshi, "Estimating the Population of Ancient Jerusalem," *Biblical Archeological Review* (June 1978): 10-15. He uses computations by several scholars, including H. Frankfort, *Town Planning Review* 21 (1950): 103-4; and J. Garstang, *Joshua-Judges* (London, 1931), pp. 121, 165.

9. Wolfgang Reinhardt, "The Population Size of Jerusalem and the Numerical Growth of the Jerusalem Church," in *The Book of Acts in Its Palestinian Setting*, ed. Richard Bauckham, vol. 4 of *The Book of Acts in Its First-Century Setting*, ed. Bruce W. Winter (Grand Rapids: Eerdmans, 1995), pp. 237-65 (263).

Reinhardt says nothing about food supply, even though the scarcity of grain would certainly have limited the year-round population of Jerusalem.

Scholars using food supply and analyses of the relationship of rural to urban areas are now calling for figures to be revised downward. A mountainous city such as Jerusalem would have been primarily dependent on its local agriculture, given the difficulty and cost of transporting grain over land. In addition, crop productivity per acre would have been less than what has been achieved today. Consequently, Douglas Oakman asserts that in Roman Palestine no city exceeded 35,000, and perhaps no more than two or three exceeded 10,000.[10] Archeologist Jonathan Reed calculated that 189 people in Roman Galilee could be fed annually on one square kilometer of cultivated grain.[11] If Jerusalem's population was even 60,000, that would have demanded over 300 square kilometers of farmland. Although a significant amount of the steep and rocky land outside Jerusalem was terraced for farming, and the land lying at the bottom of its narrow valleys was very fertile and intensely cultivated, it could hardly have fed such a large population, especially since the area would have had less rainfall and would have been less fertile than the Galilee. The rest of the food resources would have derived from tithes and taxes from elsewhere. But in spite of transportation costs and feasibility, Jerusalem was the religious capital, with the Temple system concentrating both religious and political power. If it was in the interests of the ruling party to provide grain for Jerusalem, it would have gotten there.

Jerusalem's population also fluctuated wildly due to the three great festivals — Passover, Pentecost, and Booths — the first two in the spring and the third in the fall. Jeremias puts the upper limit of visitors at 125,000,[12] but E. P. Sanders suggests 250,000 to 400,000 Palestinian Jews —

10. Quoted in Richard Rohrbaugh, "The Pre-Industrial City in Luke-Acts," in *The Social World of Luke-Acts*, ed. Jerome H. Neyrey (Peabody, Mass.: Hendrickson, 1991), p. 133.

11. Jonathan Reed, "Population Numbers, Urbanization, and Economics: Galilean Archeology and the Historical Jesus," in *SBL Seminary Papers* (Atlanta: Scholars Press, 1994), pp. 203-19 (211-12). As a parallel adjustment, Reed's own calculations of the population of Galilean Capernaum have drastically revised the 12,000 to 15,000 estimate of Meyers and Strange down to 600 to 1,500. See Reed, *Archeology and the Galilean Jesus: A Re-examination of the Evidence* (Harrisburg, Pa.: Trinity Press International, 2000), p. 152; and Eric Meyers and James Strange, *Archeology, the Rabbis, and Early Christianity* (Nashville: Abingdon Press, 1981), p. 58.

12. Jeremias, *Jerusalem in the Time of Jesus*, p. 84. He arrives at this number by calculating (among other factors) the space available for the slaughtering of Passover lambs.

half the total population — plus a large number ("tens of thousands") of pilgrims from the Diaspora at Passover, the most popular festival.[13] Sanders sees the common people of Palestine as being quite religious and under obligation to attend at least one of the festivals yearly, where they would spend the second tithe of their annual income. S. Safrai, however, says that the sources do not support the idea that Passover attracted the most pilgrims, so there is no evidence that Pentecost (the Feast of Weeks) would have had fewer than the other two feasts.[14] Reinhardt believes a more realistic figure for any one of the three feasts during the Second Temple period is a million pilgrims from all over the world.[15] However, it would seem that water requirements alone, never mind food, would render this number unrealistic.

The higher the number, the more likely it is that the travelers would have had to bring along much of their own food, perhaps even their own water. Nevertheless, Jerusalem was used to a large influx of pilgrims during the three major festivals of the year, and some pilgrims evidently stayed in community centers built especially for them.[16] Finding space for a small

13. E. P. Sanders, *Judaism: Practice and Belief: 63 b.c.e.–66 c.e.* (London: SCM Press; Philadelphia: Trinity Press International, 1992), p. 127. Herod's temple, he says, could accommodate 400,000 pilgrims. It seems unlikely to me, however, that half of the Palestinian population would have come, especially accounting for the disabled and ill, the aged, women in late pregnancy or with too many small children, and the very poor who could not afford it. Of the able-bodied, was it possible for so many to leave productive labor on the land or in the craft shop? Who watched the sheep and goats in the hills of Galilee? Who milked the goats? Sanders notes that it was a time of recreation and celebration, which is why men would come with their families.

14. Safrai, *Die Wallfahrt im Zeitalter des Zweiten Tempels* (Forschungen zum jüdisch-christlichen Dialog 3; Neukirchen-Vluyn, 1981), p. 97; quoted in Reinhardt, "The Population Size of Jerusalem and the Numerical Growth of the Jerusalem Church," p. 262.

15. Reinhardt, "The Population Size of Jerusalem and the Numerical Growth of the Jerusalem Church," p. 262; he quotes from M. Har-El, "Jerusalem and Judea: Roads and Fortifications," *Biblical Archeology* 44 (1981): 8-19 (13). But Har-El also sets the ordinary population of Jerusalem by the end of the Second Temple period at 200,000 (Reinhardt, "Population Size," p. 242).

16. David A. Fiensy points out, "Archeologists have discovered several buildings south of the Temple Mount with a large number of rooms, ritual baths, and many cisterns." See "The Composition of the Jerusalem Church," in *The Book of Acts in Its Palestinian Setting*, ed. Bauckham, p. 233. Fiensy uses B. Mazar, "Herodian Jerusalem in the Light of Excavations South and South-West of the Temple Mount," *Israel Exploration Journal* 28 (1978): 230-337. The Theodotus inscription in Greek also tells how Theodotus, ruler of this synagogue, do-

group of Galilean followers of Jesus plus any Diaspora believers who stayed on would not have been impossible, so long as some economic support system was in place to employ and feed them.

How realistic is Luke's number of about 3,000 converts in Acts 2:41? The smaller the population of Jerusalem, the less likely it is that his estimate of 3,000 people joining the original group of 120 is correct.[17] However, if the city was jammed with even 125,000 (the very lowest estimate) within the 1.1 square kilometers of the city limits and spilling out beyond its walls, the above number of 3,000 seems high but not impossible. It is anachronistic to think of these as individual conversions; many extended families and household groupings who shared Jewish religious views and a messianic hope must have been receptive, especially in the atmosphere of religious excitement.[18] Religious revivals in American history have influenced large numbers of people in a short time, and the present growth of Christianity in Africa exceeds what Western Christians today have observed or experienced. Moreover, ancient people had less accurate methods of counting large numbers of people, especially before the invention of the zero.

But even though many of the out-of-town believers must have gone home after the festival, a group of almost any size would have demanded some immediate organization. Those who stayed on for more teaching would have needed food and shelter, and those who were leaving their families had to be integrated into new systems of belonging.

Jerusalem's Wealth through Political and Religious Significance

The main source of Jerusalem's prosperity lay in its religious and political significance. First of all, the Temple received enormous revenues from all over the world in the form of various bequests, certain sacrifices, the pro-

---

nated a building for studying Torah and included guest rooms and ritual baths for pilgrims. See A. Deissmann, *Light from the Ancient East*, trans. L. R. M. Stranchan (Grand Rapids: Baker, 1965), pp. 439-40.

17. The purpose of Reinhardt's essay is to show that Luke's estimates of 3,000 and 5,000 believers (Acts 2:41 and 4:4) are reasonable within a larger population.

18. C. K. Barrett, *The Acts of the Apostles*, New International Critical Commentary (Edinburgh: T&T Clark, 1994), p. 159.

duce of lands owned by the Temple, and especially the worldwide levy of a fixed Temple tax (Exod. 30:13-16; Matt. 17:24; *Ant.* 3.8.2 [194]; *B.J.* 5.5.1 [187]; 7.6.5 [218]).[19]

Second, the religious pilgrims at the three great Jewish feasts of Passover, Pentecost, and Booths were committed to spending their so-called second tithe within the city.[20] Third, when independent rulers lived in Jerusalem (Herod, 34-4 B.C.E.; Archelaus, 4 B.C.E.–6 C.E.; Agrippa I, 41-44 C.E.), general taxes flowed in. For example, Archelaus collected six million drachmas a year, and during the short reign of Agrippa I, shortly after the events of the early chapters of Acts take place, twelve million drachmas a year were taken in by the royal court (*Ant.* 17.11.4 [320]). Fourth, Jerusalem had long been a place that attracted the wealthy — wholesalers, tax collectors, Diaspora Jews.[21] Many as well would have settled here for religious motives. Ernst Haenchen notes that Diaspora Jews would move to Jerusalem to spend the last years of their lives there in order to be buried near the Holy City.[22]

But, as in any city in an agrarian society, only a relative few were wealthy, with the great majority living at or below subsistence level. Josephus described Jerusalem as having two parts: the Lower City (*War* 5.253) and the Upper City (2.422), although he also mentioned New Town (2.530; 5.331), an area north of the city which during the thirties and forties was not enclosed by a wall. The upper class, composed of Temple nobility and lay nobility, lived in large homes in the Upper City, while most of the rest crowded into the Lower City and New Town.[23]

Urban Occupations

Beyond the farming and shepherding needed on the terraced hillsides, what other work occupied the inhabitants in and around Jerusalem? Pasture for

19. Jeremias, *Jerusalem in the Time of Jesus*, pp. 26-28.

20. Sanders, *Judaism*, p. 167.

21. Jeremias, *Jerusalem in the Time of Jesus*, p. 28.

22. Ernst Haenchen, *The Acts of the Apostles: A Commentary* (Philadelphia: Westminster Press, 1971), p. 261. This information came to him through a personal communication with K. H. Rengstorf; no original evidence was cited. But see Acts 6:1 and 9 for evidence of Hellenist Jews.

23. David A. Fiensy, "The Composition of the Jerusalem Church," pp. 218, 222.

sheep and goats in the area made wool an important industry, keeping primarily women occupied with spinning and weaving. Because weaving was women's work, male weavers were looked down upon and occupied a despised neighborhood of Jerusalem by the Dung Gate (*Ant.* 18.314; *M. Eduy.* 1.3; *Apoc. Bar.* 10.19). The cloth was then passed on to fullers and tailors.[24] The clothing market in Jerusalem would have included the products of leather workers as well. Olive oil was processed in and around Jerusalem, and butchers were needed for the cattle industry.[25] When rain was scant, water was bought and sold in pitchers and amphorae (*B.J.* 5.9.4 [410]).

Because of the huge architectural projects of the Herodians, the building trade in Jerusalem loomed large. Herod the Great alone built ten major projects, including the Temple, the palace, three towers, the fortress of Antonia, Herod's tomb, a theater, and a water channel. Under Agrippa I, the northernmost wall of the city was built strong and thick, and guarded by ninety towers. Under Agrippa II the Temple was finally completed between 62 and 64 C.E., leaving, according to Josephus, over 18,000 workers unemployed (a hyperbolic number?), who were subsequently put to work paving the streets of Jerusalem (*Ant.* 20.219-222). Pontius Pilate had an aqueduct built, though this resulted in a public uproar, since he financed it from the Temple treasury (*Ant.* 18.3.2).

Such building projects would have called for a wide range of masons, stonecutters, and well-diggers; skilled craftspersons such as goldsmiths, silversmiths, sculptors, tapestry-makers, and mosaic-makers; and maintenance persons like bakers, weavers, washers, watchmen, and money-changers.[26] However prestigious some of these occupations may be in our day, the social status of crafts persons and artisans was generally lower than that of peasant farmers, for they not only worked with their hands but also did not own the most precious possession, land.[27] Maintenance of the building projects employed more people: maintaining water channels, roads, towers, wells, and cisterns; sweeping streets, cleaning buildings, and guarding tombs. Also listed under manual workers were doctors and surgeons, barbers and money-changers.

The reader usually pictures men working at these occupations, while

---

24. Jeremias, *Jerusalem in the Time of Jesus,* p. 5.

25. Jeremias, *Jerusalem in the Time of Jesus,* p. 8.

26. M. Avi-Yonah, *The Holy Land* (Grand Rapids: Baker, 1977), p. 194.

27. Gerhard E. Lenski, *Power and Privilege: A Theory of Social Stratification* (New York: McGraw-Hill, 1966), p. 278.

women are home doing unpaid labor in the house while they raise their children. But this is more a projection of middle-class life in the United States during the 1950s than the reality in any agrarian society. It is true that women were under the power of their fathers or husbands, and they were instructed to stay out of public life (Philo). The Talmud discouraged men from talking much with women (*m. 'Abot* 1:5; cf. *m. Qidd.* 4:12; *b. Ber.* 43b). If they did go out in public, they had to be veiled.

But what was the reality? If women of wealth were secluded in roomy villas, non-elite women and children would have had to work beside their husbands and fathers in whatever industry the household produced. Thus, in addition to the regular housework of bread-baking and wool-spinning, women farmed, worked as fishers, crafts-workers, cheese-makers, wheat-grinders, spinners, weavers, tent-makers, and much more. "Since most of them lived in one-room houses that doubled as work-shops," David Fiensy explains, "the life of the retiring and pampered elites was impossible."[28]

But for the poorest families, those without land or a skill, this may not have been enough. Women and children also had to work for pay. The average wage for a man who had worked all day in the fields was a denarius (Matt. 20:1-16). But a day laborer couldn't expect to be hired every working day. Arye Ben-David has calculated the average yearly income of such a day worker at about 200 denarii. For a family of six, this income would have yielded about 1400 calories (from bread or porridge) per family member per day.[29] But such a level of nutrition would not have sustained a person's ability to work. Either the family had a small plot of land that they used for their own needs (in which case the women and children would have done most of the farming), or the rest of the family had to find paid work — which could include any of the above-mentioned occupations as well as the sex trade for women and girls. The Babylonian Talmud takes for granted that children will work from age six onward.[30] A woman's wages for paid work amounted to little more than what one person would have

28. Fiensy, "The Composition of the Jerusalem Church," p. 226.

29. Arye Ben-David, in vol. 1 of *Talmudische Oekonomie* (Hildesheim and New York, 1974), p. 301; referred to in Luise Schottroff, *Lydia's Impatient Sisters: A Feminist Social History of Early Christianity*, trans. Barbara and Martin Rumscheidt (Louisville: Westminster/John Knox Press, 1995), p. 92.

30. Samuel Krauss, vol. 2 of *Talmudische Archäologie* (Hildesheim, 1966), p. 18; cited in Schottroff, *Lydia's Impatient Sisters*, p. 93.

required for food and clothing, and somewhat less than half the yearly income (200 denarii) of a day laborer.[31]

Most commentators, including Marxists, have assumed that the Jerusalem believers, if they shared property at all, were only a community of consumption and not of production, and thus were doomed to failure. But in that culture, the household was the unit of production. Since the believers ate by households, it can be projected that they also worked at various industries by households as well. Whatever work was available in Jerusalem could be performed by the Jerusalem believers, women, men, and children.

Housing in Jerusalem

Comparatively little is known about Palestinian domestic architecture from the Persian through the Roman periods. This is the case because of massive Byzantine building operations set down into the remains of earlier cities, because of water erosion of the top strata of tells, and because of stone-robbing by local citizens, both recently and in ancient times.[32] Bradley Blue admits that "to date we cannot announce with any certainty that any of the early meeting places in Jerusalem have been identified."[33] Nevertheless, Blue believes that remains of house churches in Syria and Capernaum help in reconstructing Palestinian housing.[34]

Excavation of the old Upper City of Jerusalem after 1967 turned up a number of Herodian projects, including large residential homes. These homes were extensive, with inner courtyards that gave them the character of luxury villas.[35] These were the living quarters of the noble families of Jerusalem, headed by the high priest. Three of these — the "Herodian Resi-

---

31. Schottroff, *Lydia's Impatient Sisters*, pp. 94-95.

32. H. Keith Beebe, "Domestic Architecture and the New Testament," *Biblical Archeologist* 38 (1975): 89-103. Since 1975 significant excavation of domestic housing during the Roman period in Israel has been done, especially in Lower Galilee.

33. Bradley Blue, "Acts and the House Church," in *The Book of Acts in Its Graeco-Roman Setting*, ed. David W. J. Gill and Conrad Gempf, vol. 1 of *The Book of Acts in Its First-Century Setting*, ed. Bruce W. Winter (Grand Rapids: Eerdmans, 1994), pp. 119-222 (137).

34. Blue, "Acts and the House Church," p. 138.

35. Nahman Avigad, *Discovering Jerusalem: Recent Archaeological Excavations in the Jerusalem Area* (Oxford: Blackwell, 1984), p. 83; cited in Blue, "Acts and the House Church," p. 141.

dence," the "Palatial Mansion," and the "Burnt House" — have been described in detail by Nahman Avigad.[36]

It seems unlikely that the early Jerusalem believers lived in such homes. Most ancient urban Greco-Roman housing consisted of huge tenements called *insulae*, where people were crowded into small rooms.[37] However, a recent study by Cynthia Baker comparing floor plans of excavated domestic residences in Jewish Palestine with those in contemporaneous Italy shows that Palestinian homes tended to be more irregular, with one room attached to the next in random fashion, rather than symmetrically laid around an open courtyard.[38] Thus, enlarging one's household may have been as simple as adding an extra room extending into the courtyard or on the roof of the existing structure.

After Jesus' ascension, the 120 believers gathered to pray and wait for the coming of the Spirit in an upstairs room (ὑπερῷον; *hyperōon;* Acts 1:13; 2:1-2). It is possible that they had rented a room which was part of a domestic residence, or that this home was owned by a believer who set aside the room for use by the community. Blue suggests that the ἐπὶ τὸ αὐτό *(epi to auto)* of 1:15 may refer to an entire level or part of the building complex, especially since 2:2 compares the Spirit's coming to a rushing wind that filled the "entire house."[39] This would more easily account for the space needed for 120 believers. Although excavations in Jerusalem have shown that a house of this size is possible, it must have been at best a tight squeeze.[40] In any case, upper rooms were not uncommon in Eastern architecture and had various uses. Literature from Second Temple Pharisaism describes upper rooms as places for dining, study, guest lodging, or separate quarters for a widowed daughter or unmarried son.[41]

36. Nahman Avigad, "How the Wealthy Lived in Herodian Jerusalem," *Biblical Archeological Review* 2 (1967): 23-35.

37. Bruce W. Frier, *Landlords and Tenants in Imperial Rome* (Princeton: Princeton University Press, 1980), pp. 15, 28.

38. Cynthia Baker, "'Ordering the House': On the Domestication of Jewish Sexuality," paper presented at the annual meeting of the SBL/ASOR in Chicago, Ill., November 1994.

39. Blue, "Acts and the House Church," p. 133.

40. The space needed for groups of persons is relative. Europeans, and especially Asians, are used to crowding into far smaller spaces than are Americans. This was even more the case in the ancient world, where most homes were miniscule by our standards.

41. S. Safrai and M. Stern, eds., *The Jewish People in the First Century: Historical Geography, Political History, Social, Cultural, and Religious Life and Institutions,* 2 vols. (Philadelphia: Fortress Press; Assen: Van Gorcum, 1974-86), pp. 731-32; also cited in Blue, "Acts and the House

Was the Upper Room of Acts 1:13 the same as the place where believers met in the house of Mary, mother of John Mark, in Acts 12:12-17? That house was apparently not part of an *insulae* (tenement) complex, for it had a gateway (πυλών; *pulōn*) separating the inner courtyard from the street.[42] The fact that "many" (ἱκανοί; *hikanoi*) were gathered there probably means it was one of the larger houses available to the believers. Possibly it was a gathering place for Greek-speaking believers, since Peter refers to James and the brothers and sisters who are elsewhere (12:17).

Roger W. Gehring thinks it is more likely that the house of the Upper Room belonged to James, Jesus' brother, who stayed permanently in Jerusalem and became the leader of the Jerusalem church.[43] The fact that this place is conspicuously emphasized (Luke 22:12; Acts 1:13) indicates that it must be part of the tradition Luke inherited. Also, Luke does not mention that Jesus' mother and brothers follow him to Jerusalem, as do other women (Luke 23:55), so they may have already been staying with James. Further, the Hellenist Mary would more likely have become a believer after Pentecost. However, I am not convinced that the second son of an artisan in humble Nazareth would own such a large house in Jerusalem. The owner is never named, but it seems more likely to be a wealthier sympathizer with Jesus' program. Perhaps "James and the believers" (Acts 12:17) were staying in that house.

Bradley Blue, Brian Capper, Jerome Murphy-O'Connor, and Rainer Riesner[44] all refer to a literary tradition that places the house of the Upper

---

Church," p. 135. In addition, the dead were laid in upper rooms for a wake (1 Kings 17:19; Acts 9:39; Josephus, *Wars*, 5.7.3). The prophet Elisha was given a small upper room as a guest room (2 Kings 4:10). Daniel prayed in an upper room with a window facing Jerusalem (Dan. 6:10).

42. Ivoni Richter Reimer disagrees with some exegetes that this implies Mary had great wealth. Simon the tanner in Acts 10:17 also has a πυλών, and no one has ever supposed this despised tanner to be wealthy. See *Women in the Acts of the Apostles: A Feminist Liberation Perspective* (Minneapolis: Fortress Press, 1995), p. 241.

43. Roger W. Gehring, *House Church and Mission: The Importance of Household Structures in Early Christianity* (Peabody, Mass.: Hendrickson, 2004), pp. 63, 70-72.

44. Blue, "Acts and the House Church," p. 135; Brian Capper, "The Palestinian Context of the Community of Goods," in *The Book of Acts in Its Palestinian Setting*, ed. Bauckham, pp. 323-56 (345-49); Jerome Murphy-O'Connor, O.P., "The Cenacle and Community: The Background of Acts 2:44-45," in *Scripture and Other Artifacts: Essays on the Bible and Archeology in Honor of Philip J. King*, ed. Michael D. Coogan, J. Cheryl Exum, and Lawrence E. Stager (Louisville: Westminster/John Knox Press, 1994), pp. 296-310; Rainer Riesner, "Jesus, the Primitive Community, and the Essene Quarter of Jerusalem," in *Jesus and the Dead Sea Scrolls*, ed. James Charlesworth (New York: Doubleday, 1992), pp. 198-234.

Room on Mount Zion, the southwestern hill of old Jerusalem, which at the time of Jesus and the Jerusalem church would have been inside the city walls. This part of the city was destroyed during the Jewish War and was essentially uninhabited until Byzantine building began during the middle of the fourth century — with one apparent exception. The remains of a building that resembles synagogues of the early centuries of the Common Era have been excavated in this area. Remains containing some graffiti use language characteristic of Jewish Christians. The stone floor is assigned to the late Roman period, and stones in the wall have been reused from a Herodian structure. Thus, in the period after the Jewish War, when the Romans had renamed Jerusalem "Aelia Capitolina," there must have been a Jewish Christian place of worship on Mount Zion, referred to as "the little house of God."[45] Murphy-O'Connor provides evidence that during Roman occupation it would have been both dangerous and difficult for Christians to reach the church. "If, despite all obstacles, they maintained contact with a site there, it must have been of extreme importance to them. This means that veneration of the site must be pushed back into the first century and prior to the fall of Jerusalem."[46]

Excavations have unearthed evidence that this quarter of Jerusalem was occupied by some of the more affluent residents of the city.[47] However, the site of the possible Upper Room lies between this quarter and the (so-called) Essene Quarter, where the excavated houses are more modest, so it is impossible to make any certain statement about the value or size of the house with the Upper Room, even if it was located here.

Houses, homes, and households figure prominently in Luke-Acts, notes John Elliott.[48] They serve as both historical and metaphorical realities. The household represents mutual sharing and contrasts with the Temple, a centralized, distributive system where goods flow toward the powerful and wealthy and away from the peasants.[49]

45. Murphy-O'Connor, "The Cenacle and Community," pp. 300-301.

46. Murphy-O'Connor, "The Cenacle and Community," p. 303; he also believes that the tradition that the Christians fled to Pella before the first Jewish War is a myth (pp. 303-4).

47. M. Broshi, "Excavations on Mount Zion, 1971-72: Preliminary Report," *Israel Exploration Journal* 26: 81-88; cited in Murphy-O'Connor, "The Cenacle and Community," p. 305.

48. John Elliott, "Temple versus Household in Luke-Acts," *The Social World of Luke-Acts*, ed. Neyrey, pp. 211-40.

49. Elliott, "Temple versus Household in Luke-Acts," pp. 235-38.

Meal Settings in Peasant Family Life in Palestine

Although statistically most of the Jerusalem believers must have been from the peasant or lower classes, there is unfortunately little direct information about everyday peasant life and lower-class meal practices. Much of the information S. Safrai and M. Stern report is gleaned from hints in the Mishnah and from Josephus and other contemporaneous writings, along with archeological data.[50] The Mishnah must be used with care, since it was not compiled before 200 C.E., and Safrai and Stern have been criticized for collapsing some of their data. However, though legal formulations cannot be projected back to the first century with absolute confidence, cultural symbols are much more enduring and can be used for anthropological reconstruction of this time period.[51]

The architecture of housing for ordinary people in Palestinian villages and cities demanded a high level of communal sharing. From the narrow streets, even narrower alleys led into courtyards. The alley was public domain, and its improvement required the consent and participation of all the residents of the alley and the courtyard.[52] The basic residential unit was a courtyard around which one or more rows of houses adjoined each other.[53] Most of the courtyards were owned jointly by several families, or by a large extended family. Other structures around a courtyard, such as sheds for straw, cattle, or wood and storehouses for various commodities, could also be the common property of all the residents. Courtyards contained toilet facilities and sewage gutters, and if there was not a public water supply, cisterns were hewn under them. In larger courtyards the residents grew vegetables and fruit trees.

Though some houses were larger, many families lived in only one room. In rural areas of Palestine around this time, rabbinic sources indicate that a typical room was about five meters square, or about 255 square feet

---

50. S. Safrai and M. Stern, in cooperation with D. Flusser and W. C. van Unnik, "Home and Family," in *The Jewish People in the First Century*, pp. 728-92.

51. Jacob Neusner, *The Economics of the Mishnah* (Chicago: University of Chicago Press, 1990), p. 14.

52. Safrai and Stern, "Home and Family," p. 728.

53. Literary sources say that as few as two and as many as 24 houses could be ranged around a courtyard. Archeological excavations, however, indicate a number much smaller than 24, although only two would have been rare. Safrai and Stern, "Home and Family," p. 730.

(M. Ber. 8:12c; 3:6d; *Gen. Rab.* 31:11). The extended family often lived together in one house, including the families of married sons, who might live in an upper story or side room.[54] But for the whole family, the central and largest room was the dining room. A kitchen was not a necessity, for when weather permitted, all baking and cooking was done in the courtyard.[55]

In larger and wealthier homes, couches were stored in the dining room and used for reclining at formal and festive meals.[56] But the usual seat was a chair — a four-legged wooden one or a three-legged folding chair. Benches without backs could accommodate the most people in a room.[57] Stoves were small and could hold two pots. Ovens usually stood next to the stove. Even in large cities bread was sometimes baked at home, although professional bakers provided most of it. When it was baked at home, it was a weekly task for the whole family.[58] "The biblical picture of 'the children gathering wood, the fathers kindling the fire, and the women kneading the dough' (Jer. 7:18) remained the custom in the first century as well" (*Mekhilta Pisha* 10). Sometimes, however, the husband would do it all himself.[59] The weekly bread was baked before the Sabbath and then eaten throughout the week.

Bread was the primary food staple, although by the first century vegetables were cultivated, and the production of honey became organized. Fishing was practiced along the coast of the Mediterranean Sea and by the Sea of Galilee, and fish products such as salted fish were available more widely. If possible, families tried to have fish and vegetables on the Sabbath. Meat was a luxury, limited to feast days and festival days.[60] Wine (mixed with water) was prominent on the Sabbath and feast days. It is not clear that wine was drunk during regular daily meals.

But the very poorest people in Palestine and elsewhere ate little besides wheat or barley. Few of them would have owned or had access to an oven, so more often they crushed the grain and boiled it with water to

---

54. Safrai and Stern, "Home and Family," p. 732.
55. Safrai and Stern, "Home and Family," p. 733.
56. This would not have been true of ordinary peasants or craftspeople. See Marianne Sawicki, *Seeing the Lord: Resurrection and Early Christian Practices* (Minneapolis: Fortress Press, 1994), p. 258.
57. Safrai and Stern, "Home and Family," p. 737.
58. Safrai and Stern, "Home and Family," p. 740.
59. Safrai and Stern, "Home and Family," p. 740.
60. Safrai and Stern, "Home and Family," p. 747.

make porridge, or *puls*.[61] Ramsey MacMullen acknowledges how difficult it is to find hard evidence of the lifestyle of the poorest people of the Roman Empire, because literate people did not think poverty a fit topic to discuss. By extrapolation, however, he estimates that at least one-third of the population lived in habitual want, devoting all or most of each day's earnings to their immediate needs, able to save nothing.[62]

Conclusion: A Community of Consumption *and* Production

Between what extremes of wealth and poverty in prewar Jerusalem did the Jerusalem believers fall? Barnabas, Ananias and Sapphira, and Mary represent landowners who had more to contribute than most. The actual leaders of the community, the Galilean disciples, were peasants and artisans. At the lower end were the beggars and disabled whom Jesus or the apostles had healed (e.g., John 9; Acts 3) — although presumably they were no longer "expendable" and could now be productive. David Fiensy assumes the widows of Acts 6:1 were destitute (though I will dispute this in later chapters) and thus became some of the charity cases helped by the church.[63]

Thus we should be able to draw two vital conclusions from this chapter:

1. There is no evidence to assume that this group was only a community of consumption and that when the money ran out, they pursued another lifestyle. With the variety of types of work available in and around Jerusalem, those already living in the city would have continued with their jobs, and those moving in could either look for paid work or establish the trade they had worked at previously. In their letter to the Thessalonians, Paul, Silvanus, and Timothy speak of

61. Jo-Ann Shelton, *As the Romans Did: A Sourcebook in Roman Social History* (New York and Oxford: Oxford University Press, 1988), p. 81.

62. By comparing this period with other better-documented periods, MacMullen determines that in fourteenth- and fifteenth-century Europe, one-third of the people lived at a level of bare survival, and he assumes that life in the Roman Empire could have been no better. See Ramsey MacMullen, *Roman Social Relations, 50 B.C. to A.D. 284* (London and New Haven: Yale University Press, 1974), p. 93.

63. Fiensy, "The Composition of the Jerusalem Church," pp. 228-29.

"working night and day" in order not to burden the people they were evangelizing. Paul evidently took along his tent-making tools and used his skills along the way (see Acts 18:1-3). Many others could have done the same thing.

2. Housing conditions among the non-elite in Jerusalem were probably abysmal by contemporary middle-class standards. But given Cynthia Baker's observations on Eastern architecture, it would have been much more likely for residents to absorb new people into their homes by dividing a large room in two, adding an upper room, or building one into a courtyard.

In the following chapter I will discuss Mediterranean values and social practices that were needed to conduct a viable community of goods with communal meals in the emerging Jesus-movement.

Chapter Seven

How the Non-Elite Survived:
Social Relations and Community Values

Whaling celebrations among the Inupiaq people of Barrow, Alaska, are not commercialized. Only after the community receives the gift of a whale can the successful whaling captain declare a day of feasting. The day opens with a prayer of thanksgiving and then much time for visiting. Throughout the day, the captain and crew distribute various parts of the whale to all who are gathered. One flipper is left in the area, and anyone may carve off what they need. Everything is free. No one buys or sells any meat — that is strictly forbidden. The whaling festival revolves around giving and sharing.

James Roghair, "The Gift of the Whale: Community as Steward"

How did people in ancient agrarian, predemocratic cultures think and behave? What were the social structures and mores that bound them together? Given the huge gap between elite and non-elite, how did the latter survive? Insights from cultural anthropology now permeate biblical studies. In this chapter I will discuss several social values that directly affect our understanding of the Jesus movement and its beginnings in Jerusalem. Though we can never fully recapture the worldview and behavior of ancient Mediterranean people, anthropological comparisons bring us far closer than reading our individualist, capitalist, technological First World society back into the past.

Patronage, Benefactions, and the Concept of Honor

Throughout Mediterranean cultures, social relationships were carried on through a complex system called patronage. Patronage can be defined as a social relationship that is essentially (1) reciprocal, involving exchanges of services over time between two parties, (2) personal (as opposed to commercial), (3) asymmetrical — that is, involving an unequal relationship between two parties of different status, and (4) voluntary and not legally enforceable.[1] However, it was voluntary only in the sense that each exchange was negotiated voluntarily; the system itself was pervasive.

Patronage was entrenched in the culture because it was the way one gained honor, a core value in ancient Mediterranean society. Honor is a claim to worth that is publicly acknowledged, whereas to be shamed is to have one's claim to worth publicly repudiated. Honor is a group value, and all members of a group share in its honor. Wealth was used to gain honor by sharing it with clients in one's social group. The clients were then bound to publicly praise the patrons as a way of showing gratitude.

Some patronage can be seen in a positive light. Since Homeric times, one important way to gain honor was to become a public benefactor. Such a person was seen as good (ἀγαθός), a man (or woman) of exceptional merit.[2] Benefaction was first linked with military prowess or statesmanship, as when a ruler or deity of a certain city protected the inhabitants from their enemies. Later, such forms of benefaction and consequent public recognition were taken over by clubs and societies on the local level. Philosophers were also sometimes seen as benefactors of humanity by virtue of their integrity and wise counsel. According to Frederick Danker, Hellenistic Christian communities were quick to use this system of public benefactions. A person who combined excellent character and performance with religious piety could be seen as a benefactor who worked for

1. Andrew Wallace-Hadrill, ed., *Patronage in Ancient Society* (London and New York: Routledge, 1989), p. 3. Further insights on patronage are drawn from two essays in this book: "Patronage and Friendship in Early Imperial Rome: Drawing the Distinction" by Richard Saller (pp. 68-87), and "Patronage of the Rural Poor in the Roman World" by Peter Garnsey and Greg Woolf (pp. 153-70). See also Richard Saller, *Personal Patronage under the Early Empire* (Cambridge: Cambridge University Press, 1982).

2. See Luke 23:50 and Romans 5:7 for examples of good persons who give a benefaction to others.

the welfare of the whole group. Under this definition, even slaves and women could become benefactors.[3]

In his understanding of patronage, Bruce Malina includes the quality of kinship or family feeling. God is the ultimate patron, or benefactor, of all God's children. As patron, God gives people life and shows favor to them in numerous ways. Humans reciprocate by obeying God's commandments, showing God gratitude and praise, and in turn acting as patrons to others who need favors.[4]

An example of God's extraordinary benefaction is offered through Peter in Acts 2:38-39. Though his listeners are in some way responsible for the death of Jesus, Peter urges them to repent and be baptized. Then, he says, their sins will be forgiven and they will receive the gift of the Holy Spirit, God's promise to them and their children. Danker notes that "the generosity of the divine benefactor is subsequently echoed in the sharing of material goods by the new believers" (Acts 2:42-47).[5]

Patronage operates by means of reciprocity: if a patron does a favor for a client, the client is bound to reciprocate. Marshall Sahlins has outlined a scheme of different types of reciprocities.[6] The specific form that this exchange takes depends on the degree of closeness between the parties involved and the type of goods involved in the exchange.

1. *Generalized reciprocity* is used by members of a close kinship group. Someone may give a gift or do a favor for someone else, and the "debt" may not be collected for a long time, if at all.
2. *Balanced reciprocity* attempts to reach a near equivalence in terms of what is exchanged. Exchanges are balanced if they are done on a quid pro quo basis and the debt is liquidated fairly quickly.

3. Frederick Danker, *Benefactor: Epigraphic Study of a Graeco-Roman and New Testament Semantic Field* (St. Louis: Clayton Publishing House, 1982), pp. 26-27. Women were more likely to be public benefactors during the time of the Roman Empire, when they were gaining more legal and public social rights.

4. Bruce J. Malina, "Patronage," in *Biblical Social Values and Their Meaning*, ed. John J. Pilch and Bruce J. Malina (Peabody, Mass.: Hendrickson, 1993), pp. 133-37.

5. Danker, *Benefactor*, pp. 396, 411.

6. Marshall Sahlins, *Stone Age Economics* (Chicago: Aldine Publishing, 1972), pp. 191-96. See also Halvor Moxnes, "Social Relations and Economic Interaction in Luke's Gospel: A Research Report," in *Luke-Acts: Scandinavian Perspectives*, ed. Petri Luomanen, Publications of the Finnish Exegetical Society 54 (Helsinki: The Finnish Exegetical Society; Göttingen: Vandenhoeck & Ruprecht, 1991), pp. 58-75 (62-64).

3. *Negative reciprocity* is the unsocial extreme. It means attempting to get something for nothing through power, force, or even violence.

The types of exchange are conditioned not only by kinship distance but also by distance in rank or wealth. Kinship distance can be divided, in descending order, into household, extended family, village, tribe, and intertribal sectors. The further the distance between two parties, the more the exchange moves toward balanced and finally negative reciprocity. Unless they are the guests of a known host, strangers tend to be viewed with suspicion, and the exchange tends toward negative reciprocity. Rank and wealth also make a difference, since the more one has, the more one is expected to be generous.[7] Among goods exchanged, food is most often used in generalized reciprocity, and, because of standards of hospitality, food is extended to a wider sphere of human relationships than are other things.[8]

Concepts of patronage and reciprocity are essential in understanding how relationships operated in the Jerusalem community, especially as we come to see it as a fictive kin group.

Kin Groups and Fictive Kin Groups

In this culture, persons were not known as individuals (as in Western society today) but were embedded in a kin group, from which they derived their identity. The value of family-centeredness stems from three components: honor/shame values, tradition, and land.[9]

In a society where the well-being of the collective was of paramount importance, the social standing of the family within the community was of the highest value. The family was the center of the system of meaning. The head male, the patriarch, was responsible for procuring the honor of the family, while the head female, the matriarch, was responsible for maintaining its honor through an appropriate sense of shame that circumscribed her behavior. They both commanded great respect, although the head male was clearly pre-eminent in this strongly patriarchal society. Attacks on family honor were taken very seriously and could result in vengeance.

7. Sahlins, *Stone Age Economics*, pp. 196-215.
8. Sahlins, *Stone Age Economics*, p. 217.
9. Mark McVann, "Family-Centeredness," in *Biblical Social Values and Their Meaning*, ed. Pilch and Malina, pp. 70-72.

Children were expected to pay honor to both father and mother (Exod. 20:12), not only because their parents gave them life, but because they fed them and handed on to them time-tested communal wisdom. The land where the family originally lived provided the framework binding together honor/shame and tradition. The land was considered a gift from God and therefore sacred. Its control and maintenance were not simply matters of survival but questions of honor/shame and tradition.[10] This emphasis on family-centeredness would have prevailed throughout Mediterranean society, but was especially strong among the Jews of Palestine, who were living in continuity with their biblical history and values.

Other essential elements that grew out of such a kinship structure were loyalty and trust, truth-telling, the openness of homes to everyone in the group, and the obligation to see that the needs of everyone in the group were met. Since there was no such thing as universal democracy or belonging to universal humankind, loyalty was to the family, and telling the truth within the kin group was highly valued. Outside the group, however, no obligation existed to tell the truth except to superiors. As Bruce Malina and Jerome Neyrey explain, "It is honorable to lie in order to deceive an outsider who has no right to the truth."[11]

Malina further describes the way the ideal man in this culture lived within his kin group:

> [He] maintains a culturally predictable, transparent, socially open existence. What this means is that he lives in a way that allows others to know what he is up to. . . . One way of showing this openness, to reveal that he is no threat to others, is to allow children to roam freely in and out of his house, workplace, or any other situation that might harbor a secret threat to others. . . . Another form of signaling such openness — giving others the opportunity to check up on one — is to keep the door to one's courtyard and/or house open when the village or neighborhood is up and about.[12]

---

10. An example is the resistance of Naboth to sell his ancestral vineyard to King Ahab in 1 Kings 21:1-16.

11. Bruce J. Malina and Jerome H. Neyrey, "Honor and Shame in Luke-Acts: Pivotal Values of the Mediterranean World," in *The Social World of Luke-Acts: Models for Interpretation,* ed. Jerome H. Neyrey (Peabody, Mass.: Hendrickson, 1991), pp. 25-65 (37).

12. Bruce J. Malina, *The New Testament World: Insights from Cultural Anthropology* (Atlanta: John Knox Press, 1981), pp. 77-78.

Within the kin group, generalized reciprocity prevailed, and members were obligated to help each other in whatever way they could. However, patriarchs, or those members of an extended kin-group with substantial resources, were expected to function as patrons to the others. This in turn would increase their public honor through expressions of praise and gratitude from the recipients.

In some cultures, "pseudo-kinship" relationships develop, where persons are addressed by kin terms but are not part of a kin group through biology, marriage, or the custom of their society. One type of pseudo-kinship is called fictive kinship, where a person or persons are given the status of kin by attribution rather than by birth. In Western civilization, adoption may be thought of as a form of fictive kinship.[13]

In the Gospels, Jesus prioritizes faithfulness to God, expressed through discipleship to himself, over the natural loyalty of kinship groups (Matt. 12:46-50; Mark 3:31-35; Luke 8:19-21). Yet even as he criticizes the biological family system, he sets up its replacement. The highest loyalty is now to the community of disciples rather than to blood relatives. They are embedded in Jesus and his group and take his name for their primary identification as Christians (Acts 11:26). Within this fictive kin group, the same standards of truth-telling, keeping open homes, and practicing generalized reciprocity prevail.

Halvor Moxnes cites examples from Luke to show how Jesus expected such generalized reciprocity to work among his followers. Sometimes the religious leaders in Luke are shown practicing negative reciprocity, such as "devouring widows' houses" (Luke 20:47). Sometimes they practice balanced reciprocity with those of their own class, based on the expectation of a return. At the banquet in the house of the rich Pharisee, Jesus points out to the host that his hospitality is confined to a small circle of friends, brothers, relatives, and rich neighbors, while the poor are ignored (Luke 14:12-13).[14]

This inequality of wealth threatens the social stability of a community. Many traditional societies recognize this, says Moxnes, and put pressure on the rich to share with those who are poorer. This often takes the

13. Julian Pitt-Rivers, "Pseudo-Kinship," in *International Encyclopedia of the Social Sciences*, vol. 8, ed. D. L. Sills (New York: Macmillan, 1968), p. 408.

14. Halvor Moxnes, "Meals and the New Community in Luke," in *Svensk Exegetisk Årsbok*, ed. L. Hartman (Uppsala: Uppsala exegetiska sällskap, 1986), pp. 158-67. For further positive and negative examples, see also Luke 10:3-11, 38-39; 22:1-6; Acts 5:1-11; 2 John 7-10.

form of a great feast, or potlatch, where food and other items are shared in a form of redistribution.[15] But within the community of Jesus' fictive kin group, God is the real benefactor, and the rich are asked to forego expectations of a reward of gratitude, honor, or increased status from their poor clients. Instead, they will be repaid at the "resurrection of the just" (Luke 14:14).

From the above discussion one could conclude that nearly everyone in the ancient world belonged to some kin group, even if conditions weren't always ideal. Yet nothing could be farther from the truth, especially in urban areas of the ancient world. Dispossessed peasants and younger sons who received no land inheritance had to move away from home, usually to a city, to look for the means to support themselves.[16] Daughters were married off and possibly never made to feel a part of their new families. Impoverished parents were forced to sell their children into slavery. Girls who had been raped or had their sexuality compromised in some way were disowned. Along with widows and divorced wives, they would often be driven into the sex trade to feed themselves and their children. And families would never tolerate women who thus shamed them in their midst.

Many of these social rejects drifted toward urban centers like Jerusalem. People would settle in ethnic precincts, but the constant influx of newcomers would tend to undercut social integration both within and among ethnic groupings. As kin groups did form, their natural suspicion toward outsiders marred the social fabric and promoted urban unrest and riots.[17] In addition, death was a constant companion and threat, because people's health was poor and life expectancy was very short. Half the children born died at birth or in infancy, and those who survived lost at least one parent before maturity.[18]

15. Moxnes, "Meals and the New Community in Luke," pp. 164-65.

16. Gerhard Lenski, *Power and Privilege: A Theory of Social Stratification* (New York: McGraw-Hill, 1966), pp. 287, 290.

17. Rodney Stark, "Antioch as the Social Situation for Matthew's Gospel," in *Social History of the Matthean Community: Cross-Disciplinary Approaches*, ed. David L. Balch (Minneapolis: Fortress Press, 1991), pp. 189-210 (196); John Stambaugh, *The Ancient Roman City* (Baltimore: Johns Hopkins University Press, 1988), pp. 93-95.

18. Stark, "Antioch as the Social Situation for Matthew's Gospel," p. 198.

Fictive Kinship Structures among Jerusalem Believers

At one level, the story of the beginning of the church in Jerusalem is the story of disparate people being melded into one family, one kin group. From an economic perspective, most of them would have had no more material resources to share with each other than members in a typical lower-class extended family with meager possessions living at a subsistence level. The apostles like Peter, Andrew, James, and John had been fishermen from Galilee. Zebedee, the father of James and John, owned a fishing business prosperous enough to employ day laborers (Mark 1:20), but we do not know if they were still supported by this income.[19] Jesus' brother James was presumably a woodworker or a stoneworker. One might reasonably assume that most local members of the Jerusalem church were craftspersons or small merchants, but the text does not indicate this.[20]

Some property in the community may have been sold in order to help some of the newly arrived craftspersons and shopkeepers start businesses in Jerusalem. Some members no doubt would have had to join the throngs who worked as day laborers, competed for jobs in the buildings projects, or provided extra hands for some household industry. But here their connections to each other would prove valuable as they helped each other find work and shared in the daily tasks of survival. All members would have had all the benefits of an extended kin group: the comfort of knowing that they were part of a family with homes open to each other, a sense of trust and loyalty rather than suspicion, the gift of truth-telling, and a sense of shared destiny. They would have seen their community as the firstfruits of the New Age, the reign of God on earth, ushered in by Jesus and carried on through his Spirit in their daily relationships with each other.

Acts 4:36–5:11 records only three people who were making a substantial financial contribution to the Jerusalem community. Barnabas is a worthy example, while Ananias and Sapphira prove to be unworthy members of this fictive kin group because they do not tell the truth. Exegetes usually explain Barnabas's presence in the text by saying either that he was the only person who actually gave up substantial property for the community, or

---

19. David A. Fiensy, "The Composition of the Jerusalem Church," in *The Book of Acts in Its Palestinian Setting,* ed. Richard Bauckham, vol. 4 of *The Book of Acts in Its First-Century Setting,* ed. Bruce W. Winter (Grand Rapids: Eerdmans, 1995), p. 227.

20. Fiensy, "The Composition of the Jerusalem Church," p. 227.

that from a literary perspective it was a way to introduce him into the story, since he would play a major role thereafter. Knowing the cultural context, I think it seems more likely that Barnabas was one of the very few who owned landed wealth. Moreover, the text stresses that he is a Cypriot and a Levite (4:36). Barnabas may have sold his land because it was in Cyprus and thus of no use to the community of production in Jerusalem. But Luke may have also wanted to show Barnabas the Levite fulfilling God's original covenant with God's people. Barnabas had owned a "field" (ἀγρός), meaning a culti-vated field. However, according to Joshua 14:3b-4 and 21:1-41, Moses had given no such land to the Levites, "only towns to live in, with their [com-mon] pasture lands for their flocks and herds." In this community that was now experiencing covenant renewal, Barnabas could no longer own agri-cultural land, so he donated it to the community.[21]

S. Scott Bartchy contrasts Barnabas with the person in Jesus' Parable of the Great Banquet (Luke 14:18) who could not come to the feast because of the field he had bought, and with the young and pious ruler whose need to control his wealth kept him from joining the fictive kin group around Jesus.[22] Later in Acts 12:12 we learn that Mary, mother of John Mark (and sister or sister-in-law of Barnabas), was wealthy enough to own her own house. However, she did not sell it but used it for group meetings, which would have included the daily communal meal (Acts 2:46).

The need for trust and absolute loyalty to the kin group explains why the behavior of Ananias and Sapphira was so potentially deadly to the community. By withholding part of the money from the sale of their land and then lying about it, they revealed themselves as non-kin, as outsiders. They could no longer share an open home or live in transparent truthful-ness with the group. Their energies would be spent hiding some of their possessions from the group, keeping them forever on the margins of the group. As this poisonous attitude spread to others, the honor of the whole

---

21. Jeremiah 32:6-15 describes the priest Jeremiah specifically buying a field. However, he did this during the Babylonian siege of Jerusalem as a counterintuitive act of prophetic symbolism, to demonstrate his certainty that the people of Israel would eventually live on and cultivate their own land in freedom. In New Testament times, it was clear that Levites did have property (cf. Josephus, *Life*, 68-83), so Barnabas's act was also a political/religious statement challenging the way Levites in his day were ignoring a law that would have limited their power.

22. S. Scott Bartchy, "Community of Goods in Acts: Idealization or Social Reality?" in *The Future of Early Christianity*, ed. Birger A. Pearson (Minneapolis: Fortress Press, 1991), pp. 309-18 (16).

community would be compromised. Since the Holy Spirit had called this group into existence (Acts 2:38-42), lying within the group would be considered lying against the Holy Spirit.[23] In contrast, Barnabas protected the honor of the community by proving to be a generous and honest patron, laying his wealth at the feet of the apostles (Acts 4:37), who were his social and economic inferiors.

Ivoni Richter Reimer provides additional evidence for the priority of these fictive kin relationships over traditional family structures.[24] She asks why Ananias, as the patriarchal head of his household, could sell his property without Sapphira's involvement. Elisabeth Koffmahn's work on ancient Jewish marriage contracts *(ketubah)* gives her a clue.[25] Every respectable wife had to have a *ketubah,* which guaranteed that if the marriage were dissolved, she would have at least the minimum necessary to sustain her. If a husband wanted to sell a piece of property that was used to guarantee his wife's *ketubah,* she had to co-sign the contract and could ask for compensation.[26] Thus Sapphira had to comply with her husband's plan in order for him to sell their property legally. Her guilt, therefore, lay not in initiating the fraud but in not resisting Ananias's decision. Her first priority was her patriarchal marriage rather than the community. Comments Richter Reimer, "Here we have an example of how patriarchal marriage is an obstacle not only to the development of independent human personality, but also to the development of community life. The opportunity for a liberated life is rejected as both of the partners make themselves liable to death through their patriarchal act."[27]

How inclusive was this Jesus-centered fictive kin group? Both Hebrews and Hellenists were a part of it (Acts 6:1), including Hellenist widows, which may imply those without other kin connections or sources of support. Women were accepted on the same basis as men, as we know from Acts 5:14, which specifically mentions both. The lowest classes of Jerusalem

23. Bartchy, "Community of Goods in Acts," p. 316.

24. Ivoni Richter Reimer, *Women in the Acts of the Apostles: A Feminist Liberation Perspective,* trans. Linda M. Maloney (Minneapolis: Fortress Press, 1995), pp. 23-24.

25. Elisabeth Koffmahn, *Die Doppelurkunden aus der Wüste Juda. Recht und Praxis der jüdischen Papyri des 1. und 2. Jahrhunderts n. Chr. samt Übersetzung der Texte,* vol. 5 of *Studies on the Texts of the Desert of Judah* (Leiden, 1968), pp. 104ff.; referred to in Richter Reimer, *Women in the Acts of the Apostles,* p. 3.

26. Richter Reimer, *Women in the Acts of the Apostles,* p. 5.

27. Richter Reimer, *Women in the Acts of the Apostles,* p. 20.

society — the "expendables" and the "unclean and degraded classes"[28] — were also included, for representatives of both these classes are mentioned: the lame beggar in Acts 3, Simon the tanner[29] in chapter 10, and presumably some of the diseased people healed by the apostles in 5:12-16. David Fiensy notes that the striking thing about the Acts description of the early church is that so little is said about socio-economic class distinctions:

> The wealthy are hardly noticed at all except for a few cases of extraordinary generosity. We cannot document that any of the High Priestly family or any of the governing elite were members of the earliest church. The lower class has the fewest references, although one could speculate that they had the largest representation. The submerged [expendable] class enters the story only to indicate that the church is caring for them. The central figures are those that perform ministries of some kind, whether they come from the upper or lower class. One should stop short of concluding that class went unnoticed in this religious community, but the traditions we have certainly de-emphasize it.[30]

If indeed the Jerusalem believers were acting as a fictive kin group, without "a needy person among them" (4:34), the lack of comment about social class is what we might expect. And the most immediate and effective way for their basic needs to be met and their cross-class status to be shared would have been through the daily communal meal.

The most surprising thing about the group, observes Bartchy, was its acceptance of those who did play by the rules of fictive kinship. According to Acts 2:23 and 37-42, some of the first converts were enemies, those accused of indirectly crucifying Jesus. When they repented, they were invited to share in the spiritual and economic life of the whole community.[31]

Although Luke is concerned to present this fictive kin group in a positive light, it does not prevent him from showing some of the struggles and problems that can occur with such radical spiritual and social reorganizing. In addition to the divided hearts of Ananias and Sapphira, ethnic di-

---

28. Lenski, *Power and Privilege*, pp. 280-84.

29. Because tanning hides demanded the use of urine, a malodorous and impure pollutant, tanners were relegated to the outskirts of towns and cities and looked down upon socially.

30. Fiensy, "The Composition of the Jerusalem Church," pp. 229-30.

31. Bartchy, "Community of Goods in Acts," p. 317.

versity results in neglect of Hellenistic widows in the daily table-fellowship. This is not surprising. Given church growth and the constant incorporation of new people into groups operating as kin, many problems likely arose that Luke does not mention. Nevertheless, the kinship structure was essential, for it was the only way people in that agrarian culture and that overcrowded, dirty, chaotic city could survive. Those with no previous family connections had sunk to the bottom of the social scale as "expendables." Those who were part of a family may have been forced to leave because of their new loyalty to the crucified Jesus and the group he had first called into existence. Establishing a fictive kin group was essential — socially, economically, and spiritually.

Charity and Almsgiving

It is on the issue of almsgiving that a wide conceptual gulf must have existed between Jews and non-Jews in the Roman Empire. Apart from Jewish traditions, the idea of organized aid for the destitute was very uncommon in the Greco-Roman world. There is plenty of evidence that pity for the poor and thus attempts to help them survive had little place in the upper-class Greek character, though A. R. Hands is cautious about ascribing lack of compassion when we cannot be sure of motivation.[32] Nevertheless, there were simply no organized charities comparable to those today where people of moderate means could contribute to the needs of the destitute. No public orphanages or foundling hospitals existed.[33]

Instead, giving was integrally associated with patronage and the concepts of honor and shame. One gave a gift or a benefaction in order to receive something back. Either one received a gift in kind or was accorded a particular honor. Therefore, giving was mainly done within one's own class, or was a benefaction given to a city. The poor were not singled out for favorable treatment even during food shortages, when a dole of corn or oil may have been given to the male citizens of a city.[34] A. R. Hands cites

32. A. R. Hands, *Charities and Social Aid in Greece and Rome* (Ithaca, N.Y.: Cornell University Press, 1968), pp. 11-12.

33. Hands, *Charities and Social Aid in Greece and Rome*, pp. 73-74.

34. "The dole, even if providing a bare subsistence for a man, certainly did not cover the needs of his wife and children." See M. Cary and H. H. Scullard, *A History of Rome Down to the Reign of Constantine*, 3rd ed. (London: MacMillan Education, 1979), p. 202.

love of honor as the primary reason for benefactions, although there was a distinction between actions that were blatantly self-serving and those that showed a greater emphasis on the common good rather than self-display.[35]

This Greco-Roman attitude contrasts with the biblical attitude such as that found in Deuteronomy 15:7-11, where Hebrews are charged not to "be hard-hearted or tight-fisted toward your needy neighbor," and that found in Deuteronomy 10:17-18, where Yahweh is seen as the "great God . . . who executes justice for the orphan and the widow, and who loves the strangers, providing them food and clothing." After the Exile and under Persian rule, Proverbs and Job emphasize giving alms to the poor (e.g., Prov. 14:21; 19:17; 31:20; Job 29:12-13). Robert Grant sees the golden age of almsgiving as the second century B.C.E., when Sirach declared that "almsgiving atones for sin" (3:30), followed by numerous calls to give to needy (and deserving!) neighbors (4:10; 7:10, 32-36; 12:1-7; 17:22; 29:8-13).[36] The book of Tobit sees almsgiving as dear to God and rewarded by him (4:7, 16; 12:8, 9; 14:2, 10).

Under Hebrew law, helping the poor was also a requirement. Deuteronomy 14:27-29 explains that the agricultural tithe of every household for the third and sixth years of a seven-year cycle was to be given to the Levites and the needy — specifically, the resident aliens, orphans, and widows. E. P. Sanders is inclined to think that this tithe was given regularly, because Josephus refers to it, and because it apparently was collected by the Levites and priests in person.[37]

The agricultural tithes for the Levites and the needy were only two of the fourteen in a seven-year cycle that were required of the people. In addition, there were various taxes and revenues exacted from them by their local and Roman overlords. One wonders how many inhabitants of Palestine, barely subsisting themselves, actually gave much more than was required. Yet Joachim Jeremias notes that devout pilgrims practiced charity as they traveled to and from the annual festivals in Jerusalem, and that it was especially meritorious when practiced in Jerusalem.[38] Actually, char-

---

35. Hands, *Charities and Social Aid in Greece and Rome*, p. 45.

36. Robert Grant, *Early Christianity and Society* (San Francisco: Harper & Row, 1977), p. 125.

37. E. P. Sanders, *Judaism: Practice and Belief, 63 B.C.E.–66 C.E.* (Philadelphia: Trinity Press International, 1992), pp. 147-49.

38. Jeremias, *Jerusalem in the Time of Jesus: An Investigation into the Economic and Social Conditions during the New Testament Period* (Philadelphia: Fortress Press, 1962), p. 129.

ity dispensed in Jerusalem likely came from another annual tithe, which Deuteronomy 14:22-26 prescribed to be spent "in the place that God will choose as a dwelling" (v. 23) whenever the faithful went up for a festival. Either agricultural produce itself or money received from the sale of produce was to be given in Jerusalem as part of the celebration and for the upkeep of the city.

Luke T. Johnson especially stresses the importance of giving alms within Judaism. The *halakic* midrashim interpret the Laws to give maximum benefit to the poor, yet they also protect property owners.[39] Here, Johnson takes pains to negatively contrast a community of possessions, which he sees as Greek idealizing, to Judaism, which saw almsgiving as fulfilling the law of God. Indeed, to equalize all property would be to challenge God's disposition of the world and to make it impossible to fulfill the command to give alms.[40] Even poor Jews were expected to give charity out of their meager possessions.

It was important for Jews to give alms, says Johnson, because those with some wealth never knew when they themselves might fall into poverty (though Hands cites similar fear as a common Greek incentive for giving to social peers, not to the destitute[41]). This expresses the precarious nature of life among peasantry in the ancient world, for in such an agrarian culture, as Gerhard Lenski noted earlier, social mobility was generally downward.

Jeremias sees the early Christian community in Jerusalem dispensing charity to its widows and orphans in a form similar to the two Jewish systems that scholars have assumed were in place at that time. The *tamhuy*, or "poor bowl" (or tray), was established for wandering paupers and consisted of a daily quota of food; the *quppah*, or "poor basket" for the local poor, was distributed weekly and consisted of food and clothing (*M. Peah* 8.7; *M. Pes.* 10.1).[42] However, David Seccombe has challenged the dating of these methods of caring for the poor and proposes that they did not come into existence until later.[43] If this system was in existence among the Jews

39. Luke T. Johnson, *Sharing Possessions: Mandate and Symbol of Faith* (Philadelphia: Fortress Press, 1981), pp. 133-37.

40. Johnson, *Sharing Possessions*, p. 134.

41. Hands, *Charities and Social Aid in Greece and Rome*, pp. 78, 80.

42. Jeremias, *Jerusalem in the Time of Jesus*, pp. 130-31.

43. David Seccombe, "Was There Organized Charity in Jerusalem before the Christians?" *Journal of Theological Studies*, New Series 29 (1978): 140-43.

during the first century, it is surprising that there is such a high incidence of reports of begging and tolerance of beggars in the Gospels.[44] The beggar is despised in rabbinic teaching (*B. Bat.* 9a).

Jeremias concludes that almsgiving was an integral part of the Christian community of shared goods in Jerusalem: "It is likely that the fellowship meal that was held daily by the Christian community entailed of itself a daily distribution of aid for its poor members."[45] Jeremias visualizes this meal "in their meeting house," where "the poor and especially widows were served with the gifts that were brought in, and were also given provisions for the next day."[46] He does not explain how space would be found for the whole community to sit down to a meal, nor does he address issues of class or the shame of poverty, or the significance of the social role that food plays in a society. He does not take into account the new kinship structure and role reversals that Jesus brought into existence, and the effect that these would have had on the internal social structure of the early church.

For John Dominic Crossan, commensality and almsgiving are two different breeds altogether. Citing Gillian Feeley-Harnik's comment that food is "one of the principal ways in which differences between social groups are marked," Crossan suggests that almsgiving may be a method of salving one's conscience while still keeping those of a lower class at a distance.[47] Crossan examines Mark 6:7-11 and Luke 10:1-11, where the disciples are sent out without a purse or bag. "The missionaries," he says, "do not carry a bag because they do not beg for alms or food or clothing or anything else."[48] Instead, they are expected to share a house and table with those who receive them. Jesus' strategy here was not simply a method of supporting the mission, for he could have depended on alms, paid wages, or charged fees. Rather, it was a strategy for rebuilding peasant community on radically different principles than that of unequal patronage and clientage. Though Crossan sees changes within the tradition, as in Mat-

44. Cf. Mark 10:46; Luke 18:35; John 9:8; Acts 3:2-10.
45. Jeremias, *Jerusalem in the Time of Jesus*, p. 131.
46. Jeremias, *Jerusalem in the Time of Jesus*, p. 131.
47. John Dominic Crossan, *The Historical Jesus: The Life of a Mediterranean Peasant* (San Francisco: HarperSanFrancisco, 1991), p. 341; Gillian Feeley-Harnik, *The Lord's Table: Eucharist and Passover in Early Christianity* (Philadelphia: University of Pennsylvania Press, 1981), p. 10.
48. Crossan, *The Historical Jesus*, p. 341.

thew 10:10b ("The laborer is worthy of his hire"), he believes the original strategy of commensality came from Jesus.[49]

Halvor Moxnes defines the ancient practice of almsgiving not as a post-Jesus development but as radically different from modern notions of giving trifling sums from one's abundance.[50] Instead, almsgiving meant wealth redistribution as generalized reciprocity. (See the sections on patronage and kinship structures above.) Zaccheus, for example, returns fourfold what he has cheated, and gives half of his possessions to the poor (Luke 19:1-9). This is the way salvation comes, says Jesus (19:9). It stands in contrast to the Pharisees' behavior of negative or balanced reciprocity and harks back to the old norms of solidarity elucidated in the Old Testament.[51] Because Zaccheus was a social outcast himself, his distribution to the poor means the creation of a social bond between outsiders.

Moxnes's discussion mediates Crossan's contrast between giving alms and commensality, and shows that Crossan is thinking of alms in a modern sense. It also lessens the gap between what Luke says Jesus said, and what Jesus himself might have said. It may likewise enlighten Bo Reicke's references to poor relief (in Chapter Four). When I reflect on communal meals in Part III (Chapters Nine though Eleven), Moxnes's discussion will prove helpful.

Christian Rewards and the Logic of Communal Sharing

To modern people in capitalist societies, giving away extra capital seems foolhardy, for it shows lack of planning for the future. To invest extra earnings now means a higher rate of return later, and in the meantime one's money is put to use for all manner of profit-producing projects. But in a noncapitalist, nontechnological society, there was not much that people — especially peasants — could do with wealth accumulated beyond subsistence, other than use it for luxury items and ostentation. To share it with others in one's extended family system or clan *was* investing for the future. It provided both insurance and honor for the patriarch and his household.

---

49. Crossan, *The Historical Jesus*, p. 342.

50. Halvor Moxnes, *The Economy of the Kingdom: Social Conflict and Economic Relations in Luke's Gospel* (Philadelphia: Fortress Press, 1988), p. 114.

51. Moxnes, *The Economy of the Kingdom*, pp. 120-21.

If the giver and his household fell on hard times, others would help out. Such redistribution was occurring within the Jerusalem community, only now the kin group included all the believers, with the non-elite apostles in charge of the redistribution.

That the entire community later fell into greater poverty may have been the result of at least three factors, none of which were directly related to the concept of a community of goods: (1) the regional famine (Acts 11:28); (2) perhaps the large number of disabled people or other "expendables" being cared for within the community; and (3) the gradual and continual loss of peasant-owned land to large landholders. I repeat here from Chapter One Luise Schottroff's evaluation of the cause of Palestinian poverty:

> Acts 2:45; 4:34, 37; and 5:1-11 presuppose that money had to be raised in order to provide for all members of the original congregation in Jerusalem. The money derived from the sale of fields or houses. Had those fields been large enough that, by its own labor, the congregation could have grown sufficient food to make up for its lack, there would have been no reason to sell them. Acts 2:45 and the other verses reflect an economic situation comparable to that of Matthew 20:1-16 [Parable of the Laborers in the Vineyard]: . . . either there are no more land holdings or the land owned is too small to supply the needs of the people. What land remains must be sold so that provisions can be bought. And this means that the condition of grinding poverty escalates, becoming ever more the rule.[52]

The community in Jerusalem did survive in spite of the famine in the forties and in spite of the growing societal gap between rich and poor. This may very well be attributed to their community of goods, their "generalized reciprocity" as a fictive kin group.

Looking for sociological answers to the question of how Christianity managed to grow from this tiny sect in Jerusalem in the early 30s C.E. to the state religion 300 years later, Rodney Stark discusses the tremendous social impact of Christian theology — the idea that God loves and cares for people and thus they are expected to love and care for each other.[53] Belonging

---

52. Luise Schottroff, *Lydia's Impatient Sisters: A Feminist Social History of Early Christianity* (Louisville: Westminster/John Knox Press, 1995), p. 97.

53. Rodney Stark, *The Rise of Christianity: A Sociologist Reconsiders History* (Princeton: Princeton University Press, 1996), pp. 86-88.

to a group, making sure that everyone in the group had enough to eat, rejecting abortion and infanticide, nursing the sick through plagues and epidemics and the physical hazards of ordinary urban life simply meant that more people survived and had longer life expectancies than the general population. Stark comments,

> It was not simply the promise of salvation that motivated Christians, but the fact that they were greatly rewarded here and now for belonging. Thus while membership was expensive, it was, in fact, a bargain. That is, because the church asked much of its members, it was thereby possessed of the resources to *give* much. For example, because Christians were expected to aid the less fortunate, many of them received such aid, and all could feel greater security against bad times. . . . Because they were asked to love others, they in turn were loved. . . . In similar fashion, Christianity greatly mitigated relations among social classes — at the very time when the gap between rich and poor was growing.[54]

Stark's analysis lends credence to the idea that Jerusalem believers shared a common life, and suggests that it continued, probably in various adapted forms, for several hundred years.

A final comment should be added about the eschatological expectations of this community. It has been a common understanding that the Jerusalem church did not plan ahead and organize a community of production because they expected Jesus to return at any moment. But if we understand the Jewish worldview that the end of the Old Age and the beginning of the New Age meant not the end of the space-time universe but a renewal of this world without greed and violence, a community of shared consumption *and* production makes sense. The New Age had already begun, and they were aiming to live out its values under the guiding presence of the Holy Spirit.

Conclusion

My goal in the last three chapters has been to provide a larger social context for the early Jerusalem Christians, as described in Acts. The details

---

54. Stark, *The Rise of Christianity*, p. 188.

presented above help us reconstruct a picture of a social world far different from that experienced by present-day interpreters in the developed world. Insights from the social sciences, social history, and archeology can help us avoid some of the unconscious biases and presuppositions of European and American scholars mentioned in Chapter Two.

The earliest Christians lived in a pre-industrial, precapitalistic agrarian society where cities were relatively small because they were dependent on the outlying agricultural land for their food. Land was the most desired form of wealth, since it was the primary method of producing goods. During the first century, the gap between rich and poor was growing as more and more land passed into the possession of large landholders. Most people lived at a subsistence level, so when hard times struck, they had no reserves and had to sell land in order to survive.

The household and family was the unit of production in this society, not the individual. People in one household worked at one industry together, such as farming, a craft, or fishing. But many were day laborers who worked for wages. The wages earned by the father of the family were normally inadequate to support the whole family, so often women and children also worked for pay — a fraction of what men received for the same number of hours.

Because their culture was without a concept of universal democracy and individual rights, people survived economically and socially only through strong ties within extended families and clans. Identity was derived from one's kin group. The closer the relationship, the more generalized reciprocity was practiced, where those who had more at a given time would share with other kin who had less — with the understanding that the tables might be turned at a later time. Sharing with others and giving benefactions were honorable acts that increased one's prestige in the community. Since wealth was rarely used to produce more wealth (as in capitalism), its proper use was not to spend it on luxuries for oneself but to share it with others in order to gain honor, a core value in this society. An honorable person was open with other members of the kin group, told them the truth, and gave the group his or her full loyalty. An honorable role for a woman was to have a sense of shame and propriety.

Most of the earliest Christians were probably of the peasant or artisan classes. Some of the Galileans may have given up some of their land to follow Jesus; in any case, it was left behind. Some of those who lived in Jerusalem may have been driven there originally because they lost their land, although others must have owned small fields near the city. Some belonged to the "expendables," or submerged class, such as the disabled and the chronically sick who were without previous family support. A few believers like Barnabas and Ananias and Sapphira appear to have been wealthier, because they did own substantial property. Mary of Jerusalem shared her house with other believers.

The communal sharing which Luke describes must have been similar to the generalized reciprocity that went on all the time among an extended family. What was different — and radical — about it was *who* the kin were. No longer were they just one's blood relatives; all who believed in Jesus were now brothers and sisters together. Just as God, the primary benefactor, had given them the gift of the Holy Spirit of Jesus, so they saw their role as sharing whatever they had with each other. We can assume that those who had houses that could be used as meeting places did not sell them but made them available for other believers. Meals were eaten together in these houses, and worship and prayer followed the meals. The truly unusual aspect of the group was not its property-sharing per se, but its inclusiveness: it accepted women as well as men, people of all classes, and even the former enemies of Jesus. On the other hand, the standards of commitment were high, for even people with property, if they lied about it, could not remain part of the group.

The kind of sharing that went on was not almsgiving in the modern sense of giving loose change in one's pocket. In a community where all were seen as kin, needs were most easily and economically met by having communal meals in households, and by adding an extra room to one's house or squeezing a couple more people on the roof. If Barnabas and Mary were role models of how to share possessions in the community, others were probably following their lead as they were able.

The paradigm of a fictive kin group practicing generalized reciprocity already existed in their world. Most immediate had been the practice of Jesus and his disciples. Certainly these disciples, now in leadership roles, were in a position to explain and adapt their own experience of sharing a common life with the new believers.

However, the company around Jesus would surely have known about the Essenes, the other strongly pietist group scattered throughout Palestine and in a settlement by the Dead Sea. Over more than one hundred years they had worked out precise rules of communal sharing in order to be successful spiritually and economically. Jesus himself may have adapted

Essene practices of sharing to his itinerant ministry, practices that were now being passed on and reshaped again by a more sedentary community. It is to this deeply religious Jewish movement that we now turn for a further analog to the Jesus movement in Jerusalem.

Chapter Eight

Copycats? Essene Communal Life as Model

Each member when it has reached the wages of these so different occu-
pations gives it to one person who has been appointed as treasurer. He
takes it and at once buys what is necessary and provides food in abun-
dance and anything else which human life requires. Thus having each
day a common life and a common table, they are content with the same
conditions, lovers of frugality who shun expensive luxury as a disease of
both body and soul.

Philo, *Hypothetica*, 11:10-11

In a recent lecture, biblical scholar and archeologist James Charlesworth
commented that research on the Dead Sea Scrolls is like shining a flashlight into a dark room. On the one hand, what was previously in shadow is
now illuminated, and surprises abound. On the other hand, it is only a
flashlight, not a brilliant overhead lamp, and many shadows remain.

Until this discovery beginning in 1947, little was known about the
group called the Essenes except through the writings of Josephus and
Philo of Alexandria. There is no direct mention of them in the canonical
Gospels. Just as redaction criticism dismissed the practices of the early Jerusalem church as Lukan idealism, so many assumed that the communalism of this Jewish religious party also had little basis in historical reality.
Many scrolls and thousands of fragments later, translations and interpre-

tations are still somewhat in flux, but the historical reality of the Essene communities is no longer questioned.

Of the parallel practices of the Essenes and the early Christians, the most convincing are those of economic sharing and the sharing of communal meals. The texts in Acts 2:42-47 and 4:32–5:11, where Christian believers are said to have everything in common, show similarities to what Josephus, Philo, and Pliny the Elder say about the Essenes.[1] Josephus's account in particular sounds like the description of an especially tight-knit fictive kin group:

> There is no appearance of poverty or excess of riches, but every one's possessions are intermingled with every other's possessions; and so there is, as it were, one patrimony among all the brethren. . . . They also have stewards appointed to take care of their common affairs, who every one of them have no separate business for any, but what is for the use of them all.
>
> They have no certain city, but many of them dwell in every city; and if any of their sect come from other places, what they have lies open for them, just as if it were their own; and they go into such as they never knew before, as if they had been ever so long acquainted with them. For which reason they carry nothing with them when they travel into remote parts. (*J.W.* 2.8.3-4)

If Josephus and Philo have idealized the Essenes to some extent, their basic perceptions about communal sharing are corroborated by multiple copies of various Community Rules found among the Dead Sea Scrolls at Qumran. Various theories have been developed about Essene origins and the relationship of the Qumranites to the Essenes living in the towns of Judea. Both Geza Vermes[2] and Hans-Josef Klauck,[3] for example, see male celibacy, a common table, and a true community of goods only at Qumran, necessary because of harsh desert conditions. Married Essenes living in towns contributed two days' wages to the larger community for

---

1. Josephus, *J.W.* 2.8.2-13; *Ant.* 18.1.5; Philo, *Good Person*, 75-91; *Apology for the Jews*, quoted in Eusebius, *Praeparatio evangelica* VIII, 6-7; Pliny the Elder, *Natural History* V, 17, 4 (73).

2. Geza Vermes, *The Dead Sea Scrolls in English*, 4th ed., revised and enlarged (New York: Penguin Books, 1995).

3. H. J. Klauck, "Gütergemeinschaft in der klassischen Antike, in Qumran und im neuen Testament," *Revue de Qumran* 11 (1982): 47-79.

the care of the less fortunate, but they did not share in a communal meal or a common purse. Hartmut Stegemann[4] and Brian Capper,[5] in different ways, see a much closer relationship.

Because Essene practice relates to their origins, it is helpful to know the history of this religious organization that by the time of Jesus numbered about 4,000 men scattered throughout Judea. How did a movement nearly unknown until the past century manage to permeate the whole of southern Palestine for several hundred years?

Origins of the Essenes

Jewish homogeneity was breaking up as Judea became increasingly Hellenized by the beginning of the second century B.C.E.[6] Many Jews wanted reform of the core laws of circumcision, Sabbath-keeping, and purity, but the high priest Onias III resisted. He was deposed by his brother Jason, who built a Greek-style gymnasium in the area just below the Temple. Jason was still of the Zadokite (high priestly) line, but by 172 B.C.E. his office was bought by a lower-level priest not of this line, whose Greek name was Menelaus. Menelaus had Onias III murdered, and by 169 B.C.E. he allowed the Seleucid king Antiochus IV to strip the Jerusalem Temple of everything of value, then issued laws that forbade core Jewish practices. Menelaus finally abolished the worship of Yahweh and the use of the priestly 364-day solar calendar with all its Torah-prescribed festivals; these were replaced by the worship of Zeus Olympius and the use of the pagan 354-day lunar calendar.

Although 1 Maccabees, with its Hasmonean slant, tells us most about the revolt under Judas Maccabees, it is also clear that many other Jews re-

4. Hartmut Stegemann, *The Library of Qumran: On the Essenes, Qumran, John the Baptist, and Jesus* (Grand Rapids: Eerdmans, 1998).

5. Brian Capper, "The Church as the New Covenant of Effective Economics: The Social Origins of Mutually Supportive Christian Communities," *International Journal for the Study of the Christian Church* 2 (2002): 83-102 (90); "The Palestinian Cultural Context of Earliest Christian Community of Goods," in *The Book of Acts in Its Palestinian Setting,* ed. Richard Bauckham, vol. 4 of *The Book of Acts in Its First-Century Setting,* ed. Bruce W. Winter (Grand Rapids: Eerdmans, 1995), pp. 323-56.

6. Here I summarize the chronology and analysis supplied by Hartmut Stegemann, head of the Qumran Research Center at the University of Göttingen, Germany.

sisted either by fleeing the country or by refusing to fight on the Sabbath — for which they were cut down by the Seleucid forces (1 Macc. 2:34-38). Those who fled formed organizations in order to maintain their traditions. The largest group of those who fled east of the Jordan River were the Hasidim, the "Pious Ones," from which the name "Essene" derives.

Meanwhile, the Maccabees succeeded in gaining the right to practice most of their religious traditions. Menelaus died in 162 B.C.E., so the Seleucid government chose another priest, Alcimus, as his successor. The Hasidim across the Jordan sent a delegation to Alcimus to negotiate the situation of Temple worship, but he had them all killed, which further increased enmity between the Jewish factions. Alcimus himself died in 159, and Jonathan the Maccabee became high priest in 152. Because 1 Maccabees is silent about the seven years between them, Josephus drew the conclusion that there was no high priest during that time (*Ant.* 20:237).

Stegemann and others believe this to be impossible, since the Jewish festivals, which require an official high priest, were once again observed in the Temple. The Qumran scrolls provide clues to Alcimus's successor: the leader of the Hasidim, the "Teacher of Righteousness." His various titles named in the scrolls, says Stegemann, "place him at the pinnacle of the Temple worship in Jerusalem."[7] But by 152 B.C.E. Jonathan the Maccabee had brought Jerusalem under his power and deposed the Teacher of Righteousness, who fled to Damascus in Syria and there developed the New Covenant, which eventually became the Damascus Document (CD; see CD 7:18-20).

Certain that the Last Judgment was imminent, the Teacher contacted all the Jewish groups that had fled Palestine some years earlier and persuaded seven of them to return to the Holy Land (4QpPsa 1-10 iv 7-9; 1QpHab 11:2-8). Joined by others still in the land, this became the pan-Israelite Essene union, the largest religious group in Palestinian Judaism at that time.[8] Three smaller entities did not participate, however: those of the New Covenant in Damascus who did not want to return; the Hasidim, who developed into the group later called the Pharisees; and those loyal to Jonathan the high priest, later called Sadducees.

Although much is written about Jonathan, who becomes the "Wicked Priest" in the Qumran scrolls, no further criticism is leveled

---

7. Stegemann, *The Library of Qumran*, p. 148.
8. Stegemann, *The Library of Qumran*, p. 150.

against his Hasmonean successors. After the Teacher's hopes for his restoration as high priest were dashed, the Essenes were no longer politically active but waited for justice and vindication at the Last Judgment. Nor, apparently, were they persecuted by the Hasmoneans.[9]

Essene Community Rules

As a conservative group, the Essenes based their beliefs firmly in the Torah and the Prophets. However, since these were the "last days," the Teacher of Righteousness applied the teachings and oracles of the prophets to his own time and place. Laws that had been fleshed out in the seven groups remained in place, subject to critical review. As long as they were consonant with the Torah, Stegemann reports, "the Essenes took over from the 'New Covenant in the Land of Damascus' its laws for property administration and its Sabbath ordinance."[10] By 100 B.C.E., the final form of the Essene rules came together in the Damascus Document.

Since the site of Qumran was not established until about 100 B.C.E., the Community Rules must apply to all Essenes wherever they lived. The Teacher of Righteousness was already dead by 110 B.C.E., and it appears that this outpost was begun not to isolate the group from other Israelites but to copy the scriptures and other important writings of their movement for dissemination throughout the land. The Qumranites raised sheep and goats primarily for their hides (milk, meat, and wool were added perks), which were processed three kilometers south at Ain Feshka, a farm drawing its resources for tanning rawhide from both the Dead Sea and a freshwater spring.[11]

Stegemann asserts that a community of goods was the standard for the Essene lifestyle throughout the land, not only at Qumran, so it is important to see this economic arrangement as a practical outworking of its Torah-based theology. Though God had given the land of Palestine to God's people, they were merely tenants, and God was the proprietor.

---

9. Stegemann, *The Library of Qumran*, p. 157. It was only later, during Roman occupation, that some Essenes turned toward a more militant Zealot option, as can be seen in the *War Scroll*. See J. T. Milik, *Ten Years of Discovery in the Wilderness of Judea* (London, 1959), pp. 94-98.

10. Stegemann, *The Library of Qumran*, p. 152.

11. Stegemann, *The Library of Qumran*, p. 152.

Therefore, all an individual's material property, as well as mental and physical strength, must be devoted to God and to the whole of God's people.[12] Not only the Israelite community as a whole but also each individual must be in accord with this principle of stewardship. Thus the Teacher of Righteousness had developed in his New Covenant the idea that all members of the union must prove themselves to be true pious Jews by studying the Torah and the Prophets, by living the appropriate communal lifestyle, and finally by taking an entrance examination.[13]

Rules for the shared life of the Essenes can be found in two major scrolls (along with fragments and partial copies from various other caves). A long scroll from Cave 1 contains four different community rules: the Rule of the Community (1QS 1:1–3:12), the Manual of Discipline (1QS 5:1–11:22), the Messianic Rule (1QSa — the Essenes' oldest congregational rule), and the Rule of Blessings (1QSb). The *Damascus Document* is on a separate scroll; parts of ten copies have been found in Caves 4, 5, and 6. Copies of the same document had previously been found at the Karaite synagogue at Cairo, Egypt, in 1896.[14] All of these rules were composed during the second half of the second century B.C.E., before Qumran was settled. The *Damascus Document* contains earlier congregational rules, even some from pre-Essene times, and claims to be the last and most valid version of all the Rules. It would have been finished around 100 B.C.E., shortly after the death of the Teacher of Righteousness.[15]

As Josephus noted (above), the Essenes "have no certain city, but many of them dwell in every city." The Manual of Discipline says, "And in every place where there are ten men of the Council of the Community, there shall not lack a priest among them" (1QS 6:3-4). Thus, as few as ten men (today called a minyan) could establish an Essene community in a town or village.

The Manual of Discipline discusses the merging of a member's private property with the possessions of the group. If the guardian and the entire congregation accepted the novice, he entered the Council of the Community, but for the first year he could not touch the pure meal or share in the property of the congregation (1QS 6:16-17). At the end of a year, if the priests and the congregation approved his continuing member-

12. Stegemann, *The Library of Qumran*, p. 177.
13. Stegemann, *The Library of Qumran*, p. 152.
14. James VanderKam and Peter Flint, *The Meaning of the Dead Sea Scrolls* (San Francisco: HarperSanFrancisco, 2002), p. 215.
15. Stegemann, *The Library of Qumran*, p. 117.

ship, "his property and earnings shall be handed over to the Bursar of the Congregation who shall register it to his account and shall not spend it for the Congregation" (6:19-20). When he had successfully passed the second year, the novice could share in the drink of the congregation, and his property was merged with the community's possessions (6:22).

This entry procedure shows that during the first stages, a man did retain his own property and earnings, and that, up until the end of two years, he could have changed his mind, picked up his property, and returned to his previous life. But the Manual also indicates that the group in question did in fact have some private property. Those who failed to care for the property of the community had to restore it in full, or if they were unable to do so, they had to do penance for sixty days (7:6-8). No member could reimburse the community unless he had some private property. The same situation is suggested in 7:24-25, where members are warned against sharing their food or property with someone who has been expelled from the community. Thus James VanderKam suggests that when a new member contributed his property to the common purse, he may have retained some control over it, provided that the needs of the community were his first concern.[16]

Important fragments from eleven other manuscripts of the Manual that were found in Caves 4 and 5 contain a number of variant readings. The primary manuscript also bears the stamp of editorial modification, comments Vermes.[17] Because of these different layers of material in the texts on poverty and property-sharing, Klauck sees the community of goods as a developmental process that took many years of trial and error to work through.[18]

The Damascus Document also assumes that Essenes were living in scattered communities among other peoples, both Jews and Gentiles.[19] Like the Manual of Discipline, it includes laws for the members of a sectarian community — on the purity of priests and sacrifices, on marriage, agriculture, tithes, relations with non-Jews, entry into the covenant community, Sabbath, and communal organization.[20] The Document also includes this instruction:

16. James VanderKam, *The Dead Sea Scrolls Today* (Grand Rapids: Eerdmans, 1994), p. 83.

17. Vermes, *The Dead Sea Scrolls in English*, p. 69.

18. Klauck, "Gütergemeinschaft in der klassischen Antike," p. 64.

19. For references to Gentiles, for example, see CD 11:14 and 12:7-9.

20. VanderKam, *The Dead Sea Scrolls Today*, p. 56.

The Rule for the assembly of the towns of Israel shall be according to these precepts that they may distinguish between unclean and clean, and discriminate between the holy and the profane. (CD 12:19)

This rule makes it clear that not only are Essene communities scattered throughout the "towns of Israel," but that at some level they *are* the towns of Israel. The Essene union would have perceived itself as the true Israel, living in the midst of profane outsiders, who would eventually be destroyed. The theology behind their communal life demanded that they treat their land, possessions, strength, skills, and abilities not as their own but as belonging to God, who would soon vindicate their faithfulness in the New Age.

Property laws in the Damascus Document are somewhat different from the rules in the Rule of the Community (1QS). Most property did not seem to be held in common, though the *knowledge of it* was common. An overseer would examine the property of those new to a community (13:11), and false information about monetary affairs was punished (14:21). There was also common property in each camp, out of which something could be stolen (9:11).[21] Members were required to hand over their wages for at least two days out of every month for the support of orphans, the aged, and young women without dowries (14:12-16). The presence of women implies a community of married Essenes.

Klauck, who believes a strict community of goods existed only at Qumran, lists the following reasons: (1) the need for money from newcomers to supplement the hardscrabble farming and handwork in the desert; (2) an eschatological orientation and expectation of impending holy war, in which context earthly possessions were seen as obstacles; and (3) the priestly and Levitical tradition of receiving no land inheritance and depending on tithes. Being cut off from the Temple tithes, these priests depended on a common purse.[22] As noted above, both Stegemann and Capper challenge this theory by rethinking Essene origins.

21. "Every lost object about which it is now known who stole it from the property of the camp in which it was stolen — its owner should make a maledictory oath." See Florentino Garcia Martinez, *The Dead Sea Scrolls Translated: The Qumran Texts in English*, 2d ed. (Grand Rapids: Eerdmans, 1996), p. 40.

22. Klauck, "Gütergemeinschaft in der klassischen Antike," p. 67. To Klauck's three reasons for a community of goods at Qumran, I would add one more: the need to reconfigure kinship relationships. These celibate men had obviously left their former family ties with

Rethinking Local Essene Life

At this juncture, I want to make two important points. First, if Stegemann is right that the Damascus Document is the final version of Essene Rules, and if it was completed shortly after the death of the Teacher of Righteousness (about 110 B.C.E.) and thus before the establishment of Qumran, then the various rules for a shared communal life must apply to Essenes living throughout the land. There is not a stricter rule for remaining celibate and giving up private property at Qumran than anywhere else. As Klauck suggested, the variations may be accounted for by assuming that there was a trial-and-error period throughout the second century, but the variations would have occurred in local towns and villages, not in an isolated monastic setting. A more recent discussion by James VanderKam and Peter Flint also leans toward the similarity of both desert and town groups.[23]

But how can we imagine celibate men living and eating together in the midst of various villages of 200 to 300 people, where some of the Essenes living there are married? Rethink the puzzle, suggests Stegemann. Nowhere do the Qumran texts refer to Essene men as "celibate." Only our preconceived notions derived from later monastery life led to this conclusion. Rather, refraining from marriage was regarded as a serious infraction of the Torah, where God commanded male and female to be fruitful and multiply (Gen. 1:28). Why, then, does it look as if at least a minority of Essene men were celibate?

Rather than assuming lifelong celibacy, we need to think of periods of continence. Although other Jewish men married around sixteen or seventeen, Essene men waited until they were twenty. Even more to the point, an Essene man was permitted to marry only once in his lifetime.[24] This rule was active even if a man's wife died young or was infertile.

---

their economic base and now participated in a fictive kinship arrangement. Instead of working in a family industry and sharing the proceeds among the family members, they shared it with each other.

23. VanderKam and Flint, *The Meaning of the Dead Sea Scrolls*, pp. 242-50.

24. CD 4:20–5:2. Stegemann sees Essenes using the witness of three Torah texts to assert this: Genesis 1:27, along with the double creation of a man and a woman in Genesis 2; the narrative of the Flood, whereby Noah took animals into the ark two by two, as well as his own family in pairs; and Deuteronomy 17:17, where it says "[the king] must not acquire many wives for himself." Though these texts can be interpreted in other ways, this is an example of Essene interpretation of the Torah.

Given the social realities of the time, this rule would have meant that many men were celibate for significant periods of their lives. Overall, men lived longer than women. At twenty, an Essene man likely married a younger girl (girls could legally be married after they were twelve and a half) chosen by parents or father. At that time, pregnancy and childbirth were the most dangerous things a woman ever went through, so it would not have been unusual for some girls still in puberty to die during a pregnancy for which they were not physically ready. Others would have easily become worn down by bearing children every year or two, along with maintaining a household, helping with farm work, and supporting the industry of the household such as spinning, weaving, or making pottery. On the other hand, a number of Essene men must have lived to be sixty or older, since the Damascus Document notes that beyond this age a man could no longer hold a public office because "his spirit" would be "in decline" (CD 10:7-10; cf. 14:6-8). Stegemann estimates that the average length of a marriage was about ten years, which left most Essene men single for significant periods both before and after marriage.[25]

We must also bear in mind that all Middle Eastern culture at this time was highly patriarchal. Women were often not mentioned in texts even when they were present, since literature itself belonged to the public sphere of males. If the great majority of Essenes lived in the ordinary towns and villages of Judea, the presence of women would have been far more pervasive than the impression left by the texts themselves.

This last comment leads into my second point. Even though social history of necessity figures prominently in scroll scholarship, relatively little work has been done until recently to apply social-science analysis to it. For all of Hans-Joachim Kraus's careful examination of the scrolls and his emphasis on the concrete reality of a community of goods at Qumran, he never compares shared Essene life in the Judean villages with ordinary peasant life, nor ponders why this lifestyle may have attracted a relatively large number of people. Yet the same arguments for the necessity of the economic safety net of a kin group would also apply to Essene organization. For purity reasons, persons choosing to join this union would likely have to leave their family of origin, just as Jesus-believers were often called out of their own kin groups. Arrangements had to be made for disposal of material possessions to which the applicant had legal rights. This major

25. Stegemann, *The Library of Qumran*, p. 195.

life choice had social repercussions, so precise rules had to be developed to deal with this evolving fictive kin group.

Roughly 90 percent of the population of Palestine lived under harsh economic conditions. To people who labored each day to earn enough money to buy food for their evening meal and who often went hungry, to those who had more mouths to feed than they had sustenance, the Essene option could certainly have looked appealing. Josephus called the Essenes "lovers of one another." In a world where so many had so little, concrete love could not have been shown without mutual economic sharing. The Essene focus on the Torah — with its many commands to care for the poor — and on the Prophets — with their fierce condemnations of those who do not — is consistent with what Josephus and Philo report about the social practices of this movement. As Brian Capper puts it, "The Essenes could not claim to be the pious of Israel if they neglected the destitute."[26]

Capper's more recent analysis of the Essene presence in Judea does deal with socio-economic issues, thereby demonstrating the historical accuracy of both Philo and Josephus as they praise the Essenes for their communal lifestyles and aid to the poor. Using Magen Broshi's population estimates, along with the Community Rule for no less than ten men comprising a community, Capper asserts that, even though Josephus counts 4,000, it would take no more than 3,000 to have a viable group of 15 celibate males in each village and town of Judea.[27] (Capper uses "celibate," though I prefer to define the term as Stegemann has: men living as celibates either before marriageable age or after their wives died.)

Mindful of economic conditions, Capper sees these men as day laborers, either working the land or working as shepherds, beekeepers, or artisans. This was a vulnerable class of people, as can also be seen in Leviticus 19:13 and Deuteronomy 24:14-15, where the Torah commands wealthier employers to pay laborers at the end of each day so they can eat that night (see also James 5:4). Philo's description of the Essenes also corresponds with the picture of people living at a subsistence level:

> Each member when he has received the wages of these so different occupations gives it to one person who has been appointed as treasurer. He takes it and at once buys what is necessary and provides food in

---

26. Capper, "The Church as the New Covenant of Effective Economics," p. 90.
27. Capper, "The Church as the New Covenant of Effective Economics," p. 89.

abundance and anything else which human life requires. Thus having each day a common life and a common table, they are content with the same conditions, lovers of frugality who shun expensive luxury as a disease of both body and soul. (*Hypoth.* 11:10-11)

Philo also remarks that these people work from sunrise to sunset, another mark of a day laborer who must make every hour count (*Hypoth.* 11:6).

The Damascus Document also speaks of going beyond simply caring for the needs of the pledged members:

> And this is the rule of the Many, to provide for all their needs: the salary of two days each month at least. They shall place it in the hand of the Inspector and of the judges. From it they shall give to the orphans and with it they shall strengthen the hand of the needy and the poor, and to the elder who [is dy]ing, and to the vagabond, and to the prisoner of a foreign people, and to the girl who has no protector, and to the unma[rried woman] who has no suitor; and for all the works of the company, and [the house of the company shall not be deprived of its means]. And this is the exact interpretation of the session of [the Many, and these are the foundations which the assembly make.] And this is the exact interpretation of the regulations by which [they shall be ruled] [until there arises the messiah] of Aaron and Israel. (CD 14:12-19 [Martínez])

Most scholars assume this instruction is directed toward the married Essenes who do not participate in a full community of goods. However, the text never says this, nor does it seem necessary to do so. If these men are indeed in a celibate stage of life, and all of them are working for pay (except perhaps the one treasurer/inspector), they would have more disposable income than the laborer who has a family to support. Moreover, if there was a greater fluidity between single men and married men with families, there is no reason this rule could not apply to both. Two days' pay amounts to about a tenth or a tithe of total income.

The Document mentions "the house of the community" (CD 17). Apparently the Essenes were charged with establishing a community house in every town in which they lived, where they could minister to those less fortunate: the old, the sick, the homeless, the abandoned children. The list sounds very similar to Gerhard Lenski's description of the destitute in an advanced agrarian society (see Chapter Five).

The Essenes may have done their most effective recruiting by caring for these lower social classes. To the vagabond or prisoner, they provided teaching in the way of the Torah. The girl who may have been abandoned because her parents had no dowry to give her was saved from slavery or prostitution and may even have found a husband among the Essenes themselves.

Property-Sharing among Essenes and the Jesus Movement

What is the relationship of the community of goods at Qumran with the early Jerusalem community as recorded in Acts? Klauck sees the Lukan summaries of chapters 2 and 4 as primarily redactional, written to encourage Luke's readers, many of whom owned property, to an attitude of detachment toward material possessions and of readiness to give unbounded benevolences.[28] Yet he believes it would be a methodological mistake to throw overboard all information from Luke as unhistorical. The similarity of the Qumran texts to reports of the Essenes by Philo and Josephus has proved that reliable historical information can be hidden under many tangled traditions.[29] Nevertheless, though the early church probably knew about the Qumran community of goods, whatever communal arrangement was practiced originated from Jesus' command of love and his call to renounce possessions, and from the imminent expectation of the end of the age. Luke wrote independently and lived too far from Qumran to have made many direct connections between the two communities.[30]

But Klauck may be overly cautious. If Luke himself was removed from the situation, it doesn't necessarily mean that his sources were also so removed. Jesus' own ideas about money and sharing a common purse with his disciples were probably drawn from what he knew of Essene lifestyles. If Essenes lived in Jerusalem near the location of early Christians (see the following section), shared the same beliefs as those in Qumran, and possi-

28. "Although Luke's gospel accentuates as no other Jesus' criticism of wealth and his demands of poverty, the time of the church is different and has its own demands which are not necessarily comparable to the time of Jesus" (shades of Hans Conzelmann; see Chapter Two); Klauck, "Gütergemeinschaft in der klassischen Antike," p. 76 (my translation).

29. Klauck, "Gütergemeinschaft in der klassischen Antike," p. 76.

30. Klauck, "Gütergemeinschaft in der klassischen Antike," pp. 78-79.

bly visited the site annually,[31] various practices could have been adapted within the Christian community and the memory of them passed on. Both groups were eschatologically-oriented and would have seen their lifestyles as harbingers of the way God's people would live in the New Age on a renewed earth.

Capper agrees with Klauck that the Dead Sea Scrolls corroborate the accounts of Essenes by Josephus and Philo, and for that reason he would argue that the Lukan reports of the Jerusalem community of goods are also historical. With Stegemann but contra Vermes and Klauck, Capper believes that the property-sharing Essenes, both celibate and married, had settlements throughout Palestine.[32] Therefore, instructions in the Manual of Discipline (1QS) apply to them as well as to the Qumranites. One piece of evidence for this is 1QS 6:19-20, which specifies that not only the property but also the *wages* of the community member shall be handed over to the one who has oversight of the earnings. This cannot mean the Qumran members, since their production was communalized and they would not have received daily wages. A similar reference is made by Philo, who describes how the treasurer accepts the wages of each person at the end of each day and uses it to buy food for the common meal that evening (*Hypoth.* 11:10-11). Josephus also does not notice any difference between the property arrangements of the two types of Essene communities (*J.W.* 2:160-161).

If Capper is right, the procedure for handing over property was the same in the Essene settlements as that practiced at Qumran: a candidate had a year of testing, followed by a second examination, at which time he surrendered his property provisionally for one year while he weighed the final decision. During this year his property would be held by the overseer but would not be spent or mixed with common property (1QS 6:18-20). This protected both the candidate and the community. At the end of this

---

31. 1QS ordains a yearly ranking of the sectaries along with a solemn ritual for the Renewal of the Covenant. Vermes suggests that this feast was held for both Qumranites and Essenes of the towns together, and probably at Qumran. There are hints both in the Manual of Discipline and in the Damascus Document, as well as archeological evidence at Qumran of large deposits of animal bones that may be the remains of meals served to large groups of pilgrims. It is also possible that this Feast may explain the presence of the skeletons of women and children discovered at Qumran. See Vermes, *The Dead Sea Scrolls in English*, pp. 17-19.

32. Capper, "The Palestinian Cultural Context of Earliest Christian Community of Goods," in *The Book of Acts in Its Palestinian Setting*, ed. Bauckham, p. 331.

year the candidate could either take all possessions back if he decided he could not live in this kind of community, or he could become a full member, and thus his property would become common to the entire group.

In effect, Capper posits three different forms of Essene communities: (1) the Qumranites who practiced celibacy and communalism of production as well as consumption, (2) Essenes in settlements throughout Judea who also practiced celibacy and property-sharing but worked for wages, and (3) married Essene communities with a looser form of mutual support whereby members contributed a tax of two days' pay per month rather than a total common purse.[33]

The long establishment of Essene property-sharing and its widespread distribution throughout Palestine, says Capper, meant that its administrative structure must have been commonly understood and apparently highly respected. Since Jesus often taught about issues of wealth and poverty, "his disciples must have discussed and weighed the Essene lifestyle. Did they attempt to imitate it in Jerusalem? Such is certainly possible, if only as an attempt to prolong the common purse which Jesus' traveling disciples had kept with him prior to the crucifixion."[34] Capper comments that the story of Ananias and Sapphira assumes a phased entry into a full community of goods. Ananias hands over money from the sale of his property but lies about how much he received. In Acts 5:4, Peter responds logically, saying that there was no need to do that, since the property was still regarded as his own and he had a right to decide what to do with it. The voluntary aspect of this example of property-sharing is not in contradiction to a full community of goods, as many commentators have affirmed, but only the first step of a two-part entry into a community of goods.

Just as the Essenes practiced two forms of communal sharing, one less stringent than the other, Capper supposes something similar held true among the Christians in Jerusalem. The Hebrews must have practiced a full community of goods, while Acts 6:1-6 shows that the Hellenists "had no arrangement of any kind for the care of its poor."[35] It was at this time

33. Capper, "The Palestinian Cultural Context of Earliest Christian Community of Goods," p. 333. Stegemann's view of Essene celibacy practices would assume a more fluid relationship between these groups, especially the second and third categories.

34. Capper, "The Palestinian Cultural Context of Earliest Christian Community of Goods," pp. 334-35.

35. Capper, "The Palestinian Cultural Context of Earliest Christian Community of Goods," p. 354.

that a looser form of care was instituted among the Hellenists, based on charitable giving alone. Later, as the Hellenists fled Jerusalem, many moving to Antioch, mutual support was instituted but without a formal community of goods.[36] This looser form became a pattern throughout the churches of Mediterranean society.

I find Capper's assertion of closer ties between the Essenes and the Jerusalem community more compelling than Klauck's limited conclusions. The explanation about why Ananias and Sapphira's money was still in their power to share or hold back argues well for a two-step administrative procedure in a formal community of goods. However, this is speculative, since in the account of Barnabas's sale of his field (4:36-37), there is no indication of this pattern. In addition, such a procedure could hardly work when a community was just beginning or was accepting large numbers into its membership all at one time. The original 120 must have had some kind of shared wealth, since they were together all the time in Acts 1–2, and many originally hailed from Galilee. But even if Jesus and his disciples had had an Essene-style community, some adjustment would have had to be made to integrate the much larger group just after Pentecost. Luke does not tie events to a calendar. Ananias and Sapphira may have come along several years after a more formal plan was worked out.

More problematic is Capper's suggestion that the Hellenists had no economic sharing or care of the poor before the Seven were appointed. First, if the two groups were so separate in their economic arrangements, why did the Hellenists complain against the Hebrews about their neglected widows? Why not take care of the matter themselves? Second, what is the meaning of "all" having all things in common in Acts 2:44? Third, Barnabas himself was a Hellenist who participated in a full community of goods (4:36-37). Fourth, the daily communal meal, an integral part of communal sharing (as discussed in Chapters Three, Nine, and Ten), was practiced in Hellenist Antioch and elsewhere beyond the Jerusalem community for many years.

Neither does Capper seem to take into consideration the sort of economic and kinship structures already embedded in Palestinian society (see Chapters Five through Seven). How might these structures have been adapted, along with knowledge of Essene practices, into a community of sharing that was, and continued to be, uniquely Christian?

---

36. Capper, "The Palestinian Cultural Context of Earliest Christian Community of Goods," pp. 354-55.

Essenes in Jerusalem

As a further indication of the Jerusalem believers' connection with the Essenes, archeological evidence suggests the presence of Essenes in Jerusalem in the same area where Christians may have lived.

The Damascus Document says in 12:1, "No man shall lie with a woman in the city of the Sanctuary, to defile the city of the Sanctuary with their uncleanness." Does this mean celibate men lived in Jerusalem? Or did their wives live outside the city gates? Josephus remarks that after the reign of Herod the Great, a few Essenes offered sacrifices at the Jerusalem Temple according to their own rituals (*Ant.* 18.1.5). Josephus also gives some topographical details about the wall of Jerusalem (*J. W.* 5.4.2) that places "the gate of the Essenes" along the southwestern side of the wall. This location has been excavated to expose a three-tiered gate with three sills, the lowest of which is Herodian.[37] Since it was common to have a gate named after the group of people who lived behind it, Rainer Riesner concludes that these archeological finds "are best explained by assuming that an Essene community was established on the southwest hill at the beginning of the Herodian rule."[38] This hill has traditionally been called Mount Zion.

The evidence of a network of ritual baths in this area of the city, including a double bath outside the gate near what appear to have been latrines, adds more weight to this argument. Further mention of the "congregation of Jerusalem" in the War Scroll from Qumran (1QM 3.11, dated near the middle of the first century B.C.E.)[39] convinces Riesner that an Essene quarter on the southwest hill of Jerusalem is probable.[40]

The Essene Gate is only a few hundred meters from where "the little house of God" stood in Hadrian's day (see the section on housing in Jerusalem). If the conclusions drawn by Riesner, Jerome Murphy-O'Connor, and others are correct about the location of the Upper Room and its later

---

37. This has been dated by sealed-off pottery. See B. Pixner, D. Chen, and S. Margalit, "Mount Zion: The 'Gate of the Essenes' Re-excavated," *Zeitschrift des deutschen Palästina-Vereins* 105 (1989): 85-95, and plates 8-16; and B. Pixner, "The History of the 'Essene Gate' Area," *Zeitschrift des deutschen Palästina-Vereins* 105 (1989): 96-104; cited in Rainer Riesner, "The Essene Quarter of Jerusalem," in *Jesus and the Dead Sea Scrolls,* ed. James Charlesworth (New York: Doubleday, 1992), pp. 198-234 (209, n. 99).

38. Riesner, "The Essene Quarter of Jerusalem," p. 210.

39. Martínez, *Dead Sea Scrolls Translated,* p. 97.

40. Riesner, "The Essene Quarter of Jerusalem," p. 215.

use as a gathering place for Christian believers, and if Essenes were living in Jerusalem at least during Herodian times and possibly later, it is all the more reasonable to assume that Essene practices influenced the early Christians.

The Purity Puzzle

I've included the Essenes in my argument to demonstrate how their communal practices provided a model that showed the early Jesus-believers how to live and economically survive in a fictive kin community. Yet the purity concerns for these groups appear very different. The Essenes represent a closed community with a dualistic theology that separated the "sons of light" from the "sons of darkness" — that barred non-Essenes from table fellowship and forbade Essenes from associating with sinners. A long section in the Community Rule commands their members to "swear by the covenant to be segregated from all the men of sin who walk along paths of irreverence" (1QS 5.1-26 [10-11]; [Martínez]).

In contrast, Jesus' table was always open to outsiders: tax collectors, women perceived as "loose," even some of his opponents, the Pharisees (see Luke 7:36-50; 15:1-2; 19:1-10). He sent his disciples out with no possessions to eat and drink with whatever householders would take them in (Luke 10:1-12 [7]).

Why then is there no mention of Essenes in the Gospels? Were they so separatist that the Jesus community had no dealings with them? Or were they left out because they, unlike the Pharisees and Sadducees, did not oppose Jesus' mission? On the one hand, David Flusser argues that Jesus criticized the Essenes for their social and economic exclusivism in the Parable of the Unjust Steward (Luke 16:1-9), where Flusser believes Jesus uses the term "sons of light" ironically to refer to the Essenes in a negative way.[41]

On the other hand, Brian Capper thinks Jesus associated with the Essenes through their community poorhouses, since they and he both shared a concern for the sick and destitute. Bethany, whose name, according to Jerome, means "house of affliction" or "house of the poor," was situ-

41. David Flusser, "The Parable of the Unjust Steward: Jesus' Criticism of the Essenes," in *Jesus and the Dead Sea Scrolls,* ed. Charlesworth, pp. 176-97.

ated near but not inside the holy city for purity reasons. Capper proposes that Essenes ran a community house here that not only cared for the poor and destitute but also served as a hospice for weary travelers on their way to Jerusalem for a festival.[42]

According to Mark 11:1, 11, 12-14, 20-21; 14:1-9, Jesus and his companions stayed in Bethany during his last weekend in Jerusalem. Was it with the Essenes in their community house? Here a woman (perhaps Mary) anointed Jesus as Messiah, thus signing his death warrant, since he was sure to be challenged by the religious and political powers in Jerusalem that both he and the Essenes understood to be imposters. Only here, surrounded by marginal people, could Jesus say, "You will always have the poor with you" without sounding callous.[43]

Thus Capper ties Jesus quite intimately to the Essenes. Perhaps he is right in terms of their concern for the poor, but how this relates to their separatist purity concerns is unclear. My concern remains limited to their pioneering communal practices, which provided a practical model for the Jerusalem church, regardless of how intimately the two groups associated with each other.

Conclusion

It is obvious that Jesus and his disciples would have known about the Essenes, the other strongly pietist group scattered throughout Palestine and in a settlement by the Dead Sea. For more than one hundred years they had worked out precise rules of communal sharing in order to be successful spiritually and economically. Though they are not named in the Gospels even though their presence in that society at that time is no longer doubted, this may be because they were not seen as rivals or antagonists to the Jesus movement, as were the Pharisees and the Sadducees. In any case, Jesus himself may have adapted and expanded Essene practices of sharing in his itinerant ministry, which were now being passed on and reshaped again by a more sedentary community.

We cannot be clear about exactly how Essene practices were adapted by the Jerusalem believers. The story of Ananias and Sapphira, however,

42. Capper, "The Church as the New Covenant of Effective Economics," p. 95.
43. Capper, "The Church as the New Covenant of Effective Economics," p. 96.

does hint that there may have been a phased entrance into the property-sharing community, with a "novitiate" during which candidates offered up their property or wealth but were free to withdraw it later if they changed their minds.

Did Essene communities produce goods as well as consume them? Even in Qumran, with no opportunity for outside employment in the desert and no comment about it in their literature, archeology has shown that the community "farmed, made pots, cured hides, and reproduced manuscripts."[44] Just as Essene households in Palestine continued producing the same items as non-Essenes, so would the Jesus movement in Jerusalem have continued their economic output. With more helpers, some households may have managed even more efficiently. Some believers, if previously unemployed or from out of town, would certainly have had to seek employment as day laborers. But the usual methods of earning income needed to be no different than before. To assume that nobody worked and that the believers lived on pooled wealth until the money ran out is going far beyond what the text says or implies.

True, this was an eschatological community, but the New Age to which these believers looked forward was earthy and physical, yet where justice reigned and all had their needs met. With the coming of the Holy Spirit, this New Age had already begun. The unusual aspect of both the Essenes and the Jerusalem Christians is that they were creating new kinship structures on the basis of common religious conviction, a common hope, and generalized reciprocity — not on the basis of blood ties or the expectation of rewards for beneficence. Just as the apocalyptic hope of the Essenes did not preclude day-to-day labor in order to live, so the hope of the Christian community for Jesus' return did not mean believers stopped working. They hoped for a renewal of Israel not in some world beyond space and time, but right there in Jerusalem and Palestine, where all would have enough land, enough food, and enough work.

Nevertheless, adjusting to a larger kin-group, eating together, and sharing intimately with people of different classes and habits (some even former enemies) while seeking to continue the practices and teachings of Jesus would not have been without many problems. This is evident in the stories of Ananias and Sapphira and the Hellenist widows. No doubt there were many more that Luke did not know about or did not record.

---

44. Vermes, *The Dead Sea Scrolls in English*, p. 89.

*   *   *

The purpose of Part II has been to provide a larger social context for the early Jerusalem Christians, as described in the early chapters of Acts. (A summary of Chapters Five through Seven is found at the end of Chapter Seven.) This reconstruction confirms Luke's description of the Jerusalem community of goods as historically and sociologically plausible. It provides a context for the daily communal meals in Acts 2 and 6. Let us now use the same anthropological and sociological tools to examine meals and table fellowship in ancient Palestine.

PART III

The Social Context of Meals
in Acts 2:42-47 and 6:1-6

The next three chapters discuss the symbolic role of food and commensality in the ancient world, from meal practices in earlier times as reflected in the Hebrew Bible, to meal practices in the Hellenistic world, including the Jewish context. Yet both food and commensality are also nonsymbolic. Food nourishes physical bodies, and eating with other people enhances physical and emotional health.

Chapter Nine describes the practice of commensality in the ancient world in general. This can help us determine whether or not descriptions of Jesus' meals with many different kinds of people reflect historical reality or are idealized after the fact. In Chapter Ten I debate and critique two positions on Jesus' meal practices.

Chapter Eleven picks up on the brief mention of widows and meals in Acts 6:1-6. If women have been typically associated with meal preparation and serving, how might this tradition highlight the role of both Hebrew and Hellenist widows in this text? Kathleen Corley's book *Private Women, Public Meals* is supplemented with anthropological analysis to examine peasant women's central roles in meal preparation and serving. This background, coupled with a discussion on the meaning and role of widows in Greco-Roman and Jewish culture, suggests a quite different interpretive possibility for Acts 6:1-6. Were the neglected widows losing out on the honorable female role of *serving* food instead of *receiving* "meals on wheels"?

Chapter Nine

Never Eat Alone!
Food and Meals as Cultural Symbols

Do not reach out your hand for everything you see,
and do not crowd your neighbor at the dish. . . .
Eat what is set before you like a well brought-up person,
and do not chew greedily, or you will give offense.
Be the first to stop, as befits good manners,
and do not be insatiable, or you will give offense.

Sirach 31:14, 16-17

"You are what, how, when, and where you eat!" begins the synopsis of a doctoral dissertation on Roman meals.[1] A great deal can be learned about any culture if these questions can be answered. In no society are people permitted to eat anything, anywhere, with anyone, and in all situations. Rather, a culture's patterns of distribution and consumption of food help to define social contexts and groupings. Anthropologist Mary Douglas, in an oft-quoted statement about food symbolism, writes,

> If food is treated as a code, the messages it encodes will be found in the pattern of social relations being expressed. The message is about dif-

1. Pedar W. Foss, "Age, Gender, and Status Divisions at Mealtime in the Roman House: A Synopsis of the Literary Evidence" (http://acad.depauw.edu/romarch/hgender.html#text), from "Kitchens and Dining Rooms at Pompeii: The Spatial and Social Relationship of Cooking to Eating in the Roman Household," Ph.D. thesis, University of Michigan, 1994.

ferent degrees of hierarchy, inclusion and exclusion, boundaries and transactions across the boundaries. Like sex, the taking of food has a social component, as well as a biological one.[2]

Douglas describes the message food encodes in her British culture, where "just going out for drinks" conveys a lesser level of intimacy than inviting someone for a cold meal, which in turn implies less intimacy than inviting someone for a hot meal. Douglas's intricate details describing the meaning of eating together in a highly industrialized society like Great Britain strike a chord with all of us who come from similar cultures of Western Europe and North America.

In a pre-industrial society, symbolism around food is even more significant because such a culture has a smaller range of human-made objects.[3] Raymond Firth illustrates this through the example of twentieth-century Tikopia, a small, isolated island in the Western Pacific that at the time had no food imports and few imports of any other kind. Here all food had to be obtained raw, direct from nature, and uncleaned. Most could not be stored even for a short time. Here the people were almost totally preoccupied with problems of food supply. Firth comments, "In an industrial society, getting a meal is an interval or a conclusion to the day's work; in a society such as Tikopia, getting a meal *is* the day's work."[4]

Meal preparation in a pre-industrial society is not an individual task but one that requires highly organized, planned cooperative activity. Food is used to symbolize kinship relationships. In this respect, both division of labor and food transfers are significant. Thus Tikopia has had a rich language of terms with which to describe food and the social relationships that are involved with food. Firth points out, however, that food is not merely symbolic but serves the pragmatic purpose of providing physical sustenance. Food is not wasted. In this way, symbolic and nonsymbolic relationships are intertwined.[5]

---

2. Mary Douglas, "Deciphering a Meal," in *Myth, Symbol and Culture*, ed. Clifford Geertz (New York: W. W. Norton, 1971), pp. 61-81.

3. Raymond Firth, *Symbols Public and Private* (Ithaca, N.Y.: Cornell University Press, 1973), p. 243.

4. Firth, *Symbols Public and Private*, p. 244.

5. Firth, *Symbols Public and Private*, pp. 245-46.

From Soup to Nuts: Symbolism and Social Status in Formal Greco-Roman Meals

Because Greco-Roman society was also pre-industrial and agrarian, where most people lived at or below subsistence level, the importance of food symbolism would rank closer to that of Tikopia than that of any modern industrialized culture. Simply having enough food to eat and a great variety of it, along with proper space in which to eat it, set the upper classes apart from the vast majority of people.[6] Meals were among the best indicators of rank and status in Greco-Roman society. Here, issues of patronage were at work in every invitation to dinner from a social superior to a social inferior. Those eating with superiors were seeking social advancement, and those entertaining people below them on the social ladder used this method to gain honor or confirm their own superiority. Rules and taboos constantly dictated who would be invited to a meal, how it would be eaten, who would be served when and where, who would recline or sit where, and the like.[7]

The custom of reclining at formal meals had been known among Hebrews as early as the eighth century B.C.E. (Amos 6:4-7), and seems to have been adopted by the Greeks from the Assyrians by the sixth century B.C.E. The Romans followed suit. This custom seems to have become standardized by the first century and brought with it related practices, such as the

6. Rank was a matter of ascribed prestige, given initially by birthright. In imperial Rome, rank descended from emperor to senators to equestrians to free citizens to freedpersons, and finally to slaves. Promotion or demotion in rank was possible — for example, if a slave was manumitted, or if citizenship was conferred or lost, and so on. Status, on the other hand, was based on achievement or influence with others of higher rank. Social standing was a complex mixture of these factors, combined with wealth. See Foss, "Age, Gender, and Status Divisions at Mealtime in the Roman House."

7. Significant research has been done by biblical scholars on Greco-Roman meals. See, for example, R. Lee Cole, "Pagan Parallels of the Agape," in *Love-Feasts: A History of the Christian Agape* (London: Charles H. Kelly, 1916), pp. 18-34; Dennis Smith, "Social Obligation in the Context of Communal Meals," Ph.D. dissertation, Harvard University, 1980; Dennis E. Smith and Hal E. Taussig, *Many Tables: The Eucharist in the New Testament and Liturgy Today* (London: SCM Press; Philadelphia: Trinity Press International, 1990); Dennis Smith, *From Symposium to Eucharist: The Banquet in the Early Christian World* (Minneapolis: Fortress Press, 2003); Gene Schramm, "Meal Customs (Jewish)," in *Anchor Bible Dictionary*, vol. 4, ed. David Noel Freedman (New York: Doubleday, 1992), pp. 648-50; and Dennis Smith, "Meal Customs (Greco-Roman)," in *Anchor Bible Dictionary*, vol. 4, ed. Freedman, pp. 651-55.

need for dining rooms to accommodate couches, and servants or slaves to serve food to those reclining.[8]

The banquet was a major social event. There was considerable tension for all parties involved in the staging of a banquet. Prospective invitees risked being uninvited. Potential hosts risked both rejection of their invitations (see Luke 14:16-24) and the possibility that their social occasion might be a failure. A guest's refusal to attend signified his advancement in society as well as the host's reduced clout.[9] Dennis Smith describes some of the details involved in preparation for a banquet:

> Invitation would be extended in advance. . . . Standard customs included visiting the baths [and] dressing in special clothing. . . . A servant . . . removed the guest's sandals and washed his feet before he reclined. . . . Water would be brought for them to wash their hands, a custom that became connected with religious ritual in Judaism. . . . Banquets tended to take place in rooms especially designed for dining. . . . A "standard" dining room was designed to hold couches end-to-end along the walls in a configuration whereby the diners were all facing inward toward one another. The *triclinium,* or three-couch arrangement, which provided for nine diners or three per couch, was the most widely used.[10]

The banquet was divided into two parts: the dinner *(deipnon)* followed by a drinking party combined with entertainment and conversation *(symposium).* The dinner itself had two parts: a First Table *(prima mensa)* that involved meat and vegetables, and a final course called Second Table *(secunda mensa),* at which sweet desserts and fruit in addition to some spicy dishes and bread were served. After the tables were removed, the symposium proper would begin with a ritual mixing of wine and water, which included a libation poured out to a god or gods.[11] Besides drinking, the chief entertainment was, at least officially, conversation about all sorts of things, such as politics, religion, philosophy, and finances. The less refined meals centered around entertainment in the form of flute-playing,

8. Smith, "Meal Customs (Greco-Roman)," p. 651.

9. Horace (S. 2.8) describes a failed banquet where the host is mocked and the guests flee. See Smith, "Meal Customs (Greco-Roman)," p. 651.

10. Smith, "Meal Customs (Greco-Roman)," p. 651.

11. Martial, *Epigrams* 5.7; Peter Lampe, "The Corinthian Eucharistic Dinner Party: Exegesis of a Cultural Context (1 Cor. 11:17-34)," *Affirmation* 26, no. 4 (Fall 1991): 1-15 (2-3).

dancing girls and boys, and the companionship of higher-class hetairai (courtesans) as well as prostitutes.[12] "There was a clear connection between food and sex; one course at some dinners was the women themselves."[13] Traditionally, the *convivia*, banquets held in private homes, were basically a male activity, to which young men were first invited in their late teens when they donned the toga. (See the following chapter for women's involvement as dining companions — not the entertainment.)

Social one-upsmanship also took place at the dinner party, where the order of reclining connoted social rank and status. The guest of honor had the choice location next to the host, who assigned all other positions on the couches. If members of the host's family were present at the meal, such as his wife or freedmen, they would lie or sit on his couch in the places of lowest status. Larger dinner parties would place guests of lower rank in another room. Even the menu was not the same for all: the master of the house and his higher-status guests got the choicest foods and wine.[14]

Nor was the symposium over when it was over, for the guests were obligated to return the favor of a meal. In the tradition of balanced reciprocity, dinners were a kind of gift exchange.[15]

Such a dinner party required the work of slaves, who did all the cooking and serving. The larger and more elaborate the banquet, the more slaves — and the more specialized slaves — were needed. Thus it is clear that under ordinary circumstances, only the upper classes would have been able to afford to host either public feasts or private *convivia*.

Creating Honor: Communal Meals for the Working Classes

Many people of the working classes belonged to voluntary associations, clubs, or *collegia*, the central feature of which was a regular communal

12. Ben Witherington III, "'Making a Meal of It': The Lord's Supper in Its First-Century Social Setting," in *The Lord's Supper: Believers Church Perspectives*, ed. Dale R. Stoffer (Scottdale, Pa.: Herald Press, 1997), p. 86.

13. Martial, *Epigrams* 9.2, 5.78; Historia Augusta, Gallieni Due, 17.7; referred to in Foss, "Age, Gender, and Status Divisions at Mealtime in the Roman House."

14. Cf. Juvenal, *Satires*, 125-27.

15. J. H. D'Arms, "Control, Companionship, and Clientela: Some Functions of the Roman Communal Meal," *Echoes du Monde Classique/Classical Views* 28, no. 3 (1984): 327-48 (331-34), cited in Foss, "Age, Gender, and Status Divisions at Mealtime in the Roman House," n. 50.

meal. Greek clubs existed as far back as the sixth century B.C.E., perhaps earlier. They seem to have originated primarily as religious organizations where individuals could share in the expense of a sacrifice.[16] During the Hellenistic and Roman periods, many of these clubs placed increasing significance on the banquet as their chief activity.[17]

Roman *collegia*, however, served political, professional, and social interests as well as religious ones. Epigraphs show that professional associations existed among almost every kind of occupation and in almost every town of the Roman Empire where inscriptions remain.[18] Members came together out of a need for companionship and a desire to create positions of honor for themselves.[19] They could pool funds for their banquets, so that several times a year they could share a meal and a drinking party that rivaled those of the wealthy.

Another major type of Roman club was the burial society. These were often found among the lower classes of society, especially among slaves and freedpersons who could not otherwise be assured of a respectable burial. Dues were collected each month, at which time they sometimes had a banquet.[20] These clubs needed senate or imperial approval to meet legally, and they were restricted to meeting no more often than once a month.[21]

Nevertheless, no club or banquet organization at the time was without a religious dimension. "No body of Romans," says R. Lee Cole, "would have thought of forming any kind of organization without procuring the sanction and protection of the gods."[22] A communal meal would begin with an invocation of the gods,[23] and would end with a toast for the good spirit of the house. After the tables were removed and the wine and water mixed for the symposium, a libation to a god was poured out while the

16. Smith, *From Symposium to Eucharist*, p. 87.

17. Smith, *From Symposium to Eucharist*, p. 95.

18. Cole, *Love-Feasts*, pp. 20-21, citing Edwin Hatch, *The Organization of the Early Christian Churches* (London: Longmans, Green & Co., 1895), pp. 6-28.

19. Cole, *Love-Feasts*, p. 28; Smith, *From Symposium to Eucharist*, p. 96; Ramsey MacMullen, *Roman Social Relations: 50 B.C. to A.D. 284* (New Haven: Yale University Press, 1974), pp. 76-77.

20. Smith, *From Symposium to Eucharist*, p. 96.

21. From Justinian's sixth-century C.E. *Digesta*; cited in Smith, *From Symposium to Eucharist*, p. 97.

22. Cole, *Love-Feasts*, pp. 29-30.

23. Quintilian, *Declamationes* 301; cited in Lampe, "The Corinthian Eucharistic Dinner Party," p. 13.

people sang a religious song.[24] The primary banquet motif that was used in religious ritual was festivity. Eating together was not a solemn occasion but a time for joy and celebration.[25]

Making Friends at the Table:
The Social Value of Shared Meals

By the Hellenistic and Roman periods (ca. 200 B.C.E. to 200 C.E.), meal customs and rules of etiquette seem to have become standardized throughout the Mediterranean region in some broad details. There was a common meal tradition, particularly for the banquet, which was shared throughout the culture and adapted for specific occasions.[26] This meal tradition was also adapted for Jewish festival meals or Christian meals, as will be discussed below.

Dennis Smith and Hal Taussig note that the Greco-Roman banquet highlights three major aspects of food symbolism in the ancient world.[27] First, commensality created social equality and bonding. A meal created a special tie among the diners and served to define boundaries between various groups. Plutarch refers to this image when he speaks of "the friend-making character of the table."[28]

Second, at the same time, social stratification could be heightened. Even for those inside the boundary of a particular group in Greco-Roman culture, age, gender, and status defined how one was treated at a meal. Guests were ranked by their position at table, and by the quality or quantity of food served to them. The matter of who reclined, who sat, and who had to stand and serve was crucial. In the upper-class Roman mind, however, this aspect was not necessarily in conflict with the first. According to Augustus,[29] paying strict attention to rank and status at a dinner party contributed to the stability of the state by reminding all persons that they

24. Libation and singing belong together, according to Plato, *Symposium* 176 A, and Xenophon, *Symposium* 2.1, cited in Lampe, "The Corinthian Eucharistic Dinner Party," p. 13.
25. Smith, "Meal Customs (Greco-Roman)," p. 653.
26. Smith and Taussig, *Many Tables*, p. 21.
27. Smith and Taussig, *Many Tables*, pp. 31-34.
28. Plutarch, *Quaestionum Convivalium (Table Talk)*, 614 A-B, translated by Edwin L. Minar et al., Library of Christian Classics (Cambridge: Harvard University Press, 1961).
29. Suetonius, *The Deified Augustus* 2.74.

should know their place and be content with it. Otherwise, confusion could result, and "nothing is more unequal than the resulting equality."[30]

Third, the bonding between diners led to ethical and social obligations of each to the other. These social contracts can be understood in terms of reciprocity, either generalized, balanced, or negative. Among the Greeks there developed a tradition of "symposium laws," in which meal etiquette was included among other ethical categories like "friendship," "love," and "pleasure." These were group values, meaning the friendship or pleasure of the group as a whole. Quarreling was not allowed because it did not serve the pleasure of everyone present. "Factions" of any kind were prohibited.[31] Conversation at the meal was also to be of the sort in which everyone could participate.

Kinship Symbolism in Israelite Meals

The use of food as a religious and social symbol is especially evident in the story of Israel. Gillian Feeley-Harnik argues that "food, articulated in terms of who eats what with whom under which circumstances, had long been one of the most important languages in which Jews conceived and conducted social relations among human beings and between human beings and God. Food was a way of talking about the law and lawlessness that dated at least to the Babylonian Exile."[32]

The Jews believed that eating joins people with God or separates them (Isa. 55:1-3). Food is the most common gift in Scripture. It is given to relatives, acquaintances, kings, and prophets. Table fellowship is synonymous with fellowship in all aspects of life (e.g., Gen. 14:18-20; 26:26-31;

---

30. J. H. D'Arms, "The Roman Convivium and the Idea of Equality," in *Sympotica: A Symposium on the Symposion,* ed. O. Murray (Oxford: Oxford University Press, 1990), pp. 308-20; quote from Pliny the Younger, *Letters,* 2 vols., trans. William Melmoth and W. M. L. Hutchinson, Library of Christian Classics (London and Cambridge: Harvard University Press, 1963), 9.5.3.

31. They were, for example, forbidden by Paul for the Corinthian Christians in 1 Corinthians 11:17-34, as well as in the by-laws of the Guild of Zeus Hypsistos, as recorded in "The Guild of Zeus Hypsistos" by Colin Roberts, T. C. Skeat, and A. D. Nock, *Harvard Theological Review* 29 (1936): 40-42.

32. Gillian Feeley-Harnik, *The Lord's Table: Eucharist and Passover in Early Christianity* (Philadelphia: University of Pennsylvania Press, 1981), p. 72.

29:22, 27-28; 31:44-46, 51-54; Josh. 9:3-15; Judg. 9:26-28; 2 Sam. 3:20; 9:7, 10-11; Prov. 15:17; 17:1). On the other hand, refusal to eat together severs a relationship (1 Sam. 20:34). Those who do not eat or drink together have no obligation to each other, and may even become enemies. But the worst kind of traitor is the traitor with whom one has shared food (Ps. 41:9; Obad. 7).[33]

A century ago, W. R. Smith noted that commensality among Semitic peoples was thought of "as confirming or even as constituting kinship in a very real sense."[34] The story of Esau and Jacob competing over Isaac's blessing with food illustrates this. Joachim Jeremias affirms this close connection: "In Judaism in particular, table-fellowship means fellowship before God, for the eating of a piece of broken bread by everyone who shares in the meal brings out the fact that they all have a share in the blessing which the master of the house had spoken over the unbroken bread."[35]

Getting the Details Right:
Meals with Purity-Conscious Pharisees

Jerome Neyrey notes that meals replicate a people's symbolic universe — their system of classification.[36] In first-century Judaism, this system evolves around purity concerns: who eats with whom, what is eaten and under what conditions, where meals are eaten, and when. In this system, like eats with like, and there are places of honor around the table. Some food is clean if it comes from the right kind of animal and has been prepared with the right utensils and dishes. Appropriate places to eat are those where one can be sure the purity laws have been followed. A calendar must be kept so that meals can be eaten to conform to Sabbath and Passover times.

33. Feeley-Harnik, *The Lord's Table*, pp. 85-86.
34. W. R. Smith, *Lectures on the Religion of the Semites, First Series: The Fundamental Institutions* (Edinburgh: A. & C. Black, 1889), p. 257; cited in Feeley-Harnik, *The Lord's Table*, p. 86.
35. Joachim Jeremias, *The Proclamation of Jesus*, vol. 1 of *New Testament Theology* (London, 1971), p. 115.
36. Jerome H. Neyrey, "Ceremonies in Luke-Acts: The Case of Meals and Table Fellowship," in *The Social World of Luke-Acts*, ed. Jerome H. Neyrey (Peabody, Mass.: Hendrickson, 1991), pp. 361-87 (363).

This can be most clearly seen among first-century Pharisees.[37] Of the 341 rabbinic rules attributed to the houses of Shammai and Hillel, 229 of them relate to table fellowship.[38] Pharisees were committed to tithing all their food and to eating every meal (either in their own homes or together as a formal meal) with the same degree of purity as the priests officiating in the Temple. This involved washing their hands before each meal and insuring that the food was not defiled during preparation or serving. A prospective member of a Pharisaic fellowship (havurah) made this commitment during his initiation period, after which he became a full member.

This double emphasis on purity and tithing in connection with meals put limitations on commensality. First, one could not be the guest of a person who was not scrupulous in paying tithes and properly preparing foods (though a Pharisee could host non-Pharisees if they were provided with clean garments upon entering the house and if they were not among that class of people whose presence would defile the house and all within it).[39] Second, one could not share a table with people whose presence might defile the meal.[40]

This concern for table fellowship crystallized the quest for holiness that developed during and after the Exile, where holiness was understood as separation. Therefore, disputes about commensality concerned the shape of the community that was truly loyal to Yahweh. The havurah symbolized what was expected of the nation of Israel.[41] Commensality also symbolized Israel's future, which was often pictured as a meal (e.g., Isa. 25:6; Zeph. 3:13).

In principle, no Jew was excluded from havuroth, but in fact it was impossible for many people to observe these regulations because of poverty, social habits, or "unclean" occupations.[42] So the net effect was to con-

37. Marcus Borg, Conflict, Holiness, and Politics in the Teachings of Jesus, vol. 5 of Studies in the Bible and Early Christianity (Lewiston, N.Y.: Edwin Mellen Press, 1984), p. 80.

38. Jacob Neusner, "Pharisaic Law in New Testament Times," Union Seminary Quarterly Review 26 (1971): 337.

39. Borg, Conflict, Holiness, and Politics in the Teachings of Jesus, p. 81.

40. Neusner, "The Fellowship in the Second Jewish Commonwealth," Harvard Theological Review 53, no. 2 (April 1960): pp. 125-42 (134-35).

41. Borg, Conflict, Holiness, and Politics in the Teachings of Jesus, p. 81.

42. There were seven kinds of tradespeople who were despised: gamblers who used dice, usurers, organizers of games of chance, dealers in produce of the sabbatical year, shepherds, tax collectors, and revenue farmers. See Sanh. 25b; Joachim Jeremias, Jerusalem in the Time of Jesus: An Investigation into the Economic and Social Conditions during the New Testament Period (Philadelphia: Fortress Press, 1962), pp. 310-12.

struct social barriers between those who were part of *havurah* and those who were not.[43]

Daily Meals, Daily Prayers: The Essenes at Table

A major difference between the meal practices of the Pharisees and the Essenes is that the Pharisees usually practiced their purity regulations at meals in their own homes or at various formal dinners, whereas the Essenes ate communally each day, apparently in groups of no fewer than ten men.

All references to these meals show that they had religious significance for the sect. Josephus describes the Essenes as having two meals a day at which these rituals were practiced (*J.W.* 2.8.5). At the fifth hour of the day, the members would bathe in cold water and put on "white veils," after which they went to the dining room, where they were served bread and one other kind of food on plates. A priest said grace before the meal and again at the end of the meal. After this midday meal, they would again change clothes and resume work until the same ritual was repeated for the evening meal. At both of these meals the group would praise God as the one who gives food.

It is not clear whether or not this procedure was carried on by married Essenes. Near the end of the same chapter, Josephus (*J.W.* 2.8.13) refers to the married order, how they "agree with the rest as to their way of living, customs, and laws," but differ only on the issue of marriage. Since some of the financial arrangements described in the Damascus Document seem somewhat different for married communities of Essenes, their meal patterns probably were also adjusted to allow for families to eat together. Brian Capper suggests the possibility of frequent communal meals for married Essenes.[44]

43. One did not have to be part of a *havurah* in order to be a Pharisee, but all *haverim* were Pharisees. The writers of the Synoptic Gospels treat most Pharisees as if they were *haverim* or at least supporters of their aims. See John Koenig, *New Testament Hospitality: Partnership with Strangers as Promise and Mission* (Philadelphia: Fortress Press, 1985), p. 18.

44. Brian Capper, "The Palestinian Cultural Context of Earliest Christian Community of Goods," in *The Book of Acts in Its Palestinian Setting*, ed. Richard Bauckham, vol. 4 of *The Book of Acts in Its First-Century Setting*, ed. Bruce W. Winter (Grand Rapids: Eerdmans, 1995), p. 333.

Philo praises the Essene communities for their communal sharing from a common treasury. It is only natural, then, that their food is also held in common "through their institution of public meals" (*Good Person*, 86). These common meals in turn further the unity of the members: "They live together formed into clubs, bands of comradeship with common meals, and never cease to conduct all their affairs to serve the general weal" (*Hypoth.* 11.5)

The Community Rule found in the caves near Qumran speaks of a meal ceremony very similar to what Josephus describes. The religious ritual before the meal and the seating according to rank also reflect general banquet practices throughout the Mediterranean during this period:

> They shall eat in common, and pray in common, and deliberate in common. Wherever there are ten men of the Council of the community there shall not lack a Priest among them. And they shall all sit before him according to their rank. And when the table has been prepared for eating, the Priest shall be the first to stretch out his hand to bless the first fruits of the bread and new wine. (1QS 6:3-6)[45]

Still another reference to a formal communal meal is found in a fragment called the Messianic Rule Fragment, also from a Dead Sea cave. Here the structure of the meal is very similar to 1QS (with the priest blessing the bread and wine first), but the meal occurs in the presence of two Messiahs, the King-Messiah and the Priest-Messiah. It is not known, therefore, whether this refers to an actual meal or whether it is an eschatological meal that is to take place when the Messiahs appear.[46] James Dunn sees it as both and compares it to Jesus' meals (recorded in the Synoptics) in this respect. The current practices of table fellowship are an expression and foretaste of the age to come.[47]

Dunn also points out differences between Jesus' practice and what is described in the Community Rule (1QS). In the latter, restrictions were placed on who could participate in the communal meals of the Essenes.

---

45. Geza Vermes, *The Dead Sea Scrolls in English* (London and New York: Penguin Books, 1990), p. 77.

46. Leonard F. Badia, *The Dead Sea People's Sacred Meal and Jesus' Last Supper* (Washington, D.C.: University Press of America, 1979), p. 14.

47. James D. G. Dunn, "Jesus, Table-Fellowship, and Qumran," in *Jesus and the Dead Sea Scrolls*, ed. James H. Charlesworth (New York: Doubleday, 1992), pp. 254-72 (262-63).

The stages of the novitiate described both in Josephus (*J. W.* 2.8.7) and in 1QS (6:16-17, 20-21) involve a one-year probation before a novice can touch "the purity of the Many," and a two-year period before he can "touch the drink of the Many." This purity rule set firm boundaries around the community, the inner boundary being even stricter than that of the Pharisaical *havurah* fellowships.[48]

In previous chapters I have shown that the Jerusalem community would most certainly have known about the Essenes and their communal meals. Clearly the entry requirements to meals in the two communities were quite different. Yet there were unmistakable similarities. In a setting where meals had deep religious and eschatological significance, Essene meals provided an example of how daily meals can be held in common with groups of committed persons, and can become the central ceremony tying the community, or groups of communities, together. These meals symbolized God's ability to provide for each member of the believing community in the present, and gave a foretaste of the future Messianic banquet. But the Christian meals had the added feature of the presence of the risen Messiah, which gave their meals an atmosphere of joy not noted in the texts on Essene meals.

Conclusion

Not only is food physically important, but eating food together is also symbolically important. In the Greco-Roman world, the banquets of the upper classes were highly structured events, where seating arrangements — and even the quality of food — were dictated by the social status of the participants. The system of hierarchical patronage prevailed at these meals. Even those in lower classes aspired to honor by holding banquets, although this was more often done through their *collegia*. Such meals always had a religious dimension, and the bread-breaking and drink-mixing at the beginning and end of the main courses were done to honor and invoke the presence of a particular god or goddess.

The Hebrew meal tradition also involved kinship. Sharing bread or salt bound one to another in a special way. Concerns of purity developed from this thinking as well. First-century Pharisees endeavored to live care-

---

48. Dunn, "Jesus, Table-Fellowship, and Qumran," p. 262.

fully within the constraints of Hebrew law, including food laws, and thus strict rules developed concerning those with whom one could and could not eat. Theoretically, every Jew should have been able to eat with every other Jew, but the practical realities of poverty and "unclean" occupations and gender ruled out many people. Essene regulations were apparently even stricter, calling for daily communal meals in groups of no less than ten men and presided over by a priest.

Like any other first-century Jew, Jesus would have grown up understanding Greco-Roman and Jewish customs, including Essene practices. In what ways did his meals with Israelites reflect his cultural and religious background — and in what ways did he break with custom? Why did Jesus say he was accused of being "a glutton and a drunkard, a friend of tax collectors and sinners"? How was his theology expressed through his commensality?

Chapter Ten

"A Glutton and a Drunkard": Jesus and Table Fellowship

I don't believe in charity. I believe in solidarity. Charity is so vertical. It goes from the top to the bottom. Solidarity is horizontal. It respects the other person and learns from the other. I have a lot to learn from other people.

Eduardo Galeano, Uruguayan social-justice activist

When he was at the table with them, [Jesus] took bread, blessed and broke it, and gave it to them. Then their eyes were opened, and they recognized him. . . . Then they told [the other disciples] what had happened on the road, and how he had been made known to them in the breaking of the bread.

Luke 24:30-31, 35

How do Jesus' meal experiences, as described in the canonical Gospels, compare to the meals of the Essenes and the Pharisees? Although the New Testament does not mention the Essenes by name,[1] the Synoptic Gospels

1. Diane Jacobs-Malina suggests that the reference to persons who have made themselves eunuchs for the kingdom of heaven in Matthew 19:12 refers to celibate Essenes who have thus disqualified themselves both from Temple worship and from marriage. See *Beyond Patriarchy: The Images of Family in Jesus* (New York and Mahwah, N.J.: Paulist Press, 1993), p. 71. If we use Hartmut Stegemann's definition of celibate males from Chapter Eight,

set Jesus' meal practices in sharp contrast to those of the Pharisees. Rather than excluding people, Jesus especially welcomed those who could not or did not meet Pharisaic regulations. This strongly suggests that Jesus' open table fellowship was a strategy used to challenge social and religious exclusivism wherever it was officially sanctioned or accepted as normal.[2]

In previous chapters I have remarked that the meals of the Jerusalem believers mentioned in Acts 2:42 and 46 were a continuation of Jesus' inclusive table fellowship. But this case can be made only if the Gospels are recording the table fellowship of the historical Jesus rather than an idealization. More than a generation ago, Norman Perrin had proposed that Jesus' table fellowship with "outcasts" such as "tax collectors and sinners" (Matt. 11:16-19) was historical because it explains how Jesus came to die as a defiler of community boundaries. It also accounts for how the early Christian churches came to practice an agape meal together.[3] Today, with few exceptions, there is a high level of scholarly consensus that Jesus did practice a radically inclusive commensality as a key tactic in announcing and redefining the Kingdom of God.[4] The evidence is strong, being found in multiple sources and in various forms. The sources include Mark, Q, Luke's unique material, and probably the *Gospel of Thomas*. The forms include controversy stories (Mark 2:15-17, par. Matt. 9:9-13 and Luke 5:29-32), kingdom parables (Luke 14:15-24, par. Matt. 22:1-13; *Gos. Thom.* 64), pronouncement stories (Luke 7:36-50; 19:1-10), brief sayings (Matt. 8:11-12, par. Luke 13:28-29; 14:12-14), opponents' criticism (Matt. 11:18-19, par. Luke 7:33-34), and a summary (Luke 15:1-2).[5]

John Koenig calls particular attention to the odd saying of Jesus found in Q (Matt. 11:16-19; Luke 7:31-35) about John the Baptist, who "has a

---

this would have applied only to Essene males after the death of their wives. See also David Flusser on the "sons of light" in Luke 16:1-9 in his essay "The Parable of the Unjust Steward: Jesus' Criticism of the Essenes," in *Jesus and the Dead Sea Scrolls*, ed. James H. Charlesworth (New York: Doubleday, 1992), pp. 176-97.

2. John Koenig, *New Testament Hospitality: Partnership with Strangers as Promise and Mission* (Philadelphia: Fortress Press, 1985), p. 20.

3. Norman Perrin, *Rediscovering the Teaching of Jesus* (New York: Harper & Row, 1967), pp. 102-8.

4. These scholars include E. P. Sanders, James Dunn, Marcus Borg, John Dominic Crossan, Scott Bartchy, Bruce Chilton, and others.

5. This list was compiled by S. Scott Bartchy, "Table Fellowship," in *The Dictionary of Jesus and His Gospels*, ed. Gerald F. Hawthorne, Ralph P. Martin, and Daniel G. Reid (Downers Grove, Ill.: InterVarsity Press, 1993), pp. 796-800 (797).

demon," and about Jesus, who is "a glutton and a drunkard" and a friend of tax collectors and sinners. The charges made here against both John and Jesus are unique and must have been an embarrassment for the early church, since here the insults are not rebutted. In no other Christian tradition is Jesus' open table fellowship denounced so sharply. Koenig suggests that Jesus may be using it as a self-insult to take the wind out of his opponents' sails. In any case, this word-play seems to fit the circumstances of the historical Jesus rather than those of the post-Resurrection Christian communities. Moreover, Jesus is called a "friend of toll collectors." The term is nowhere else used by Jesus or as a charge against him. This charge would plausibly place Jesus in a Galilean context, where Herod's toll collectors were shunned primarily because they defrauded everyone.[6] It is thus quite probable that Jesus did associate with such immoral people, at table and elsewhere.

The earliest securely dated reference to a "Lord's Supper" is 1 Corinthians 11:17-34. Paul includes the tradition about Jesus' last supper in verses 23 to 25 not only to show "the historical Jesus' practice of blessing and breaking bread with his disciples but also Jesus' eagerness to share table fellowship with all persons, especially the poor and the outcasts."[7] The abuses taking place in the Corinthian congregation (vv. 18-21) result from disregarding Jesus' practice of open commensality. Some of the members are eating before everyone gets there, so there is no food left for those who work longer hours and "have nothing" (v. 22). That, declares Paul emphatically, is not a κυριακὸν δεῖπνον (literally, "Lord-style supper"; v. 20). In other words, it is not the way Jesus eats a meal.

Suzanne Watts Henderson and Beverly Gaventa both agree. Even the line "You proclaim the death of the Lord" connects Jesus' execution as a lawbreaker with his sacrificial breaking of certain purity regulations to eat with outcasts. By eating together across social boundaries, believers actually teach and preach Jesus' theology. The Supper itself becomes an act of proclamation.[8]

6. Koenig, *New Testament Hospitality,* pp. 20-26.

7. S. Scott Bartchy, "Table Fellowship with Jesus and the 'Lord's Meal' at Corinth," in *Increase in Learning: Essays in Honor of James G. Van Buren,* ed. Robert J. Owens Jr. and Barbara E. Hamm (Manhattan, Kans.: Manhattan Christian College, 1979), pp. 45-61 (54).

8. Suzanne Watts Henderson, "'If Anyone Hungers . . .': An Integrated Reading of 1 Cor. 11:17-34," *New Testament Studies* 48 (2002): 195-208 (202); Beverly Roberts Gaventa, "'You Proclaim the Lord's Death': 1 Cor. 11:26 and Paul's Understanding of Worship," *Review and Expositor* 80 (1983): 380-85.

Eating with Jesus: Historical Fact or Literary Creation? Two Views

I have chosen to discuss in some detail the positions of two other scholars regarding Jesus' commensality, those of John Dominic Crossan and Dennis E. Smith. Both are somewhat skeptical about the Gospels' accuracy regarding the historical Jesus, and both regard him as a Cynic-like teacher[9] who had no intention of starting a movement distinct from Judaism. However, Crossan sees Jesus' meal practices as an essential part of his program, whereas Smith highlights the literary, nonhistorical character of these meal descriptions in the Gospels.

Crossan centers his argument on Mark 6:7-11 (par. Luke 10:1-12), where Jesus sends his disciples out with nothing but a staff. That means they take no food with them, nor do they beg, but they are to eat whatever they are served in whatever house receives them. Crossan sees Jesus as a peasant with a revolutionary social program of which egalitarianism is an essential part. This is primarily expressed through "open commensality," sharing a table across boundaries that persons were previously forbidden to cross through custom or law.[10] This merging of two classes of people (itinerant = destitute; householder = poor) results in generalized reciprocity. The itinerant disciples heal the sick and cast out demons in exchange for their food and lodging (Mark 6:7, 13; Luke 10:9).[11] In this way the reign of God is announced.

Crossan is firm about the difference between almsgiving and commensality, for the former keeps people separated in their own class and status, whereas the latter communicates equality and unity.[12] Open commensality, then, originates with and is practiced by the historical Jesus as an integral part of his program. With this understanding, it is not hard

---

9. Crossan's emphasis on Jesus' similarity to Cynics seems to have dropped out of his more recent books co-authored with the archeologist Jonathan L. Reed: *Excavating Jesus: Beneath the Stones, Behind the Texts* (San Francisco: HarperSanFrancisco, 2001); and *In Search of Paul: How Jesus's Apostle Opposed Rome's Empire with God's Kingdom* (San Francisco: HarperSanFrancisco, 2004).

10. John Dominic Crossan, *The Historical Jesus: The Life of a Mediterranean Jewish Peasant* (San Francisco: HarperSanFrancisco, 1991), pp. 338-44.

11. Crossan and Reed, *Excavating Jesus*, p. 124.

12. Crossan, *The Historical Jesus: The Life of a Mediterranean Jewish Peasant* (San Francisco: HarperSanFrancisco, 1991), p. 341.

to picture the disciples carrying on post-Easter the open commensality in which they had personally participated in their mission in Galilee. They would have perceived it as part of their mission to continue proclaiming Jesus' message. Organizing small groups of such commensality in Jerusalem not only would have been practical in terms of meeting physical needs, but also would have been seen as an integral part of Jesus' program.

Smith is more skeptical than Crossan about the table practices of the historical Jesus. In his extensive study of the banquet in the Greco-Roman world and early Christianity, he discusses the historical reality of the banquet tradition but also shows how the literary tradition, in Greek, Roman, Jewish, and Christian writings, shapes descriptions of meals by the literary motif of the banquet.[13] Just as Jesus had no intention of starting a movement distinct from Judaism, he did not develop a distinct table fellowship with a different clientele. Not until later did the various Christian communities develop a communal meal with their surrounding ideological groups. Jesus' "Last Supper," for instance, is part of Mark's passion narrative, which "has been shown in recent research to be largely a creation of the gospel writer."[14] Smith understands the text in Mark 2:15-17 (par. Matt. 9:10-13; Luke 5:29-32), about Jesus eating with tax collectors and sinners, to be a *chreia*, a form of rhetoric used to characterize a famous person or hero. Mark, says Smith, uses the *chreia* to suit his own literary aims and is not concerned about being historically accurate. "The tradition represented in this text in both its . . . form as found in Mark and in its basic *chreia* form can be seen to have its origin in the early church."[15]

Smith rightly stresses that descriptions of some banquets in Greco-Roman literature are literary creations and do not refer to specific meals.[16]

13. Dennis E. Smith, *From Symposium to Eucharist: The Banquet in the Early Christian World* (Minneapolis: Fortress Press, 2003). This volume draws together various essays and papers Smith has published since his landmark dissertation entitled "Social Obligation in the Context of Communal Meals," Ph.D. diss., Harvard University, 1980.

14. Dennis Smith, "Table Fellowship and the Historical Jesus," in *Religious Propaganda and Missionary Competition in the New Testament World: Essays Honoring Dieter Georgi*, ed. Lukas Borman, Kelly del Tredici, and Angela Standhartinger (Leiden and New York: E. J. Brill, 1994), p. 142. Smith follows Burton Mack in seeing Mark's plot as "a mythological framework . . . 'the wisdom story of the persecution and vindication of the righteous one.'" See Burton Mack, *A Myth of Innocence: Mark and Christian Origins* (Philadelphia: Fortress Press, 1988), pp. 315-31; see also Smith, *From Symposium to Eucharist*, p. 247.

15. Smith, *From Symposium to Eucharist*, pp. 228-30 (230).

16. Smith, *From Symposium to Eucharist*, pp. 47-48.

In the same way, he says, descriptions of Jesus' meals in the Gospel are literary creations. "None of the texts in which Jesus teaches by means of his table customs can be clearly affirmed as historical."[17] On the other hand, Smith admits that "all of the characteristics of meals utilized in these texts are historically and socially valid. It *is* the case that meals defined community boundaries and . . . carried implications of the messianic kingdom. . . . Thus, these texts certainly represent social reality."[18]

An Idealized Jesus as Philosopher at a Meal Symposium

The question is this: Where should that social reality be located? Smith thinks that the early Christian community got the social realities right, but that they placed an idealized Jesus, not a historical Jesus, in the midst of table gatherings where he taught in parables through his table practice and presided as host over Messianic meals that could not possibly have happened during his lifetime. The main consistency Smith sees between the literary traditions and the historical Jesus is that he "was known to have chosen a lifestyle different from the monastic lifestyle of John and that this lifestyle was understood to be consistent with the tenor of his teachings as a whole."[19] Thus the later Christians could have interpreted him as having taught through his meal practices.

The strongest argument for an idealized rather than a historical Jesus being placed in table fellowship by the Gospel writers is that they use the literary motif of the Greek symposium, which reflects a literate, upperclass culture. Luke, the most literary of all the Gospels' writers, often presents Jesus as teaching at table in the manner of a philosopher at a symposium.[20] Smith thinks that the ideal for a proper meal for all levels of social strata is the model of the symposium, *but only for a ceremonial or formal meal.* Otherwise we are in the dark about lower-class meal customs.[21] And

17. Smith, *From Symposium to Eucharist,* p. 238.
18. Smith, *From Symposium to Eucharist,* p. 238.
19. Smith, *From Symposium to Eucharist,* p. 239.
20. Smith, *From Symposium to Eucharist,* p. 253.
21. However, Plutarch does assume symposium practices, such as symposium games after the *deipnon,* among the lower classes: "After dinner even common, unliterary people allow their thoughts to wander to other pleasures. . . . They take up conundrums and riddles, of the Names and Numbers game." See *Quaest. Conv.* 673A; cited in Dennis Smith,

if Jesus was a peasant, as Crossan and others have recently stressed, we cannot possibly know what kind of meal customs he practiced.[22] Smith also argues that if Jesus was a peasant eating with "tax collectors and sinners" — an outcast eating with other outcasts — the meal would lose its symbolic value. "This theme works best if Jesus is not of the same social class with tax collectors and sinners. If all parties involved, including Jesus, are peasants, then the motif fails, for there is no experience of social stratification at the table."[23]

Arguments for Historicity

Yet Smith is essentially arguing from silence. If we cannot know what lower-class meal customs were like in first-century Palestine, and if the descriptions of meals in the Gospels assume an upper-class symposium atmosphere, why must we assume these meals didn't happen? I do not find his argument convincing for several reasons.

First, many of the meals mentioned in the Gospels *are* special events, so they would be more likely to take on a formal ambiance. At the meal in the house of Simon the Pharisee (Luke 7:36) or the banquet with tax collectors and others (Luke 5:29-31), the host would be expected to go to great lengths to do things properly, according to convention.[24] Moreover, though tax collectors were despised because of their occupation, they would not necessarily have been poor or of the lowest classes. And since they were hired by the Romans, they would likely have been well-acquainted with Roman meal customs.

Second, even very poor people will put on a formal meal when a guest is coming, and if it is a holy man or a sage such as Jesus was, so much

---

"What Really Happened at Ancient Banquets? Evaluating the Evidence for Ancient Meal Practices," paper read at SBL Annual Meeting, Washington, D.C., 21 November 1993, p. 11, n. 16.

22. Marianne Sawicki suggests that Jesus did not recline at meals because peasants in his day did not recline, and that this context was added later. See *Seeing the Lord: Resurrection and Early Christian Practices* (Minneapolis: Fortress Press, 1994), p. 258.

23. Smith, *From Symposium to Eucharist*, p. 238; in opposition to Crossan, *The Historical Jesus*, pp. 261-64.

24. This explains Jesus' comment that Simon the Pharisee had neglected the kiss and the water for footwashing.

the more. In *The City of Joy*, an account of life in Calcutta's largest and utterly miserable slum, Dominique Lapierre describes the lavish celebrations of destitute people, including lepers, at weddings, on religious holidays, and for the visit of a special guest.[25]

Third, one of the meal practices that divided the poor from the rich was being able to recline at the table. The majority of people would have had neither the space in their houses nor the furniture upon which to recline. Yet every time a position at a meal is mentioned, it is always a reclining position. This would be the strongest case for Jesus' meals being idealized in the Gospels, for if he were a peasant and ate with outcasts, it is hardly likely that they would be able to recline at all their meals. I would suggest, however, that the terms *anaklino* (ἀνακλίνω), *katakeimai* (κατάκειμαι), and *anapipto* (ἀναπίπτο) were used to refer to being at table, regardless of what position one was able to take. The Gospel writers must have used these terms even in situations where reclining would have been impossible, just as in English translations of the Gospels, "sit" is always used rather than "recline" to make sense to English speakers. Further, the crowds are asked to recline at the outdoor feedings described in all the Gospels (Matt. 14:19, 15:35; Mark 6:39, 8:6; Luke 9:14-15; John 6:10). Here the atmosphere is anything but an upper-class dining room with couches and slaves to cook and serve.

Smith thinks that Crossan weakens his case by casting Jesus as a peasant, for what message could possibly come across about equality when Jesus ate with other peasants of the same status?[26] But Smith ignores the huge gaps between peasants — the layers of status between those with a little land and those with none, those with respectable occupations and those with unclean or despised jobs, and those who were free and those who were bondservants to others through debt.[27] Even Pharisees were

---

25. Dominique Lapierre, *The City of Joy* (New York: Doubleday, 1985). North American Christians visiting churches in the Two-Thirds World always comment on the rich hospitality they receive in spite of great poverty.

26. Smith, *From Symposium to Eucharist*, p. 238.

27. It is my theory that the more hierarchical and stratified a society, the more this stratification occurs at every level. Pedar Foss speaks of slaves in Roman households having their own social hierarchy, where each task had its own rank and no slave would perform a task below him or her in rank. See Pedar W. Foss, "Age, Gender, and Status Divisions at Mealtime in the Roman House: A Synopsis of the Literary Evidence," in "Kitchens and Dining Rooms at Pompeii: The Spatial and Social Relationship of Cooking to Eating in the

peasants, but they perceived an unbreachable gap between themselves and "sinners." Note also Crossan's observation above about the difference between "poor" (the householder) and "destitute" (the itinerant). Smith also overlooks Bruce Malina's discussion of the suspicion everyone had of strangers of whatever social status — whoever was not of their village or kin group or a guest of a villager.[28] Thus, when Jesus practiced open commensality all over Palestine — even as a peasant or a village artisan — he was making a strong political and religious statement.

Although Crossan's analysis of Jesus' table practice and ministry is more favorable to my own argument about actual daily commensality among early Jerusalem believers, neither Smith nor Burton Mack (another skeptic about the Gospels' account of the historical Jesus)[29] denies the symbolic value of meals in first-century Palestine. If Jesus and his traveling disciples had practiced open commensality in *any* way, it would have been an important model to follow in a situation where loving one's neighbor in the context of a growing group of fellow believers took on concrete reality. In a culture with such strong food symbolism, the practice of communal meals beyond one's kin group would have served to break down walls of mistrust and suspicion between peasants of many social levels and different regions of the land. I agree with S. Scott Bartchy that, by using the language of meals, "Jesus challenged the inherent exclusivism and status consciousness of accepted social and religious custom and presented a living parable of a renewed Israel."[30]

The description of the daily meals in Acts 2:42, 46 does not refer to a body position. The everyday occurrence of these meals would preclude many characteristics of the special meals described in the Gospels. No doubt in good weather many of these household meals took place in the

---

Roman Household." Ph.D. diss., University of Michigan, 1994, pp. 45-56. Online: http://www.arts.usyd.edu.au/departs/classical/dropbox/hgender.html.

28. Bruce J. Malina and Jerome H. Neyrey, "Honor and Shame in Luke-Acts," in *The Social World of Luke-Acts: Models for Interpretation*, ed. Jerome H. Neyrey (Peabody, Mass.: Hendrickson, 1991), p. 32: "No one outside the family of blood can be trusted until and unless that trust can be validated and verified. So men of the same village or town who are not blood relatives relate to each other with an implied deep distrust that in practice prevents any effective form of cooperation. Strangers to the village, that is, people of the same cultural group but not resident in the same place, are looked upon as potential enemies, while foreigners, those of other cultural groups just passing through, are considered certain enemies."

29. Mack, *A Myth of Innocence.* See n. 14 above.

30. Bartchy, "Table Fellowship," p. 796.

courtyards where extended families or more than one family living in surrounding houses shared a meal with whoever was attached to that household and courtyard. From the brief description, it sounds as if wine was not drunk regularly, which would be typical of the ordinary meal of peasants. But what apparently was happening was the inclusion of nonblood kin and the mixing of those of different layers of social classes and occupations around the same table. In his class analysis of the composition of the Jerusalem church, David Fiensy concludes that all classes, from wealthy to impoverished, were represented, and that, amazingly, class differences were barely commented upon.[31]

Being united around one cause and one beginning-to-be-realized Messianic hope would certainly have leveled out some previous social and religious gaps and prompted Luke to characterize this first community as being of one heart and soul with each other. What was continued was the religious significance of the meal, the prayers and bread-breaking that were part of the "living parable of a renewed Israel." Inclusive commensality with all Jesus-believers from a range of social strata made a powerful statement about changing group boundaries of who was in and who was out.[32] If food symbolism was so powerful in this nonindustrial, agrarian culture, and if Jesus indeed used this symbolism to make a major theological statement, it is only to be expected that his followers would have continued the practice.

Conclusion

It is obvious that the daily communal meals of the early Jerusalem church were a continuation of Jesus' meal practices with all who accepted him at their table. Evidence that Jesus' inclusive meals were worth commenting on shows up often in the Synoptic Gospels, in multiple sources and various forms. The earliest evidence is found in Paul's first letter to the Corinthians (11:17-34), where he insists that, unless all are eating together —

31. David Fiensy, "The Composition of the Jerusalem Church," in *The Book of Acts in Its Palestinian Setting*, ed. Richard Bauckham, vol. 4 of *The Book of Acts in Its First-Century Setting*, ed. Bruce W. Winter (Grand Rapids: Eerdmans, 1995), pp. 213-36 (226-30).

32. John Koenig observes that, though meals are restricted to believers in Acts 2:46-47, Luke intends to show how these meals attract nonbelievers. See *New Testament Hospitality*, p. 111.

those who come early and those who work for a living until sunset — it is not a "Jesus-style supper."

Here I have compared the work of two scholars who have written about Jesus' meals: John Dominic Crossan and Dennis Smith. Crossan sees Jesus' meal practices as an essential part of this program, which involved bringing together different classes of people for a renewal within Israel. Smith tends to see Jesus' meals in the Gospels as literary creations, since they sound more like upper-class banquets at which participants recline and where Jesus teaches like a philosopher. However, because the actual practice of sharing meals across boundaries becomes a powerful theological lesson, S. Scott Bartchy believes that Jesus' meals were a direct challenge to the status consciousness and hierarchy that kept Israelites from fulfilling their role as the people of God.

But if these meals were actual historical events, food did not appear on tables by magic. Who grew the food, obtained the food, prepared and served the food? The following chapter takes us to the kitchen and the role of women in relationship to first-century Mediterranean meals.

Chapter Eleven

"Upstairs, Downstairs": Widows and Other Women in Dining Room and Kitchen

Wisdom has built her house,
she has hewn her seven pillars.
She has slaughtered her animals,
she has mixed her wine,
she has also set her table.
She has also sent out her servant girls. . . .

Proverbs 9:1-3

Luke's reference to widows in Acts 6:1 provides a window into a hidden world lying behind the social reality of communal meals in the Gospels and Acts. It is the "downstairs" complement to the "upstairs" of a more public meal. It is the labor of freedwomen and men, and female and male slaves, which is absolutely necessary if a meal is to be shared at all. At the least, the widows in Acts 6:1 bring into focus the question of women at meals in the Greco-Roman world and in Palestine. What were their roles in ordinary family meals, in the meals Jesus shared with a motley assortment of fellow Israelites, and especially in the communal meals of the early Jerusalem community? If these daily meals in Jerusalem were family meals eaten in fictive kin groups, what role did women play in them? What hints do the widows in Acts give us about the essential role of women in relation to meals?

Women at Public Meals: Protecting Chastity

Kathleen Corley's *Private Women, Public Meals*[1] presents research on the
status of women in relation to public meals in the Greco-Roman world.
The Greek custom among the upper classes had been that public meals
were for men only, not for their wives. The only women who attended were
entertainers and the prostitutes of higher status called *hetairai*. A respectable matron would be respectable no longer if she were present.[2] Although
the Romans adopted the Greek custom of public dining, it gradually became more acceptable for married women to attend with their husbands.
In some instances, they would sit at the end of their husband's couch,
along with their children, if the latter were also invited. Later, some women
did recline with their husbands, although this never became a universal,
standard practice.[3] Wives and daughters might attend the feast in their
home and then leave before the heavy drinking began.[4]

The erotic nature of some banquets, for which (slave) prostitutes
would be hired, precluded the presence of respectable women. There was a
clear connection between food and sex; one course at some dinners was
the women themselves.[5] During the late Republican period, it was not appropriate to even mention the name of a respectable matron in public.[6]
Such banquets are noted in Greco-Roman literature well into the second
century C.E..[7] Other meals, however, did include women. Pedar Foss notes
that Roman women and men commonly dined together: "In the early Re-

1. Kathleen Corley, *Private Women, Public Meals: Social Conflict in the Synoptic Tradition* (Peabody, Mass.: Hendrickson, 1993).

2. Corley, *Private Women, Public Meals*, pp. 25-28.

3. Corley, *Private Women, Public Meals*, pp. 28-31.

4. Corley, *Private Women, Public Meals*, p. 30; Plutarch, *Quaest. Conv.* 612F-613A;
653A-D; *Sept. Sap. Conv.* 150-55; Pedar W. Foss, "Age, Gender, and Status Divisions at Mealtime in the Roman House: A Synopsis of the Literary Evidence," in "Kitchens and Dining
Rooms at Pompeii: The Spatial and Social Relationship of Cooking to Eating in the Roman
Household," Ph.D. diss., University of Michigan, 1994, pp. 45-56. Online: http://
www.arts.usyd.edu.au/departs/classical/dropbox/hgender.html.

5. Foss, "Age, Gender, and Status Divisions at Mealtime in the Roman House."

6. David Schaps, "The Women Least Mentioned: Etiquette and Women's Names,"
Catholic Quarterly 27 (1977): 323-30; Eve Cantarella, *Pandora's Daughters: The Role and Status
of Women in Greek and Roman Antiquity*, trans. Maureen B. Fant (London and Baltimore:
Johns Hopkins University Press, 1987), pp. 124-26.

7. Corley, *Private Women*, p. 53.

publican period, women are said to have been seated at dinner, but by the Empire custom dictated that both sexes recline."[8]

Among the lower classes who celebrated banquets through their voluntary associations, evidence for women's attendance is mixed. It is not clear that women were members of *collegia* and other associations, but they apparently did attend club meals. Their attendance at certain cultic *symposia* would have been innovative, and it is quite possible that if they were present at all, they would have been seated together as a group, perhaps in a separate room.[9] But freedwomen and slaves were already classed as public women, "available to all."[10] Since they were held to a different sexual standard than higher-class matrons, their presence at these meals may not have been proscribed.

Ramsey MacMullen also indicates that patronesses of various social strata were included at the banquets of associations they sponsored. Roman women seem to have been excluded from no social role or aspiration in the public affairs of their communities. However, there were few female patrons compared to the number of male patrons, so there would have been relatively few of them at such meals.[11]

Historians have noted that Roman women seem to have been more "liberated" during the late Republic and early Empire than at any other time, which would have included their attending banquets more frequently and even drinking alcohol there. This "liberation," however, would have involved only aristocratic women and would have been tolerated only so long as it did not interfere with the "real world" of male politics. The writings of Virgil, Livy, Tacitus, and Juvenal are critical of women's emancipated behavior and perceive it as sexually licentious.[12] Once Roman men recognized the political ramifications of women's changing behavior, they again tried to restrict women's liberties through legislation and by insisting on women's traditional virtues.[13]

---

8. Foss, "Age, Gender, and Status Divisions at Mealtime in the Roman House."

9. Corley, *Private Women, Public Meals*, p. 31.

10. According to Carolyn Osiek, "This sexual availability of slaves seems to have been completely taken for granted." See her essay "Female Slaves, *Porneia*, and the Limits of Obedience," in *Early Christian Families in Context: An Interdisciplinary Dialogue* (Grand Rapids: Eerdmans, 2003), pp. 236-64 (263-64).

11. Ramsey MacMullen, "Women in Public in the Roman Empire," *Historia* 29 (1980): 208-18 (213).

12. Corley, *Private Women, Public Meals*, p. 54.

13. Cantarella, *Pandora's Daughters*, p. 143.

Jewish formal meals were patterned after Greco-Roman formal meals, and David Balch notes that Jews were also criticized during this era for the sexual immorality of their women.[14] Women (primarily upper-class women) were required to be present at the Passover seder and to recline beside their husbands. However, they were excluded from participating in the Passover liturgy, comparable to excluding Greco-Roman women from the *symposium*.[15] One unusual example of women dining regularly with men at a weekly formal meal is Philo's account of the Therapeutae, an Alexandrian Jewish monastic community, where both men and women reclined in a double room with a partition between them that did not reach all the way to the ceiling. Both women and men fully participated in the after-dinner proceedings, which would have been unusual. Philo notes the great contrast between the solemnity of these meals and the gaiety and looseness of pagan meals, with their "unrestrained merrymaking" and promiscuous sex with both men and women.[16]

Evidence for Jewish meal practices generally corresponds to that of their Greco-Roman contemporaries. Care is taken to guard against perceiving women who are dining as targets for sexual advances.[17] Both Philo and Josephus show concern for Greco-Roman propriety.[18]

The experiences of Christian women can be paralleled with those of women in the larger Greco-Roman world as well. Since Christians were slandered for their inclusive dining practices,[19] it is not surprising that Christian art and literature of the early centuries reflect concern for women's behavior and posture at meals. A significant piece of evidence is the late second-century fresco from the catacomb of St. Priscilla in Rome,

14. David Balch, *Let Wives Be Submissive: The Domestic Code in 1 Peter* (Atlanta: Scholars Press, 1981), chaps. 5-6.

15. S. Stein, "The Influence of Symposia Literature on the Literary Form of the Pesah Haggadah," *Journal of Jewish Studies* 8 (1984): 379-94.

16. Philo, *On the Contemplative Life*, 58.

17. Barbara H. Geller Nathanson, "Reflections on the Silent Woman of Ancient Judaism and Her Pagan Roman Counterpart," in *The Listening Heart: Essays in Wisdom and the Psalms in Honor of Roland E. Murphy*, ed. Kenneth Hoglund et al. (Sheffield: JSOT Press, 1987), pp. 259-79.

18. Corley, *Private Women, Public Meals*, p. 74.

19. For example, Minucius Felix, a third-century Christian writer, lists such charges in *Octavius* 8.4–12.5, translated in Jo-Ann Shelton, *As the Romans Did: A Sourcebook in Roman Social History* (Oxford: Oxford University Press, 1988), pp. 417-18.

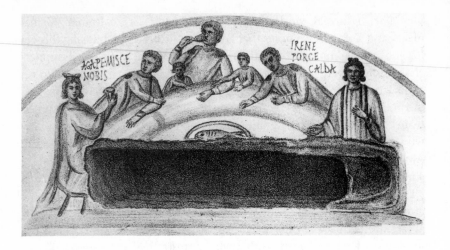

where seven women share in a meal. Six are reclining while the seventh is sitting, breaking the bread.[20]

Corley believes that the social innovation of including women at public meals pervaded all of Hellenistic society from roughly the second century B.C.E. through the third century C.E. However, the ideology about women's table etiquette was not advancing at the same rate as women's actual behavior, and consequently criticism of women entering this "public" arena was harsh. Corley does not see gender-inclusive meal practices of Christians deriving from their theology; they only partook of the social milieu of their time.[21]

But Corley is not able to determine from her data what were *everyday* meal practices of first-century Jews or Christians.[22] Nor has she showed clear awareness of the class restrictions on some of her data. Public meals described in the literature were upper-class phenomena (except for the less-frequent banquets of associations and *collegia*). Pedar Foss assumes that in the Roman Empire communal family meals were the normal state of affairs, since Caligula, in grief at his sister Drusilla's death, forbade

20. *Women's Ordination: "The Hidden Tradition"* (Houston, Tex.: Reel Spirit Productions in association with British Broadcasting Corporation, 1992), video recording; John Beckwith, *Early Christian and Byzantine Art* (Baltimore: Penguin Books, 1970), Plate 2: "The Breaking of Bread."

21. Corley, *Private Women, Public Meals*, pp. 78-79.

22. Corley, *Private Women, Public Meals*, p. 71.

anyone on pain of death from eating with their parents, wives, or children during the period of public mourning.[23]

Since nearly all extant literature from Hellenistic society of this period was written by, about, and for males of the upper class, it is impossible to find direct information on lower-class women and meal preparation, serving, eating, and clean-up. Besides reading between the lines of ancient literature, we must use analogies from cultures and peoples that are better known and extrapolate backward from the experiences of those not in obvious positions of power and authority. One method of analysis uses modern anthropological research into present societies that appear to share a symbolic universe similar to that of the ancient Mediterranean world. It is to some of this research that we turn next for a better understanding of women's contributions to the meal practices of the Jerusalem community, and a possible role for the widows of Acts 6:1.

Holding up Half the Sky: Women in the Private Sphere

Making cross-cultural analogies is a complex process. Anthropologists have not agreed on whether or not gender roles are universal, but they have found a strong association of women within the domestic sphere. Understanding the division between private and public spheres is critical in contemporary Middle Eastern societies, where the public/private dichotomy is strongly linked to gender. This is especially evident in villages and rural areas, except where economic forces are driving women from home to the workplace.[24] Gender expectations in these societies conform closely to those expressed in the Hebrew Bible and Christian Testament, as well as in Jewish writings around the time of Jesus.[25] The continuity of traditional gender roles among nonelite women and men was apparently maintained

23. C. Suetonius Tranquillus, *Lives of the Twelve Caesars: Caligula* 24.

24. A helpful book on this topic is *Gender and Power in Rural Greece*, ed. Jill Dubisch (Princeton: Princeton University Press, 1986).

25. Further descriptions of women's roles around the time of Jesus can be found in S. Safrai, "Home and Family," in *The Jewish People in the First Century*, 2 vols., ed. S. Safrai and M. Stern (Philadelphia: Fortress Press, 1976-1986), pp. 728-93; Joachim Jeremias, *Jerusalem in the Time of Jesus* (Philadelphia: Fortress Press, 1962); and Leonard Swidler, *Women in Judaism: The Status of Women in Formative Judaism* (Metuchen, N.J.: Scarecrow Press, 1976). These studies, however, lie in the area of social description and are not concerned with analyzing or synthesizing or explaining these facts in social-scientific fashion.

throughout history. Using documents from the tenth to the thirteenth century C.E., S. D. Goitein's five-volume work, *A Mediterranean Society*, describes the world of medieval Jews and Arabs, which also reflects a strong connection between women and domestic life.[26]

In a culture where there is a wide gap between the public and private spheres, can it be assumed that women necessarily have a much lower status than men? There are two opinions on this question. Early feminist anthropology had declared that the subjection of women was actually universal because of women's major role in the reproduction and nurture of young children. The benchmark statement of this position was made by Michelle Z. Rosaldo.[27]

But more recent theory has criticized this conceptualization, pointing out that such binary pairing creates a value and a disvalue, and reductively defines the private sphere in terms of the public sphere.[28] Field anthropologists and archeologists have also been unable to use this construct in any simple way. Space is more public or private depending on many factors — for example, how was an activity understood, and what was the gender or kin status of the people doing it? In fact, in contemporary traditional societies the gender of a place can shift with the time of day or week. (See below an illustration from Yemen.)

Some feminist anthropologists argue that when the private/public distinction is highly developed in a particular culture, such roles give women a separate sphere of power and authority where they may actually be dominant.[29] When the domestic realm is neglected or devalued (as it is

26. S. D. Goitein, *The Family*, vol. 3 of *A Mediterranean Society: The Jewish Documents of the Arab World as Portrayed in the Documents of the Cairo Geniza* (Berkeley and Los Angeles: University of California Press, 1978).

27. Michelle Z. Rosaldo, "Women, Culture, and Society: A Theoretical Overview," in *Woman, Culture, and Society,* ed. Michelle Z. Rosaldo and Louise Lamphere (Stanford: Stanford University Press, 1974), pp. 17-42. See also Sherry B. Ortner, "Is Female to Male as Nature Is to Culture?" in *Woman, Culture, and Society,* ed. Rosaldo and Lamphere, pp. 67-88; Peggy Reeves Sanday, *Female Power and Male Dominance: On the Origins of Sexual Inequality* (Cambridge: Cambridge University Press, 1981).

28. Rosaldo has taken these criticisms into account in a later essay, "The Use and Abuse of Anthropology: Reflections on Feminism and Cross-Cultural Understanding," *Signs* 5 (1980): 389-417.

29. See, for example, Louise Lamphere, "Strategies, Cooperation, and Conflict among Women in Domestic Groups," in *Woman, Culture, and Society,* ed. Rosaldo and Lamphere, pp. 97-112.

in our Western or North American cultures), an important source of status and power for women is overlooked, and a distorted view of women's position in a particular society results.[30] Comments Ernestine Friedl,

> From the standpoint of the ceremonial mores of the community, there may be many cultures in which male activity is accorded pre-eminence in the public sector. But if a careful analysis of the life of the community shows that, pragmatically, the family is the most significant social unit, then the private and not the public sector is the sphere in which the relative attribution of power to males and females is of the greatest real importance.[31]

Friedl describes her experiences in the Greek village of Vasilika, where the public display of male prestige and honor is obvious, where women and men are clearly segregated in public space, and where women accord men ritual deference in public situations.[32] But underneath the social prestige of the men lies the economic power of the women through their dowries, usually in the form of land. Within the household they participate fully in decision-making about the land — what crops to plant, when to sell, what credit to accept, and the like. This same control over property gives women power in the marriages of their children, since a woman's property would be passed on to her daughters in the form of dowries. Friedl calls this power informal, but she insists that this is not a trivial statement.[33] She sees an additional avenue of power for women in the fact that men's honor rests primarily on the behavior of their womenfolk. In the privacy of the home, women remind men of the labor and trouble they endure to preserve the honor of the family, and they can thus threaten to disrupt the order of the men's world. Concludes Friedl, "For the weaker partner in a social structure, the ability to create and maintain such a sense of obligation in the stronger is a real exercise of power, and one in which Greek village women are past masters."[34]

---

30. This argument is well stated in Jill Dubisch's introduction to *Gender and Power in Rural Greece*, ed. Dubisch, pp. 3-41 (13-15).

31. Ernestine Friedl, "The Position of Women: Appearance and Reality," in *Gender and Power in Rural Greece*, ed. Dubisch, pp. 42-52 (42).

32. Friedl, "The Position of Women," p. 43.

33. Friedl, "The Position of Women," pp. 49-51.

34. Friedl, "The Position of Women," p. 52.

Carla Makhlouf's description of traditional life in Yemen similarly shows a culture in which sex roles are rigidly defined, and the women are strictly secluded and wear the veil in the presence of all men who are not family members.[35] Yet the *tafrita* (afternoon visit) is a regular ritual and the principal leisure activity. It is arranged in advance that the women receive their guests while the men are out, and vice versa.[36] This traditional women's world offers little chance of achievement, but it does provide a separate sphere of life where women gain a great deal of support from each other and have unexpected decision-making power: they influence their brothers and sons by controlling the circulation of information about other females gained through visiting and gossip. In actuality they arrange marriages, because only they know what other females are like and can suggest whom their sons or brothers should marry.[37] In this way, like the women of the Greek village of Vasilika, they gain some power over the alliances that keep society together.[38]

Indeed, when there is a wide gender separation, male authority can turn into a measure of male subordination in the home. During his fieldwork in a village on the island of Rhodes, Michael Herzfeld was accepted into one home fully enough to observe a woman slapping her drunken husband, something that would never have been deemed appropriate in public.[39] Some have suggested that, ironically, women's power may stem from submission to the system that seeks to deny it to them. Juliet de Boulay confirms that in rural Greece a woman increasingly exercises power as she succeeds in embodying the maternal ideal which is open to her. She can be compared to the "Mother of God." But the flip side is that a woman resisting this ideal is seen as Eve from whom springs all kinds of evil.[40]

But Herzfeld thinks something important is missed when scholarship too closely identifies women with private space ("inside"), and men with

---

35. Carla Makhlouf, *Changing Veils: Women and Modernization in North Yemen* (London: Croom Helm, 1979).

36. Makhlouf, *Changing Veils*, pp. 22-23.

37. Makhlouf, *Changing Veils*, p. 42.

38. Makhlouf, *Changing Veils*, p. 43.

39. Michael Herzfeld, "Within and Without: The Category of 'Female' in the Ethnography of Modern Greece," in *Gender and Power in Rural Greece*, ed. Dubisch, pp. 215-33 (219-20).

40. Juliet de Boulay, "Women — Images of Their Nature and Destiny in Rural Greece," in *Gender and Power in Rural Greece*, ed. Dubisch, pp. 139-68 (158-61).

public space ("outside"). If woman symbolizes interior space, he says, the reverse can also be true. "The categories of 'male' and 'female' . . . can be manipulated as symbols of exterior and interior identities of other kinds."[41] Within a village, town, or nation, then, women can stand for the intimate, interior aspect of that entity. Herzfeld discusses two disparate images that Greeks have of their national culture. The "Hellenic" model is the heroic, classic, archaic ideology of the establishment and political right wing. This is the outer, public image that displays national pride to foreigners. But opposed to this is what he calls the "Romeic" model, which is the familiar self-image Greeks assume when conversing among themselves. This "warts and all" self-image shares the main characteristics of the Greek model of female identity — cunning, illiterate, and lacking in self-control, but also warm and welcoming. There is a sense in which all Greeks, male and female, partake of the "female" national self-identity. As Herzfeld observes, "There are circumstances under which a true Greek man should not emulate women and others under which his very Greekness is enhanced by his doing so."[42]

The patriarchal, agrarian culture of first-century Judea sounds very similar to the above descriptions of Mediterranean societies today. Though not usually exercising much obvious influence in the public sector, some women — at least the matrons in their homes — must have exercised considerable authority in their extended families. Most but not all of this is hidden because it was not considered the sort of thing people wrote about in those days. Men operating in the public sphere of life wrote the New Testament documents.

Crossing the Divide: Jesus and Women's Roles

Nevertheless, both Diane Jacobs-Malina and Karen Torjesen do not think women's authority is as hidden under the New Testament writings as we might suppose, and their interpretations can have profound theological implications. Jacobs-Malina interprets the Jesus of the Gospels as having the qualities of a mother in a patriarchal society.[43] She proposes that as we

41. Herzfeld, "Within and Without," p. 217.
42. Herzfeld, "Within and Without," p. 231.
43. Diane Jacobs-Malina, *Beyond Patriarchy: Images of Family in Jesus* (Mahwah, N.J.: Paulist Press, 1993).

understand the domestic role of the ideal wife/mother in ancient Palestinian culture, we will better understand Jesus' character and mission. Using anthropological insights from contemporary Mediterranean societies, Jacobs-Malina sees the ideal wife and mother integrating all the facets of her life around domestic life within her husband's household. In that role, her most important achievements are those that lead to the creation and nurturing of children.[44] Her second most important duty is to turn the produce and meat that enter the house into meals. Says Jacobs-Malina,

> Because food is the general idiom which symbolizes bonds and relationships among those on the inside, it is an integral part of every woman's responsibilities. The significance of meals extends beyond the household to include outsiders who enter into relations with the family. The kind and amount of food the family eats, its preparation, the quality and quantity served to outsiders, symbolize how the family sees itself in relation to outsiders.[45]

In a patriarchal society, the ideal wife and mother is also the primary socializing agent of the household. She must comfort and sustain those members who go out into the harsh public world, as well as "toughen" the younger members so they will be able to function in a society that demands sacrifice for the good of the group and household. The woman is also in charge of the economic aspects of the household, responsible for the goods that the family might produce to sell in the marketplace. Such a woman is given no real power as it is defined in the public world. Her influence is indirect, yet (as noted above by Friedl) nonetheless substantial. Jacobs-Malina compares this anthropological description of a wife/mother in a patriarchal society with the portrait of a "good wife" in Proverbs 31:10-31.[46]

Each of the four Gospels presents an image of Jesus that resembles the above description. As women relied on male family members to maintain their honor, so Jesus relied on God for his honor. The realm of God as portrayed by Jesus called for the nurturing roles of women to be just as appropriate for men because this showed God's love for God's children. God's love was what was important, not the maintenance of honor through rigid gender roles. Jacobs-Malina continues,

44. Jacobs-Malina, *Beyond Patriarchy,* pp. 2-3.
45. Jacobs-Malina, *Beyond Patriarchy,* p. 4.
46. Jacobs-Malina, *Beyond Patriarchy,* pp. 4-6.

This radical alteration of the male role invites a closer look at each Gospel from the domestic standpoint, the world of nature and nurture. From this perspective, God's testing of Jesus, Jesus' complete loyalty to the Father who authorized him, the unique role Jesus enjoys as he brings children into the household of God, his role of socializing these "children" as well as meeting their physical needs, Jesus' example of hard work and suffering in order to maintain the household according to the will of the Father, and Jesus' designation of his own body and blood as food are but a few examples of activities that Jesus performed as part of his unique role in the household of God. The role of the eldest son in a patriarchal family is quite different from the multiple roles just described.[47]

Jesus' reinterpretation of the household of God permits men to perform the same roles as women and thus breaks down the traditional patriarchal family structure. The inside (private sphere) becomes as important as the outside because God sees what happens in private as well as in public (i.e., Matt. 6:2-6).[48] With food as the main idiom of the household, Jesus expands the walls of his house by eating with those who would never have been invited to his table under traditional mores. More than once, at the end of a long teaching session, rather than sending his listeners back out into the public sphere, Jesus turns outside space into domestic space by preparing to feed the crowd (Matt. 14:19 and par.; Matt. 15:35 and par.). He "allows food to be the medium which transforms strangers into household members or 'friends of the family.'"[49] In addition, his male disciples serve the food to the reclining crowds of women, men, and children. Jesus' actions thus pave the way for the common sharing of property and communal meals in the early church and affect traditional gender roles about who does the serving.

Economic or Political? Shifting Gender Roles

This anthropological analysis of Jesus' character in the Gospels has points of connection with Karen Torjesen's historical investigation comparing

47. Jacobs-Malina, *Beyond Patriarchy*, p. 7.
48. Jacobs-Malina, *Beyond Patriarchy*, p. 17.
49. Jacobs-Malina, *Beyond Patriarchy*, p. 21.

leadership models within early church congregations to household management in the Greco-Roman culture.[50] Since the church began in the private sphere where women lived and worked, many duties that were typical
of women's work, such as preparing and serving food, became the same
duties of church leaders.

But it is more complex than that. In "Household Management and
Women's Authority" (co-written with Virginia Burrus), Torjesen notes inconsistencies in the ancient sources. Perspectives on the household and the
status and roles of women would vary depending on the context. When
the household was seen as part of the political structure of society (polis),
the legal authority of the male was underscored, and women were portrayed as strictly subordinate. But when writers attempted to contrast gender roles by aligning the male role with the state and the female role with
the household, the result was a portrayal of women as the sole rulers of the
household. A third view represented the husband and wife as comple-
menting each other in household management, the man working outside
and the woman managing the interior space.[51]

Torjesen sees all three views as ideological and prescriptive, and she
attempts to sort out the social realities from among them. In doing so, she
notes a high degree of role interchangeability between men and women
who functioned as heads of households. For example, she sees the household authority taken by the man Cornelius in Acts 10 as very similar to that
taken by the woman Lydia in Acts 16 — even to the fact that members of
both households converted to Christianity out of deference to their
head![52]

When households are described in the ancient literature as economic
units rather than as part of the polis, role complementarity tends to be
stressed. This is not surprising, since the public duties of Greek and Roman men would call them away and require their wives to manage both
the indoor and the outdoor parts of a household. (One may think first of
senators and governors with large estates, but this would also have been
true for many farmers with small holdings who were conscripted into the

50. Karen Torjesen, When Women Were Priests: Women's Leadership in the Early
Church and the Scandal of Their Subordination in the Rise of Christianity (San Francisco:
HarperSanFrancisco, 1993).

51. Karen Torjesen and Virginia Burrus, "Household Management and Women's Authority," When Women Were Priests, pp. 53-87 (58).

52. Torjesen and Burrus, "Household Management," pp. 53-55.

military.) In addition, women retained control over their marriage dowries, often in the form of land. Comments Torjesen, "In her capacity as householder, [a woman] was free to buy and sell, contract day laborers, and conduct household — hence, 'private' — business in the 'public' sphere."[53]

A second-century letter from an Egyptian woman named Ptolema to her brother shows how much oversight she had over the land they held in common:

> All the fields are in good condition. The southern basin of the 17 arurae has been sold for the use of cattle. Your cattle have eaten one arura and have gone off to Pansoue. All the land there has been given over for grass cutting. We have sold the grass in the cleruchies excepting the six eastern basins for 112 drachmas. Grass is exceedingly cheap.[54]

A much later description of the activities of two wives of a Middle Eastern sheik shows the continuing involvement of rural women in the economic management of a household — even in an Islamic region where women are separated from men and relegated to the "private sphere." Whether or not the sheik was present, the senior wife would travel with the flocks of sheep to their grazing lands each spring, supervising both men and women who were doing the manual labor around lamb-birthing, milking, cheese-processing, wool-shearing, and the marketing of surpluses. While she was gone, the second wife took over the management of the household, organizing the feeding of twenty to fifty people a day, providing shelter and food for strangers, interviewing the foreman and laborers looking for work, supervising local agricultural and shepherding activities, and supervising village weddings, house-building, and care of the sick. She announced many of her decisions by saying, "This is the wish of the Sheik," although he had not been home in a long time.[55] Both of the above examples are congruent with the depiction of Jesus in the Gospels, as he does the work of the (absent) Father in heaven.

---

53. Torjesen, *When Women Were Priests*, p. 76.

54. Mary R. Lefkowitz and Maureen B. Fant, *Women's Life in Greece and Rome* (Baltimore: Johns Hopkins University Press, 1982), p. 236.

55. Marjorie Wall Bingham and Susan Hill Gross, *Women in Islam in Ancient Middle East to Modern Times* (St. Louis Park, Minn.: Glenhurst Publications, Inc., 1980), p. 55.

Torjesen also looks at leadership in the early house churches (as prescribed in the *Didache* and 1 Timothy 5 and 6) from the perspective of household management such as that described above, and finds the similarities striking. Both positions required supervising, educating, disciplining, and nurturing the members of the community. Both household managers and bishops were responsible for receiving, storing, and distributing the common goods of the community. Both derived their authority not only from their ascribed positions but from their personal abilities to persuade and win respect by constant involvement in the community.[56] In terms of women's leadership in house churches, Torjesen deduces another similarity: the public gender ideology does not always conform to social reality.[57] Though prescriptive roles place men in authority and women in submission, there are many conflicting representations of women's roles in early church literature. Certainly, leadership by Lydia, Prisca, and a number of women referred to as Paul's co-workers in his letters challenges a simple prescriptive stereotype.

Responsibilities of church leaders included receiving, organizing, and distributing the common goods of the community. This would also involve table ministry, tied in with the Eucharistic meal ceremonies at the center of Christian worship. For obvious reasons, there were cautions to both household managers and church leaders not to be greedy or addicted to wine (*Didache* 15; 1 Tim. 3:4-5). Capable management of other persons in the community was also essential for both roles. Torjesen concludes that the role of household manager cannot be tied to one gender in ancient Greco-Roman society; therefore, "so long as church leadership continued to model itself on the familiar role of household manager, there was no cultural barrier to women assuming leadership roles."[58]

The characterization of Jesus in the Gospels and the later job descriptions of church leaders can be used to add to the realism of the communal life of the early Jerusalem community. The commensality would have involved the labor of many members, both women and men, although what was happening in the households was taking place on what was ordinarily women's turf.

56. Torjesen, *When Women Were Priests*, pp. 76-80.
57. Torjesen, *When Women Were Priests*, p. 81.
58. Torjesen, *When Women Were Priests*, p. 82.

"Wash up before you come in!"
Women in the Kitchen and the Work World

If there is one area within the private space of the home that is tradition-ally associated with women, particularly servant women, it is the kitchen — or whatever space in which food is prepared. Even ancient Jewish rabbis recognized women's superior knowledge of laws related to the home and kitchen. Two legal rulings in the *Tosefta* connected with the house are given by women. One is about a door bolt (*tKel. BM* 1.6), and the other is about an oven (*tKel. BQ* 4.17).[59] Rabbis have passed on two other stories pertaining to women's superior knowledge of laws about the kitchen, one having to do with treatment of an egg laid on a festival day (yShab. 4.1, 6d; yBets. 4.4, 62c), and the other about food left on one's plate (*bErub.* 53b; *Lam. R.* 1.19).[60]

Ethnographers and anthropologists have generally explained this connection of women and food preparation in terms of women's closer re-lationship to nature, natural processes, and pollution. This in turn ac-counts for their devaluation in relation to men, who are equated with cul-ture.[61] Jill Dubisch turns this explanation on its head, however. In her provocative essay entitled "Culture Enters through the Kitchen," Dubisch interprets women in the kitchen (and in the house generally) as *controllers* of pollution, both their own and that of others, and as those who trans-form natural products and processes into cultural ones.[62] (Dubisch did her research in Tinos, an island in the Greek Peloponnesus, where strong be-liefs exist about women's sexuality and bodily processes being polluting — not unlike concepts about female pollution in ancient Israelite and Pales-tinian society.)

As Torjesen described some of the literature about women's relation to house management, so Dubisch describes a family's house as the special responsibility of the woman.[63] It is her job to keep it orderly and clean, the

---

59. Tal Ilan, *Jewish Women in Greco-Roman Palestine* (Peabody, Mass.: Hendrickson, 1996), p. 195.

60. D. Goodblatt, "The Beruriah Traditions," *Journal of Jewish Studies* 26 (1975): 83; cited in Ilan, *Jewish Women in Greco-Roman Palestine,* p. 195.

61. Ortner, "Is Female to Male as Nature Is to Culture?" pp. 67-87.

62. Jill Dubisch, "Culture Enters through the Kitchen: Women, Food, and Social Boundaries in Rural Greece," *Gender and Power in Rural Greece,* ed. Dubisch, pp. 195-214.

63. Dubisch, "Culture Enters through the Kitchen," p. 197.

opposite of the "outside," or street, which is a place of dirt and immorality. A woman's house reflects her moral character, for if a woman has an orderly house and is a good cook, she obviously has not had time to engage in immoral behavior. The kitchen is her special area, the place where not only food preparation occurs, but family and friends gather for informal or intimate socializing.

Transitional space between the kitchen and the street is the porch, or courtyard. This area is also used for much informal socializing, especially while work is being done. Certain types of dirt can be controlled in this area so they need not enter the house. Here laundry is done, and here men coming in from the fields take off dirty clothes and wash up before they enter the house. As guardians of the kitchen and porch, or courtyard, women control the amount of pollution and dirt that enter the house, literally, symbolically, and morally. This also includes food. Claude Levi-Strauss compared the relationship between cooking and culture with the analogy of raw to cooked and nature to culture. Men bring raw food from the fields to women, who transform it by cleaning and cooking it.[64]

As noted above, food is intimately related to social life and the family and carries rich symbolism. In pre-industrial cultures, food preparation consumes the greater part of each day. Dubisch also observes the spiritual aspect of food in Greek family life. A meal is a sacred event, especially so at holidays and when hospitality is shown to guests. At such times, it is the woman's products that represent the household to the public world. However, men also participate in food ceremonies during these occasions, hosting meals and serving food, sometimes in a most "feminine" manner.[65]

Dubisch concludes that one cannot make a simple analogy between females and nature, and then extrapolate women's lower status. Rather, women are "controllers of nature and maintainers of cultural boundaries."[66] Moreover, agreeing with Herzfeld (above), she notes that feminine qualities can be considered valuable and appropriate in certain contexts for both men and women.

---

64. Claude Levi-Strauss, *The Raw and the Cooked* (New York: Harper & Row, 1969); in Dubisch, "Culture Enters through the Kitchen," pp. 203-5.

65. Dubisch, "Culture Enters through the Kitchen," p. 207.

66. Dubisch, "Culture Enters through the Kitchen," p. 212.

Once a Widow, Always a Poor Widow?

In Chapter Four I discussed various options for who might be the widows of Acts 6:1, so I will not repeat that discussion here. In this section I will concentrate on the social background of actual widowhood in the Mediterranean and Palestinian culture.

If a woman whose husband had died had one or more adult living sons, she would likely be cared for in their home(s) until she died or remarried. Although the ancient Mosaic law did not make legal provision for widows, as did Babylonian, Hittite, and Assyrian codes of law, afflicting widows, orphans, and other poor was a crime (Exod. 22:21-25), and a tithe was to be gathered for them every three years (Deut. 14:28-29).

In the Greco-Roman world a bride was given a dowry, usually by her father, which was to provide for her maintenance. If her husband died, the laws governing use of the dowry were clearly defined. She could either live in her deceased husband's house with her children, or return to her parents.[67] According to Z. W. Falk, during the Hellenistic Jewish period, a Jewish wife was allowed a share in her own property during marriage, and if she became a widow, she could retain part of her dowry, or *ketubah*.[68] But the *ketubah* was only two hundred denarii, which would have assured the woman's livelihood for only one year after divorce or her husband's death.[69] In a subsistence economy with no government safety net, it is obvious that some women from poor families or those with no family connections or with only daughters and no sons could easily fall through the legal cracks and become destitute without any respectable source of income.

What percentage of the Jerusalem community does it seem realistic to think of as destitute widows? How many of them would be younger, with dependent children? Probably not many. Although widowhood be-

---

67. David M. Schaps, *Economic Rights of Women in Ancient Greece* (Edinburgh: Edinburgh University Press, 1979), p. 81.

68. Z. W. Falk, *Introduction to Jewish Laws of the Second Commonwealth* (Leiden: E. J. Brill, 1978), p. 290. See also Elisabeth Koffmahn, *Die Doppelurkunden aus der Wüste Juda. Recht und Praxis der jüdischen Papyri des 1. und 2. Jahrhunderts n. Chr. samt Übersetzung*, vol. 5 of *Studies on the Texts of the Desert of Judah* (Leiden, 1968), pp. 11, 29, 104-10; cited in Ivoni Richter Reimer, *Women in the Acts of the Apostles* (Minneapolis: Fortress Press, 1995), pp. 3-4 ; Tal Ilan, *Jewish Women*, pp. 167-70.

69. Luise Schottroff, *Lydia's Impatient Sisters: A Feminist Social History of Early Christianity* (Louisville: Westminster Press, 1995), p. 93.

came a highly respected status in later Christian communities,[70] in Judaism it was in most instances a temporary situation. In all Jewish literature of this time there are only a very few accounts of women remaining widows long after the death of their husbands.[71] Anonymous widows are also very rare in the sources. Rabbinical stories about widowhood usually describe the special efforts rabbis would make to confirm that a woman's husband was dead so that she could remarry again. Although the law required two male, Jewish witnesses, there are numerous accounts of rabbis who declared a husband dead on the strength of only one witness, or the testimony of a Gentile or a woman, in one case even a woman innkeeper[72] (who would have been considered immoral). On the one hand, this information testifies to the fact that widowhood could indeed be a dismal state for a woman to fall into because of the risk of poverty. On the other hand, it was usually a temporary condition.

But some women without husbands would have fared well enough. Since women in wealthier families often managed the economic affairs of their households when their husbands were away, some could have kept on doing the same things after a husband's death. If, as Ernst Haenchen noted (see Chapter Six), some older Jewish couples from the Diaspora moved to the Holy City in order to die and be buried there, Jerusalem may have had a higher number of elderly widows, some of whom were adequately provided for, and some of whom were not. However, since

---

70. Orders of ascetic widows are known probably by the late first or early second century. Both Stevan L. Davies and Ross Kraemer note the predominance of women's concerns and preferences for female characters in the Apocryphal Acts. While Kraemer interprets these stories as having developed out of oral traditions originating from orders of ascetic women, Davies takes the written Acts themselves to be the work of women. See Ross S. Kraemer, "The Conversion of Women to Ascetic Forms of Christianity," *Signs: Journal of Women in Culture and Society* 6 (Winter 1980): 298-307; Kraemer, "Autonomy, Prophecy, and Gender in Early Christianity," in *Her Share of the Blessings: Women's Religions among Pagans, Jews, and Christians in the Greco-Roman World* (New York and Oxford: Oxford University Press, 1992), pp. 128-56; Stevan L. Davies, *The Revolt of the Widows: The Social World of the Apocryphal Acts* (Carbondale and Edwardsville: Southern Illinois University Press, 1980). Robert McNair Price asserts that the widow traditions of both Luke and Acts come from the same milieu — circles of women storytellers who belong to orders of widows. But Price dates Luke-Acts to the early or mid–second century and is skeptical that any information in it is historically accurate. See Robert McNair Price, "The Widow Traditions of Luke-Acts," Ph.D. diss., Drew University, 1993.

71. Ilan, *Jewish Women in Greco-Roman Palestine*, p. 149.

72. Ilan, *Jewish Women in Greco-Roman Palestine*, p. 151.

women's life expectancy in the ancient world was generally shorter than that of men because of the high risk of death related to childbirth, more men would have lost their wives than vice versa.[73] It is unrealistic to suppose that most widows and widowers did not remarry. We even have one example of polygamy in the early second century c.e. Personal papers of a Jewish woman named Babatha found in a cave near the Dead Sea show that after her first husband died, she married a man who already had a living wife and daughter.[74]

There is another possibility that could explain why the widows of Acts 6:1 may have been poor and why there may have been a substantial group of them. To prevent starvation, one of the few options available for poor unattached women was prostitution.[75] Jesus was known as a friend of these people (e.g., Matt. 21:31-32). Surely some of these women became believers in the Jerusalem community, but they may not have been deemed marriageable. If they did leave their occupation, they may not have been able to survive without the support of the community.

But the long and short of it is that *nobody* in that culture would have been able to survive without the support of a community or kin group. Bruce J. Malina has shown that in Mediterranean cultures, poverty is as much a result of a lack of social connections as a lack of material provisions.[76] What better way to incorporate previously unattached (and thus underpaid) widows into the community than to put them to work on the

73. Rodney Stark, "Antioch as the Social Situation for Matthew's Gospel," in *Social History of the Matthean Community: Cross-Disciplinary Approaches,* ed. David L. Balch (Minneapolis: Fortress Press, 1991), p. 195. In Rome at this time, the male/female ratio was estimated at 131 males per 100 females, and in Italy and North Africa at 140 to 100. However, part of this imbalance is accounted for by abortions and female infanticide, which Jews did not usually practice. See also Hartmut Stegemann, who thinks the reason so many Essene men were celibate is that their wives had died and they were forbidden to remarry. See *The Library at Qumran: On the Essenes, Qumran, John the Baptist, and Jesus* (Grand Rapids: Eerdmans, 1998), pp. 193-96.

74. Ross Kraemer, "Typical and Atypical Jewish Family Dynamics," in *Early Christian Families in Context: An Interdisciplinary Dialogue,* ed. David L. Balch and Carolyn Osiek (Grand Rapids: Eerdmans, 2003), pp. 130-56 (137-39).

75. Luise Schottroff, *Let the Oppressed Go Free: Feminist Perspectives on the New Testament,* trans. Annemarie S. Kidder (Louisville: Westminster/John Knox Press, 1993), pp. 151-52.

76. Bruce J. Malina, "Interpreting the Bible with Anthropology: The Case of the Poor and the Rich," *Listening: Journal of Religion and Culture* 21 (1986): 148-59.

daily communal meals that were the primary activity around which the physical, social, and spiritual life of the believers took place?

Conclusion

Only one verse in the early chapters of Acts ties women to communal meals. I have explained this through an analysis of how public and private space was owned, understood, and written about in ancient cultures. Women have always been associated with indoor space and with food preparation. Yet the more separate the gender roles are in a society, the more power women have within the roles assigned to them, since men do not or may not transgress women's spheres of activity. At the same time, New Testament texts portray Jesus transcending traditional masculine expectations, and leadership roles in the early church parallel women's roles in household organization.

The widows mentioned in Acts 6:1 no doubt represented a far more diverse group than our stereotypes of old, poor, lonely women sitting helplessly in little shacks waiting for "meals on wheels." What are possible outcomes for widows who are part of a fictive kin community centered on a risen Jesus who had included many women among his traveling companions and who himself did not conform to the male stereotypes of his day? The last section of this study will incorporate these insights into an exegetical analysis of the two passages in Acts that refer to communal meals in the Jerusalem church.

PART IV

Back to the Texts: Putting It All Together

The Open Door strives to create an alternative community — a community of discipleship that is anti-racist, feminist, and nonviolent. . . . With faith in Jesus' promise of resurrection and new life, and inspiration from Dr. King's vision of Beloved Community, we embark together on a transformation.

Many people who come to live at the Open Door bear scars of violence, racism, sexism, poverty, wealth, heterosexism, and addiction. . . . Building the Beloved Community takes time, energy, and love. . . . From a common pot, each resident shares in the resources of the community. All residents receive a small monthly stipend, not a salary. The Open Door relies entirely upon donations from individuals, church agencies, and small family foundations. Their generosity makes the Open Door's ministries possible — and is a sign of the new Beloved Community for which we hunger.

Open Door Community, Atlanta, Georgia

In Chapter Two we looked at the history of typical Western interpretations of the community of goods in Acts and noted how various cultural and political attitudes have often biased these interpretations. In Chapters Three and Four we saw how these attitudes, combined with various methods of reading, produced a range of opinions on the relationship of the communal meals in Acts 2 and 6 with the community of goods, with Jesus' meal practices, Essene meals, and the churchwide Christian agape meal with the Eucharist. In Chapters Five through Nine and Eleven, I used insights from the social sciences to reconstruct, as much as possible, the daily lives of ancient Palestinian people, especially those in Jerusalem, in order to provide a plausible sociological background for the commensality of Acts 2 and 6. In Chapter Ten I discussed the question of the historical Jesus at meals.

In the next two chapters I will combine textual analysis with previous social and historical material in order to arrive at a plausible historical scenario for daily commensality in the earliest Christian community in Jerusalem. Two preliminary assumptions and observations are in order.

From Redaction to Narrative to Reader-Response Criticism

When so much emphasis is placed on Luke's sources and how he has edited them, attention is drawn away from the overall narrative that Luke tells with great literary artistry. Even "composition criticism," which emphasizes Luke's overarching theology — soteriology, Christology, eschatology, or ecclesiology — can muffle what F. Scott Spencer calls "the symphony of multiple literary themes and patterns echoing throughout Luke's work."[1]

Maria Anicia Co has analyzed the three summaries of Acts 2:42-47, 4:32-37 (the community of goods) and 5:12-16 (the report of apostles' "signs and wonders") from a literary perspective. She demonstrates that the linguistic and thematic evidence support the view that the summaries are to be ascribed entirely to Luke himself and were not edited later.[2] I find her evidence convincing and will be treating Acts 2:42-47 as a whole, cohesive literary unit.[3] Thus the summaries provide the reader with material contributing to Luke's overall message.

This conclusion says nothing either way about the historicity of

1. F. Scott Spencer, "Acts and Modern Literary Approaches," in *The Book of Acts in Its Ancient Literary Setting*, ed. Bruce W. Winter and Andrew D. Clarke, vol. 1 of *The Book of Acts in Its First-Century Setting*, ed. Bruce W. Winter (Grand Rapids: Eerdmans, 1993), pp. 381-414 (386).

2. Maria Anicia Co, "The Major Summaries in Acts," *Ephemerides Theologicae Lovanienses* 68, no. 1 (April 1992): 49-85.

3. Against Jeremias, Cerfaux, Benoit, and others.

Luke's summary information.[4] But it does recognize our limitations in finding specific sources of tradition under the text, and it avoids complicating an interpretation with a hypothetical later redactor.

The more recent reader-response method may also provide a perspective on the communal meals and the community of goods in the early chapters of Acts. John Darr's use of this model for Luke-Acts is "attuned to the Greco-Roman literary culture of the first century."[5] Closely allied with narrative criticism, it pays attention to sequential reading or hearing, "the ways in which a first-time reader progressively 'builds' characters and events over the course of the narrative."[6]

Darr's interest is primarily in how readers or listeners would develop an attitude toward characters as they progress from the beginning to the end of the narrative. For example, scholars, especially those using redaction criticism, perceive Luke's attitude toward Pharisees as somewhat positive because of the way they are portrayed in Acts 5:33-39, 15:5, and 23:6-9. However, this is based on a reverse reading — seeing the Pharisees in Luke's Gospel through Acts, which a once-through reader would not be doing. Such readers would already form their negative opinions of the Pharisees through the sequential reading of the Gospel, and would bring that attitude into the book of Acts.[7]

I would suggest that a similar thing would have happened with first-century readers regarding the summaries of the community of goods and the communal meals. Commentators have argued that we never hear of these practices after the first few chapters of Acts; therefore, they must have been discontinued. But a reader-response model suggests otherwise. Luke certainly does not tell us of their demise, and Greco-Roman readers in their precapitalist agrarian society would be more likely than not to as-

---

4. As Co points out, "That some words or expressions may ultimately go back to Luke's sources is not a proof against his redactional creativity since the vocabulary of his sources may be reflected even in summaries he freely composed. Similarly, the affirmation of Lucan redaction does not constitute an immediate argument for or against tradition or historicity." See "The Major Summaries in Acts," p. 58.

5. John Darr, *On Character Building: The Reader and the Rhetoric of Characterization in Luke-Acts*, Literary Currents in Biblical Interpretation (Louisville: Westminster/John Knox Press, 1992), p. 14.

6. Spencer, "Acts and Modern Literary Approaches," p. 403.

7. Darr, "Observers Observed: The Pharisees and the Rhetoric of Perception," chap. 4 in *On Character Building*, pp. 85-126.

sume Christians continued to relate to each other within fictive kin group structures of reciprocity. If inclusive table fellowship was the way that Jesus communicated his theology and mission (as in Luke's Gospel), and if the Jesus-believers' communal meals carried on that theology and mission, this practice may be implied in many later texts that do not explicitly discuss meals and property-sharing.[8]

An Imminent Parousia?

Many commentators who argue for an actual community of goods in Jerusalem propose that such lavish and reckless generosity occurred because the believers expected Jesus to return at any moment. Their underlying assumption, then, is that the Parousia means the end of history, social life, and economics as we know it, so there is no reason to plan ahead financially.

There are two problems with this assumption. First, traditional Jewish understanding at that time held that the created world was good and the physical body was good. Consistent with this, those who believed in an afterlife would have held the notion of the bodily resurrection of the righteous in the New Age — which would take place on the same physical earth. I agree with N. T. Wright, who after extensive research concludes that "there is virtually no evidence that the Jews were expecting the end of the space-time universe." Instead, Jews believed in a theopolitical revolution, where "the present world order would come to an end — the world order in which pagans held power, and Jews, the covenant people of the creator god, did not."[9]

As Jews, the Jerusalem believers would have had similar eschatological expectations, except that their Messiah would already have come the first time. Continuity with his lifestyle — a common purse, radical shar-

---

8. A parallel pattern seems to be happening within Acts itself with regard to the Holy Spirit. The Holy Spirit dominates the first half of Acts, but Luke includes far fewer references to the Spirit in the second half. However, because the stage is set at the beginning for the Spirit's powerful activity, we as readers assume it continues, even though Luke does not verbally emphasize it as much.

9. N. T. Wright, *The New Testament and the People of God* (Minneapolis: Fortress Press, 1992), p. 333. Here Wright follows E. P. Sanders, especially in *Judaism: Practice and Belief, 63 B.C.E.-66 C.E.* (London: SCM; Philadelphia: Trinity Press International, 1992).

ing, and commensality — would surely have seemed like the most obvious way to live in expectation of his return. Pharisees, Essenes, and Zealots shared the same hope of a new age and a new world order. But there is no evidence that any of these groups succumbed to a mismanaged community of goods that resulted in economic ruin. In fact, the Essenes — perhaps the most eschatologically oriented of all — apparently practiced a successful community of goods for 150 to 200 years.

Second, Acts itself provides no evidence that communal sharing and eating together resulted from an expectation of the imminent Parousia. Though the two men in white (1:11) promised the disciples that Jesus would return *in the same way* he was taken up into heaven (as an event that implies the same space-time universe), Peter's sermon emphasizes the present exaltation of Jesus at God's right hand and the Holy Spirit poured out in the *here and now* (2:33). When Ananias lied to Peter about the amount of money he had received from the sale of his property, Peter did not remind him of the uselessness of saving wealth for himself because the end of the world was upon them; instead, Peter chided Ananias for lying to the Holy Spirit, who had called the *present* community into existence (5:3-4). There is no textual, historical, or theological evidence, therefore, that the expectation of Jesus' imminent return led to financial irresponsibility that drove the community into poverty.

Chapter Twelve

The Intentional Community:
An Exegesis of Acts 2:41-47

For the Greek text, I am using the United Bible Societies' *Greek New Testament,* fourth revised edition (1983). I will note the significant differences between the Alexandrian and Western versions (Codex Bezae) that affect my topic.[1] Below is a visual layout of Acts 2:41-47 in both Greek and English, which will highlight patterns and relationships in the text. I have lined up verbs and phrases that have parallel weight in the text. I include verse 41 because it provides the transition into the following summary account. (Exegesis of verse 43 is omitted because it does not directly deal with my topic.) The translation is my own. Because this exegesis draws on previous material in this book, chapter or page numbers for reference are included in the text.

1. The United Bible Societies' Committee was of the opinion that neither of the two forms always preserves the original text. Therefore, the members compared them point by point, and in each place where they diverged they selected the version that seemed most likely to be the original. There are seven variations for Acts 2:42-47 and seven for Acts 6:1-6 that are significant enough to be commented upon in Bruce M. Metzger's *A Textual Commentary of the Greek New Testament* (London and New York: United Bible Societies, 1975), but most of these do not affect my interpretation. Those that may have some bearing on my interpretation or emphasis I will note throughout this and the next chapter.

Acts 2:41
Οἱ μὲν οὖν   ἀποδεξάμενοι τὸν λόγον αὐτοῦ
                  ἐβαπτίσθησαν
           καὶ
                  προσετέθησαν   ψυχαὶ ὡσεὶ τρισχίλιαι.
                  ἐν τῇ ἡμέρᾳ ἐκείνῃ
2:42   ἦσαν δὲ προσκαρτεροῦντες
                         τῇ διδαχῇ τῶν ἀποστόλων
                                καὶ
                         τῇ κοινωνίᾳ,
                         τῇ κλάσει τοῦ ἄρτου
                                καὶ
                         ταῖς προσευχαῖς.
2:43
Ἐγίνετο δὲ πάσῃ ψυχῇ φόβος,
      τε
πολλά τέρατα καὶ σημεῖα   ἐγίνετο.
                  διὰ τῶν ἀποστόλων
2:44
δὲ
πάντες οἱ πιστεύοντες ἦσαν ἐπὶ τὸ αὐτὸ
                  καὶ
                  εἶχον ἅπαντα κοινὰ
2:45   καὶ
                  ἐπίπρασκον   τὰ κτήματα καὶ τὰς ὑπάρξεις
                  καὶ
                  διεμέριζον αὐτὰ
                         πᾶσιν καθότι ἄν τις χρείαν εἶχεν·
2:46
καθ' ἡμέραν τε προσκαρτεροῦντες
                  ὁμοθυμαδὸν ἐν τῷ ἱερῷ,
                  κλῶντές τε κατ' οἶκον ἄρτον,
                  μετελάμβανον τροφῆς
                         ἐν ἀγαλλιάσει
                         καὶ
                         ἀφελότητι καρδίας,
2:47   αἰνοῦντες τὸν θεὸν
                  καὶ

221

ἔχοντες χάριν
πρὸς ὅλον τὸν λαόν.
ὁ δὲ κύριος   προσετίθει τοὺς σῳζομένους
καθ' ἡμέραν
ἐπὶ τὸ αὐτό.

2:41

                    Welcoming his [Peter's] message,
they   were baptized,
                    and
about 3,000 persons were added
                    in that day.

2:42
They   were continuing faithfully
                    in the teachings of the apostles
                    and
                    in the communal sharing,
                    in the breaking of the bread
                    and
                    in the prayers.

2:43
Awe   was coming to every soul,
                    and
                    many wonders and signs were happening
                               through the apostles
2:44 and
all the believers were together/of one accord
                    and
                    were sharing everything
2:45   and
                    were selling possessions and property
                    and
                    were distributing them
                            to all according as any were having need.
2:46
Day by day, continuing faithfully
                    together in the temple,
                    breaking bread by households,

(they)	were sharing food in great gladness	
	and	
	simplicity of heart,	
2:47	praising God,	
	and	
	having favor with all the people.	
And day by day		
the Lord	was adding	those who were being saved
	to their number.	

Taking It Verse by Verse

Verse 41

Οἱ μὲν οὖν ἀποδεξάμενοι τὸν λόγον αὐτοῦ ἐβαπτίσθησαν καὶ προσετέθησαν ψυξαὶ ὡσεὶ τρισχίλιαι ἐν τῇ ἡμέρᾳ ἐκείνῃ. (Welcoming his [Peter's] message, they were baptized, and about 3,000 persons were added in that day.)

Peter's Pentecost sermon in Acts 2:14-36 was so persuasive that about 3,000 listeners were "stabbed to the heart" (κατενύγησαν), repented, and were baptized. Verse 41 is transitional; it is these new believers who devoted themselves to the various tasks mentioned in verse 42 that incorporated them into the core group of disciples. In the visual layout the two main verbs in verse 41 — "were baptized" (ἐβαπτίσθησαν) and "were added" (προσετέθησαν) — along with the participle "welcoming" (ἀποδεξάμενοι) which functions similarly, are parallel to "were" in verse 42.

There are several other reasons why verse 41 should be seen as a transition into the rest of the summary. First, μὲν οὖν is a favorite formula in Acts when a new unit is begun in continuity with what precedes it — for example, 1:6; 5:41; 8:4, 25; 9:31; 11:19; 13:4; 15:3, 30; 16:5; 23:31.[2] Second, verse 42 begins with an understood subject that must be supplied from verse 41.

---

2. Kirsopp Lake and Henry J. Cadbury, *The Acts of the Apostles: English Translation and Commentary*, vol. 4 of *The Beginnings of Christianity*, ed. F. J. Foakes Jackson and Kirsopp Lake (Grand Rapids: Baker, 1965), p. 27; C. K. Barrett, *The Acts of the Apostles*, International Critical Commentary, ed. J. A. Emerton, C. E. B. Cranfield, and G. N. Stanton (Edinburgh: T&T Clark, 1994, 2004), p. 159.

Third, the concept of being "added" in verse 47 echoes the being "added" in verse 41, thus forming an *inclusio*.[3]

ψυξαὶ ὡσεὶ τρισχίλιαι (about 3,000 persons). Luke uses the same qualifying term "about" in Luke 9:14 (men at the feeding of the 5,000) and Acts 1:15 (the original group of 120). The accuracy of this large number is not impossible; it depends on the size of Jerusalem and the number of pilgrims present for Pentecost (see pp. 110-13). Ψυξαί (literally, "souls") is used here in the sense of "persons." (See Acts 7:14; Gen. 46:27.) It would appear to be a term including women and children as well as men (that is, only men — ἄνδρες — are numbered at the feeding of the 5,000; Luke 9:14 and par.). This helps explain the large number involved, since family groups who became believers probably included children and other relatives in extended families,[4] and in some cases servants or slaves. Presumably the number also includes some of the "widows" of 6:1. Moreover, these were not people making a full conversion from a pagan religion to a totally new faith expressed in a radical moral and lifestyle change. These were Jews who already had a religious background with Messianic expectations.[5]

Verse 42

ἦσαν δὲ προσκαρτεροῦντες τῇ διδαχῇ τῶν ἀποστόλων καὶ τῇ κοινωνίᾳ, τῇ κλάσει τοῦ ἄρτου καὶ ταῖς προσευχαῖς. (They were continuing faithfully in the teachings of the apostles and in the communal sharing, in the breaking of the bread and in the prayers.)

According to Gerd Lüdemann's redactional analysis, the summary in this verse may go back to tradition (pp. 66-67). It is historically likely that the apostles played a leading role in the Jerusalem community (Gal. 1–2) and that the believers stayed together through their common meals. These meals were either a continuation of Jesus' table fellowship with his disciples or a regular repetition of his last meal with them, or an ordinary Jewish meal.[6] Further, κοινωνία *(koinonia)* is only used once in Luke-Acts, sig-

3. Gregory E. Sterling, "'Athletes of Virtue': An Analysis of the Summaries in Acts," *Journal of Biblical Literature* 113, no. 4 (1994): 680-81.

4. See the discussion on kin groups in Chapter Seven.

5. Barrett, *The Acts of the Apostles*, p. 159.

6. Gerd Lüdemann, *Early Christianity according to the Traditions in Acts: A Commentary*, trans. John Bowden (Minneapolis: Fortress Press, 1989), pp. 48-49.

nifying that it is likely pre-Lukan. Because some of these actions are repeated in verse 46, especially bread-breaking, it is possible that Luke first repeated information from the tradition and then elaborated on it himself.[7]

But Luke avoids simple repetition by first portraying just the new believers of verse 41 engaged in these activities. The visual layout makes clear that they are the implied subject of the verb ἦσαν προσκαρτεροῦντες ("were continuing faithfully"). Προσκαρτερέω is used here and in verse 46. Luke uses it six times in the first ten chapters of Acts (1:14; 2:42, 46; 6:4; 8:13; 10:7), although never elsewhere; it is used only four other times in the entire New Testament. Προσκαρτερέω connotes remaining faithfully attached to a person or applying oneself to a certain thing, devoting oneself to it tirelessly. According to Ceslas Spicq, "The idea is constant diligence, effort that never lets up, confident waiting for results."[8] If Luke is idealizing, the exaggeration may primarily lie in this verb.

But perhaps so much constant, daily spiritual activity only seems unrealistic when viewed through our modern lenses. In our world, daily times of corporate prayer, worship, and teaching can be practiced only by those who are intentionally counter-cultural. But ancient Mediterranean life was centered on religion; it pervaded every aspect, including work. Along with family relationships, it was their social life and "entertainment." Furthermore, among the Pharisees and Essenes of that time, daily and hourly attention was paid to keeping God's law in the most perfect way possible. In order for this new group to survive, their daily perseverance must have been similar. If they were transferring their primary loyalties away from their extended family of blood kin and to the gathering of fictive kin as the new Israel, performing the same activities day after day would be the most effective way to do so. One is reminded of the present practice among some Korean Christians of holding common prayer meetings at 5:30 every morning before people go to work as an effective means for church growth.

"In the teachings of the apostles and in the communal sharing, in the breaking of the bread and in the prayers." All four of these activities are nouns, direct objects to the verb, each preceded by the dative definite

7. Lüdemann, *Early Christianity according to the Traditions in Acts,* p. 48.
8. Ceslas Spicq, *Theological Lexicon of the New Testament* (Peabody, Mass.: Hendrickson, 1995), p. 191.

article. The most logical explanation is that they are parallel to each other, standing for four different (though related) activities to which the new members are devoted. This interpretation is not universally accepted, however. The Vulgate reading omits the comma and translates κοινωνία as the "communion of bread-breaking," the sacramental rite of the Eucharist performed by the apostles along with their teaching and prayers. In other words, the traditional Roman Catholic reading affirms an apostolic hierarchy (see pp. 49-50). This translation has been strongly refuted by M. Manzanera (pp. 53-54).[9]

κοινωνία: Although Luke uses this specific term only once, other κοινος (koinos) words occur below in 2:44 and 4:32. If this term is traditional, what kind of "common life" was experienced by the early believers?

In secular usage, κοινωνία referred usually to two or more people's joint sharing of a common property, such as that of a married couple, or of common ownership in equal parts, whether in legal or other terms.[10] Yet ever since John Calvin, many commentators have interpreted κοινωνία in Acts 2:42 primarily as fellowship, a *spirit* of communion and unity that existed among the early believers.[11] Friedrich Hauck puts it as baldly as anyone:

> In Acts 2:42 κοινωνία does not denote the concrete community or society of Christians. . . . Nor can it signify the community of goods. It is rather an abstract and spiritual term for the fellowship of brotherly concord established and expressed in the life of the community.[12]

9. M. Manzanera, "Koinonia en Hch 2,42. Notas sobre su interpretacion y origen historico-doctrinal," *Estudios Eclesiasticos* 52, no. 202 (July-September 1977): 307-29.

10. Friedrich Hauck, "κοινωνία," *Theological Dictionary of the New Testament*, ed. Gerhard Kittel and Gerhard Friedrich, trans. Geoffrey W. Bromiley, 10 vols. (Grand Rapids: Eerdmans, 1964-1976), 3:789-810 (790).

11. See Chapter Two and the discussions of John Calvin, Ernst Troeltsch, and the neo-orthodox theologians. See also Gerhard A. Krodel, *Acts*, Augsburg Commentary on the New Testament (Minneapolis: Augsburg Press, 1986), pp. 92-93; and French Arrington, *The Acts of the Apostles: Introduction and Commentary* (Peabody, Mass.: Hendrickson, 1988), p. 33. Both Hauck ("κοινωνία," *TDNT*) and Manzanera ("Koinonia en Hch 2,42") refer to H. Seesemann, *Der Begriff KOINONIA im N.T.*, BZNW 14 (Giessen, 1933), regarding his emphasis on an abstract spirit of community. Hauck leans heavily on Seesemann, while Manzanera is strongly critical, attributing Seesemann's attitude to the anticommunistic, dogmatic, kerygmatic theology of the times (p. 310).

12. Hauck, "κοινωνία," p. 809.

However, as Hackett had pointed out earlier, this interpretation destroys the parallelism of verse 42, since all the other nouns denote an *activity*, not a state of feeling.[13]

A second option is that κοινωνία refers to the collection and distribution of money for the needy in the community.[14] Joachim Jeremias and Bo Reicke see this happening in the context of a worship service (pp. 57-59; 62). Most interpreters disagree, but C. K. Barrett walks a middle path. In an ideal community (which is what Luke is portraying), the worship service is the particular focus of the community, so the major activities of the community's life will be brought into the public worship.[15] Barrett sees charity as an important meaning but not the sole meaning of κοινωνία, though he says that "Calvin is not far wrong with 'mutual association, alms, and other duties of brotherly fellowship.'"[16]

Kirsopp Lake and Henry Cadbury suggest four possible meanings of κοινωνία: (1) fellowship with the apostles, as in Galatians 2:9; (2) the communism of verse 44; (3) an activity equivalent to the "breaking of bread"; and (4) an activity almost equivalent to almsgiving.[17] They lean toward the first or the fourth, which they say is supported by the fact that the words are arranged in two groups; thus, "the teaching and fellowship of the apostles" and "the breaking of bread and the prayers."

Their first option is unconvincing. Luke is a careful enough writer that if he had meant that, he would have written "to the teaching and to the κοινωνία of the apostles" in that order so as not to be ambiguous. Even use of the definite article τῇ ("to the") suggests something distinctive. Moreover, Galatians 2:9 is not a comparable example, since the emphasis there is on the shared agreement, not necessarily that it is with certain apostles. Also, "the breaking of bread and the prayers" are still two distinct activities that are not parallel to "the teaching and the fellowship of the apostles." Finally, this interpretation does not go very far

13. Horatio B. Hackett, *A Commentary on the Acts of the Apostles* (Philadelphia: American Baptist Publication Society, 1882), p. 55.

14. Ernst Haenchen, *The Acts of the Apostles* (Philadelphia: Westminster, 1971), p. 191. Haenchen ties this term more closely to 6:1 than to the sharing of property in 2:45.

15. Barrett, *The Acts of the Apostles*, p. 162.

16. Barrett, *The Acts of the Apostles*, p. 164. See also John Calvin, *The Acts of the Apostles*, trans. John W. Fraser and W. J. G. McDonald (London & Edinburgh: Oliver & Boyd, 1965), p. 85.

17. Lake and Cadbury, *The Acts of the Apostles*, pp. 27-28.

in defining what τῇ κοινωνίᾳ means, other than an abstract spiritual communion.

It is far simpler to understand the activities of verse 42 in light of verses 43-47 (and 4:32, 34-35), where the four activities are further defined. Not only the new believers but everyone together is now participating in these activities. The κοινωνία of verse 42, then, is shown to be the ἅπαντα κοινά (everything common) of verse 45, where property and possessions are concretely shared so that all believers have their needs met.[18] The emphasis is nowhere implied to be charity for the poor, but sharing by and for everyone.

The κοινός term with this meaning is repeated at three places in Paul's letters, where he uses it to describe sharing financial resources through his collection for the Jerusalem Christians (Rom. 15:26; 2 Cor. 8:4; 9:13). He also urges sharing (κοινωνέω) in the needs of the saints in Rome (Rom. 12:13).[19] Though these texts are often interpreted to imply that κοινωνία in Pauline contexts is more closely related to almsgiving, Paul's idea is hardly that the middle class should provide handouts for the poor. Rather, the goal is mutuality. The Gentile churches now have a chance to repay their debt to the Jerusalem Christians, since it was from them that they first received the Gospel (e.g., Rom. 15:27; 2 Cor. 8:12-15). It is communal sharing practiced in one geographical location that is now adapted to a broader arena. Moreover, Paul's encouragement to the Roman Christians to "share in the needs of the saints" is not a general exhortation to contribute money to the poor but a particular charge on a specific occasion when Jewish Christians are returning to Rome after exile. They are returning refugees who need to be fully incorporated into the house churches that presently exist in Rome (Rom. 16:5, 10, 11, 14, 15).

18. Jacques Dupont, *The Salvation of the Gentiles: Studies in the Acts of the Apostles*, trans. John Keating (New York and Ramsay, N.J.: Paulist Press, 1979), pp. 86-87.

19. Κοινωνία always has a practical sense in the New Testament. In Philippians, Paul uses it twice in what may seem an abstract, spiritual sense (1:5; 3:10), but in 2:1-11 he says that this κοινωνία leads to looking out for the interests of others. The bread and wine of 1 Corinthians 10:16, with all the social implications of such eating, is a κοινωνία in the *body* of Christ (double meaning intended). The usage in Philemon 6 may sound abstract, but Paul has a very specific social reason for writing to Philemon: the treatment of his slave Onesimus. In Galatians 2:9-10, Paul and Barnabas were given the right hand of κοινωνία, and in the same breath told to remember the poor. 1 John 1:3, 6, 7 insist that vertical κοινωνία with the Father and the Son is intimately tied to κοινωνία with each other. The Pastor in 1 Timothy 6:18 calls on the rich to share with others (κοινωνικός).

Compelling evidence for the meaning of κοινωνία as sharing of communal property and for its historicity in the Jerusalem community has been presented by M. Manzanera and previously described in Chapter Three (pp. 53-54). This is a technical term for the sharing of property that goes back in Jewish history as far as Leviticus and that was historically realized among the Essenes, who used their biblical writings as a blueprint for their own community of goods.[20] Manzanera points to the same use of this term in both the Manual of Discipline (1QS 3:13-14, 26) and two Christian writings (*Epistle of Barnabas* 19:8 and *Didache* 4:8), where property-sharing is also in view. Both are taken from a now-lost document called "The Two Ways," which is Jewish in origin. Since Luke uses κοινωνία only in this context (Acts 2:41-47), he must be referring to a historical reality of property-sharing in the first Jerusalem community, which in turn was inspired by the biblical ideal currently practiced among the Essenes. Evidence in the writings of the *Epistle of Barnabas* and the *Didache* shows that this practice did not stop in Jerusalem but was known and encouraged elsewhere. (I will discuss further connections with the Essenes below.)

τῇ κλάσει τοῦ ἄρτου — "the breaking of the bread" is the third activity listed in 2:42. Five early Greek manuscripts have inserted καί ("and")[21] before the phrase, which further stresses κοινωνία as a separate object of the verb, as in the visual layout above. Either way, the activities present a chiasm, where the inner terms represent horizontal, social activities, while the outer two — learning from the apostles and praying — are more vertical. None is presented as superior or inferior to any other.

Breaking bread was an ancient custom in Palestine (see Jer. 16:7; pp. 176-77). At the beginning of any meal, ordinary or special, the head of the household would give thanks and then tear pieces from a loaf of bread and hand them to the others at the table.[22] It is clear from this and other New Testament texts that Christians used this description of an opening meal ritual to stand for the entire meal.

Commentators have been divided over whether or not to view the bread-breaking in Acts 2 as sacramental. On the one hand, because of its placement among other major "spiritual" activities in verse 42, it has been

---

20. Manzanera, "Koinonia en Hch 2,42," p. 91.
21. Barrett, *The Acts of the Apostles*, p. 164.
22. Johannes Behm, "κλάω," *Theological Dictionary of the New Testament*, 3:726-43 (728).

interpreted as the Eucharist (see the Vulgate translation for one extreme). However, another reference to breaking bread occurs in Acts 27:35 (Paul with pagan sailors), so other interpreters express uncertainty and suggest it refers to an ordinary meal.

To make such a marked separation, however, is to misunderstand the symbolism of meals in Palestinian culture (see Chapter Nine), where *every* meal eaten with others has religious and social significance. An ordinary meal eaten with people of different social positions is in reality *not* an ordinary meal. The bread-breaking ritual at the beginning signifies the unity and community of those who lay aside status for the sake of equal access to sustenance and a sense of belonging. Meals, along with κοινωνία in the form of generalized reciprocity (Chapter Seven, p. 127), would have been necessary in order to reconstitute the believers into a fictive kin group (p. 130) that could meet their social, economic, and spiritual needs. This network effectively prevented those who had had to forsake a previous kin group from falling into social isolation and economic destitution or even starvation.

Berndt Kollmann differentiates between the term τῇ κλάσει τοῦ ἄρτου (the breaking of bread) in verse 42 and κλῶντες ἄρτον (breaking bread) in verse 46, suggesting that the former refers to the Jewish ritual at the opening of a meal and the latter to the Christian meal itself.[23] Barrett suggests that τῇ κλάσει τοῦ ἄρτου is probably an old traditional Christian term that predates Paul. Luke uses it here in its appropriate ancient context.[24] But both may be hair-splitting. Textually, the only apparent reason for Luke's use of different phrases in 2:42 and 46 is sentence structure. In verse 42 it is more appropriate to use "the breaking of the bread" in noun form with three other nouns, whereas in verses 46-47 "breaking bread" is one of three participles (the other two being "praising God" and "having favor") that are parallel to the imperfect verb "taking food."

---

23. Berndt Kollmann, *Ursprung und Gestalten der frühchristlichen Mahlfeier*, GTA 43 (Göttingen: Vandenhoeck & Ruprecht, 1990), pp. 72-73.

24. Barrett, *The Acts of the Apostles*, p. 165. His way of expressing it is to say that Luke uses it here "to give his narrative the impression of antiquity."

Verse 44

πάντες οἱ πιστεύοντες ἦσαν ἐπὶ τὸ αὐτὸ καί (all the believers were "epi to auto" and . . .). The phrase *epi to auto* cannot be translated literally. The NRSV says, "All the believers were together . . ." Lake and Cadbury observe that *epi to auto* occurs three times in the Western text, "and in none of them is it really a natural phrase."[25] A few manuscripts omit ἦσαν ("were") and καὶ ("and"), a difficult reading that Barrett (against Bruce Metzger) thinks is almost certainly correct.[26] This reading implies more strongly the use of *epi to auto* as a technical term for a particular type of community. "Those who believed believed themselves, as it were, into a society," explains Barrett.[27]

Research on the Dead Sea Scrolls has shown that ἐπὶ τὸ αὐτο is similar to the term יחד (*yḥd*) in the Manual of Discipline from Qumran (1QS 1:11-12), where "all those who freely devote themselves to His truth shall bring all their knowledge, powers, and possessions into the Community [היחד] of God."[28] Ἐπὶ τὸ αὐτό is also used of the original group of 120 believers in 1:15 and 2:1, which also implies an organized community. Even though nothing specific is said about possessions in these earlier texts, the Gospel accounts portray the community around Jesus as sharing resources and a common purse.

εἶχον ἅπαντα κοινά (were sharing everything). This is clearly a Greek expression, about which much has been said in previous chapters. "Friends have everything in common" is the language of Greek idealism,[29]

25. Lake and Cadbury, *The Acts of the Apostles*, p. 29.
26. Barrett, *The Acts of the Apostles*, p. 167.
27. Barrett, *The Acts of the Apostles*, p. 167.
28. Geza Vermes, *The Dead Sea Scrolls in English*, 4th ed. (London and New York: Penguin Books, 1995), p. 70; Barrett, *The Acts of the Apostles*, p. 167; Brian Capper, "The Palestine Cultural Context of Earliest Christian Community of Goods," in *The Book of Acts in Its Palestinian Setting*, ed. Richard Bauckham, vol. 4 of *The Book of Acts in Its First-Century Setting*, ed. Bruce W. Winter (Grand Rapids: Eerdmans, 1995), p. 336; Richard Longenecker, "The Acts of the Apostles," in *John-Acts*, Expositor's Bible Commentary, ed. Frank E. Gaebelein (Grand Rapids: Zondervan, 1981), pp. 205-573 (308); Richard Bauckham, "The Early Jerusalem Church, Qumran, and the Essenes," in *The Dead Sea Scrolls as Background to Postbiblical Judaism and Early Christianity*, ed. James R. Davila (Leiden: E. J. Brill, 2003), pp. 63-89.
29. *Life of Pythagoras* VIII:10; *Nicomachean Ethics* VIII:11; 1159 B, 31; IX:8, 1168 B, 8; Euripides, *Andromache* 376f; Josephus, *War* II:122; *Ant.* XVIII:20; quoted in Dupont, *The Salvation of the Gentiles*, p. 90.

but it also implies that *only* friends who are of the same socio-economic class can share everything in common. Here the term "believers" is used instead of "friends," which has a radical cross-class implication.[30] The κοινά here harks back to the κοινωνία of verse 42.

It appears that the Greek phrase ἅπαντα κοινά was supplied (perhaps even in the tradition Luke received) to explain to Greek readers/listeners the expression ἐπὶ τὸ αὐτό, which did not have a technical meaning in Greek and would have sounded obscure.[31] In order to explain to the readers that this social grouping of Jerusalem believers also included a formal community of goods, Luke included the Greek phrase that carried the same meaning. Using such a literary device by no means implies that this community of goods was a figment of Luke's imagination any more than Josephus's use of Greek terminology to describe the Essenes for Greek-speaking readers implies that the Essenes were a figment of his imagination.[32] John Chrysostom also finds ἐπὶ τὸ αὐτό awkward, showing that it is not natural Greek, so he deduces that it must refer to the ἅπαντα κοινά in the next line.[33] Ironically, B. W. W. Dombrowski argues that the use of היחד at Qumran probably was an attempt to translate the Greek term τὸ κοινὸν into Hebrew![34]

The verb εἶχον ("were having") is iterative imperfect, as are all the verbs in verses 42-47 (except those that are present participles). In this tense, the writer views the action as being in progress in the past, and as having been repetitive.[35] The believers' sharing of possessions was a continuous act, in the sense of generalized reciprocity within the community (p. 127).

30. Alan C. Mitchell, "The Social Function of Friendship in Acts 2:44-47 and 4:32-37," *Journal of Biblical Literature* 111, no. 2 (Summer 1992): 255-72; Manzanera, "Koinonia en Hch 2,42," p. 310.

31. Capper, "The Palestinian Cultural Context of Earliest Christian Community of Goods," p. 336.

32. Dupont, *The Salvation of the Gentiles*, p. 89.

33. "And they speedily came, *epi to auto,* to the same thing in common, even to the imparting to all"; "Homily VII on Acts 2:44," in *The Homilies of St. John Chrysostom on the Acts of the Apostles,* vol. 2 of *The Nicene and Post-Nicene Fathers of the Christian Church,* ed. Philip Schaff, trans. J. Walker, J. Sheppard, and H. Browne (New York: Christian Literature Company, 1889; Grand Rapids: Eerdmans, 1956), pp. 46-47.

34. B. W. W. Dombrowski, "היחד in 1QS and τὸ κοινόν: An Instance of Early Greek and Jewish Synthesis," *Harvard Theological Review* 59 (1966): 293-307.

35. James A. Brooks and Carlton L. Winbery, *Syntax of New Testament Greek* (Lanham, Md.: University Press of America, 1975), p. 93.

Verse 45

καὶ ἐπίπρασκον τὰ κτήματα καὶ τὰς ὑπάρξεις καὶ διεμέριζον αὐτὰ πᾶσιν καθότι ἄν τις χρείαν εἶχεν· (and [they] were selling possessions and property and were distributing them to all according as any were having need). Κτήματα is usually interpreted as "land or fields" (Acts 5:1, 3, 8, where κτῆμα is equivalent to χωρίον, a piece of land; see also Sir. 28:24; 51:21; Hos. 2:15; Joel 1:11). Ὑπάρξεις (or ὑπαρχόντων) is understood to be personal possessions or resources, and is used frequently in the LXX (2 Chron. 35:7; Prov. 8:21; 13:11; 18:11; 19:14). Luke 8:3 provides a precedent for this text: the group of women who travel with Jesus and the male disciples who provide for them ἐκ τῶν ὑπαρχόντων αὐταῖς ("out of their own resources"). However, this phrase may also be translated "according to what was possible for them in their circumstances."[36] Luise Schottroff prefers this alternate translation because it shows women providing for others in concrete works of love like preparing them a meal rather than handing them coins.[37] Thus there is a precedent in Luke's narrative for previous ἄπαντα κοινὰ in a community around Jesus of both women and men disciples. (And, as I will explain later, διακονέω ["to serve"] of Luke 8:3 almost certainly refers to serving a meal.)

Codex B limits the sales to "as many as had property and possessions," implying that not everyone owned property.[38] In light of the fact that land would have been owned by only a few percent of the wealthiest people anywhere in the Greco-Roman world, this would have been obvious to Luke's audience without the qualification.

Recent translations of the Bible tend to translate αὐτά ("them") as meaning the money received from the sales (NRSV, NIV, TEV, New Jerusalem).[39] For example, the NRSV says, "They would sell their possessions

---

36. In *A Greek-English Lexicon* (Oxford: Clarendon, 1961), Henry George Liddell and Robert Scott translate the phrase this way: "under the circumstances, according to one's means" in the general and not specifically financial sense. This is noted in Luise Schottroff, *Lydia's Impatient Sisters: A Feminist Social History of Early Christianity*, trans. Barbara and Martin Rumscheidt (Louisville: Westminster/John Knox Press, 1993), p. 272, n. 121.

37. Schottroff, *Lydia's Impatient Sisters*, p. 210.

38. Luke T. Johnson, *The Acts of the Apostles*, ed. Daniel J. Harrington, vol. 5 of Sacra Pagina (Collegeville, Minn.: Michael Glazier, 1992), p. 59; Barrett, *The Acts of the Apostles*, p. 169.

39. Other versions preserve the ambiguity of the text. KJV = "sold their possessions

233

and goods and distribute *the proceeds* to all" (my italics). This looks like an interpretive attempt to make sense out of the whole sentence.[40] The visual layout, however, shows that ἐπίπρασκον is parallel to διεμέριζον, meaning that they sold some things and distributed others within the community, as any had need. Lake and Cadbury suggest "they sold the land [κτήματα] and divided up their other possessions [ὑπάρξεις]."[41] But the text does not say this, and it seems more likely that they sold whatever real estate or other possessions they had that would not be of use to the community, keeping what was useful and distributing it to or sharing it with any who needed it. Barnabas provides an example. Since he was from Cyprus, it is possible the field he owned was located there, which of course would not have been of any use to the Jerusalem community — thus his reason for selling it (see p. 133 for another possibility). Some land or fields would not have been large enough for production and were sold for this reason. As Luise Schottroff notes elsewhere (p. 141), "Had those fields been large enough that, by its own labor, the congregation could have grown sufficient food to make up for its lack, there would have been no reason to sell them."[42] Bradley Blue assumes that some homes were sold but enough others were retained for purposes of gathering; thus he concludes that the early church was financially solvent.[43] However, understanding something about the high density of population in ancient cities and the scarcity of adequate housing, I am skeptical that any homes would have been sold, unless very small ones were sold to purchase ones where larger groups of people could live and gather together. The same could be true of fields: some very small ones could have been sold to buy a larger field to cultivate.

The final clause of v. 45 — καθότι ἄν τις χρείαν εἶχεν (according as any were having need) — further explains the various activities of distri-

---

and goods and divided them among all"; RSV = "sold their possessions and goods and distributed them to all"; NEB = "sell their property and possessions and make a general distribution"; NAB = "would sell their property and goods, dividing everything on the basis of each one's need."

40. See also Barrett, *The Acts of the Apostles*, p. 169; I. H. Marshall, *The Acts of the Apostles* (Grand Rapids: Eerdmans, 1980), p. 84.

41. Lake and Cadbury, *The Acts of the Apostles*, p. 29.

42. Schottroff, *Lydia's Impatient Sisters*, p. 97.

43. Bradley Blue, "Acts and the House Church," in *The Book of Acts in Its Graeco-Roman Setting*, ed. David W. J. Gill and Conrad Gempf, vol. 2 of *The Book of Acts in Its First-Century Setting*, ed. Bruce W. Winter (Grand Rapids: Eerdmans, 1994), p. 137.

bution. In kin groups now characterized by belief in Jesus as Messiah rather than entirely by blood relation, generalized reciprocity would have been practiced. That much can be assumed by knowledge of ancient Mediterranean and Palestinian sociological structures of family life (Chapter Seven, pp. 126-31). Perhaps this happened in smaller groups, among those who lived in the same neighborhood or around the same courtyard, or who spoke the same language (see 6:1), along with the out-of-town believers or formerly homeless persons who had moved in with them. But this more informal procedure may just as well have quickly become organized and systematized. The original group would also have been able to adapt and demonstrate their experience of having lived in the Jesus community. And everyone would have known about the Essene patterns of communal sharing, which could also be adapted for their new situation (Chapter Eight, pp. 150-58).[44]

Although Barrett thinks it quite reasonable to conclude that the Christians must have followed a plan of property-sharing similar to that of the Essenes, he wonders *why* they would have done so. First, he suggests the traditional reason: because of their eschatological beliefs. "If the world was to end shortly, an immediate pooling and common charitable use of all resources might well seem prudent. There was no need to take thought for the morrow, since there would not be one."[45] Since Luke himself did not hold this view (here Barrett is influenced by Hans Conzelmann and the notion that Luke is coming to terms with a delayed eschatology), perhaps that is why he did not give any reasons for the community of goods. On the other hand, perhaps the Christians were under pressure from the unbelieving Jewish authorities who had cut off Jewish charities from the poor, and a common life was the only viable one.[46]

But, as I've noted several times before, there were no organized Jewish charities at this time,[47] and even if there had been, they would not have taken care of the influx of Galileans and others from out of town who stayed on. Nor would any charities have taken care of all the poor people,

---

44. 1QS 7:5-8 assumes some retention of personal property when it speaks of members paying fines within the community and carrying on business dealings with one another and with the community itself. See Longenecker, "The Acts of the Apostles," pp. 311-12.

45. Barrett, *The Acts of the Apostles*, p. 168.

46. Barrett, *The Acts of the Apostles*, p. 168.

47. David Seccombe, "Was There Organized Charity in Jerusalem before the Christians?" *Journal of Theological Studies*, new series 29 (1978): 140-43.

since ninety percent of them already lived at subsistence level. In his gospel, Luke had already demonstrated how Jesus reconstituted the family on the grounds of doing the will of God rather than by blood kinship (Luke 8:19-21 and par.; 12:51-53 and par.; also many narrative examples of traveling and eating with disciples). The need for socio-economic sharing among this fictive kin group (Chapter Seven, pp. 125-45) was obvious enough to Luke's readers that he didn't have to explain why the common life developed after Jesus' ascension.

Verses 46-47a

καθ' ἡμέραν τε προσκαρτεροῦντες ὁμοθυμαδὸν ἐν τῷ ἱερῷ, κλῶντές τε κατ' οἶκον ἄρτον, μετελάμβανον τροφῆς ἐν ἀγαλλιάσει καὶ ἀφελότητι καρδίας αἰνοῦντες τὸν θεὸν καὶ ἔχοντες χάριν πρὸς ὅλον τὸν λαόν. (Day by day, continuing faithfully together in the temple, breaking bread by households, [they] were sharing food in great gladness and simplicity of heart, praising God, and having favor with all the people.)

This sentence describes five actions of the believers, but only one — μετελάμβανον (taking/sharing) — is the main finite verb. It is again in the iterative imperfect, showing that the believers kept on taking/sharing their food, while at the same time they were together in the Temple, breaking bread at home, praising God, and having favor with all the people.

It is not immediately clear how this sentence is structured. Luke clearly intends for καθ' ἡμέραν ("day by day") to refer to all the following activities, since it is placed prominently at the beginning of the sentence, along with προσκαρτεροῦντες ("being together/of one accord"). In other words, the believers were every day continuing faithfully in what follows. But ὁμοθυμαδόν ("together") refers only to ἐν τῷ ἱερῷ (in the Temple). Ὁμοθυμαδόν often occurs with statements about number (such as πάντες — "all") and place of participation.[48] Luke uses it nine times in Acts (1:14; 4:24; 5:12; 7:57; 8:6; 12:20; 15:25; 18:12; 19:29), and it is used only one other time in the New Testament (Rom. 15:6). Each time in Acts it is used to describe a group of people being together in one place who agree internally

---

48. Hans W. Heidland, "ὁμοθυμαδόν," *Theological Dictionary of the New Testament*, 5:185.

about a particular issue and are engaged in an externally similar action.[49] This does not mean the group necessarily has the same disposition or personal feeling; rather, it means that they work together at a common action.[50] In this verse, ὁμοθυμαδόν, to be consistent with its usage in the rest of Acts, refers only to the believers being together *in the Temple*, because the Temple is the only place large enough for all the believers to be together.[51] This provides a contrast to the next activity, breaking bread, which occurs in various homes.

κατ' οἶκον ("relating to house or home"). Older commentaries have questioned whether the emphasis is on one home where the believers eat,[52] or "now in one house, now in another," or in private homes in contrast to the public Temple worship,[53] or whether it means "by household," where the group of people in one household operate as a unit.[54] The visual layout and the above discussion make it clear that κατ' οἶκον ("at home") must be seen as a contrast to ὁμοθυμαδόν ("together") in the Temple. Luke does have a fondness for the distributive use of the preposition κατὰ and uses it in 8:3, which means that Saul hounded out the Christians from one house

49. Heidland, "ὁμοθυμαδόν," 5:185. Lake and Cadbury assert that this term is appropriate only to a collected group (Lake and Cadbury, *The Acts of the Apostles*, p. 29); against Luke Johnson, who mentions only unanimity of spirit (*The Acts of the Apostles*, p. 59).

50. Heidland here reminds the reader of "the many personal and material tensions in the first congregations," but they are unanimous about praising one Lord ("ὁμοθυμαδόν," 5:186). Both Heidland and Walter Bauer (*A Greek-English Lexicon of the New Testament and Other Early Christian Literature*, 2d ed. [Chicago: University of Chicago Press, 1979], p. 566) emphasize the unanimity over against the physical togetherness in one place, but the examples in Acts demonstrate each time that the group under consideration was all in one place as well.

51. The use of ἱερόν here must mean the entire Temple precincts rather than the Temple proper, since the group as a whole would not have been permitted to enter the latter (Gottlob Schrenk, "ἱερόν," *Theological Dictionary of the New Testament*, 3:235). They most likely met in Solomon's Portico (see 3:11).

52. H. A. W. Meyer, *Handbook to the Acts of the Apostles*, 2d ed., trans. Paton J. Gloag (New York: Funk & Wagnalls, 1889), p. 71; Henry Alford, *The Acts of the Apostles, Romans, Corinthians*, vol. 2 of *The Greek Testament* (Boston and New York: Lee & Shepard, 1872), p. 29; Johannes Weiss, *Earliest Christianity: A History of the Period A.D. 30-150*, trans. Frederick C. Grant (Gloucester, Mass.: Peter Smith, 1970), p. 56, on the basis of 1:13.

53. Richard John Knowling, *The Acts of the Apostles*, Expositor's Greek Testament (Edinburgh: n.p., 1900; Grand Rapids: Eerdmans, 1951), p. 97.

54. Lake and Cadbury, *The Acts of the Apostles*, p. 29; F. F. Bruce, *The Acts of the Apostles* (Grand Rapids: Eerdmans, 1990), p. 160.

to the next.[55] However, the use of the plural κατὰ τοὺς οἴκους ("house after house," NRSV) and the context make clear that Saul's action was consecutive, whereas the singular suggests a quite different nuance.[56] The possibility of the entire congregation eating in one place cannot be considered, since the size of the group and the small homes of ordinary citizens preclude this, even if the much smaller original group did meet in one large upper room. In light of what we know about first-century Palestine, the most accurate term for where bread-breaking took place is "by household." The emphasis is on the group of people who live together, not on the house itself. This could mean several families who share the same courtyard and have invited previously homeless or out-of-town believers to live with them (Chapter Six, pp. 118, 124).

Evidence that the Christian movement began by believers gathering in the private sphere of the household is undisputed (Rom. 16:5; 1 Cor. 16:19; Col. 4:15; Phil. 4:22; 2 Tim. 4:19; cf. 1 Cor. 1:11 and 16:15). In explaining the eventual triumph of Christianity in the Mediterranean world, Robin Lane Fox has proposed that "it was through the household and the house church that Christianity . . . first put down its roots."[57] This phenomenon has been conceptualized as wealthy patrons opening large homes to possibly 30 or 40 members of one "house church"[58] or shop space on the ground floor of a tenement building that might accommodate 10 or 20 believers.[59] Robert Jewett's work in Romans and 1 and 2 Thessalonians has led him to hypothesize that there were church groups in tiny tenement rooms functioning without a patron.[60]

Bradley Blue has suggested that a precedent for the Jerusalem believers meeting in homes can be found in contemporary Judaism. At that time most synagogues were single rooms in houses:

55. Lake and Cadbury, *The Acts of the Apostles*, p. 29.

56. But Codex Bezae does use κατ' οἴκους in 2:46.

57. Robin Lane Fox, *Pagans and Christians* (New York: Knopf, 1989), p. 89. It was this household structure that eventually "grew to undermine the old civic values and the very shape of the pagan city."

58. Jerome Murphy-O'Connor, *St. Paul's Corinth: Texts and Archaeology* (Wilmington, Del.: Michael Glazier, 1983), p. 156. See also Robert Banks, *Paul's Idea of Community: The Early House Churches in Their Historical Setting* (Grand Rapids: Eerdmans, 1980), pp. 35-36.

59. Jerome Murphy-O-Connor, "Prisca and Aquila," *Bible Review* 8 (December 1992): 49-50.

60. Robert Jewett, *Paul, the Apostle to America: Cultural Trends and Pauline Scholarship* (Louisville: Westminster/John Knox Press, 1994), pp. 77-80.

Because the majority of the early believers were converts from Judaism . . . it would not be inconsistent to propose that some of the Jewish believers had formerly opened their houses (or parts thereof) to the synagogue community. In turn, having espoused the Christian faith, it would have been natural for these patrons to use the same facilities as a gathering place for the Christian community.[61]

In addition, Palestinian homes were often enlarged by adding an extra room on the roof or in the courtyard (Chapter Six, p. 118). Blue also notes that early Christians met in homes not only because there was nowhere else to meet, but also because the house setting contained the kitchen and dining facilities for the common meal on which worship centered.[62] In light of research on the house church structure of early Christianity, Luke's descriptions of the Jerusalem believers meeting in homes for daily worship and commensality is entirely plausible.

Much debate has centered on the relationship of κλῶντές . . . ἄρτον ("breaking bread") and μετελάμβανον τροφῆς ("sharing/taking food"). If in verse 42 "the breaking of the bread" stood for the entire meal, here it seems more likely that it refers to the ritual of bread-breaking at the beginning of any kind of meal, while "taking food" or "sharing food" would be the general commensality that was happening in the community. This may be Luke's way of further explicating his terse statement "the breaking of the bread" in verse 42.

Μεταλάμβανω is used seven times in the New Testament, four times in Acts alone. It covers meanings from "receiving one's share in something" to "taking one's share."[63] The only other place in the New Testament where it is associated with a meal is Acts 27:33-38. Here Paul the prisoner is aboard a sinking ship with crew and passengers who are almost entirely pagan. They have not eaten for two weeks because of the trauma of the fierce Mediterranean storm. Paul urges them to take food — μετελαβεῖν τροφῆς (vv. 33-34) — after which he takes bread, gives thanks to God, breaks it (κλάσας), and eats. Many interpreters have been hesitant to see any "sacramental" meanings in either bread-breaking or sharing food in Acts 2:46, primarily because of this later Acts text where

---

61. Blue, "Acts and the House Church," p. 136.
62. Blue, "Acts and the House Church," p. 121.
63. Bauer, *A Greek-English Lexicon of the New Testament and Other Early Christian Literature*, p. 511.

the act cannot be sacramental in the traditional sense, since the ship's passengers are not believers.

However, though the two accounts differ with relation to the *vertical* meaning of bread-breaking, there are significant similarities on the *horizontal* level. In Acts 2, a common belief in Jesus as Messiah has brought together around a common table people who for social or religious reasons would never otherwise eat together. Their commensality creates their unity and common hope of salvation. They do not eat by themselves. Together they participate in the opening ritual of breaking bread, and they receive food from or share food with each other. Likewise, the ship's passengers in Acts 27, who come from various social strata (including prisoners), have become one group whose lives are saved or lost together. They experience social reversal as one who has been in chains among them takes the lead in hosting a meal and urging commensality. By eating together they ensure that not a single one of them will be lost from the group of 276.

Though breaking bread in this verse may refer specifically to the ritual at the beginning of a meal, Luke is using a term that later (probably by his day) stood for the entire agape meal shared by groups of believers throughout the Mediterranean region. Berndt Kollmann notes that Acts 20:7, Ignatius's letter to the Ephesians 20:2, and *Didache* 14:1 all refer to "breaking bread," by which is meant an entire meal, or agape.[64] Does this mean that Luke was simply taking a practice from his time period and anachronistically reading it back into the thirties in Jerusalem? Kollmann says no. The term ἐν ἀγαλλιάσει ("with great gladness; exultation") is a reference to the tradition of eating joyful meals with Jesus. As long as the Bridegroom is present with them, now resurrected and glorified, they can rejoice.[65] These meals, then, continue the former practice of Jesus and are thus historical. Here Luke does not present the community in an upper-class *symposium* setting, but describes it in the simple language of "breaking bread" and "taking food."[66]

And they continue every day, καθ᾽ ἡμέραν, which leads the sentence at the beginning of verse 46. In that cultural situation it would only make sense to have daily meals together to ensure that everyone got fed. This is

---

64. Kollmann, *Ursprung und Gestalten der frühchristlichen Mahlfeier*, pp. 71-75.

65. Kollmann, *Ursprung und Gestalten der frühchristlichen Mahlfeier*, pp. 71-75.

66. Dennis Smith says that because Luke's Gospel presents Jesus in such *symposia* settings, the meals must be only literary creations. See *From Symposium to Eucharist: The Banquet in the Early Christian World* (Minneapolis: Fortress Press, 2003), ch. 4, n. 62.

confirmed by the work of Robert Jewett on the Thessalonian texts and the command "The one who does not work shall not eat," which reflects a daily meal practice twenty years later in a Macedonian city (Chapter Three, pp. 73-75).

Textual exegesis, then, concurs with sociological and historical analysis. As discussed in Chapters Nine and Ten, commensality symbolizes unity, solidarity, and equality among those who partake, especially in a socially stratified society like ancient Mediterranean Palestine. The poor do not remain outcast street beggars who accept small handouts from those somewhat better off. Daily commensality is also the most economical approach in a subsistence economy among a group who are reconstituted as fictive kin. Organizing daily suppers in homes where everyone has a place at a table saves money. It is easier to share a bowl of porridge from a large pot than to set aside scarce coins to give away.

The congregation also ate their food with ἀφελότητι καρδίας ("simplicity of heart"; NRSV: "generous hearts"). Ἀφελότης occurs nowhere else in the New Testament or the Septuagint, and is rare otherwise. Bo Reicke argues that it is equivalent to ἁπλότης, which means "simplicity."[67] Ernst Haenchen suggests that Luke emphasizes this because by his time these Christian communal meals were already under grave suspicion.[68] But Reicke thinks this verse may be connected with Acts 2:13-15, where Peter confirms that the believers are not drunk: "their rejoicing is of a harmless kind."[69] As discussed in the last chapter, communal meals in the Greco-Roman world could often descend into raucous drinking bouts, which could have been an issue both in Luke's day and long before. So "simplicity of heart" was needed to offset the "great gladness" of the previous phrase, so that Luke's readers would not get the wrong impression of these meals.

The last two phrases of the sentence in verses 46-47a — "praising God, and having favor with all the people" — compare with the previous two. With great joy the people praise God at their meals, but because of their simplicity of heart they do not incur the displeasure of other people. Ancient cities like Jerusalem were very crowded, with streets no wider than

---

67. Bo Reicke, *Diakonie, Festfreude und Zelos in Verbindung mit der Altchristlichen Agapenfeier*, Uppsala Universitets Årsskrift 5 (Uppsala: A.-B. Lundequistska Bokhandeln, 1951), p. 204; Reicke uses Vettius Valens 153:30; 240:15 and Cicero (*Ad Atticum* 1:18.1). The Vulgate concurs by using *simplicitas*.

68. Haenchen, *The Acts of the Apostles*, p. 193.

69. Reicke, *Diakonie*, p. 204; also mentioned in Barrett, *The Acts of the Apostles*, p. 171.

15 feet and houses packed wall to wall, and even in some cases joining together over the streets.[70] Many neighbors would have overheard activity around a communal meal in a small room or an open courtyard that was characterized by great joy (singing? laughter?). In the midst of the urban chaos and misery that characterized every ancient Mediterranean city,[71] such a gathering must have sounded inviting indeed.

Verse 47b

ὁ δὲ κύριος προσετίθει τοὺς σῳζομένους καθ' ἡμέραν ἐπὶ τὸ αὐτό (And day by day the Lord was adding those who were being saved to their number). Luke speaks of community growth on the heels of his description of the communal meals. Just as the believers ate together every day, so the Lord was adding those who were being saved "every day." What was an attraction as much as anything else were these meals that were watched and overheard by hungry neighbors. Like Jesus' meals, the suppers themselves were proclamations that God's kingdom was at hand. Like a good king, the risen Jesus was feeding his people.

The inclusion of ἐπὶ τὸ αὐτό *(epi to auto)* at the end of this sentence seems very awkward, both in Greek and in attempts to translate it into English. The Western text tried to remedy the situation by adding ἐν τῇ ἐκκλησίᾳ ("in the church") after *epi to auto,* and the Antiochian improved this by omitting ἐν so that the text read "added to the church," and by moving *epi to auto* to the beginning of the next sentence.[72] This shows how difficult the earliest Greek readers found the sentence. Henry Cadbury noted that in the papyri *epi to auto* was used in financial statements to mean "in total." In that case a number should follow, as it does in 1:15.

Other exegetes have pointed to an Aramaic background for the term. Lake and Cadbury refer to Torrey, who believed the early chapters of Acts were translated from an Aramaic source. Torrey thought *epi to auto* repre-

---

70. Most of the streets of the capital city of Rome were eight feet wide or less, so Jerusalem's were likely even narrower. See John E. Stambaugh, *The Ancient Roman City* (Baltimore: Johns Hopkins University Press, 1988), pp. 188-89; and Jerome Carcopino, *Daily Life in Ancient Rome* (New Haven: Yale University Press, 1940), p. 46.

71. Rodney Stark, *The Rise of Christianity: A Sociologist Reconsiders History* (Princeton: Princeton University Press, 1996), pp. 147-62.

72. Lake and Cadbury, *The Acts of the Apostles*, p. 30.

sented an Aramaic word that in Judean Aramaic could only mean "greatly" when it came at the end of a sentence.[73]

However, M. Wilcox showed that προσετίθει . . . ἐπὶ τὸ αὐτὸ was an idiom meaning "to add together," reflecting the Qumran idiom לְיַחַד לִהְיוֹת, which meant the process of expansion of the community.[74] The possibility of Semitic source material behind this summary strongly suggests its historicity.

Several texts in the Manual of Discipline (1QS) and the Damascus Document (CD) from Qumran describe the process of adding persons to an Essene community:

Every man, born of Israel, who freely pledges himself to join the Council of the Community shall be examined by the Guardian at the head of the Congregation concerning his understanding and his deeds. (1QS 6:14)

No man . . . who deliberately, on any point whatever, turns aside from all that is commanded, shall touch the pure Meal of the men of holiness or know anything of their counsel until his deeds are purified from all injustice and he walks in perfection of way. And then, according to the judgment of the Congregation, he shall be admitted to the Council and shall be inscribed in his rank. This rule shall apply to whoever enters the Community. (1 QS 8:19)

[The Guardian of the Camp] shall examine every man entering his Congregation with regard to his deeds, understanding, strength, ability and possessions, and shall inscribe him in his place according to his rank in the lot of L[ight]. (CD 13:11)[75]

How exactly were people being added to the number of Christian disciples? How did the process of entering the community in Jerusalem compare with rigorous Essene examination? Luke says nothing specific in this text, except that women were equally a part of the group. But he does

73. Lake and Cadbury, *The Acts of the Apostles*, p. 30.

74. M. Wilcox, *The Semitisms of Acts* (Oxford, 1965), pp. 93-100; noted in Capper, "The Palestinian Cultural Context of Earliest Christian Community of Goods," p. 336, n. 41, and approved by Matthew Black in *An Aramaic Approach to the Gospels and Acts*, 3rd ed. (Oxford: Oxford University Press, 1967), p. 10.

75. Vermes, *The Dead Sea Scrolls in English*, pp. 78, 81, 112.

repeat Jesus' statement in Mark 8:34-38 about self-denial and taking up one's cross (Luke 9:23-27). In a situation of daily commensality and pooled resources, organization and rigorous ethical standards would have had to be in force. One reason the story of Ananias and Sapphira was passed down in the tradition was surely to remind everyone of how high the standards of loyalty and truth-telling were in this fictive kin group brought into being by the Holy Spirit.

Conclusion

We know historically that one key place the church began was Jerusalem and that apostles had administrative authority there for some period of time. We know that the church grew and spread out from there. How did it grow? What attracted people to the community? In a crowded city where most people lived marginal and often desperate lives, many cut off from previous kin-groups back on the land,[76] Luke has truthfully portrayed what was probably one of the great attractions of the new movement: the inclusive and joyful daily communal meals held in the next courtyard.

In 1933 Henry Cadbury's conclusion about the summaries in Acts was that they were written later than the narrative material and were generalized from this material.[77] Luke had a natural tendency to exaggerate the growth and influence of Christianity, and the summaries served as connective tissue to draw together his disparate traditions into one continuous narrative. Thus their historical value is open to question. On the other hand, Cadbury cautioned, we don't know how much data Luke and his sources knew beyond the Acts narratives. Some items hint that Luke knew more details than he offered.[78] Unlike Dibelius, Haenchen, and Conzelmann, Cadbury preferred to leave the question open.

However, in light of what can now be known — about contemporary Essene property-sharing, about ancient Mediterranean kinship groupings

---

76. See Chapter Five. Most social mobility was downward, as younger sons got pushed off the land and drifted to the cities in search of work. This often left them bereft of necessary group solidarity and support.

77. Kirsopp Lake and Henry J. Cadbury, *Additional Notes to the Commentary*, vol. 5 in *The Beginnings of Christianity*, ed. F. J. Foakes Jackson and Kirsopp Lake (Grand Rapids: Baker, 1965), pp. 392-401.

78. Lake and Cadbury, *Additional Notes to the Commentary*, p. 402.

and generalized reciprocity, about house- and tenement-church structures, and about unfair and exploitative economic practices which drove so many into poverty and against which Jesus certainly protested — it seems woefully inadequate to think that Luke drew his overall picture of a community of goods from one brief positive account of Barnabas and one negative story about Ananias and Sapphira.

The point can be made even more strongly about daily commensality in the early Jerusalem community, since there is no mention of meals in any narrative accounts until we come to widows in 6:1-6. (Even then, scholars argue over whether the text refers to food tables at all.) Here no reference is made to meals eaten "by household" or with "great gladness." So where does Luke get his description of commensality? Either he was generalizing from practices in his own community — in which case daily commensality was probably a tradition that went back to Jesus' lifetime and continued as a widespread practice for many years (see Reicke in Chapter Three, pp. 67-70) — or he had access to traditions about early Jerusalem practices — which also would have derived from Jesus, and perhaps from Essene structures as well. Considering the status of research at this point, the burden of proof should rest on those who maintain that Luke's summary is merely literary, symbolic, and probably nonhistorical.

Chapter Thirteen

The Widows' Complaint:
An Exegesis of Acts 5:42–6:1-6

> *I start out with the beautiful, heroic idea of handling the two jobs at once, and for two days I almost do it: working the breakfast/lunch shift at Jerry's from 8:00 till 2:00, arriving at the Hearthside a few minutes late, at 2:10, and attempting to hold out until 10:00. . . . There is a problem, though. When, during the 3:00-4:00 dead time, I finally sit down to wrap silver, my flesh seems to bond to the seat. I try to refuel with a cup of purloined clam chowder . . . but Stu catches me and hisses "No eating!" although there's not a customer around to be offended by the sight of food making contact with a server's lips.*

> Barbara Ehrenreich,
> *Nickel and Dimed: On (Not) Getting by in America*

In the public sphere of the Temple precincts, the apostles have shown great power in healing and preaching but have also endured arrest, interrogation, and flogging for the sake of Jesus' name (Acts 3–5). Apart from the shocking deaths of Ananias and Sapphira, the private household sphere has provided comfort, joy, and single-mindedness. But now — months or years later — cracks begin to show in the harmony of the earliest community as Hellenists complain that their widows are being overlooked in some way. How can the brief account in Acts 6:1-6 open a window into the table practices and role of women in this intentional community?[1]

Unlike the previous text, Acts 6:1-6 is not a summary. It recounts a pivotal event in the life of the Jerusalem community. Besides concluding Luke's narrative of the early years of the Jerusalem church, it provides a transition useful for introducing Stephen and the Hellenists and moving the witnesses outward beyond Jerusalem. According to Luke, the problem provoking the event arises from the διακονίᾳ τῇ καθημερινῇ, the daily (table?) service.

Why does Luke include this particular episode? Kirsopp Lake and Henry Cadbury were certain that it "is clearly intended by the writer to explain why the communistic experiment broke down. There was dissension among the recipients of help, and the officers appointed to administer the dole were either killed or driven out of Jerusalem."[2] But nearly all other twentieth-century commentators refer to this pericope as the selection, election, installation, or appointing of "the Seven," thus already skewing their exegesis toward the male Hellenists whose actions will affect the future church, and away from the conflict that underlies the choice of these men.[3] Though Adolf Harnack thought that here the narrative finally entered historical ground,[4] redaction critics like Ernst Haenchen suspect the widows' complaint only covers up a deeper rift between Hebrews and Hellenists, or, like Hans Conzelmann, claim that the conflict was artificially constructed.[5]

---

1. As in the previous chapter, I use the United Bible Societies' *Greek New Testament*, 4th rev. ed. (1983).

2. Kirsopp Lake and Henry J. Cadbury, *The Acts of the Apostles: English Translation and Commentary*, vol. 4 of *The Beginnings of Christianity*, ed. F. J. Foakes Jackson and Kirsopp Lake (Grand Rapids: Baker, 1965), p. 63.

3. For example, Hans Conzelmann, *Acts of the Apostles* (Philadelphia: Fortress Press, 1987), p. 44; Ernst Haenchen, *The Acts of the Apostles: A Commentary* (Philadelphia: Westminster Press, 1971); F. F. Bruce, *The Acts of the Apostles* (Grand Rapids: Eerdmans, 1956, 1990); Gerhard Krodel, *Acts*, Augsburg Commentary on the New Testament (Minneapolis: Augsburg Press, 1986); I. H. Marshall, *Acts of the Apostles*, Tyndale New Testament Commentaries (Grand Rapids: Eerdmans, 1980); Luke Johnson, *The Acts of the Apostles*, Sacra Pagina 5 (Collegeville, Minn.: Michael Glazier, 1992); John B. Polhill, *Acts*, New American Commentary 26 (Nashville: Broadman Press, 1992).

4. Adolf Harnack, *Expositor* 5, 3rd series, p. 324; referred to in Richard John Knowling, *The Acts of the Apostles*, Expositor's Greek Testament, ed. W. Robertson Nicoll (Edinburgh: n.p., 1900; Grand Rapids: Eerdmans, 1951), p. 164.

5. Haenchen, *The Acts of the Apostles*, pp. 260-62; Conzelmann, *Acts of the Apostles*, p. 44.

None of these scholars, however, has attempted to reconstruct the social situation behind the complaint of the widows.

Below is a visual layout of Acts 5:42–6:1-6 in both Greek and English, which will highlight patterns and relationships in the text. I have lined up verbs and phrases that have parallel weight. The translation is my own. Because this exegesis draws on previous material in this book, chapter and page numbers for reference are included in the text. As before, I begin with the verse immediately preceding our text. It is not part of this pericope, but it sets the stage for it.

Acts 5:42
Πᾶσάν τε ἡμέραν
     ἐν τῷ ἱερῷ
       καὶ
     κατ᾽ οἶκον
οὐκ ἐπαύοντο διδάσκοντες
          καὶ
     εὐαγγελιζόμενοι   τὸν Χριστόν, Ἰησοῦν.

Acts 6:1
Ἐν δὲ ταῖς ἡμέραις ταύταις πληθυνόντων τῶν μαθητῶν
ἐγένετο γογγυσμὸς
     τῶν Ἑλληνιστῶν
     πρὸς τοὺς Ἑβραίους,
ὅτι
παρεθεωροῦντο   αἱ χῆραι αὐτῶν.
     ἐν τῇ διακονίᾳ τῇ καθημερινῇ.
6:2   προσκαλεσάμενοι δὲ οἱ δώδεκα τὸ πλῆθος τῶν μαθητῶν
εἶπαν,
Οὐκ ἀρεστόν ἐστιν
     ἡμᾶς   καταλείψαντας τὸν λόγον τοῦ θεου
          διακονεῖν τραπέζαις.
6:3   ἐπισκέψασθε δέ, ἀδελφοί, ἄνδρας ἑπτά,
     ἐξ ὑμῶν
          μαρτυρουμένους
          πλήρεις πνεύματος καὶ
              σοφίας,
     οὓς καταστήσομεν
          ἐπὶ τῆς χρείας ταύτης,

6:4   ἡμεῖς δὲ προσκαρτερήσομεν
          τῇ προσευχῇ καὶ
          τῇ διακονίᾳ τοῦ λόγου.
6:5   καὶ ἤρεσεν ὁ λόγος
          ἐνώπιον παντὸς τοῦ πλήθους
          καὶ ἐξελέξαντο
          Στέφανον,
                  ἄνδρα πλήρης πίστεως καὶ
                        πνεύματος ἁγίου, καὶ
                  Φίλιππον καὶ Πρόχορον καὶ Νικάνορα καὶ
                  Τίμωνα καὶ Παρμενᾶν καὶ Νικόλαον
                              προσήλυτον Ἀντιοχέα,
6:6   οὓς
          ἔστησαν
              ἐνώπιον τῶν ἀποστόλων, καὶ
          προσευξάμενοι
          ἐπέθηκαν αὐτοῖς τὰς χεῖρας.

5:42
And every day
          in the temple and
          by households
     they did not stop teaching and
          telling the good news   that (the) Messiah was Jesus.
6:1 Now during these days while the disciples were increasing (in number),
     there came about a complaint
                    of the Hellenists
                    against the Hebrews
          because
     their widows were being overlooked
                    in the daily waiting (on persons at tables).
6:2   The Twelve,
               having called to themselves the assembly of the disciples,
               said, "It is not right [in the sight of God],
                    that we should have given up the word of God
                    to serve tables.
6:3   Select, then, brothers and sisters,
               seven men from among yourselves

well-spoken of,
full of Spirit and
wisdom,
whom we will appoint
for this matter,

6:4   and we will devote ourselves
to the prayer and
to the service
of the word."

6:5   The word found favor in the eyes of all the assembly, and
they chose for themselves
Stephen,
a man full of faith and
the Holy Spirit, and
Philip and Prochorus and Nicanor and
Timon and Parmenas and Nicolaus,
a proselyte of Antioch,

6:6   whom
they placed
before the apostles, and,
having prayed,
they laid hands on them.

Verse-by-Verse Analysis

Acts 5:42

Πᾶσάν τε ἡμέραν ἐν τῷ ἱερῷ καὶ κατ' οἶκον οὐκ ἐπαύοντο διδάσκοντες καὶ εὐαγγελιζόμενοι τὸν Χριστόν Ἰησοῦν. (And every day, in the temple and by households, they [apostles] did not stop teaching and telling the good news that [the] Messiah was Jesus.)

The public sphere of the Temple is set alongside the private sphere of the household. There is no mention of the apostles serving at the daily meals, not necessarily because they did not help in this task, but because the emphasis is on public proclamation. Yet it is the apostles' constant teaching and preaching (the verb is imperfect) that ultimately lead to an administrative crisis in the community — both in the sense that the apostles obviously do not have enough time to serve meals, and in the sense that their proclamations are attracting more people to the group, with need for further organizational structure.

τὸν Χριστόν Ἰησοῦν (to Christ Jesus). C. K. Barrett suggests that τὸν Χριστόν is "an implied subject: they proclaimed the good news that the Christ was Jesus."[6] Presumably, as eyewitnesses themselves, they were demonstrating this truth by telling stories from Jesus' ministry and teaching, as well as his resurrection from death and his ascension. In a meal setting κατ' οἶκον ("by household"), it was also likely that stories about Jesus at meals were told by both men and women who had been his disciples.

Stating the message in this way — that "the Messiah is Jesus" — implicitly sets up an eschatological framework. The figure of the Messiah, awaited by so many and most intensely by the Essenes, had now arrived in the person of Jesus, proclaimed the apostles. The message must have been explosive, eliciting strong reactions either pro or con. "How can you prove that?" thinking people must have asked. By Luke's accounting through Peter's sermons, it was Jesus' resurrection that confirmed the authenticity of his life as God's emissary and placed his killers on the side of evil. But without a marked change in behavior of the gathering community, I doubt that many would have been convinced. The joy at the daily meals, the inclusion of many kinds of people who heretofore would never have eaten together, must have confirmed to many the reality of the imminent reign of God. Hence the gravity of the internal crisis around these communal meals.

Acts 6:1

ἐν δὲ ταῖς ἡμέραις ταύταις (Now during these days).

From the perspective of the larger narrative, 6:1-6 is a transitional episode. It provides the final report about internal activities of the Jerusalem community as a whole and introduces leaders who will push the story out beyond Jerusalem. But the actual events themselves must be taken seriously in their own right, not simply as a setup to introduce new characters.

"During these days" can be interpreted with emphasis on continuity or on a change of topic. When ταύταις is translated "these" (instead of "those," as in the NRSV), continuity seems primary. The same phrase is

6. C. K. Barrett, *Acts 1–14*, International Critical Commentary (London and New York: T&T Clark, 2004), p. 301.

used in 1:15 and 11:27 in order to bind together two episodes.[7] Luke, however, does not give any sense of how much time has elapsed since Pentecost. Because 5:42 segues into 6:1-6, Luke means to show that the internal problem arises around the same time as the external persecution by religious authorities, on the grounds that the apostles had less time to devote to internal organizational affairs.

πληθυνόντων τῶν μαθητῶν (while the disciples were increasing [in number]). This participial phrase is an attendant circumstance explaining why a problem is arising. When an intentional community is forming through fictive kin relationships like this one, growth can outstrip adequate organization. Ethnic and cultural differences arise when collective sharing is intensely practiced across these boundaries.

This is the first time that believers are called disciples, although the term has been used many times in Luke's Gospel and will be repeated 28 more times in Acts. This could imply a new source, but Luke's literary skill is such that it is not possible to know. More likely it serves to show a lapse of time since the beginning days of the movement. One can become a "believer" more easily than one can become a "disciple." Discipleship implies being a pupil of a master over the long haul and changing one's lifestyle according to the master's teaching. With the high standards of communal sharing in 2:42-47 and 4:32-37 across social boundaries and the shocking results when those standards are not met, it is to be expected that some "believers" would drop out, even as the total number of true disciples increased and those who stayed gradually learned about the costs of discipleship.

Discipleship also implies study and proclamation. In Jewish understanding, all disciples devote themselves to the study of the Torah,[8] with the expectation of teaching others. In this case, Luke's use of the term "disciples" is a subtle indication of the missionary thrust outward from Jerusalem that will begin just after this episode.[9]

7. Haenchen, *The Acts of the Apostles*, p. 260; Gerd Lüdemann, *Early Christianity According to the Traditions in Acts: A Commentary*, trans. John Bowden (Minneapolis: Fortress Press, 1989), p. 74.

8. K. H. Rengstorf, μαθητής, κτλ," *Theological Dictionary of the New Testament*, ed. Gerhard Kittel and Gerhard Friedrich, trans. Geoffrey W. Bromiley, 10 vols. (Grand Rapids: Eerdmans, 1964-1976), 4:458.

9. Ivoni Richter Reimer connects Tabitha's discipleship with her "good works" as a missionary. See *Women in the Acts of the Apostles: A Feminist Liberation Perspective* (Minneapolis: Fortress Press, 1995), p. 54.

The Widows' Complaint: An Exegesis of Acts 5:42–6:1-6

ἐγένετο γογγυσμὸς τῶν Ἑλληνιστῶν πρὸς τοὺς Ἑβραίους (there came about a complaint of the Hellenists against the Hebrews). Luke has not previously spoken about Hellenists and Hebrews in those terms, although ethnic groups with different languages and cultural backgrounds are present from the beginning of Acts. Galileans mixed with native Judeans, along with Jews and proselytes from fourteen other regions of the known world (2:9-11). Acts 6:9 speaks of Cyrenians, Alexandrians, and others from Cilicia and Asia who are ex-slaves belonging to the Synagogue of Freedmen.

As discussed earlier, there is now strong agreement that Hebrews and Hellenists were both Jewish, and the distinction is one of linguistics. The latter were Greek-speaking Jews who spoke *only* Greek, and the former were Aramaic-speaking Jews who might be bilingual.[10] Such consensus is fairly recent. In 1992 Craig Hill examined both scholarly and popular material over the previous 75 years to demonstrate that there has been a general opinion in favor of F. C. Baur's 1845 proposal — that the Hebrews and the Hellenists made up distinctive ideological groups within Judaism.[11] The Hebrews were stricter Jews with a more positive view of the Temple, while Stephen, representing the Hellenists as a whole, was hostile toward the Temple and maintained a more liberal outlook. This presupposition has led some to argue that the controversy over the "daily *diakonia*" only disguises the deeper ideological split within the early church. The fact that all of the Seven chosen to help resolve the problem have Greek names and are never portrayed as serving tables (while two of them become missionaries and preachers) contributes to this perspective.

Hill's monograph effectively challenges this position (pp. 91-92). Al-

10. C. F. D. Moule, "Once More, Who Were the Hellenists?" *Expository Times* 70 (1958-59): 100-102. Henry J. Cadbury, however, considers the Hellenists to be Gentiles, primarily because of the strange terminology and because Jerusalem at that time would have contained many foreigners who were not necessarily Jewish. See "Note VII" in *Additional Notes to the Commentary*, ed. Kirsopp Lake and Henry J. Cadbury, vol. 5 of *The Beginnings of Christianity*, ed. F. J. Foakes Jackson and Kirsopp Lake (Grand Rapids: Baker, 1965), pp. 59-74. But narrative analysis confirms that these Hellenists cannot be Gentiles, since Luke takes such pains to trace the gradual development of the Gentile mission after this early stage of development of the church.

11. Craig Hill, *Hellenists and Hebrews: Reappraising Division within the Earliest Church* (Minneapolis: Fortress Press, 1992), pp. 12-15. He includes Bultmann, J. Christiaan Beker, Helmut Koester, C. S. C. Williams, Hans Conzelmann, Gerhard Krodel, Gerhard Schneider, Richard Longenecker, F. F. Bruce, Christopher Rowland, *The New Oxford Annotated Bible*, *The NIV Study Bible*, and *Eerdmans Handbook to the History of Christianity*.

though language itself surely affected the interaction between the believers, there is no basis in the New Testament texts for an ideological split
along Hebrew/Hellenist lines. However, we can imagine a nuanced cultural diversity among the community, simply because at that time there
was no such thing as pure Judaism. Greek influence since Alexander the
Great had pervaded Eastern cultures, creating all kinds of amalgamated
"Hellenisms." As Shane J. D. Cohen puts it, "'To Hellenize or not to
Hellenize' was not a question the Jews of antiquity had to answer. They
were given no choice. The questions that confronted them were 'how?'
and 'how far?'"[12]

It is possible that there were noticeable cultural differences between
the core group of formerly rural Galileans and the mixture of Jews from
Jerusalem, Judea, and the Diaspora. Acts 4:13 says that the Temple rulers
noticed that Peter and John were ἀγράμματοί (lit., "those without writing"; NRSV: "uneducated"). Tensions could have arisen between those
who could read and write and those who could not, especially if the less
educated were the main leaders. But language differences alone can create
miscommunications, especially as groups increase. It is entirely natural,
concludes Hill, that the growth in numbers of the Jerusalem church would
have occasioned the need for more leaders.[13] It also goes without saying
that the larger a tight-knit community grows, the more complex are the issues that must be worked out.

ὅτι παρεθεωροῦντο ἐν τῇ διακονίᾳ τῇ καθημερινῇ αἱ χῆραι αὐτῶν (because their widows were being overlooked in the daily waiting [on persons at tables]). For those who do not immediately dismiss this complaint
as too trivial to be the real issue, there are two traditional interpretations of
this phrase. Either this episode chronicles the breakdown of the
communalism described in 2:42-47 and 4:32-37, or it refers to a problem
with care of the poor within the community. Some have envisioned daily
handouts that were not reaching Hellenist widows. This is inferred from
rabbinic descriptions of the Jewish system of care for the poor, where the
Kuppah (basket) was circulated once a week to the local poor so they could

12. Shane J. D. Cohen, *From the Maccabees to the Mishnah* (Philadelphia: Westminster
Press, 1989), p. 45. James D. G. Dunn refers to the second-century B.C.E. Maccabean Revolt
and the "residue of suspicion" between the devout Torah Jews and Hellenist Jews. See *The
Acts of the Apostles* (Valley Forge, Pa.: Trinity Press International, 1996), p. 82.

13. Hill, *Hellenists and Hebrews*, p. 26. There is no definite proof that all the Seven
were Hellenists.

have food for the following week, and a *Tamhui* (tray) was daily distributed to transient poor (pp. 82, 92, 138).[14] The Acts description does not exactly correspond with the Jewish system, since here local widows are involved with something that happens every day.[15] Thus it must mean that already the Christians were cut off from Jewish charities and had to set up their own system of poor relief.[16] Those who interpret the διακονία as food envision a kind of soup kitchen, where the widows and other poor sat down at tables and were given a meal. Even Bo Reicke, who insists on tying together the agape meals with care of the poor, assumes that there is little difference between feeding the poor at a meal and giving them alms in the context of a meal (p. 89).

Modern Bible translations also interpret the action in 6:1 as almsgiving. Although the KJV literally translates διακονία into "ministration," and another literal translation, the New American Standard, calls it "the daily serving of food," most use the term "distribution" (i.e., NIV, RSV, NRSV, NKJV) even though Luke uses two different words to describe distribution of property: διαμερίζω (*diamerizo;* 2:45) and διαδίδωμι (*diadidomi;* 4:35).

All of these translations, interpretations, and visualizations have been marred by at least four significant misunderstandings: (1) the notion of who is poor, (2) the meaning of διακονία (*diakonia*), (3) the significance of an androcentric text discussing females, and (4) the various definitions of χήρα ("widow").

First, who is poor? The culture and economics of first-century Palestine are assumed to be no different from those of the modern West, where most Christians belong to an affluent, educated middle class in a market capitalist economy, and the poor are an underclass to whom Christians should extend charity, but who are definably "the other" (pp. 88-91). Interpreters are usually not visualizing a situation in which 90 percent of the population lived at or below subsistence level. The poor were not "the other" in this community, for nearly everyone was poor (pp. 99-

14. Joachim Jeremias, *Jerusalem in the Time of Jesus* (Philadelphia: Fortress Press, 1969), p. 131.

15. Kirsopp Lake insists that the two systems were almost the same. See "Note XII" in *Additional Notes to the Commentary,* ed. Lake and Cadbury, p. 148.

16. Haenchen therefore deduces that this episode must have occurred much later, after the Christians no longer considered themselves a part of Judaism. See *The Acts of the Apostles,* p. 262.

107).[17] It is true that there were different levels of poverty. But with the cultural practices of kin-group cohesion now transferred to the fictive kin community, the issue — if it did concern destitute widows — was not "Are we giving enough charity?" but "Are we including everyone in our households?"

The second misunderstanding concerns the *diakonia*. John N. Collins's intensive study of the meaning of *diakonia* challenges the contemporary conception of the diaconate as humble service to the poor and needy.[18] He compares the New Testament usages of *diakonia* and its related forms with non-Christian usage in the ancient Greek and Greco-Roman contexts, and concludes that the essential meaning is of a go-between in three different contexts. First, in the context of a message to be communicated, the one performing *diakonia* is the spokesperson or courier. Second, in the area of agency, the word and its forms have to do with mediating, carrying out a task or commission, being an agent for someone else. And third, in the context of attendance upon a person or within a household, the meaning relates to waiting on, fetching, carrying, or performing a task.[19] The word that *diakonia* best translates into in English is "ministry." The English language uses this term for many status levels as well, and many times a *diakon*-word from the New Testament is translated as "minister" or "ministry" to refer to apostles and church leaders (i.e., Rom. 11:13; Eph. 3:7, etc.), as well as those who minister by preparing meals and waiting on tables.

Since the use of *diakonia* in isolation does not say much in the Greek language about the status or specific task of the person involved in it, the

17. Gerhard Lenski, *Power and Privilege: A Theory of Social Stratification* (New York: McGraw-Hill, 1966). Richard Rohrbach, "Agrarian Society," in *Biblical Social Values and Their Meaning: A Handbook*, ed. John J. Pilch and Bruce J. Malina (Peabody, Mass.: Hendrickson, 1993); Douglas Oakman, *Jesus and the Economic Questions of His Day*, vol. 8 in Studies in the Bible and Early Christianity (Lewiston, N.Y.: Edwin Mellen Press, 1986); M. I. Finley, *The Ancient Economy* (London: Penguin, 1982); Ramsey MacMullen, *Roman Social Relations, 50 B.C. to A.D. 284* (London and New Haven: Yale University Press, 1974); and others.

18. John N. Collins, *Diakonia: Re-Interpreting the Ancient Sources* (New York: Oxford University Press, 1990). He disputes Hermann Wolfgang Beyer's statements in "διακονία" (*Theological Dictionary of the New Testament*, 2:82, 87) that διακονία can be used in the wider sense of "provide or care for."

19. A concise description of various usages is found in Appendix I in Collins, *Diakonia*, p. 335.

context is extremely significant.[20] As a Hellenistic writer, Luke is aware of these various meanings of *diakon-* and uses different nuances of it in 6:1-6. Thus the "daily *diakonia*" of verse 1 is further elaborated by διακονεῖν τραπέζαις ("to serve at tables," v. 2) and the διακονία τοῦ λόγου ("service of the word," v. 4). According to the apostles, there is a ministry that involves tables and a ministry that involves speaking.

What kind of tables are in view in verse 2? In the New Testament, τραπέζαις *(trapezais)* are used for both money and dining. Both have a transference sense in that dining tables refer to meals, while money tables serve as banks.[21] The only two occasions where money tables are clearly referred to are when Jesus overturns them when cleansing the Temple (Mark 11:15 and par.) and when, in the Lukan parable of the pounds, the slave is chastised for not putting the master's pound "on the table" where it could earn interest. All other references are to meals or dining tables.[22]

Some commentaries consider the tables of Acts 6:2 to be money tables (p. 81, n. 4). However, when there is a *diakonia* of tables, the only possible context is that of meals. Here *diakonia* must mean the fetching and carrying that is involved in serving meals at tables (which also probably refers to preparing the meal and cleaning up afterward), since no such activity is associated with money tables.

Since meals are thus in view in 6:1-2, they must refer back to the daily bread-breaking and communal meals of 2:42, 46, which include *everyone* in various household situations. There is no indication whatsoever that "the needy" are singled out and given a daily sit-down meal at a table. Rather, there are no needy (4:34) because possessions are shared and meals are eaten in common.[23]

αἱ χῆραι αὐτῶν (their widows). Third, why does an androcentric text talk about women? On the one hand, it is not surprising to read about women here, since a *diakonia* of tables is usually associated with women

---

20. Collins, *Diakonia*, p. 336.

21. Leonard Goppelt, "τράπεζα," *Theological Dictionary of the New Testament*, 8:211. While other artisans or traders put their wares on the ground, money-changers put their coins on a table and thus came to be called "table-men" — that is, money-changers or bankers.

22. See Matt. 15:27; Mark 7:28; Luke 16:21; 22:21, 30; Acts 16:34; Rom. 11:9; 1 Cor. 10:21. The one exception is Heb. 9:2, which refers to the Temple "shewbread." This also involves food, but only in a liturgical sense.

23. See the discussion of Reicke's thesis of διακονία and meals on pp. 88-91.

(i.e., Luke 10:38-42).[24] On the other hand, in literature written from a male-oriented point of view (which includes the entire New Testament), women are never mentioned unless they are exceptional or have become a problem (for men).[25] Therefore, the issue must be the widows themselves, rather than Luke using this issue to cover up some "deeper" theological conflict.[26] Syntactically, αἱ χῆραι αὐτῶν ("their widows") comes at the end of both the phrase and the sentence itself, thus placing even more emphasis on the widows.[27]

There are only two possible reasons why poor relief is assumed to be the issue here. The first is the common modern assumption that διακονία was understood in the ancient world as care of the poor, a fallacy discussed above. The second reason is that the text refers to the neglect of widows, who are assumed to always be the poorest and most vulnerable sector of ancient Palestine.

As we have seen in Chapter Four, one cannot always assume all widows at that time were destitute, nor can one make a definitive statement about the social status of a widow. In Judaism, widowhood was often a temporary status. Widows were encouraged to marry as soon as the period of mourning was over,[28] since the patriarchal economic system did not provide adequately for most women to live on their own.[29] Nevertheless, Christian writings are not consistent on this matter. When writing to Corinthian widows (1 Cor. 7:8, 39-40), Paul urges them to remain unmarried

24. Beyer, "διακονία," p. 82.

25. Elisabeth Schüssler Fiorenza, *In Memory of Her: A Feminist Theological Reconstruction of Christian Origins* (New York: Crossroad, 1983), p. 44. See Chapter Four, p. 91.

26. This is wrongly asserted by Conzelmann, *Acts of the Apostles*; Haenchen, *The Acts of the Apostles*, pp. 264-69; and Lüdemann, *Early Christianity According to the Traditions in Acts*, p. 78.

27. Benjamin Chapman, *New Testament Greek Notebook*, 2d ed. (Grand Rapids: Baker, 1983), p. 86: "If still more emphasis is intended, the writer may put the subject last of all in the sentence."

28. Tal Ilan, *Jewish Women in Greco-Roman Palestine* (Peabody, Mass.: Hendrickson, 1996), p. 149: "Widowhood in Judaism was in most instances a temporary situation, and the sources describe many cases of widows remarrying."

29. Luise Schottroff, *Lydia's Impatient Sisters: A Feminist Social History of Early Christianity* (Louisville: Westminster/John Knox Press, 1995), p. 93: "The sources consistently show that the levels of payment for women's work are such that, as a rule, the income earned by women and girls could not support an independent economic existence. Women worked in the rural economy and, most often, in textile production. Their wages at times matched only what they had to spend on food."

so they can give themselves most fully to the things of the Lord (v. 34). Clearly there is a group of women in the church at Corinth who have a choice in determining their future, one not wholly dictated by economics.

Though New Testament writings other than 1 Timothy say little about widows, Luke-Acts includes many references. Only two have Markan parallels: the widow's coin of Luke 21:1-4 (Mark 12:41-44), and widows as victims of scribes' greed (Luke 20:47; Mark 12:40). The other four narratives and examples are unique to Luke: the prophetess Anna (2:36-38), the widow at Zarephath (4:25-26), the widow at Nain (7:11-17), and the persistent widow (18:1-8). In Acts, widows are mentioned twice, and in each case they are a distinct group: in 6:1, and in 9:36-42 in connection with Tabitha. Though it is clear from the contexts that most of the widows in Luke's Gospel are poor, it is not their poverty and helplessness that Luke is emphasizing.[30] In the case of Anna, nothing is said about need; it is her piety that dominates the pericope. Both the generous widow (21:1-4) and the persistent widow (18:1-8) are used as examples of what both male and female disciples ought to be like.[31] Yet none of these traits have been brought into play when discussing the widows of Acts 6:1 or of 9:36-41.[32]

Some exegetes have suggested that other women in Luke-Acts who appear independently and without husbands were also widows: Peter's mother-in-law (Luke 4:38-39), Martha (Luke 10:38-42), Lydia (Acts 16:14-15), Mary, the mother of John Mark (Acts 12:12), and Tabitha herself.[33] The same unresolved tension is also found in sociohistorical descriptions of the ancient world. On the one hand, there was no fate worse than widowhood, especially if one was childless. On the other hand, for the first time in her life a widowed woman — unless she was destitute — had the right of self-determination, or at least the right to be consulted in matters that

---

30. Marla J. Selvidge, *Daughters of Jerusalem* (Scottdale, Pa.: Herald Press, 1987), p. 109.

31. Gustav Stählin, "χήρα," *Theological Dictionary of the New Testament,* 9:448-51 (450-51).

32. Turid Karlsen Seim, *The Double Message: Patterns of Gender in Luke and Acts* (Nashville: Abingdon Press, 1994), p. 231; Stählin, "χήρα," p. 451.

33. Seim, *The Double Message,* p. 230; Lilian Portefaix, *Sisters Rejoice: Paul's Letter to the Philippians and Luke-Acts as Received by First-Century Philippian Women* (Stockholm: Almqvist & Wiksell, 1988), p. 159; Leonard Swidler, *Biblical Affirmations of Woman* (Philadelphia: Westminster Press, 1979), pp. 304-5.

concerned her own life.[34] The social reality in that culture was that a widow's position was ambiguous.[35]

It is consequently impossible to be sure, simply from the term itself, what meaning Luke intends for the widows of Acts 6:1. We must look to the context. Here several clues can be drawn from the larger narrative of Acts 1–12, from a Qumran fragment, and from references to property-sharing and commensality that we have already examined.

The first clue emerges from the women in the story of Tabitha in Acts 9:36-42. The disciple Tabitha appears to be unrelated to a man, is doing active service in the church, and is surrounded at her death by widows who weep for her. She was evidently a craftswoman working in textiles, for she herself had made the clothes that a group of widows show to Peter (v. 39). There is no evidence that these widows were objects of charity, for the text does not say that Tabitha made the clothes *for* the widows, only that she made them *while she was with the widows* (v. 39). It is more likely that Tabitha employed these women to work in the shop in her home as a way of helping them support themselves and at the same time evangelized and did "works of mercy."[36] This may also explain why Tabitha was so important to the church at Joppa that messengers were immediately sent to Peter for help when she died (9:38).

Though Tabitha is not connected to a διακονία of tables, her life reflects the same integration of practical and spiritual activity that characterizes the Jerusalem church. Seen in this light, Tabitha's textile work provides an example of the "community of production" that so many exegetes think is missing from the early church. It also means that such ventures of shared production had spread beyond Jerusalem to other parts of Judea.[37]

34. Seim, *The Double Message*, p. 231; Jane F. Gardner, *Women in Roman Law and Society* (Bloomington: Indiana University Press, 1986), pp. 54-55.

35. Ilan, *Jewish Women in Greco-Roman Palestine*, p. 147; Seim, *The Double Message*, p. 231.

36. Here one is reminded of the apostle Paul's trade as a tentmaker. He used the workday in the shop as a time to teach workers and customers alike about Jesus. See Ronald F. Hock, *The Social Context of Paul's Ministry: Tentmaking and Apostleship* (Philadelphia: Fortress Press, 1980), pp. 24-49.

37. Further, if widows are banded together to work in an industry, they immediately possess an autonomy they would not have if they were working for wages individually. If they are sharing food and shelter, they can live more economically as well. If this option is open to the widows of Corinth (see above), Paul can realistically encourage the alternative of remaining unmarried. See also Bruce J. Malina's assertion that poverty is based on the lack

After Peter raises Tabitha, he calls the saints and widows to show them she is alive. Bonnie Bowman Thurston observes that the widows are mentioned separately from the "saints." Since the text gives no reason to suggest that these widows were not members of the Christian community, she conjectures that "Peter is calling the Christians, and a special group of Christians, the widows, to witness Tabitha's restoration. The friends of Tabitha may have belonged to a society."[38] Turid Seim goes further: "It is probable that both the daily service in Acts 6:1 and the widows in Tabitha's house in Acts 9 reflect an established order of widows in Luke-Acts."[39]

The second clue derives from fragments from the Damascus Document found in Cave 4 at Qumran (4QD). Several lines reveal the presence of "a group of women singled out for special honor, the 'Mothers'"[40]:

> Whoever murmurs against the Fathers [shall be expelled] from the congregation and shall not return; [but if] against the Mothers, then he shall be punished te[n] days, because the Mo[th]ers do not have "authority" in the midst. 4QDc 71, 13-17

There is debate about the meaning of the Hebrew word that Sidnie White Crawford here translates "authority." In any case, she concludes that "Fathers" are highly respected in the Essene community, while "Mothers" have a less exalted status (since the punishment for "murmuring" against them is less severe), but some status nevertheless. This fragment demonstrates the presence of a distinct group of women who commanded respect in the Essene communities.

Perhaps the widows of Acts 6:1 were a group patterned after the Essene Mothers, though without such formal gender stratification. Whether or not they were an "order," I suggest that both Hellenist and He-

---

of social connections and not merely the lack of material provisions: "Interpreting the Bible with Anthropology: The Case of the Poor and the Rich," *Listening: Journal of Religion and Culture* 21 (1986): 148-59.

38. Bonnie Bowman Thurston, *The Widows: A Women's Ministry in the Early Church* (Minneapolis: Fortress Press, 1989), p. 32.

39. Seim, *The Double Message*, p. 241.

40. Sidnie White Crawford, "Mothers, Sisters, and Elders: Titles for Women in Second Temple Jewish and Early Christian Communities," in *The Dead Sea Scrolls as Background to Postbiblical Judaism and Early Christianity*, papers from an international conference at St. Andrews, Scotland, 2001, ed. James R. Davila (Boston and Leiden: E. J. Brill, 2003), pp. 177-91.

brew widows were organized to work together on a particular task appropriate in that culture for their gender — although in both cases the task itself took on dimensions that considerably stretched the role.

The third clue to the widows' situation concerns the juxtaposition of διακονία in the same phrase in which the widows are mentioned. I have clarified that the daily διακονία in verse 1 cannot be limited to alms for the poor or feeding the poor, but instead is connected to the διακονία ("table service") in verse 2, which, according to 2:46, includes everyone. A common meal eaten daily in various households of the congregation involves organizing, preparation, serving, and cleaning up — activities that take place primarily in the kitchen or in spaces where women work and are in charge (pp. 209-10). Just as spinning, weaving, and sewing clothes are normally seen in that culture (and most others) as primarily women's work (Acts 9:36-42), so is kitchen work and food preparation. Whether these widows were poor (and it is likely most of them were, given the general economic situation), it hardly meant that they sat around lamenting their poverty and expecting handouts from the community. Many of them would not necessarily have been old, especially those who had been married to men who were considerably older and who had not yet remarried.[41] Some may not have been marriageable because of previous work as prostitutes (p. 213). Instead, they would have been given work within the community, the most obvious being meal preparation and serving.

If some widows did not have homes of their own to manage, it is natural that they could have been assigned as liaisons between the various households, organizing the meals so that everyone had a place to eat and so that there was adequate food for each of the meals. This arrangement may have been especially true of the Hellenist widows, if they had lived abroad most of their lives and had few blood-ties in Jerusalem.[42] The same thing would likely have been true of the Galilean women like Mary, Jesus' mother, and others mentioned in the Gospels who were without husbands and who were also uprooted from their kin groups in Galilee (pp. 132-36).

That women are connected in some way with the διακονία of Acts

41. Girls were often married at puberty, between ages 12 and 15, while Jewish men were 18 or 20, and Greek men married around 30. See Everett Ferguson, *Backgrounds of Early Christianity*. 2d ed. (Grand Rapids: Eerdmans, 1993), p. 68. If Jewish Hellenist men married young girls when they were older than 20, widowhood would be statistically more likely for these women than for Palestinian women.

42. Haenchen, *The Acts of the Apostles*, p. 261.

6:1-6 is not surprising, given their association in Luke's Gospel. E. Jane Via notes that "the instance of διακονέω in Luke's gospel falls into two distinct groups: διακονέω [the verb form "to serve"] as role for women; [the participle] διακονῶν as model for discipleship."[43] In both groups, the content and imagery involve serving tables and eating. In the Gospel, women prepare and serve meals for Jesus and the male disciples around him (Luke 4:39 and par.: 8:1-3, 10:38-42). And the traditional passage about the one who serves being greater is set in the context of the Last Supper (22:24-27), where Jesus makes it clear that discipleship is service at a meal, a culturally feminine task.[44] In light of the association of women, *diakonia,* and discipleship in Luke's Gospel, the issue in 6:1 could just as well have concerned problems about women and serving as about poor women receiving handouts.

παρεθεωροῦντο (being overlooked). For some reason the Hellenist widows were being "overlooked" or "neglected" in the daily διακονία. We cannot know very specifically what this means, since the word is used nowhere else in the LXX or the New Testament. Given my reconstruction, it seems likely there was some conflict among the women involved in meal organization, preparation, or serving. Language differences could have exacerbated it, as well as variations in meal customs between Galilean, Judean, and Diaspora Jews from other parts of the known world.

Elisabeth Schüssler Fiorenza suggests the problem may be that the Hellenist women were not being served at the meal because it was more acceptable in the Diaspora than in Palestine for women to eat with men at social gatherings (p. 93). Following her, Luise Schottroff is more explicit. She assumes that both men and women were serving and being served at tables, but that Hebrew men began to dominate Hellenist women by not preparing food and serving it to them.[45]

I cannot rule out this possibility, but it doesn't explain why only widows were involved and why they were seated in a group. If unattached women had been absorbed into various households or were living with an employer-patron like Tabitha, it seems more natural to picture them joining together to organize and arrange for daily common meals among all the

---

43. E. Jane Via, "Women, the Discipleship of Service, and the Early Christian Ritual Meal in the Gospel of Luke," *St. Luke's Journal of Theology* 29 (1985): 37-60 (38).

44. Via, "Women, the Discipleship of Service, and the Early Christian Ritual Meal in the Gospel of Luke," p. 57.

45. Schottroff, *Lydia's Impatient Sisters,* p. 209.

believers. Out of this work, then, tension between ethnic groups of women could have arisen. Remembering the importance of household and meal management to Cicero's wife (p. 94, n. 51), it is not at all unlikely that there was competition between groups of women for certain honors associated with the daily common meal experience, which was the physical, social, and spiritual highlight of the day for the entire community (pp. 93-94).[46]

It is also possible that both men and women participated in the daily διακονία. Male slaves waited on tables in upper-class households throughout the Empire.[47] Perhaps young Hebrew men did the fetching and carrying involved in serving the daily meals, and they refused to serve Hellenist widows, who, as meal organizers, did eat together as a group. In any case, the Hellenist widows had enough clout in the community that they could complain as a group and get results.

Acts 6:2

οἱ δώδεκα (the twelve). This is the first time this term occurs in Acts, although it is often used in Luke's Gospel. The Twelve are indirectly mentioned in Acts 1:26 and 2:14 as the Eleven, before Matthias's election. The term cannot be exactly equivalent to "the apostles," since the latter probably included others from the group of 120 in Acts 1:15, from which Matthias was chosen. The use of "the Twelve" does not necessarily mean Luke is using a new source here. Luke may want to juxtapose the Twelve with the Seven, who are to be appointed and installed subsequently. The Twelve may also refer to the inner group of apostles who actually call the meeting together.[48]

Προσκαλεσάμενοι . . . τὸ πλῆθος τῶν μαθητῶν (having called to themselves the assembly of the disciples). In light of the common understanding that poor relief was the problem in verse 1, this is a truly astonishing phrase. The main leaders of the community, the Twelve, call together the

46. Mary L. McKenna, *Women of the Church: Role and Renewal* (New York: P. J. Kennedy & Sons, 1967), pp. 39-41.

47. Pedar W. Foss, "Age, Gender, and Status Divisions at Mealtime in the Roman House: A Synopsis of the Literary Evidence" (http://www-personal.umich.edu/'pfoss/ROMARCH.html), from "Kitchens and Dining Rooms at Pompeii: The Spatial and Social Relationship of Cooking to Eating in the Roman Household," Ph.D. thesis, University of Michigan, 1994.

48. See the discussion of organizational structure below in exegesis of verse 3.

entire assembly of the disciples (probably in the Temple precincts, since no other area would have been large enough) and, for the sake of a group of widows who weren't getting their daily supply of food, propose to restructure the entire administrative organization! Given this scenario, it is no wonder that exegetes like Ernst Haenchen, Hans Conzelmann, and Gerd Lüdemann suspect a deeper conflict lies below what Luke has said up front in verse 1. That the entire group needs to solve the problem indicates that it was indeed bound up with a core activity of the community, the sacred communal meals — and thus also the symposium/worship that followed the food and was an integral part of the meal.[49]

Οὐκ ἀρεστόν ἐστιν ἡμᾶς καταλείψαντας τὸν λόγον τοῦ θεοῦ διακονεῖν τραπέζαις (It is not right that we should have given up the word of God to serve tables). The expression Οὐκ ἀρεστόν ἐστιν ("it is not right") is also used in the LXX to mean "it is not proper in the sight of God" (see Deut. 6:18; 12:25, 28; 13:18; Exod. 15:26) — a rather presumptuous statement in this context, as we shall see below.

Καταλείψαντας *(kataleipsantas)* is an aorist (past tense) participle of the verb "to give up." To translate it as past action implies that the Twelve have previously been involved in meal responsibilities to the detriment of preaching. We do know from 4:35, 37 that they've been holding the purse strings. Yet 5:42 says that they are "not ceasing to teach and preach," and they've obviously missed some meals because of arrest and imprisonment. It sounds more like their table service is slipping than the other way around. On the basis that καταλείψαντας does not express past action, Seim thinks Acts 6:2 takes for granted that God would be displeased if the Twelve would *henceforth* abandon God's word to serve at table.[50]

The Twelve's statement is reminiscent of the tension between table and word in Luke 10:38-42, where two sisters are involved. According to some interpretations of this Gospel text, the word must come before table service, even for a woman, whose normal role in that society was table service.[51] In contrast, F. Scott Spencer's gavel falls harshly on the apostles and

---

49. One is reminded of another situation in Philippians 4:2, where Paul pleads with two women, Euodia and Syntyche, to get along with each other. Evidently their disagreement was significant enough that Paul heard about it many miles away and was concerned that it would threaten the unity of the church as a whole.

50. Seim, *The Double Message*, p. 108.

51. Gerhard Schneider, *Die Apostelgeschichte*, vol. 1 (Freiburg, Basel, Vienna: Herder, 1980), p. 426, n. 48.

the whole church. Assuming these widows are powerless and poor (he compares them with other oppressed widows in Luke's double narrative), Spencer declares that "when it comes to caring for poor Hellenist widows, the church finds itself in an unholy alliance with unjust judges (Luke 18:1-8), hypocritical scribes (20:45-47), and an exploitative temple system (21:1-6)"! Even though the apostles take action to remedy the crisis, they still trivialize the widows' concerns. When they say, "It is not right to give up the word of God to serve tables," Spencer notes, "What is 'not right' is not as much the widows' predicament as it is the prospect that the Twelve might have to curtail their teaching ministry in order to help widows."

Though I disagree with Spencer on the plight of the widows, I'm inclined to follow his narrative logic about the equal importance of table service and preaching. Past references to meals in Acts 2:42, 46 have placed no preference on preaching and prayers; all activities are listed equally. Nor does Acts as a whole elevate the apostles' status far above that of the Seven, since the former soon disappear from the narrative altogether. Moreover, readers of Luke's Gospel would have already noticed Jesus' emphasis on meals and table service (i.e., Luke 12:37; 22:24-27; "I am among you as one who serves" — 22:27). Much of his teaching ministry had taken place around meals. As stated above, Jesus had communicated his theology by means of his inclusive table fellowship, just as the communal meals of these believers were conveying the inbreaking of God's reign and inviting others to join in.

Thus, Luke may be more critical of the Twelve here than is usually noted. It is ironic that the Twelve, who thought they should be relieved of table service in order to preach, no longer have a public preaching role! After this incident, Luke moves them off the public stage, and only Peter reappears later, though he is granted no more public speeches in the Temple. Rather, table servers dominate the next three chapters.

But this event does point up the tension that can arise between practical, concrete ministry and a verbal teaching/preaching ministry, between male roles in the public arena and female roles in private space. Perhaps the Galilean disciples of both genders first organized the daily meals, since they had participated in and best understood Jesus' practice of meal fellowship — with teaching as an integral part of the preparation and meal conversation. In time the growth of the congregation and the demands of constant public teaching and preaching likely became so heavy that the men were not able to do both, and women took over completely. Tensions may have arisen between the Galilean women (Hebrew widows?) who organized and prepared these meals and the Hellenist widows. Their services were also important, but their language and perhaps some of their table customs were different. If these differences related to questions of Jewish law, this could have especially provoked strong arguments among the women who were responsible for these meals. Women often were more aware of what the Law said about issues relating to the kitchen than were the rabbis (p. 209).[52] It is often in seemingly small details that arguments and divisions arise. If Hellenist women felt they were losing out on the honor of preparing and serving these meals in any significant way, this problem could easily have affected the community as a whole, and the issue moved into the public sphere.

The fact that the Twelve call a general assembly to solve the problem certainly speaks for the significance of the common meals in the life of the congregation and the importance of the work involved in preparing, serving, and cleaning up after them.

Acts 6:3

ἐπισκέψασθε δέ, ἀδελφοί, ἄνδρας ἐξ ὑμῶν μαρτυρουμένους ἑπτά (Select, then, brothers and sisters, seven [well-regarded] men from among yourselves). Ἐπισκέπτομαι (*episkeptomai*) is a Lukan word (in Luke three times; in Acts four times; in the rest of the New Testament four times) with a range of meanings. Here the sense is "to search out or select." Μαρτυρέω (*martureo*) in the active voice means "to bear witness to," but here in the passive it is "to be well spoken of, approved."[53] It is the same term used in 1 Timothy 3:7, where bishops are to be well thought of by outsiders.

All of the Twelve and the proposed Seven are men. Commentators are generally agreed that these lists of names were part of the bedrock of tradition Luke received.[54] However, the way Luke built the lists into his

---

52. Ilan, *Jewish Women in Greco-Roman Palestine*, pp. 195, 204. Ilan says, "Commandments and laws relevant to keeping a *kosher* Jewish household were meticulously repeated, at least in the households of the Pharisaic and *tannaitic* sages. This intensive training could result in women's specialized knowledge of laws extending beyond the rabbis' own kin."

53. Walter Bauer, *A Greek-English Lexicon of the New Testament and Other Early Christian Literature*, 2d ed. (Chicago: University of Chicago Press, 1979), p. 493.

54. Lüdemann, *Early Christianity According to the Traditions in Acts*, pp. 29, 77.

narrative (1:15-26; 6:1-6) implies that the criterion of gender had to be specifically stated and was not automatically taken for granted.[55] But why were only men chosen for table service?

Several interpreters have evaluated Luke as concerned to keep women in their subordinate roles in society.[56] Here it appears that Luke was accepting or promoting the cultural assumption that men belonged in the public sphere and women in the private sphere. Though women would be natural candidates for the διακονία of tables, seven *men*, at the request of the Twelve, were to be brought forward by the entire congregation to be publicly appointed to this task. Women held valued roles in domestic life, but this work was part of the private sphere in which they were normally expected to stay. Since the problem over the διακονία of tables concerned the entire group and thus became an issue in the public sphere, men were given overall administration. One might draw a parallel between this development and the way women's missionary societies in most Christian denominations were taken over by male administration during the 1920s.[57]

This is a valid consideration, but it does not do justice to the call in Luke's Gospel for male leaders to become table servers. When men are appointed to an actual διακονία of tables, which by definition includes fetching and carrying food, the public and private spheres interpenetrate each other. Here it is just as possible that appointing men to be involved with communal meals was part of the role change for men called for by Jesus, who demonstrated at the Last Supper (Luke 22:24-27; John 13:1-20) that following him meant becoming ὡς διακονῶν ("like the ones serving"). This appointment is a good example of the involvement of men in domestic administration, which Diane Jacobs-Malina discusses (pp. 203-5). Though Luke places the choosing and appointing of these men in the public sphere, their actual tasks

---

55. Seim, *The Double Message*, p. 111.

56. For example, Elisabeth Schüssler Fiorenza and Kathleen Corley, *Private Women, Public Meals: Social Conflict in the Synoptic Tradition* (Peabody, Mass.: Hendrickson, 1993). Both of these scholars, however, generally interpret Lukan texts about women as negatively as possible. See, for example, Schüssler Fiorenza's "Martha and Mary: Luke 10:38-42," *Religion and Intellectual Life* 3, no. 2 (1986): 21-36.

57. Rosemary Skinner Keller, "Lay Women in the Protestant Tradition," in vol. 1 of *Women and Religion in America*, ed. Rosemary Radford Ruether and Rosemary Skinner Keller (San Francisco: Harper & Row, 1981), pp. 242-53; Sharon Klingelsmith, "Women in the Mennonite Church, 1900-1930," *Mennonite Quarterly Review* 54 (July 1980): 163-207. See also histories of women's missionary societies in all major denominations that include this time period.

were located in the private sphere. Though Luke never records the appointment of a woman to any specific office, he is interested in having men take on traditionally female roles. As Seim notes, "The leaders remain leaders, but new ideals for their leadership are established."[58]

πλήρεις πνεύματος καὶ σοφίας (full of Spirit and wisdom). Although only "Spirit" is mentioned here, it must refer to the Holy Spirit, since Stephen in verse 5 is said to be full of the Holy Spirit.[59]

"Sophia" is a multifaceted word,[60] and here it appears that Luke is playing on different definitions of it. In the context of a διακονία of tables, it likely refers to practical wisdom, the kind possessed by the capable wife of Proverbs 31. Any traditional woman would immediately know what kind of wisdom would be needed for organizing, preparing, and serving meals, although she might be suspicious about whether any man had it. Of course, in the midst of some interpersonal conflict, good people skills would also be required, but μαρτυρουμένους — "being well-spoken of" — would speak to this kind of wisdom.

Οὓς καταστήσομεν ἐπὶ τῆς χρείας ταύτης (whom we will appoint for this matter). The twelve apostles call the meeting and present the problem. Then they ask the whole group to choose extra helpers, whom the Twelve formally appoint. The process of decision-making described in 6:1-6 sounds very orderly for a group that has been characterized by some commentators as living from day to day without any plans for the future. Thus Haenchen believes it would be rash to draw conclusions about the early church from this procedure and the nature of the office created here, for Luke likely has depicted the scene in accordance with models used in his own congregation.[61]

An essay by Bo Reicke challenges Haenchen's facile assumption by carefully examining the method of decision-making of this assembly and concluding that it is neither Greek (Luke's milieu) nor modern. "It looks as though the Jerusalem church had a mixed or 'complex' constitution, where inclinations toward monarchy, oligarchy, and democracy were present to-

58. Seim, *The Double Message*, p. 85.

59. Some scribes did add ἁγίου after πνεύματος, and the word passed into the Textus Receptus. See Bruce M. Metzger, *A Textual Commentary on the Greek New Testament* (London and New York: United Bible Societies, 1975), p. 337.

60. Ulrich Wilckens and Georg Fohrer hold forth for 63 pages in "σοφία," *Theological Dictionary of the New Testament*, 7:465-528.

61. Haenchen, *The Acts of the Apostles*, p. 263.

gether, without being mutually exclusive or even in conflict."[62] Reicke uses the 1932 dissertation of O. Linton, which contrasts Greek and modern concepts of government — the latter a governing body consisting of individuals who are treated as equal — with an Eastern non-egalitarian legislative assembly. Early Christianity must be understood in its Eastern context, he says, where apostles, elders, and the whole church reach decisions together, as in Acts 15:22. "The apostles and elders did not stand over against the congregation, but there was rather a single congregation, unequally constituted. . . . Linton finds reason to believe that the unequally structured legislative assembly was identical with the worshiping congregation . . . the people of God."[63] This structure is also seen partially in Acts 6:2-6, where the Twelve have the authority to call together the whole assembly and suggest a solution, but the choice of the Seven is made by the whole group.

Though in 1932 Linton had no proof of such a constitutional form, Reicke uses evidence from the Manual of Discipline from Qumran (1QS) and the Damascus Document (CD) to identify just such a hierarchical order within these communities, an order that at the same time preserves unity. In 1QS the congregation is divided into classes: the priests at the head, then the Levites, then the entire community of Israel. Even in a group of only ten, a priest must recite grace before and after meals, and the others must follow in their proper order. In decision-making, the men may speak (though only in the exact order of their rank [1QS 6:4]), but the group as a whole decides on all questions.[64]

Early Christianity does not indicate such rigidity of structure, but there are some parallels. 1QS 8:1 speaks of a "council" in the community consisting of twelve men and three priests, though it is not clear whether the three are part of the twelve or outside the circle. If they are inside, this looks like an analogy to the "college of the twelve apostles of Jesus, with the inner group composed of three — Peter, James, and John."[65]

62. Bo Reicke, "The Constitution of the Primitive Church in the Light of Jewish Documents," in *The Scrolls and the New Testament*, ed. Krister Stendahl (New York: Crossroad, 1992), 143-56 (146).

63. Reicke, "The Constitution of the Primitive Church in the Light of Jewish Documents," p. 147.

64. Reicke, "The Constitution of the Primitive Church in the Light of Jewish Documents," pp. 149-50.

65. Reicke, "The Constitution of the Primitive Church in the Light of Jewish Documents," p. 151.

Although probably Hellenist himself, Luke nevertheless depicts an assembly structured along Eastern organizational lines, where monarchic, oligarchic, and democratic tendencies exist side by side without open contention. This is another example where the text more accurately describes a plausible event in the earliest Jerusalem church rather than in Luke's own congregation. Furthermore, Luke avoids calling the Seven "deacons," an office that was in existence when he wrote Acts but that did not exist when these events were happening. The task of serving tables is what they have been appointed to do. Connotations of the later title "deacon" would deflect attention from that task.

Acts 6:4

ἡμεῖς δὲ τῇ προσευχῇ καὶ τῇ διακονίᾳ τοῦ λόγου προσκαρτερήσομεν (and we will devote ourselves to the prayer and to the service of the word). A repetition of προσκαρτερέω ("devote, continue faithfully") ties this text with 2:42-47 and underlines the perseverance of the apostles in their ministry of teaching and prayer.

The phrase διακονίᾳ τοῦ λόγου ("service of the word") occurs nowhere else in Luke-Acts. Rather, Luke plays with different meanings of διακονία. In this context, it fits best with John Collins's first definition: when a message is to be communicated, the one performing διακονία is the spokesperson.[66] The Twelve now propose to be go-betweens, or agents, verbally carrying out a commission from God to the people and, through their prayers, from the people to God — though, as stated above, we don't know if anyone but Peter actually continued to do this.

If this is a community of production as well as of consumption, the "diakonia of tables" may even refer to more male-oriented tasks of food production: planting, cultivating, and harvesting crops in the nearby fields; threshing barley or wheat; building fires to bake the bread. Perhaps here the Twelve are asking to be released from this work in order to devote all their time to preaching and teaching.

---

66. Collins, *Diakonia*, p. 335.

Acts 6:5

Καὶ ἤρεσεν ὁ λόγος ἐνώπιον παντὸς τοῦ πλήθους (The word found favor in the eyes of all the assembly). Ἤρεσεν ἐνώπιον ("found favor in the eyes of") is a Semitism used in the LXX (2 Sam. 3:36). Robert Tannehill comments that the idealizing tendency of Acts has less to do with avoiding community problems than with exaggerating the ease with which they were solved.[67] This phrase may be an example of that, since we can imagine that most decisions are not reached so easily and quickly. On the other hand, given the Eastern method of reaching decisions described by Reicke above, the process may not have been that difficult. But actually putting it into practice — men working with women on table service — is where all kinds of difficulties can be imagined, although of this the text says nothing. However, if the issue was one of language and ethnic customs relating to meals, using men as go-betweens for organizing table service to minimize these problems would have brought some relief. These men may have been among the few non-Palestinians who were bilingual.

καὶ ἐξελέξαντο Στέφανον, ἄνδρα πλήρης πίστεως καὶ πνεύματος ἁγίου, καὶ Φίλιππον καὶ Πρόχορον καὶ Νικάνορα καὶ Τίμωνα καὶ Παρμενᾶν καὶ Νικόλαον προσήλυτον Ἀντιοχέα (and they chose for themselves Stephen, a man full of faith and the Holy Spirit, and Philip and Prochorus and Nicanor and Timon and Parmenas and Nicolaus, a proselyte of Antioch). How did the community choose these seven men? Were they already leaders who stood out among the Greek-speaking Diaspora Jews? All the names are Greek, but only one is a proselyte from non-Jewish background. The great majority of interpreters believe the Seven are all Hellenists because of their names and because the problem is one where Hellenist widows have been treated unjustly. However, Johannes Munck cautions against attaching too much importance to the names, since many Jews had Greek names when other members of their families had Semitic names.[68] "To assume that the primitive church would choose a committee for social services in which only one of the feuding parties was represented would be to underestimate its efficiency in practical matters. Such a proce-

---

67. Robert Tannehill, vol. 2 of *The Narrative Unity of Luke-Acts* (Minneapolis: Fortress Press, 1990), p. 81.

68. Johannes Munck, *The Acts of the Apostles*, revised by William F. Albright and C. S. Mann (Garden City, N.Y.: Doubleday, 1967), p. 57. This was discovered through excavation of Jewish tombs in Jerusalem and its vicinity.

dure would probably have given rise to complaints from the Hebrews."[69] Again, bilingual skills may have been the deciding factor.

From a historical perspective, says Craig Hill, "it is wholly natural to assume that the Greek-speaking Christians of Jerusalem would have had leaders. Luke's description in 6:3 does not debase them but presupposes their recognition and authority. . . . It was, after all, a Jewish practice to set up boards of seven men to administer some task."[70]

Acts 6:6

οὓς ἔστησαν ἐνώπιον τῶν ἀποστόλων, καὶ προσευξάμενοι ἐπέθηκαν αὐτοῖς τὰς χεῖρας (whom they placed before the apostles, and, having prayed, they laid hands on them). The apostles approve of these men. That they officially and publicly pray and lay hands on them shows how critical the problem was regarding the widows and table service, and how important commensality was to the entire community.

We do not hear any more about how the Seven performed their duties, but neither do we hear that they neglected them. Far too much has been made of the inconsistencies between Stephen's and Philip's appointment to the διακονία of tables and their subsequent preaching and missionary work. The fact that the apostles set themselves apart for prayer and the διακονία of the word does not preclude these activities on the part of others, whether the Seven or other women and men in the community. Nor do we know how much time elapsed between their appointment and the events described in 6:8-15. The following verse (6:7) is one of Luke's mini-summaries about the continuing growth of the church (see also 2:47; 9:31; 12:24; 19:20), one purpose of which is to allow for the passage of time. There were likely many opportunities for organizing meals and serving tables before Stephen's confrontational sermon and martyrdom recorded in the next chapter — and afterwards for the remaining six.

The prominence Luke gives to the importance of households through-

69. Munck, *The Acts of the Apostles*, p. 57. However, "a committee for social services" is an anachronistic description!

70. Hill, *Hellenists and Hebrews*, p. 26. See also David Daube, *The New Testament and Rabbinic Judaism*, 2d ed. (New York: Arno, 1973), p. 237: "It was customary for the Jewish inhabitants of a Palestinian city to choose seven worthies to look after the common affairs."

out Acts[71] and the vital role played by the house church and communal Eucharistic meal in the growth of Christianity would suggest that this task was taken very seriously. The only other person of the Seven mentioned subsequently is Philip, who took on missionary work among despised Samaritans (8:5-40). Later we find he has four daughters who are all prophets (21:8-9). His work with the διακονία of tables — quite likely with his wife and daughters — no doubt prepared him for nontraditional relationships and tasks. Possibly through working with the widows and recognizing the great contributions they made to the community because of their autonomy, Philip was able to forego arranging marriages for his daughters and to encourage them to freely use their prophetic gifts for the sake of the church.

Conclusion

A number of conclusions can be drawn from this analysis of Acts 6:1-6. First, the charge that the Hellenists bring against the Hebrews concerns the daily table service (διακονία), not poor relief, and not some deeper theological problem that Luke is trying to cover up. The daily meal is a core activity of the community (2:42, 46), and the problem must be solved in the presence of the entire community.

Second, the problem must somehow concern the women who are called widows in verse 1, since women are not mentioned in androcentric literature unless they are exceptional or a problem.

Third, in a culture where meal management, preparation, and serving is a female task, it is significant that women are mentioned in this context, suggesting that the issue centers on women's administration of the meals.

Fourth, the widows are mentioned as a group. This also implies some community structure and suggests that the widows are working together on meal service. The position of a widow in that culture was ambiguous. On the one hand, she might be driven to destitution without the support of a man, but on the other, she could be free to make choices about her own life for the first time. Since part of the reason for poverty in that soci-

71. The term οἰκία ("house/household") appears 25 times in Luke and 12 times in Acts; οἶκος ("house/household") appears 34 times in Luke and 25 times in Acts. According to John Elliott, "These terms comprise family and kin, personnel and property." See his "Temple Versus Household in Luke-Acts," in *The Social World of Luke-Acts: Models for Interpretation*, ed. Jerome H. Neyrey (Peabody, Mass.: Hendrickson, 1993), pp. 211-40 (225).

ety was lack of social connections, the fact that these widows are working together suggests they are not poor but have been given tasks which help them survive and thrive in the community.

Fifth, I accept the consensus that "Hellenists" and "Hebrews" refer to linguistic differences between native Aramaic speakers (who may also know some Greek) and Diaspora Jews who know only Greek. There are no implications that the Hebrews are more conservative and law-observant while the Hellenists are more liberal. Mention of these groups, however, may point to the tensions that can arise when meals with deep symbolic meaning are eaten across class and ethnic boundaries — and when such women working and eating together have different ethnic customs surrounding meal preparation and organization.

Sixth, women's roles were more restricted than men's roles in Mediterranean culture, but they took pride in their work. Performing their duties well brought them honor in the household. It is possible that Galilean women working on meal service were receiving more honor than Hellenist women, since the former had been followers of and eyewitnesses to Jesus. It is also possible that Hebrew men were not serving Hellenist women at table; perhaps Hebrew men felt it was beneath their dignity to serve women. We cannot know the exact problem, but knowledge of the culture and situation can provide educated guesses.

Seventh, the decision-making procedure suggests a high level of organization in the young community. The description fits an Eastern-style, non-egalitarian legislative assembly, not unlike similar forms delineated in Qumran writings such as the Manual of Discipline and the Damascus Document. The level of organization does not, therefore, imply that Luke depicts the scene with models from his own community — especially since he is likely from a Greek, non-Eastern milieu.

Eighth, that men were chosen for table service could mean that they were appointed to supervise quarreling women. It is just as possible, however, that the choice is in conformity with the Gospels' portrayal of Jesus calling male leaders in his community to act as those serving others at table. The appointment was public, but the task to which they were called was in the private sphere, which probably explains why we don't hear any more about it. It does not mean that the men never served tables, nor does it mean that their task precluded preaching and teaching. Acts 6:7 denotes the passage of time, so there were probably many opportunities for table service before Stephen's martyrdom and the move outward from Jerusalem.

Chapter Fourteen

Daily Commensality:
A Necessity Then, Impractical Today?

God, when we come to share the riches of your table, we cannot forget the rawness of the earth. We cannot take bread and forget those who are hungry. Your world is one world, and we are stewards of its nourishment.

We cannot take wine and forget those who are thirsty. The ground and the rootless, the earth and its people, cry out for justice.

We cannot celebrate the feast of your family and forget our divisions. We are one in the spirit, but not in fact. History and hurt still dismember us.

Communion liturgy at LaSalle Street Church,
Chicago, Illinois, June 19, 2005

Summarizing the Thesis

In addition to exegetical analysis, I have done research in four major areas in an attempt to understand the social reality behind Luke's summary description of communal meals set in a shared community of goods in Acts 2:41-47. The first area is cross-cultural. If Luke is describing a unique situation in first-century Jerusalem, against what "normal" background does this portrayal stand? Using social-scientific criticism at various levels (both descriptive and analytical), I have created a scenario of the economic conditions, worldviews, and social/religious values belonging to these ancient Mediterranean people. This culture knew nothing of universal democracy, the rights of the individual, the theory that all people are created equal, or the workings of market capitalism. There was no middle class in the sense that we understand it today. Rather, the great majority of people were living at a subsistence level in this agrarian society, surviving by means of their kin-group network and family connections, sharing primarily through generalized reciprocity with the in-group, and treating outsiders with suspicion. In this honor/shame society with zero-sum economics, wealth was not invested to create more wealth but was meant to be shared among the in-group so that greater honor would be attributed to the patron. It was entirely natural that those living in extended households in this cultural milieu would eat together daily.

It is against this background that we must see the first Christian community, many of whom for geographical or religious reasons had to leave their kin group and re-create a new one with fellow believers. The choice was not between communism and a capitalist individualism, as so many Western interpreters unconsciously assume, but between a previous kin group defined by blood relations and a fictive kin group defined as those who follow Jesus as Messiah. The reconstitution of the fictive kin group meant physical as well as spiritual survival, since without it the lack of relationships and connections doomed first-century Mediterraneans to destitution and starvation. And as households formed, it was only natural that communal meals would be served to all who belonged to a household.

The three other areas I have explored must also be seen in light of this general cultural worldview. Chronologically, the first is the presence of Essene communities in the Jewish Mediterranean first-century culture of Palestine. Since the discovery of the Dead Sea Scrolls, it has become clear that the "idealized" descriptions of Essene communities in Josephus, Philo, and Pliny were historically actualized in these religious communities who based their economic sharing on biblical ideals and eagerly awaited the coming Messiah(s) in cultic purity. Here individual men left their former kin groups and joined themselves to a fictive kin group with whom they shared their property and possessions and with whom they ate a daily communal meal of bread and wine. The Manual of Discipline and the Damascus Document also imply the presence of such communities throughout Palestine, as well as some who practiced marriage and lived in families. The Qumran writings detail specific procedures for entering an Essene community, for dealing with property, for living with others in community, and for having daily meals.

Since the Essenes seem to have lived in this manner for approximately 150 to 200 years by the time of Jesus and were well-regarded by Jewish people as a whole, it is hard to imagine that the early Christians would not have borrowed and adapted communal and social practices for their own growing group. There are various indications in the early chapters of Acts which lead to this conclusion, as well as Semitic terms reminiscent of language in the Qumran documents. Although the Gospels are for the most part silent about the Essenes, their very silence indicates that there was not an antagonistic relationship between them and the Jesus movement as there was with the Pharisees and the Sadducees.

The second connection is with the common purse and table fellowship of Jesus and his disciples, both women and men. Some scholars have raised questions about the historicity of Jesus' meal practices as described in the Gospels. I have found it instructive to reflect on Jesus' own communal practices in light of the Mediterranean Jewish worldview described above and the fact that he also would have known about Essene communal life. As a religious leader calling disciples out of their previous kin groups, it was essential to form a new fictive kin group, and eating together was an important aspect of the cohesion of this group. However, Jesus' interpretation of purity laws resulted in more socially inclusive meal practices than are evident in most descriptions of Essene meals. This inclusive behavior modeled his proclamation of the nature of the coming kingdom of God. Continuation of this meal tradition with people from all social strata would have been a mark of the Jesus community that gathered in Jerusalem in the power and presence of Jesus' Spirit after he had physically left them. It was an integral part of their theology.

The last major focus (though the one with the most direct literary evidence) is the attested historical reality of the agape meal tradition that spread far beyond Jerusalem and was celebrated throughout the church for hundreds of years. I accept the thesis that there was only one meal tradition, where the Eucharist (also called bread-breaking or the Lord's Supper) was celebrated in the context of a communal meal at which everyone, poor and less poor, ate. Later, as the agape meal became separated from the celebration of the Eucharist in different regions, alms were given for the poor at the Eucharistic ritual, indicating the original connection with the daily communal meal where all were fed and the poor sustained. There is also evidence in the Thessalonian letters for daily communal meals years after the Jerusalem community began.

This practice of daily communal meals is also attested in Acts 6:1, where Hellenists complain against the Hebrews because their widows are being overlooked in the "daily *diakonia*." An analysis of the meaning of *diakonia* makes clear that what is in view here is a table service which includes the entire community, and not simply the care of the poor. That females are specifically mentioned in what is ordinarily male-oriented literature signifies that the problem does concern the widows and is not a smokescreen hiding some deeper ideological issue. But even if widows are involved, this does not mean that the problem is poor relief or that all widows in that society were poor. The reality was that the widow's position was ambiguous. On the one hand, many women alone could not have survived economically without a man. On the other hand, many widows would have retained their dowries *(ketubah)* and thus have had some freedom to make choices about their future.

The reference to widows as a group in a structured community like this one hints that the women in question are not as likely to be poor recipients (the text says there are no needy). The fact that they are being overlooked in the context of daily table service suggests that they were women who were helping to manage and organize the meals in various households, since meal preparation and administration was a typically female role in Mediterranean society. Possibly they were complaining about the injustice of not being served by Hebrew men at the daily meals. Or both.

Choosing seven administrators in a public gathering of the whole community indicates that the issue was very important to the entire group. This points much more clearly to the issue being the daily communal meal, the core activity of the group, rather than simple alms for the poor, which could be handled by a subcommittee. The fact that men would be working with women in a typically female role conforms to the Gospels' portrayal of Jesus as practicing and teaching the importance of table service for community leaders.

Interpreted appropriately, the text in Acts 6:1-6 confirms the existence of daily commensality in the Jerusalem community. In turn, Acts 2:42-47 provides the generalized backdrop against which the problem over the widows and the appointment of the Seven must be seen. The four factors of Mediterranean culture, Essene communal meal practice, Jesus' meal practice, and the later agape meal tradition all point clearly to Luke's description in Acts 2:42-47 and 6:1-6 as a plausibly accurate historical description of the daily communal meal practices of the early Jerusalem community.

The Value of Communal Meals Today

Anyone with historical and cultural sensitivity knows that social practices cannot be imported whole from an earlier time and place to our present modern and postmodern societies. What, for example, would parallel Jesus walking along a road, finding a man in a tree, and inviting himself to dinner — resulting in the salvation of that man through immediate economic repentance and sharing? (Luke 19:1-10). The picture of joyful, daily meals of a group of disparate people in a crowded city cannot be easily replicated when people with more opportunities and wealth keep moving into suburbs and exurbs. Even if this practice was tried with great effort, the theological meaning of those meals might change or look forced.

Nevertheless, food, meals, and eating together continue to convey strong symbolism. If theology is communicated through meals, what kind of theology is the church communicating today? Through two thousand years the church has retained a meal of sorts — a ritual or ceremony we've called Mass, the Eucharist, the Lord's Supper, or Holy Communion. It is a sacrament, an ordinance, a means of grace for the believer. It is typically interpreted as a time to privately confess one's individual sins and to reflect on Jesus' (substitutionary) death for their forgiveness. A vertical element remains, but for most the horizontal element is missing. We do not usually confess our sins to each other and reflect together on "the death of the Lord" as a self-giving act that we are to emulate. The relational aspect of a communal meal is gone, along with any attempt to eat together across social boundaries. This meal has nothing to do with feeding the poor and the less poor alike so that no one is hungry. Instead, our real meals take place (when we don't grab something on the run or at a fast-food restaurant) with family or friends or co-workers who are social equals. Church potlucks and picnics, also with social equals, are the closest we come to agape meals of the past — and how many of us view an all-you-can-eat church potluck meal as a sacrament?

Because the church as a whole has not linked its sacred meal with the need for Christians of all social classes and ethnic backgrounds to come together around food, we are geographically separated from each other more than ever. American culture pulls more strongly, and we generally live with socio-economic equals and give a tiny percentage of our income to charity. The poor remain "the other."

A supreme irony also exists in the many church groups who do not ordain women and do not allow them to share bread and wine/juice at the Table of the Lord. Women are barred from administering the so-called "sacraments" of their faith, though they are expected to prepare and serve actual food at church gatherings and soup kitchens and to show hospitality through sharing food in their homes. Yet where is the more authentic re-creation of "a supper of the Lord" — a Jesus-supper — taking place? To separate "Holy Communion" from fellowship meals by gender is to further depart from the theology of the table taught and exemplified by Jesus in his meals and his stress on the spiritual value of humble table service for men as well as women.

A lengthy study on how churches today can develop a theology and spirituality of the table is beyond the scope of this study on communal meals in Acts. A number of such resources already exist (though they rarely include gender analysis).[1] An attractive new ecumenical educational curriculum, *Just Eating? Practicing Our Faith at the Table,* has recently become available through the Presbyterian Distribution Service.[2] It discusses food and eating from a wide range of perspectives — as sacrament, as nutrition, as communal sharing — and how our eating habits relate to the environment and to world hunger. However, I want to close by citing a few examples of how some Christians today use table fellowship to enlarge their mission.[3]

1. See, for example, John Koenig, *The Feast of the World's Redemption: Eucharistic Origins and Christian Mission* (Harrisburg, Pa.: Trinity Press International, 2000); L. Shannon Jung, *Food for Life: The Spirituality and Ethics of Eating* (Minneapolis: Fortress Press, 2004); Arthur Simon, *How Much Is Enough? Hungering for God in an Affluent Culture* (Grand Rapids: Baker, 2003); and Christine D. Pohl, *Making Room: Recovering Hospitality as a Christian Tradition* (Grand Rapids: Eerdmans, 1999).

2. Jennifer Halteman Schrock, *Just Eating? Practicing Our Faith at the Table* (Advocate Health Care, Church World Service, Presbyterian Hunger Program [PCUSA], 2005).

3. These descriptions are adapted from my essay entitled "Table Fellowship: The Spirituality of Eating Together," in *Vital Christianity: Spirituality, Justice, and Christian Practice,* ed. David L. Weaver-Zercher and William H. Willimon (New York: T&T Clark, 2005), pp. 188-200.

Protestant and Orthodox Christians would be well served by considering the witness of the Catholic Worker movement. Inspired by Dorothy Day's vision of Jesus' commitment to the poor, many Catholic Worker houses in this country can be found in low-income, often multiracial areas of cities where workers live with and share meals with transient, transitional guests. The rationale for this sort of work is simple, straightforward, and biblically based. "Jesus is in the poor," says Jeremy Winder, a worker in the Casa Juan Diego Catholic Worker house in Houston, Texas. "When we serve and live with the poor, we are doing it for Jesus." Because this theological claim is rooted in Jesus' parable of the sheep and the goats in Matthew 25, this passage is often read in the worship liturgy at Casa Juan Diego.[4]

Another such house can be found in East Oakland, California, an area teeming with immigrants from Mexico and Central and South America. Begun in 1986 to provide sanctuary for refugees fleeing the violence in El Salvador and Guatemala, the house now serves as a community center and transitional shelter, welcoming guests for up to two months as they seek jobs and permanent housing. Each weekday, staff members and guests take turns preparing and serving a communal dinner. Both staff and guests share responsibility for cleaning and maintaining the household. In this way, Hispanics — especially women, who are used to serving others — come to see that there are no superior or inferior roles. Rather, everyone operates on an equal level.[5]

Although Catholic Worker programs and personnel vary from city to city, their houses invariably reflect the spirituality of eating together. For instance, the sixteen or so people who live in the Catholic Worker house in Denver, Colorado, share a common meal together every evening.[6] The Casa Juan Diego Catholic Worker house in Houston is quite a bit larger, with space for fifty men and forty women and children, but it too serves common meals once a day, with Mass once a week. Of course, in light of our study, the true supper of the Lord may actually be occurring each evening as all eat together around one table.

Intentional table fellowship is not limited to Catholic Workers. The Witmer Heights Mennonite Church, located in Lancaster County, Pennsylvania, likewise ministers through meals, though in a different way. Each

---

4. Jeremy Winder, phone conversation with author, 28 October 2003.
5. Melody Cline, phone conversation with author, 22 October 2003.
6. Sue Gomez, e-mail message to author, 20 October 2003.

Sunday a Witmer Heights member plans to be a host family, preparing a meal for unknown guests. When Miriam Eberly's Sunday comes around, she sets her table for twelve and tries her best to fill it. One Sunday her table companions included the visiting pastor and her husband; a Seventh-Day Adventist neighbor who does not attend church; a couple who recently experienced a house fire and their daughter, who resides in a community for mentally challenged adults; two government employees from Washington, D.C.; and the son of a local Presbyterian minister. Since Miriam needed one more person to fill the table, she invited a young, disabled African-American man from her church. "When we sat down to eat," she recalls, "I suddenly had a moment of anxiety about how this was going to work with such a mix of people. After the blessing and before food was passed, I asked each person to tell their name and tell us something interesting about themselves. That took care of everything! I no longer was concerned about keeping conversation going; it just happened."[7]

A few hundred miles to the south, in Harrisonburg, Virginia, an unusual restaurant called the Little Grill provides table fellowship in yet another way. A collectively owned business that focuses on healthful cuisine, the Little Grill closes for regular business each Monday in order to prepare and serve free meals to anyone who wants to come. Diners are invited to come early to help prepare food or stay late to clean up. These meals often draw a wide variety of people, from those lacking basic necessities to ordinary working people to college students and professors. Jason Wagner, one of the collective's members, delights in the variety of people who come as well as the abundance of food that seems to appear. From gardens, from unsolicited contributions, from leftovers, and from shopping with a mere thirty dollars, participants create a wonderful meal for fifty people.[8]

Ron Copeland, who with his wife originally owned the Little Grill, has now sold it to the people who work there. At first a collective in practice, it is now legally organized as a worker-owned cooperative. According to Copeland, his vision for the Little Grill is rooted in his "understanding of the Way as articulated by Jesus." Writes Copeland, "I see Christ renouncing the ideas of exclusive ownership and collecting material wealth for one's own self. In fact, the early church, as described in the book of Acts, held all possessions in common and had no destitute people among

---

7. Miriam Eberly, e-mail message to author, 20 October 2003.
8. Jason Wagner, interview with author, 31 October 2003.

them."[9] In planning to expand its table ministry beyond the table itself, the collective is now renovating a nearby building (to be called Our Community Place) that will host events aimed at attracting people from different classes and arenas of life.[10]

In 2003, Lasalle Street Church, an independent evangelical church on the near north side of Chicago, began an outreach ministry to poor and homeless people in their area called Breaking Bread. The core of this program is the hot, nutritious meal served one evening a week to seventy-five guests. Volunteers prepare and serve the food, most of which is either donated or purchased from the Greater Chicago Food Depository.[11]

What makes this radically different from a food pantry or soup kitchen is that the volunteers sit at tables and share the meal with the guests. The meal is served restaurant-style in an atmosphere of hospitality and friendship. Director Mike Post asserts, "Our volunteer training stresses this aspect of Breaking Bread as the heart of our program. We believe that this simple act of eating a meal together fosters trusting relationships and that this in turn leads to positive growth and change for both the guests and the volunteers." Of course, table fellowship of this kind limits the number of guests. Since it often happens that more people show up than can be accommodated, students at an alternative high school in the same building make sack lunches so no one goes away hungry. Breaking Bread works in conjunction with other outreach programs of Lasalle Street Church as well as with the Chicago Department of Human Services. In this way, homeless people not only receive hospitality with a meal but are connected to resources and services available to them. Some guests have also begun attending Sunday worship services.

One final example of a community with a shared, worshipful life across economic and racial divides is the Open Door Community in Atlanta, Georgia, which was begun by two Presbyterian couples. Influenced by the Catholic Worker model, members of the Open Door Community currently share living quarters in an old apartment building in what used to be a rough urban neighborhood. Through their common life and work,

9. Ron Copeland, "Why I Think the Little Grill Collective Will Work," *Our Community Place* 9 (Summer 2002): 24.

10. "OCP Building Renovations," *Our Community Place* 9 (Summer 2002): 4.

11. Information on this ministry comes from reports and other materials by Mike Post and Deanna Finley sent from Lasalle Street Church and its Breaking Bread outreach program, 1111 N. Wells Street, Suite 404, Chicago, IL 60610.

the community endeavors to "perform the Scriptures" in a contemporary urban context, seeking to incarnate the biblical text in much the way that vocalists sing musical scores. The community serves nearly 100,000 meals per year to Atlanta's homeless community. More than simply providing food, however, the community offers a variety of compassionate, humanizing services: showers, changes of clothing, telephone access, mail delivery to people without mailing addresses, and restroom facilities. Recognizing that homelessness is both a personal issue and a political one, the community also engages in various forms of public advocacy work.[12]

While drawing on the Catholic Worker model, the Open Door Community departs from it in its efforts to train committed Christian leaders from the people who come to them and who are then supported by the community. This practice has not only fostered shared leadership across lines of race and class, but also has enabled the core community to fully integrate worship into its common life.[13] This core community worships together regularly, at lunchtime twice a week and at each evening meal. On Sunday, community members celebrate the Lord's Supper around a table in the center of their circle.[14] In all these ways, this contemporary equivalent of an ancient house church mirrors the early believers' commensality in Jerusalem: gathering together across race and class, with the goal of everyone being fully and equally fed.

It is obvious that most of the above examples could not be realized without a larger vision of intentional community, which usually involves downward socio-economic mobility — Christians moving into areas of greater poverty and need. We are not likely to eat with people from different classes and backgrounds if we do not live in diverse neighborhoods. But such movement runs counter to the Great American Dream and to the growth of sprawl as new developments of large homes and gated communities move into the countryside. That, however, is a subject for another book.[15]

---

12. For a more comprehensive description of the Open Door Community, see www.opendoorcommunity.org.

13. Hannah Loring-Davis, phone conversation with author, 28 October 2003.

14. Footwashing is also considered a sacrament and is practiced regularly. See Murphy Davis, "Liturgy and Life, Sacrament and Struggle," in *A Work of Hospitality: The Open Door Reader, 1982-2002*, ed. Peter R. Gathje (Atlanta: Open Door Community, 2002), 205-11.

15. For recent theological reflections on economics and property-owning, see the collection of essays edited by William Schweiker and Charles Mathewes, *Having: Property and Possession in Religious and Social Life* (Grand Rapids: Eerdmans, 2004).

The daily meals of the Jesus movement, the continuing agape supper tradition in house churches throughout the Greco-Roman world, and the powerful example of creative, committed communities like the Open Door should challenge us to consider the racial and economic divisions that so casually and maliciously structure our lives. They should help us see the Eucharist as more than a device to nurture one's private, individual relationship with God. Luke 24:30-31 tells us that the couple who met the risen Jesus on the road to Emmaus did not recognize him until they broke bread together. We too may not recognize Jesus unless we break bread with each other until all are satisfied and none are in need.

Bibliography

Ancient Authors

Aristotle. *Nicomachean Ethics.* Translated by H. Rackham. Loeb Classical Library. London and Cambridge: Harvard University Press, 1962.

Athanasius. *De Vita Antonii; Epistulae; Regula Magistri.* Vol. 4 of *The Nicene and Post-Nicene Fathers of the Christian Church,* edited by Philip Schaff, translated by H. Ellershaw. Grand Rapids: Eerdmans, 1956.

Augustine. *De Opere Monachorum; De Sancta Virginitate.* Vol. 1 of *The Nicene and Post-Nicene Fathers of the Christian Church,* edited by Philip Schaff. Grand Rapids: Eerdmans, 1956.

Benedict. *Rule.* Vol. 2 of *The Dialogues of Gregory the Great.* Translated by Myra L. Uhlfelder. Indianapolis: Bobbs-Merrill, 1967.

Cassian, John. *Institutes* and *Conferences.* In Owen Chadwick, *John Cassian.* Cambridge: Cambridge University Press, 1968.

Chrysostom, John. *Homilies on the Acts of the Apostles and the Epistle to the Romans.* Vol. 11 of *The Nicene and Post-Nicene Fathers of the Christian Church,* edited by Philip Schaff, translated by J. Walker, R. Sheppard, and H. Browne. New York: The Christian Literature Company, 1889; Grand Rapids: Eerdmans, 1956.

————. *Homilies on the Epistles of Paul to the Corinthians.* Vol. 12 of *The Nicene and Post-Nicene Fathers of the Christian Church,* edited by Philip Schaff. Grand Rapids: Eerdmans, 1956.

Cicero. *Letters to Atticus.* 3 vols. Translated by E. O. Winstedt. Loeb Classical Library. Cambridge, Mass.: Harvard University Press, 1962.

Didache. Vol. 6 of Ancient Christian Writers series, translated by James A. Kleist. New York and Mahwah, N.J.: Paulist Press, 1948.

Epistle of Barnabas. Vol. 6 of Ancient Christian Writers series, translated by James A. Kleist. New York and Mahwah, N.J.: Paulist Press, 1948.

Euripides. *Andromache*. Edited and with an introduction and commentary by P. T. Stevens. Oxford: Clarendon Press, 1971.

Eusebius. *Ecclesiastical History: Complete and Unabridged*. Translated by C. F. Cruse. Peabody, Mass.: Hendrickson, 1998.

Hippolytus. *The Statutes of the Apostles (Canones ecclesiastici)*. Vol. 5 of *The Ante-Nicene Fathers*, edited by Alexander Roberts and James Donaldson. American reprint of the Edinburgh edition. Grand Rapids: Eerdmans, 1985.

Horace. *The Satires and Epistles of Horace*. Translated by Smith Palmer Bovie. London and Chicago: University of Chicago Press, 1959.

Iamblicus. *Life of Pythagoras*. Translated by Thomas Taylor. London: A. J. Valpe, 1818.

Ignatius. *Epistle to the Ephesians*. 2 vols. Early Christian Literature. Loeb Classical Library. Cambridge, Mass.: Harvard University Press, 1959, 1970.

Josephus. *Antiquities of the Jews; Wars of the Jews: The Works of Josephus Complete and Unabridged*. Translated by William Whiston. Peabody, Mass.: Hendrickson, 1987.

Justin. *Apology*. Vol. 6 of *The Fathers of the Church*, translated by Thomas B. Falls. Washington, D.C.: Catholic University, 1948.

Juvenal. *Juvenal and Persius; The Satires of Juvenal*. Translated by G. G. Ramsay. Loeb Classical Library. Cambridge, Mass.: Harvard University Press.

Martial. *Epigrams*. 2 vols. Translated by Walter C. A. Ker. Loeb Classical Library. London and Cambridge: Harvard University Press, 1968.

Minucius Felix. *Octavius*. Vol. 4 of *The Ante-Nicene Fathers*, edited by Alexander Roberts and James Donaldson. Grand Rapids: Eerdmans, 1956.

Philo. *Every Good Man Is Free; Hypothetica; On the Contemplative Life*, vol. 9, translated by F. H. Colson. Loeb Classical Library. London and Cambridge: Harvard University Press, 1967.

Plato. *The Symposium of Plato*. Edited by John A. Brentlinger. Translated by Suzy Q. Groden. Boston: University of Massachusetts Press, 1970.

Pliny the Elder. *Natural History*, vol. 2, translated by H. Rackham. Loeb Classical Library. London and Cambridge: Harvard University Press, 1961.

Pliny the Younger. *Letters*. 2 vols. Translated by William Melmoth and W. M. L. Hutchinson. Loeb Classical Library. London and Cambridge: Harvard University Press, 1963.

Plutarch. *Table Talk; Quaest. Conv. Sept. Sap. Conv.*, vol. 8, translated by Edwin L. Minar et al. Loeb Classical Library. Cambridge, Mass.: Harvard University Press, 1961.

Quintilian. *Declamationes,* vol. 1, translated by H. E. Butler. Loeb Classical Library. Cambridge, Mass.: Harvard University Press, 1958.

Suetonius. *Lives of the Twelve Caesars.* 2 vols. Translated by J. C. Rolfe. Loeb Classical Library. London and Cambridge: Harvard University Press, 1964.

Tertullian. *Apology; De Spectaculis.* Vol. 3 of *The Ante-Nicene Fathers,* edited by Alexander Roberts and James Donaldson. Grand Rapids: Eerdmans, 1956.

Xenophon. *Symposium.* Translated by E. C. Marchant. Loeb Classical Library. London and Cambridge: Harvard University Press, 1968.

General

Alexander, Joseph A. *The Acts of the Apostles.* New York: Scribner, Armstrong & Co., 1875. Reprint, Minneapolis: Klock & Klock Christian Publications, 1980.

Alford, Henry. "The Acts of the Apostles, the Epistles to the Romans and Corinthians." In *The Greek Testament,* vol. 2. Boston and New York: Lee & Shepard, 1872.

Ardener, Shirley, ed. *Perceiving Woman.* New York: John Wiley & Sons, 1975.

Arrington, French. *The Acts of the Apostles: Introduction and Commentary.* Peabody, Mass.: Hendrickson, 1988.

Avery, Catherine B., ed. *The New Century Classical Handbook.* New York: Appleton-Century-Crofts, Inc., 1962.

Avigad, Nahman. *Discovering Jerusalem: Recent Archeological Excavations in the Jerusalem Area.* Oxford: Blackwell, 1984.

———. "How the Wealthy Lived in Herodian Jerusalem." *Biblical Archeological Review* 2 (1967): 23-25.

Badia, Leonard F. *The Dead Sea People's Sacred Meal and Jesus' Last Supper.* Washington, D.C.: University Press of America, 1979.

Baker, Cynthia. "'Ordering the House': On the Domestication of Jewish Sexuality." Paper presented at the SBL/ASOR Annual Meeting, Chicago, November 1994.

Balch, David. *Let Wives Be Submissive: The Domestic Code in 1 Peter.* Atlanta: Scholars Press, 1981.

Banks, Robert. *Paul's Idea of Community.* Rev. ed. Peabody, Mass.: Hendrickson, 1994.

Barker, Paula Datsko. "Caritas Perckheimer: A Female Humanist Confronts the Reformation." *The Sixteenth-Century Journal* 26, no. 2 (1995): 259-72.

Barrett, C. K. *The Acts of the Apostles.* International Critical Commentary. General Editors: J. A. Emerton, C. E. B. Cranfield, and G. N. Stanton. Edinburgh: T&T Clark, 1994.

Bartchy, S. Scott. "Community of Goods in Acts: Idealization or Social Reality?"

Pages 309-18 in *The Future of Early Christianity*, edited by Birger A. Pearson. Minneapolis: Fortress Press, 1991.

———. "Table Fellowship with Jesus and the 'Lord's Meal' at Corinth." Pages 45-61 in *Increase in Learning: Essays in Honor of James G. Van Buren*, edited by Robert J. Owens Jr. and Barbara E. Hamm. Manhattan, Kans.: Manhattan Christian College Press, 1979.

Bauckham, Richard. "Jude." Page 1184 in *Harper Collins Bible Commentary*, rev. ed., edited by James L. Mays. San Francisco: HarperSanFrancisco, 2000.

———. *Jude, 2 Peter*. Word Biblical Commentary, edited by David A. Hubbard and Glenn W. Barker, no. 50. Waco: Word Books, 1983.

Bauer, Walter. *A Greek-English Lexicon of the New Testament and Other Early Christian Literature*. 2d ed. Chicago: University of Chicago Press, 1979.

Beck, Rosalie. "The Women of Acts: Foremothers of the Christian Church." Pages 297-308 in *With Steadfast Purpose: Essays on Acts in Honor of Henry Jackson Flanders Jr.*, edited by Naymond H. Keathley. Waco: Baylor University Press, 1990.

Beckwith, John. *Early Christian and Byzantine Art*. Baltimore: Penguin, 1970. Plate 2: "The Breaking of Bread."

Beebe, H. Keith. "Domestic Architecture and the New Testament." *Biblical Archeologist* 38 (1975): 89-103.

Behm, Johannes. "κλάω, κλάσις." In vol. 1 of *Theological Dictionary of the New Testament*, edited by Gerhard Kittel, translated by Geoffrey W. Bromiley. Grand Rapids: Eerdmans, 1965.

Bender, Harold S. *Conrad Grebel, c. 1498-1526: The Founder of the Swiss Brethren Sometimes Called Anabaptists*. Scottdale, Pa.: Herald Press, 1950, 1971.

Bettenson, Henry, ed. *Documents of the Christian Church*. New York and Oxford: Oxford University Press, 1943, 1967.

Beyer, Hermann Wolfgang. "διακονέω, διακονία, διάκονος." Pages 81-92 in vol. 2 of *Theological Dictionary of the New Testament*, edited by Gerhard Kittel, translated by Geoffrey W. Bromiley. Grand Rapids: Eerdmans, 1964.

Bingham, Marjorie Wall, and Susan Hill Gross. *Women in Islam in Ancient Middle East to Modern Times*. St. Louis Park, Minn.: Glenhurst Publications, 1980.

Black, Matthew. *An Aramaic Approach to the Gospels and Acts*. Oxford: Clarendon, 1954, 1967.

Blue, Bradley. "Acts and the House Church." Pages 119-222 in *The Book of Acts in Its Graeco-Roman Setting*, edited by David W. J. Gill and Conrad Gempf, vol. 2 of *The Book of Acts in Its First-Century Setting*, edited by Bruce W. Winter. Grand Rapids: Eerdmans, 1994.

———. "The House Church at Corinth and the Lord's Supper: Famine, Food Supply, and the Present Distress." *Criswell Theological Review* 5 (Spring 1991): 221-40.

Boecker, Hans Jochen. *Law and the Administration of Justice in the Old Testament and Ancient Near East.* Translated by J. Moiser. Minneapolis: Augsburg, 1980.

Borg, Marcus. *Conflict, Holiness, and Politics in the Teaching of Jesus.* Studies in the Bible and Early Christianity 5. Queenston, Ont., and Lewiston, N.Y.: Edwin Mellen Press, 1984.

Boring, M. Eugene, Klaus Berger, and Carsten Colpe. *Hellenistic Commentary to the New Testament.* Nashville: Abingdon Press, 1995.

Bormann, Lukas, Kelly Del Tredici, and Angela Standhartinger. *Religious Propaganda and Missionary Competition in the New Testament World: Essays Honoring Dieter Georgi.* Leiden, New York, and Cologne: E. J. Brill, 1994.

Boulay, Juliet de. "Women — Images of Their Nature and Destiny in Rural Greece." Pages 139-68 in *Gender and Power in Rural Greece,* edited by Jill Dubisch. Princeton, N.J.: Princeton University Press, 1986.

Bovon, François. *Luke the Theologian: Thirty-three Years of Research, 1950-1983.* Princeton Theological Monograph Series. Edited by Dikran Y. Haddidian. Translated by Ken McKinney. Allison Park, Pa.: Pickwick Press, 1987.

Brooks, James A., and Carlton L. Winbery. *Syntax of New Testament Greek.* London and Lanham, Md.: University Press of America, 1975.

Brooten, Bernadette J. "Early Christian Women and Their Cultural Context: Issues and Method in Historical Reconstruction." Pages 65-91 in *Feminist Perspectives on Biblical Scholarship,* edited by Adela Yarbro Collins. Chico, Calif.: Scholars Press, 1985.

———. "Jewish Women's History in the Roman Period: A Task for Christian Theology." *Harvard Theological Review* 79 (1986): 22-30.

———. *Women Leaders in the Ancient Synagogue.* Brown Judaic Studies 36. Edited by J. Neusner. Atlanta: Scholars Press, 1982.

Broshi, Magen. "Estimating the Population of Ancient Jerusalem." *Biblical Archeological Review* (June 1978): 10-15.

Browne, Laurence E. *Acts of the Apostles.* The Indian Church Commentaries. London: Society for Promoting Christian Knowledge; Madras, India: Diocesan, 1925.

Bruce, F. F. *The Acts of the Apostles.* Grand Rapids: Eerdmans, 1956, 1990.

Brunner, Emil. *The Christian Doctrine of the Church, Faith, and the Consummation: Dogmatics,* 3. Translated by David Cairns with T. H. L. Parker. Philadelphia: Westminster Press, 1962.

Bultmann, Rudolf. *The History of the Synoptic Tradition.* Translated by John Marsh. New York: Harper & Row, 1963.

Cadbury, Henry J. "The Summaries in Acts." Pages 392-402 in *Additional Notes to the Commentary,* vol. 5 of *The Beginnings of Christianity,* edited by Kirsopp Lake and Henry J. Cadbury. Grand Rapids: Baker, 1933, 1965.

Calvin, John. *The Acts of the Apostles: 1–13.* Translated by John W. Fraser and W. J. G. McDonald. London and Edinburgh: Oliver & Boyd, 1965.

———. *Institutes of the Christian Religion.* The Library of Christian Classics, vols. 20-21. Edited by John T. McNeill. Translated by Ford Lewis Battles. Philadelphia: Westminster Press, 1960.

Cantarella, Eva. *Pandora's Daughters: The Role and Status of Women in Greek and Roman Antiquity.* Translated by Maureen B. Fant. London and Baltimore: Johns Hopkins University Press, 1987.

Capper, Brian. "The Church as the New Covenant of Effective Economics: The Social Origins of Mutually Supportive Christian Communities." *International Journal for the Study of the Christian Church* 2 (2002): 83-102.

———. "The Palestinian Context of the Community of Goods." Pages 105-52 in *The Book of Acts in Its Palestinian Setting,* edited by Richard Bauckham, vol. 4 of *The Book of Acts in Its First-Century Setting,* edited by Bruce W. Winter. Grand Rapids: Eerdmans, 1995.

Carcopino, Jerome. *Daily Life in Ancient Rome: The People and the City at the Height of the Empire.* New Haven: Yale University Press, 1940.

Cary, M., and H. H. Sculland. *A History of Rome Down to the Reign of Constantine.* 3rd ed. London: MacMillan Education, 1979.

Case, Shirley Jackson. *The Social Triumph of the Ancient Church.* London: G. Allen & Unwin, 1934.

———. "Whither Historicism in Theology?" Pages 63-97 in *The Process of Religion,* S. Shailer Mathews festschrift, edited by M. H. Krumbine. New York: Macmillan, 1933.

Chapman, Benjamin. *New Testament Greek Notebook.* 2d ed. Grand Rapids: Baker, 1983.

Charlesworth, James H. "The Dead Sea Scrolls and the Historical Jesus." Pages 1-74 in *Jesus and the Dead Sea Scrolls,* edited by James H. Charlesworth. New York: Doubleday, 1992.

Co, Maria Anicia. "The Major Summaries in Acts." *Ephemerides Theologicae Lovanienses* 68 (April 1992): 49-85.

Cole, R. Lee. *Love-Feasts: A History of the Christian Agape.* London: Charles H. Kelly, 1916.

Collins, John N. *Diakonia: Re-interpreting the Ancient Sources.* New York and Oxford: Oxford University Press, 1990.

Colpe, Carsten. "The Oldest Jewish-Christian Community." Pages 75-102 in *Christian Beginnings: Word and Community from Jesus to Post-Apostolic Times,* edited by Jürgen Becker, translated by Annemarie S. Kidder and Reinhard Krauss. Louisville: Westminster/John Knox Press, 1993.

Conzelmann, Hans. *Acts of the Apostles.* Philadelphia: Fortress Press, 1987.

———. *Die Mitte der Zeit: Studien zur Theologie des Lukas.* Beiträge zur historischen Theologie 17. Tübingen: Mohr, 1954. ET: *The Theology of St. Luke.* New York: Harper, 1961.

Copeland, Ron. "Why I Think the Little Grill Collective Will Work." *Our Community Place* 9 (Summer 2002): 2-3.

Corley, Kathleen E. "Jesus' Table Practice: Dining with 'Tax Collectors and Sinners,' Including Women." In *SBL Seminar Papers, 1993,* 444-59. Society of Biblical Literature Seminar Papers 32. Atlanta: Scholars Press, 1993.

—————. *Private Women, Public Meals: Social Conflict in the Synoptic Tradition.* Peabody, Mass.: Hendrickson, 1993.

Crawford, Sidnie White. "Mothers, Sisters, and Elders: Titles for Women in Second Temple Jewish and Early Christian Communities." Pages 177-91 in *The Dead Sea Scrolls as Background to Postbiblical Judaism and Early Christianity.* Papers from an international conference at St. Andrews, Scotland, 2001. Edited by James R. Davila. Leiden, The Netherlands; Boston: Brill, 2003.

Crossan, John Dominic. *The Historical Jesus: The Life of a Mediterranean Jewish Peasant.* San Francisco: HarperSanFrancisco, 1991.

Crossan, John Dominic, and Jonathan Reed. *Excavating Jesus: Beneath the Stones, Behind the Texts.* San Francisco: HarperSanFrancisco, 2001.

—————. *In Search of Paul: How Jesus's Apostle Opposed Rome's Empire with God's Kingdom.* San Francisco: HarperSanFrancisco, 2004.

Crowe, Jerome. *The Acts.* New Testament Message 8. Wilmington, Del.: Michael Glazier, 1979.

Crown, Alan D., and Lena Cansdale. "Qumran: Was It an Essene Settlement?" *Biblical Archeological Review* (Sept./Oct. 1994): 25-35, 73-77.

Danker, Frederick W. *Benefactor: Epigraphic Study of a Graeco-Roman and New Testament Semantic Field.* St. Louis: Clayton Publishing House, 1982.

D'Arms, John H. "Control, Companionship, and Clientela: Some Functions of the Roman Communal Meal." *Echos du Monde Classique/Classical Views* 28, no. 3: 327-48.

—————. "Slaves at Roman Convivia." Pages 171-83 in *Dining in a Classical Context,* edited by William J. Slater. Ann Arbor: University of Michigan Press, 1991.

Daube, David. *The New Testament and Rabbinic Judaism.* Jordan Lectures, 1952. London: Athlone Press, 1956.

Davies, Stevan L. *The Revolt of the Widows: The Social World of the Apocryphal Acts.* Carbondale and Edwardsville: Southern Illinois University Press, 1980.

Davis, Murphy. "Liturgy and Life, Sacrament and Struggle." Pages 204-11 in *A Work of Hospitality: The Open Door Reader,* edited by Peter R. Gathje. Atlanta: Open Door Community, 2002.

Degenhardt, H. J. *Lukas, Evangelist der Armen, Besitz und Besitzverzicht in den lukanisch Schriften. Eine traditions- und redaktionsgeschichtliche Untersuchung.* Stuttgart: Katholisches Bibelwerk, 1965.

Dibelius, Martin. *Studies in the Acts of the Apostles.* Edited by Heinrich Greeven. Translated by M. Ling. New York: Charles Scribner's Sons, 1956.

Dombrowski, B. W. W. "היחד in 1QS and τὸ κοινόν: An Instance of Early Greek and Jewish Synthesis." *Harvard Theological Review* 59 (1966): 293-307.

Douglas, Mary. "Deciphering a Meal." In *Myth, Symbol, and Culture,* edited by Clifford Geertz. New York: W. W. Norton, 1971.

Dubisch, Jill. "Culture Enters through the Kitchen: Women, Food, and Social Boundaries in Rural Greece." Pages 195-214 in *Gender and Power in Rural Greece,* edited by Jill Dubisch. Princeton: Princeton University Press, 1986.

————, ed. *Gender and Power in Rural Greece.* Princeton: Princeton University Press, 1986.

Dunn, James D. G. "Jesus, Table-Fellowship, and Qumran." Pages 254-72 in *Jesus and the Dead Sea Scrolls,* edited by James H. Charlesworth. New York: Doubleday, 1992.

————. *Unity and Diversity in the New Testament: An Inquiry into the Character of Earliest Christianity.* Philadelphia: Trinity Press International, 1977, 1990.

Dupont, Jacques, O.S.B. *The Salvation of the Gentiles: Studies in the Acts of the Apostles.* Translated by John Keating, S.J. New York and Ramsey, N.J.: Paulist Press, 1967.

Edelstein, Gershon, and Shimon Gibson. "Ancient Jerusalem's Rural Food Basket." *Biblical Archeological Review* (July/August 1982): 46-54.

Elliott, John H. "Temple versus Household in Luke-Acts." Pages 211-40 in *The Social World of Luke-Acts: Models for Interpretation,* edited by Jerome H. Neyrey. Peabody, Mass.: Hendrickson, 1991.

————. *What Is Social-Scientific Criticism?* Minneapolis: Fortress Press, 1993.

Engels, Friedrich. *The Peasants' War in Germany.* Moscow: Foreign Languages Publishing House, 1956.

Esler, Philip Francis. *Community and Gospel in Luke-Acts: The Social and Political Motivations of Lucan Theology.* New York, Melbourne, and Cambridge: Cambridge University Press, 1987.

Falk, Z. W. *Introduction to Jewish Laws of the Second Commonwealth.* Leiden: E. J. Brill, 1978.

Feeley-Harnik, Gillian. *The Lord's Table: Eucharist and Passover in Early Christianity.* Philadelphia: University of Pennsylvania Press, 1981.

Ferguson, Everett. "Agape Meal." Pages 90-121 in *The Anchor Bible Dictionary,* vol. 1, edited by David Noel Freedman. New York: Doubleday, 1992.

Fernea, Elizabeth Warnock, ed. *Women and the Family in the Middle East: New Voices of Change.* Austin: University of Texas Press, 1985.

Finger, Reta Halteman. "Table Fellowship: The Spirituality of Eating Together." Pages 188-200 in *Vital Christianity: Spirituality, Justice, and Christian Prac-*

tice, edited by David L. Weaver-Zercher and William H. Willimon. New York: T&T Clark International, 2005.

Finley, M. I. *The Ancient Economy*. 2d edition. London: Penguin, 1985, 1992.

Firth, Raymond. *Symbols Public and Private*. Ithaca, N.Y.: Cornell University Press, 1973.

Fitzmyer, Joseph A., and Norman Golb. "Scroll Origins: An Exchange on the Qumran Hypothesis." *Christian Century*, 24-31 March 1993, pp. 326-32.

Flusser, David. "The Parable of the Unjust Steward: Jesus' Criticism of the Essenes." Pages 176-97 in *Jesus and the Dead Sea Scrolls*, edited by James H. Charlesworth. New York: Doubleday, 1992.

Foss, Pedar W. "Age, Gender, and Status Divisions at Mealtime in the Roman House: A Synopsis of the Literary Evidence" (http://www.personal.umich.edu/'pfoss/ROMARCH.html). Pages 45-56 from "Kitchens and Dining Rooms at Pompeii: The Spatial and Social Relationship of Cooking to Eating in the Roman Household." Ph.D. thesis, University of Michigan, 1994.

Fox, Robin Lane. *Pagans and Christians*. New York: Alfred A. Knopf, 1987.

Friedl, Ernestine. "The Position of Women: Appearance and Reality." Pages 42-52 in *Gender and Power in Rural Greece*, edited by Jill Dubisch. Princeton: Princeton University Press, 1986.

Friedman, Robert. "Community of Goods." Pages 658-62 in *The Mennonite Encyclopedia*, edited by C. Henry Smith et al. Scottdale, Pa.: Scottdale Publishing House, 1969, 1982.

————. "Hutterian Brethren." Pages 854-65 in *The Mennonite Encyclopedia*, edited by C. Henry Smith et al. Scottdale, Pa.: Scottdale Publshing House, 1969, 1982.

Frier, Bruce W. *Landlords and Tenants in Imperial Rome*. Princeton: Princeton University Press, 1980.

Fuller, R. H. "The Double Origin of the Eucharist." *Biblical Research* 8 (1963): 60-72.

Gardner, Jane F. *Women in Roman Law and Society*. Bloomington: Indiana University Press, 1986.

Gardner, Jane F., and Thomas Wiedemann. *The Roman Household: A Sourcebook*. London and New York: Routledge, 1991.

Garnsey, Peter, and Greg Woolf. "Patronage of the Rural Poor in the Roman World." Pages 153-70 in *Patronage in Ancient Society*, edited by Andrew Wallace-Hadrill. London and New York: Routledge, 1989.

Gasque, W. Ward. *A History of the Interpretation of the Acts of the Apostles*. Peabody, Mass.: Hendrickson, 1975, 1989.

Gaventa, Beverly. "The Peril of Modernizing Henry Joel Cadbury." Pages 7-26 in *Cadbury, Knox, and Talbert*, edited by Mikeal C. Parsons and Joseph B. Tyson. Atlanta: Scholars Press, 1992.

Gehring, Robert W. *House Church and Mission: The Importance of Household Structures in Early Christianity*. Peabody, Mass.: Hendrickson, 2004.

Gese, H. "The Origin of the Lord's Supper." Pages 117-40 in *Essays on Biblical Theology*, translated by Keith Crim. Minneapolis: Augsburg, 1981.

Goitein, S. D. *The Family*. Vol. 3 of *A Mediterranean Society: The Jewish Communities of the Arab World as Portrayed in the Documents of the Cairo Geniza*. Berkeley and Los Angeles: University of California Press, 1978.

Golb, Norman. "The Qumran-Essene Hypothesis: A Fiction of Scholarship." *Christian Century*, 9 December 1992, pp. 1138-43.

Gonzáles, Justo. *Faith and Wealth: A History of Early Christian Ideas on the Origin, Significance, and Use of Money*. San Francisco: HarperSanFrancisco, 1990.

Goodblatt, G. "The Beruriah Traditions." *Journal of Jewish Studies* 26 (1975): 83.

Goodman, Martin. *The Ruling Class of Judea*. Cambridge: Cambridge University Press, 1987.

Grant, Robert M. *Early Christianity and Society: Seven Studies*. San Francisco: Harper & Row, 1977.

Grimm, Harold J. *The Reformation Era, 1500-1600*. London: Macmillan, 1965.

Grossman, Susan. "Women and the Jerusalem Temple." Pages 15-37 in *Daughters of the King: Women and the Synagogue: A Survey of History, Halakah, and Contemporary Realities*, edited by Susan Grossman and R. Haut. Philadelphia: Jewish Publication Society, 1992.

Guthrie, Donald. *The Apostles*. Grand Rapids: Zondervan, 1975.

Haas, Peter J., ed. *Recovering the Role of Women: Power and Authority in Rabbinic Jewish Society*. Atlanta: Scholars Press, 1992.

Hackett, Horatio B. *A Commentary on the Acts of the Apostles*. Philadelphia: American Baptist Publication Society, 1882.

Haenchen, Ernst. *The Acts of the Apostles: A Commentary*. Philadelphia: Westminster Press, 1971.

———. "Das 'Wir' in der Apostelgeschichte und das Itinerar." *Zeitschrift für Theologie und Kirche* 58 (1961): 329-66.

Hands, A. R. *Charities and Social Aid in Greece and Rome*. Ithaca, N.Y.: Cornell University Press, 1968.

Henderson, Suzanne Watts. "'If Anyone Hungers . . .': An Integrated Reading of 1 Cor. 11:17-34," *New Testament Studies* 48 (2002): 195-208.

Hengel, Martin. *Acts and the History of Earliest Christianity*. Translated by John Bowden. Philadelphia: Fortress Press, 1980.

———. *Between Jesus and Paul: Studies in the Earliest History of Christianity*. Translated by John Bowden. Philadelphia: Fortress Press, 1983.

———. *The "Hellenization" of Judea in the First Century after Christ*. Translated by John Bowden. London: SCM Press; Philadelphia: Trinity Press, 1989.

————. *Property and Riches in the Early Church: Aspects of a Social History of Early Christianity.* Translated by John Bowden. London: SCM Press, 1974.

Herzfeld, Michael. "Within and Without: The Category of 'Female' in the Ethnography of Modern Greece." Pages 215-33 in *Gender and Power in Rural Greece*, edited by Jill Dubisch. Princeton: Princeton University Press, 1986.

Hill, Craig C. *Hellenists and Hebrews: Reappraising Division within the Earliest Church.* Minneapolis: Fortress, 1992.

Hock, Ronald F. *The Social Context of Paul's Ministry: Tentmaking and Apostleship.* Philadelphia: Fortress Press, 1980.

Holmberg, Bengt. *Paul and Power: The Structure of Authority in the Primitive Church as Reflected in the Pauline Epistles.* Philadelphia: Fortress Press, 1980.

Horsley, Richard. *Archeology, History, and Society in Galilee: The Social Context of Jesus and the Rabbis.* Valley Forge, Pa.: Trinity Press International, 1998.

————. *Sociology and the Jesus Movement.* New York: Crossroad, 1989.

Hsia, R. Po-Chia. *The German People and the Reformation.* Ithaca, N.Y.: Cornell University Press, 1988.

Ilan, Tal. *Jewish Women in Greco-Roman Palestine.* Peabody, Mass.: Hendrickson, 1996.

Jacobs-Malina, Diane. *Beyond Patriarchy: The Images of Family in Jesus.* New York and Mahwah, N.J.: Paulist Press, 1993.

Jeremias, Joachim. *The Eucharistic Words of Jesus.* Translated by Norman Perrin. London: SCM Press Ltd., 1966.

————. *Jerusalem in the Time of Jesus: An Investigation into the Economic and Social Conditions during the New Testament Period.* Philadelphia: Fortress Press, 1962.

Jewett, Robert. "Tenement Churches and Pauline Love Feasts." Pages 73-86 in *Paul the Apostle to America: Cultural Trends and Pauline Scholarship.* Louisville: Westminster/John Knox Press, 1994.

Johnson, Luke T. *The Acts of the Apostles.* Sacra Pagina 5. Edited by Daniel J. Harrington. Wilmington, Del.: Michael Glazier, 1992.

————. *The Literary Function of Possessions in Luke-Acts.* SBL Dissertation Series 39. Missoula, Mont.: Scholars Press, 1977.

————. *Sharing Possessions: Mandate and Symbol of Faith.* Philadelphia: Fortress Press, 1981.

Jung, L. Shannon. *Food for Life: The Spirituality and Ethics of Eating.* Minneapolis: Fortress Press, 2004.

Kautsky, Karl. *Foundations of Christianity: A Study in Christian Origins.* Translated from the 13th German edition. New York and London: Monthly Review Press, 1925.

Keathley, Naymond H., ed. *With Steadfast Purpose: Essays on Acts in Honor of Henry Jackson Flanders, Jr.* Waco: Baylor University Press, 1990.

Keating, John F. *The Agape and the Eucharist in the Early Church: Studies in the History of the Christian Love-Feasts.* London: Methuen, 1901; New York: AMS Press, 1969.

Keck, Leander. "The Poor among the Saints in Jewish Christianity and Qumran." *Zeitschrift für die neutestamentliche Wissenschaft* 57 (1966): 54-78.

Kee, Howard Clark. *Knowing the Truth: A Sociological Approach to New Testament Interpretation.* Minneapolis: Fortress Press, 1989.

————. *Medicine, Miracle, and Magic in New Testament Times.* Cambridge: Cambridge University Press, 1986.

Keller, Rosemary Skinner. "Lay Women in the Protestant Tradition." Pages 242-53 in *The Nineteenth Century,* vol. 1 of *Women and Religion in America,* edited by Rosemary Radford Ruether and Rosemary Skinner Keller. San Francisco: Harper & Row, 1981.

Keyssar, Alexander. "Reminders of Poverty, Soon Forgotten." *The Chronicle Review* of *The Chronicle of Higher Education* 52, no. 11 (4 November 2005): B6-B8.

Kittel, Gerhard, and Gerhard Friedrich, eds. *Theological Dictionary of the New Testament.* Translated by Geoffrey W. Bromiley. 10 vols. Grand Rapids: Eerdmans, 1964-1976.

Klauck, Hans-Josef. "Gütergemeinschaft in der klassischen Antike, in Qumran und im neuen Testament." *Revue de Qumran* 11 (1982): 47-79.

————. "Lord's Supper." Translated by David Ewert. Pages 362-72 in *The Anchor Bible Dictionary,* vol. 4, edited by David Noel Freedman. New York: Doubleday, 1992.

Klingelsmith, Sharon. "Women in the Mennonite Church, 1900-1930." *Mennonite Quarterly Review* 54 (July 1980): 163-207.

Klosinski, Lee E. "The Meals in Mark." Ph.D. diss., Claremont College, California, 1988.

Knowling, Richard John. *The Acts of the Apostles.* Expositor's Greek Testament. Edinburgh: n.p., 1900; Grand Rapids: Eerdmans, 1951.

Kodell, Jerome. *The Eucharist in the New Testament.* Wilmington, Del.: Michael Glazier, 1988.

Koenig, John. *The Feast of the World's Redemption: Eucharistic Origins and Christian Mission.* Harrisburg, Pa.: Trinity Press International, 2000.

————. *New Testament Hospitality: Partnership with Strangers as Promise and Mission.* Philadelphia: Fortress Press, 1985.

Koffmahn, Elisabeth. *Die Doppelurkunden aus der Wüste Juda. Recht und Praxis der jüdischen Papyri des 1. und 2. Jahrhunderts n. Chr. samt Übersetzung.* Studies on the Texts of the Desert of Judah 5. Leiden: E. J. Brill, 1968.

Kraemer, Ross S. "Autonomy, Prophecy, and Gender in Early Christianity." Pages 128-56 in *Her Share of the Blessings: Women's Religions among Pagans, Jews, and Christians in the Greco-Roman World.* New York and Oxford: Oxford University Press, 1992.

————. "The Conversion of Women to Ascetic Forms of Christianity." *Signs: Journal of Women in Culture and Society* 6 (Winter 1980): 298-307.

Kraus, Hans-Joachim. "Aktualität des 'Urchristlichen Kommunismus'?" *Freispruch und Freiheit* (1973): 306-27.

Kraybill, Donald B., and Dennis M. Sweetland. "Possessions in Luke-Acts: A Sociological Perspective." *Perspectives in Religious Studies* 10 (1983): 215-39.

Krodel, Gerhard A. *Acts.* Augsburg Commentary on the New Testament. Minneapolis: Augsburg, 1986.

————. *Acts.* Proclamation Commentaries. Philadelphia: Fortress Press, 1981.

Kuhn, Karl Georg. "The Lord's Supper and the Communal Meal at Qumran." Pages 1-17 in *The Scrolls and the New Testament,* edited by Krister Stendahl. New York: Crossroad, 1992.

Lake, Kirsopp, and Henry J. Cadbury. *The Acts of the Apostles: English Translation and Commentary.* Vol. 4 of *The Beginnings of Christianity,* edited by F. J. Foakes Jackson and Kirsopp Lake. London: n.p., 1920-33; Grand Rapids: Baker, 1965.

————. *Additional Notes to the Commentary.* Vol. 5 of *The Beginnings of Christianity,* edited by F. J. Foakes Jackson and Kirsopp Lake. London: n.p., 1920-33; Grand Rapids: Baker, 1965.

Lambert, J. C. "Agape." In *The International Standard Bible Encyclopedia,* vol. 1, edited by Geoffrey W. Bromiley. Grand Rapids: Eerdmans, 1979.

Lampe, Peter. "The Corinthian Eucharistic Dinner Party: Exegesis of a Cultural Context (1 Cor. 11:17-34)." *Affirmation* 4 (Fall 1991): 1-15.

————. *From Paul to Valentinus: Christians at Rome in the First Two Centuries.* Translated by Michael Steinhauser. Minneapolis: Fortress Press, 2003.

————. "The Roman Christians of Romans 16." Pages 216-30 in *The Romans Debate,* edited by Karl P. Donfried. Peabody, Mass.: Hendrickson, 1991.

Lamphere, Louise. "Strategies, Cooperation, and Conflict among Women in Domestic Groups." Pages 97-112 in *Women, Culture, and Society,* edited by M. S. Rosaldo and L. Lamphere. Stanford: Stanford University Press, 1974.

Lapierre, Dominique. *The City of Joy.* New York: Doubleday, 1985.

Laverdiere, Eugene. *Dining in the Kingdom of God: The Origins of the Eucharist According to Luke.* Chicago: Liturgy Training Publications, 1994.

Lechler, Gotthart Victor. *Acts.* Lange's Commentary on the Holy Scriptures 5. Translated by Philip Schaff. German edition, 1857; Grand Rapids: Zondervan, 1886.

Lefkowitz, Mary R., and Maureen B. Fant, eds. *Women's Life in Greece and Rome.* Baltimore: Johns Hopkins University Press, 1982.

Lenski, Gerhard. *Power and Privilege: A Theory of Social Stratification.* New York: McGraw-Hill, 1966.

Lenski, R. C. H. *The Interpretation of the Acts of the Apostles.* Columbus, Oh.: Wartburg Press, 1944.

Léon-Dufour, Xavier, S.J. *Sharing the Eucharistic Bread: The Witness of the New Testament.* New York: Paulist Press, 1987.

Liddell, Henry George, and Robert Scott. *A Greek-English Lexicon.* Oxford: Clarendon, 1948, 1961.

Lienhard, Joseph T. "Acts 6:1-6: A Redactional View." *Catholic Biblical Quarterly* 37 (April 1975): 228-36.

Lietzmann, Hans. *Mass and Lord's Supper: A Study in the History of Liturgy.* Translated by D. H. G. Reeve. Leiden: E. J. Brill, 1979.

Lightfoot, J. B., and J. R. Harmer, editors and translators. *The Apostolic Fathers: Greek Texts and English Translations of Their Writings.* London: Macmillan, 1891; rev. ed.: Grand Rapids: Baker, 1992.

Longenecker, Richard. Pages 205-573 in *The Gospel of John and the Acts of the Apostles.* Expositor's Bible Commentary. Zondervan: Grand Rapids, 1981.

Löning, Karl. "The Circle of Stephen and Its Mission." Pages 103-31 in *Christian Beginnings: Word and Community from Jesus to Post-Apostolic Times,* edited by Jürgen Becker, translated by Annemarie S. Kidder and Reinhard Krauss. Louisville: Westminster/John Knox Press, 1993.

Luccock, Halford E. *The Acts of the Apostles.* New York: Willett, Clark & Co., 1938.

Lüdemann, Gerd. *Early Christianity According to the Traditions in Acts: A Commentary.* Translated by John Bowden. Minneapolis: Fortress Press, 1989.

Lumby, J. Rawson. *The Acts of the Apostles.* Cambridge Bible for Schools and Colleges. Cambridge: Cambridge University Press, 1893.

Luther, Martin. "The German Mass and Order of Service." Pages 61-90 in *Liturgy and Hymns,* edited by Ulrich S. Leupold, vol. 53 of *Luther's Works,* edited by Helmut T. Lehmann. Philadelphia: Fortress Press, 1965.

———. "Ordinance of a Common Chest, Preface, 1523." Pages 159-94 in *The Christian in Society,* vol. 2, edited by Walther I. Brandt, vol. 45 of *Luther's Works,* edited by Helmut T. Lehmann. Philadelphia: Muhlenberg Press, 1963.

———. "Predigt am Mittwoch nach Pfingsten, Juni 12, 1538." Pages 428-32 in *Predigten des Jahres 1538.* Martin Luthers Werke: Kritische Gesamtausgabe 46 Band. Herman Böhlaus: Weimar Nachfolger, 1912, 1967.

Mack, Burton. *A Myth of Innocence: Mark and Christian Origins.* Philadelphia: Fortress Press, 1988.

Mackowski, Richard M. *Jerusalem, City of Jesus: An Exploration of the Traditions, Writings, and Remains of the Holy City from the Time of Christ.* Grand Rapids: Eerdmans, 1980.

MacMullen, Ramsey. *Enemies of the Roman Order: Treason, Unrest, and Alienation in the Empire.* Cambridge, Mass.: Harvard University Press, 1966.

———. *Paganism in the Roman Empire.* New Haven: Yale University Press, 1981.

———. *Roman Social Relations 50 b.c. to a.d. 284.* London and New Haven: Yale University Press, 1974.

———. "Women in Public in the Roman Empire." *Historia* 29 (1980): 208-18.

Macy, Gary. *The Banquet's Wisdom: A Short History of the Theologies of the Lord's Supper.* New York: Paulist Press, 1992.

Makhlouf, Carla. *Changing Veils: Women and Modernization in North Yemen.* London: Croom Helm, 1979.

Malina, Bruce J. "Interpreting the Bible with Anthropology: The Case of the Poor and the Rich." *Listening: Journal of Religion and Culture* 21 (1986): 148-59.

———. *The New Testament World: Insights from Cultural Anthropology.* Atlanta: John Knox Press, 1981.

Malina, Bruce J., and Jerome H. Neyrey. "Honor and Shame in Luke-Acts." Pages 25-66 in *The Social World of Luke-Acts: Models for Interpretation,* edited by Jerome H. Neyrey. Peabody, Mass.: Hendrickson, 1991.

Manzanera, M. "Koinonía en Hch 2,42. Notas sobre su interpretación y orígen histórico-doctrinal." *Estudios Eclesiasticos* 52 (July-September 1977): 307-29.

Marshall, I. Howard. *Acts of the Apostles.* Tyndale New Testament Commentaries. Grand Rapids: Eerdmans, 1980.

———. *Last Supper and Lord's Supper.* Grand Rapids: Eerdmans, 1981.

Martinez, Florentino Garcia. *The Dead Sea Scrolls Translated: The Qumran Texts in English,* 2d ed. Grand Rapids: Eerdmans, 1996.

McGee, Daniel B. "Sharing Possessions: A Study in Biblical Ethics." Pages 163-78 in *With Steadfast Purpose: Essays in Honor of Henry Jackson Flanders, Jr.,* edited by Naymond H. Keathley. Waco: Baylor University Press, 1990.

McVann, Mark. "Family-Centeredness." Pages 70-72 in *Biblical Social Values and Their Meaning: A Handbook,* edited by John J. Pilch and Bruce J. Malina. Peabody, Mass.: Hendrickson, 1993.

Metzger, Bruce M. *A Textual Commentary on the Greek New Testament.* London and New York: United Bible Societies, 1975.

Metzger, Bruce M., and Michael D. Coogan, eds. *The Oxford Companion to the Bible.* New York and Oxford: Oxford University Press, 1993.

Meyer, Heinrich August Wilhelm. *Handbook to the Acts of the Apostles.* 2d ed. Translated by Paton J. Gloag. New York: Funk & Wagnalls, 1889.

Mikhail, Mona, and G. Asfor. *Images of Arab Women: Fact and Fiction.* Washington, D.C.: Three Continents Press, 1979.

Milavec, Aaron. *The Didache: Faith, Hope, and Life of the Earliest Christian Communities, 50-70 c.e.* Mahwah, N.J.: Newman Press, 2003.

Mitchell, Alan C. "The Social Function of Friendship in Acts 2:44-47 and 4:32-37." *Journal of Biblical Literature* 111 (Summer 1992): 255-72.

Moessner, David P. *Lord of the Banquet: The Literary and Theological Significance of the Lukan Travel Narrative.* Minneapolis: Fortress Press, 1989.

Moule, C. F. D. "Once More, Who Were the Hellenists?" *Expository Times* 70 (1958-59): 100-102.

Moxnes, Halvor. *The Economy of the Kingdom: Social Conflict and Economic Relations in Luke's Gospel.* Philadelphia: Fortress Press, 1988.

————. "Meals and the New Community in Luke." Pages 158-67 in *Svensk Exegetisk Årsbok* 51-52, edited by L. Hartman. Uppsala: Uppsala exegetiska sällskap, 1986.

————. "Social Relations and Economic Interaction in Luke's Gospel: A Research Report." Pages 58-75 in *Luke-Acts: Scandinavian Perspectives,* edited by Petri Luomanen. Publications of the Finnish Exegetical Society 54. Helsinki: The Finnish Exegetical Society/Göttingen: Vandenhoeck & Ruprecht, 1991.

Munck, Johannes. *The Acts of the Apostles.* Revised by Rev. William F. Albright and C. S. Mann. Anchor Bible. Garden City, N.Y.: Doubleday, 1967.

Murphy-O'Connor, Jerome. "The Cenacle and Community: The Background of Acts 2:44-45." Pages 296-310 in *Scripture and Other Artifacts: Essays on the Bible and Archeology in Honor of Philip J. King,* edited by Michael D. Coogan, J. Cheryl Exum, and Lawrence E. Stager. Louisville: Westminster/John Knox Press, 1994.

————. "Prisca and Aquila." *Bible Review* 8 (December 1992): 49-50.

————. *St. Paul's Corinth: Texts and Archaeology.* Wilmington, Del.: Michael Glazier, 1983.

Myers, Eric, and James Strange. *Archeology, the Rabbis, and Early Christianity.* Nashville: Abingdon Press, 1981.

Nathanson, Barbara H. Geller. "Reflections on the Silent Woman of Ancient Judaism and Her Pagan Roman Counterpart." Pages 259-79 in *The Listening Heart: Essays in Wisdom and the Psalms in Honor of Roland E. Murphy,* edited by Kenneth Hoglund et al. *Journal of the Study of the Old Testament,* Supplement 58. Sheffield: JSOT Press, 1987.

Neil, William. *The Acts of the Apostles.* New Century Bible. Grand Rapids: Eerdmans, 1973.

Neusner, Jacob. *The Economics of the Mishnah.* Chicago Studies in the History of Judaism. Chicago: University of Chicago Press, 1990.

————. *From Politics to Piety: The Emergence of Pharisaic Judaism.* New York: Ktav Publishing House, 1979.

————. "Pharisaic Law in New Testament Times." *Union Seminary Quarterly Review* 26 (1971): 337.

Newsome, James D. *Greeks, Romans, Jews: Currents of Culture and Belief in the New Testament World*. Philadelphia: Trinity Press International, 1992.

Neyrey, Jerome H. "Ceremonies in Luke-Acts: The Case of Meals and Table-Fellowship." Pages 361-87 in *The Social World of Luke-Acts: Models for Interpretation*, edited by Jerome H. Neyrey. Peabody, Mass.: Hendrickson, 1991.

Nicholson, G. C. "Houses of Hospitality: 1 Cor. 11:17-34." *Colloquium: The Australian and New Zealand Theological Review* 19 (October 1986): 1-6.

North, Gary. *An Introduction to Christian Economics*. Nutley, N.J.: Craig Press, 1976.

Oakman, Douglas. "The Countryside in Luke-Acts." Pages 151-80 in *The Social World of Luke-Acts: Models for Interpretation*. Edited by Jerome H. Neyrey. Peabody, Mass.: Hendrickson, 1991.

———. *Jesus and the Economic Questions of His Day*. Studies in the Bible and Early Christianity 8. Lewiston/Queenston: Edwin Mellen Press, 1986.

Ortner, Sherry. "Is Female to Male as Nature Is to Culture?" Pages 67-87 in *Woman, Culture, and Society*, edited by Michelle Z. Rosaldo and Louise Lamphere. Stanford: Stanford University Press, 1974.

Osiek, Carolyn. "Female Slaves, Porneia, and the Limits of Obedience." Pages 255-74 in *Early Christian Families in Context: An Interdisciplinary Dialogue*, edited by David L. Balch and Carolyn Osiek. Grand Rapids: Eerdmans, 2003.

O'Toole, Robert F. "Last Supper." Pages 234-41 in *The Anchor Bible Dictionary*, vol. 4, edited by David Noel Freedman. New York: Doubleday, 1992.

Page, Thomas Ethelbert. *The Acts of the Apostles*. London and New York: Macmillan, 1895.

Parpart, Jane L., and Kathleen A. Staudt, eds. *Women and the State in Africa*. Boulder/London: Lynne Rienner Publishers, 1989.

Parsons, Mikeal C., and Joseph B. Tyson, eds. *Cadbury, Knox, and Talbert: Contributors to the Study of Acts*. Atlanta: Scholars Press, 1992.

Peristiany, J. G., ed. *Honor and Shame: The Values of Mediterranean Society*. London: Weidenfeld & Nicolson, 1965.

Perkins, Pheme. "Women in the Bible and Its World." *Interpretation* 42 (1988): 33-44.

Perrin, Norman. *Rediscovering the Teaching of Jesus*. New York: Harper & Row, 1967.

Pervo, Richard. "On Perilous Things: A Response to Beverly R. Gaventa." Pages 37-43 in *Cadbury, Knox, and Talbert*, edited by Mikeal C. Parsons and Joseph B. Tyson. Atlanta: Scholars Press, 1992.

———. *Profit with Delight: The Literary Genre of the Acts of the Apostles*. Philadelphia: Fortress Press, 1987.

Pilch, John J., and Bruce J. Malina, eds. *Biblical Social Values and Their Meaning: A Handbook*. Peabody, Mass.: Hendrickson, 1993.

Pitt-Rivers, Julian. "Pseudo-Kinship." Page 408 in *International Encyclopedia of the Social Sciences,* vol. 8, edited by D. L. Sills. New York: Macmillan, 1968.

Pixner, Bargil. "Church of the Apostles Found on Mt. Zion." *Biblical Archeology Review* 16, no. 3 (1990): 16-35, 60.

—. "The History of the 'Essene Gate' Area." *Zeitschrift des deutschen Pälastina-Vereins* 105 (1989): 96-104.

Pixner, Bargil, D. Chen, and S. Margalit. "Mount Zion: The 'Gate of the Essenes' Re-excavated." *Zeitschrift des deutschen Pälastina-Vereins* 105 (1989): 85-95 and plates 8-16.

Pohl, Christine D. *Making Room: Recovering Hospitality as a Christian Tradition.* Grand Rapids: Eerdmans, 1999.

Polhill, John B. *Acts.* The New American Commentary 26. Nashville: Broadman Press, 1992.

Portefaix, Lilian. *Sisters Rejoice: Paul's Letter to the Philippians and Luke-Acts as Received by First-Century Philippian Women.* Coniectanea Biblica New Testament Series 20. Stockholm: Almqvist & Wiksell, 1988.

Post, Mike, and Deanna Finley. "Breaking Bread: An Outreach Ministry of Lasalle Street Church." Reports and letters from Lasalle Street Church, Chicago, Illinois, 2003-2005.

Price, Robert McNair. "The Widow Traditions of Luke-Acts." Ph.D. diss., Drew University, 1993.

Quesnell, Quentin. "The Women at Luke's Supper." Pages 59-79 in *Political Issues in Luke-Acts,* edited by Richard J. Cassidy and Philip J. Scharper. Maryknoll, N.Y.: Orbis Books, 1983.

Rackham, Richard Belward. *The Acts of the Apostles.* London: Methuen, 1901; Grand Rapids: Baker, 1964.

Rausch, Thomas P. *Radical Christian Communities.* Collegeville, Minn.: Liturgical Press, 1990.

Reed, Jonathan. *Archeology and the Galilean Jesus: A Re-examination of the Evidence.* Harrisburg, Pa.: Trinity Press International, 2002.

—. "Population Numbers, Urbanization, and Economics: Galilean Archeology and the Historical Jesus." Pages 203-19 in *SBL Seminar Papers, 1994.* Society of Biblical Literature Seminar Papers 33. Atlanta: Scholars Press, 1994.

Reghair, James E. "The Gift of the Whale: Community as Steward." Master's diss., Garrett-Evangelical Theological Seminary, 2000.

Reicke, Bo. "The Constitution of the Primitive Church in the Light of Jewish Documents." Pages 143-56 in *The Scrolls and the New Testament,* edited by Krister Stendahl. New York: Crossroad, 1992.

—. *Diakonie, Festfreude und Zelos in Verbindung mit der Altchristlichen Agapenfeier.* Uppsala Universitets Årsskrift 5. Uppsala: A.-B. Lundequistska Bokhandeln, 1951.

Reimer, Ivoni Richter. *Women in the Acts of the Apostles: A Feminist Liberation Perspective.* Minneapolis: Fortress Press, 1995.

Rempel, John. *The Lord's Supper in Anabaptism: A Study in the Christology of Balthasar Hubmaier, Pilgram Marpeck, and Dirk Philips.* Scottdale, Pa.: Herald Press, 1993.

Reumann, John. *The Supper of the Lord: The New Testament, Ecumenical Dialogues, and Faith and Order on Eucharist.* Philadelphia: Fortress Press, 1985.

Rideman, Peter. *Confession of Faith: Account of Our Religion, Doctrine, and Faith.* Originally published in 1565. Rifton, N.Y.: Plough, 1950, 1970.

Riesner, Rainer. "Jesus, the Primitive Community, and the Essene Quarter of Jerusalem." Pages 198-234 in *Jesus and the Dead Sea Scrolls,* edited by James Charlesworth. New York: Doubleday, 1992.

Roberts, Colin, T. C. Skeat, and A. D. Nock. "The Guild of Zeus Hypsistos." *Harvard Theological Review* 29 (1936): 39-88.

Robinson, Olivia F. *Ancient Rome: City Planning and Administration.* London and New York: Routledge, 1992.

Rohrbaugh, Richard L. "Agrarian Society." Pages 4-7 in *Biblical Social Values and Their Meaning: A Handbook,* edited by John J. Pilch and Bruce J. Malina. Peabody, Mass.: Hendrickson, 1993.

———. "The Pre-Industrial City in Luke-Acts: Urban Social Relations." Pages 125-50 in *The Social World of Luke-Acts: Models for Interpretation,* edited by Jerome H. Neyrey. Peabody, Mass.: Hendrickson, 1991.

Ron, Zvi. "Agricultural Terraces in the Judean Mountains." *Israel Exploration Journal* 16 (1966): 33-49.

Rordorf, Willy, et al. *The Eucharist of the Early Christians.* Translated by Matthew J. O'Connell. New York: Pueblo, 1978.

Rosaldo, Michelle Z. "The Use and Abuse of Anthropology: Reflections on Feminism and Cross-Cultural Understanding." *Signs* 5 (1980): 389-417.

Rosaldo, Michelle Z., and Louise Lamphere. "Women, Culture, and Society: A Theoretical Overview." Pages 17-42 in *Woman, Culture, and Society,* edited by Michelle Z. Rosaldo and Louise Lamphere. Stanford: Stanford University Press, 1974.

Rosaldo, Michelle Z., and Louise Lamphere, eds. *Woman, Culture, and Society.* Stanford: Stanford University Press, 1974.

Safrai, S., and M. Stern, eds. *The Jewish People in the First Century: Historical Geography, Political History, Social, Cultural, and Religious Life and Institutions.* 2 vols. Philadelphia: Fortress Press; Assen: Van Gorcum, 1976-86.

Sahlins, Marshall. *Stone Age Economics.* Chicago: Aldine Publishing, 1972.

Saller, Richard. "Patronage and Friendship in Early Imperial Rome: Drawing the Distinction." Pages 49-62 in *Patronage in Ancient Society,* edited by Andrew Wallace-Hadrill. London and New York: Routledge, 1989.

————. *Personal Patronage under the Early Empire.* Cambridge: Cambridge University Press, 1982.

Sanday, Peggy Reeves. *Female Power and Male Dominance: On the Origins of Sexual Inequality.* Cambridge: Cambridge University Press, 1981.

Sanders, E. P. *Judaism: Practice and Belief, 63 BCE–66 CE.* London: SCM Press; Philadelphia: Trinity Press International, 1992.

Sawicki, Marianne. *Seeing the Lord: Resurrection and Early Christian Practices.* Minneapolis: Fortress Press, 1994.

Schaps, D. M. *Economic Rights of Women in Ancient Greece.* Edinburgh: Edinburgh University Press, 1979.

————. "The Women Least Mentioned: Etiquette and Women's Names." *Catholic Quarterly* 27 (1977): 323-30.

Schneider, Gerhard. *Die Apostelgeschichte I. Teil.* Freiburg, Basel, Vienna: Herder, 1980.

Schottroff, Luise. *Let the Oppressed Go Free: Feminist Perspectives on the New Testament.* Translated by Annemarie S. Kidder. Louisville: Westminister/John Knox, 1993.

————. *Lydia's Impatient Sisters: A Feminist Social History of Early Christianity.* Translated by Barbara and Martin Rumscheidt. Louisville: Westminster/John Knox Press, 1995.

Schramm, Gene. "Meal Customs (Jewish)." Pages 648-50 in *The Anchor Bible Dictionary,* vol. 4, ed. David Noel Freedman. New York: Doubleday, 1992.

Schrock, Jennifer Halteman. *Just Eating? Practicing Our Faith at the Table.* Advocate Health Care, Church World Service, Presbyterian Hunger Program [PCUSA], 2005.

Schürmann, Heinz. *Eine quellenkritischen Untersuchung des lukanischen Abendmahlsberichtes Lk 22:7-38. I. Der Paschamahlbericht Lk 22:(7-14) 15-18. II. Der Einsetzungsbericht Lk 22:19-20. III. Jesu Abschiedsrede Lk 22:21-38.* Neutestamentliche Abhandlungen XIX, 5; XX, 4; XX, 5. Münster: Aschendorff, 1953, 1955, 1957.

Schüssler Fiorenza, Elisabeth. *In Memory of Her: A Feminist Theological Reconstruction of Christian Origins.* New York: Crossroad, 1983.

————. *Jesus: Miriam's Child, Sophia's Prophet.* New York: Continuum, 1994.

————. "Martha and Mary: Luke 10:38-42." *Religion and Intellectual Life* 3, no. 2 (1986): 21-36.

Schweiker, William, and Charles Mathewes. *Having: Property and Possession in Religious and Social Life.* Grand Rapids: Eerdmans, 2004.

Schweizer, Eduard. *The Lord's Supper According to the New Testament.* Translated by James M. Davis. Facet Books. Philadelphia: Fortress Press, 1967.

Seccombe, David P. *Possessions and the Poor in Luke-Acts.* Linz, Austria: Studien zum Neuen Testament und Seiner Umwelt, 1982.

————. "Was There Organized Charity in Jerusalem Before the Christians?" *Journal of Theological Studies*, new series 29 (1978): 140-43.

Seim, Turid Karlsen. *The Double Message: Patterns of Gender in Luke and Acts.* Nashville: Abingdon Press, 1994.

Selvidge, Marla J. *Daughters of Jerusalem.* Scottdale, Pa.: Herald Press, 1987.

Shelton, Jo-Ann. *As the Romans Did: A Sourcebook in Roman Social History.* Oxford: Oxford University Press, 1988.

Simon, Arthur. *How Much Is Enough? Hungering for God in an Affluent Culture.* Grand Rapids: Baker, 2003.

Simons, Menno. "Reply to False Accusations." Pages 542-77 in *The Complete Writings of Menno Simons*, vol. 2, edited by John C. Wenger, translated by Leonard Verduin. Scottdale, Pa.: Herald Press, 1956.

Sjoberg, Gideon. *The Pre-Industrial City.* New York: Free Press, 1960.

Smith, Dennis E. *From Symposium to Eucharist: The Banquet in the Early Christian World.* Minneapolis: Fortress Press, 2003.

————. "Meal Customs (Greco-Roman)." Pages 650-53 in *The Anchor Bible Dictionary*, vol. 4, edited by David Noel Freedman. New York: Doubleday, 1992.

————. "Social Obligation in the Context of Communal Meals." Ph.D. diss., Harvard University, 1980.

————. "Table Fellowship and the Historical Jesus." Pages 135-62 in *Religious Propaganda and Missionary Competition in the New Testament World: Essays Honoring Dieter Georgi*, edited by Lukas Borman, Kelly del Tredici, and Angela Standhartinger. Leiden and New York: E. J. Brill, 1994.

————. "What Really Happened at Ancient Banquets? Evaluating the Evidence for Ancient Meal Practices." Presentation at the Society of Biblical Literature Annual Meeting, Washington, D.C., 21 November 1993.

Smith, Dennis E., and Hal E. Taussig. *Many Tables: The Eucharist in the New Testament and Liturgy Today.* Philadelphia: Trinity Press International, 1990.

Smith, Preserved. *The Age of the Reformation.* New York: Holt, 1920.

Smith, W. R. *Lectures on the Religion of the Semites, First Series: The Fundamental Institutions.* Edinburgh: A. & C. Black, 1889.

Snyder, Graddon F. "Love Feast." Pages 762-64 in *The Brethren Encyclopedia*. Elgin, Ill.: Brethren Press, 1983.

Soffan, Linda Usra. *The Women of the United Arab Emirates.* London: Croom Helm; New York: Barnes & Noble, 1980.

Soulen, Richard N. *Handbook of Biblical Criticism.* Atlanta: John Knox Press, 1978.

Spencer, F. Scott. "Acts and Modern Literary Approaches." Pages 381-414 in *The Book of Acts in Its Ancient Literary Setting*, edited by Bruce W. Winter and Andrew D. Clarke, vol. 1 of *The Book of Acts in Its First-Century Setting*, edited by Bruce W. Winter. Grand Rapids: Eerdmans, 1993.

————. "Neglected Widows in Acts 6:1-7." *Catholic Biblical Quarterly* 56, no. 4 (October 1994): 715-33.

Spicq, Ceslas. *Theological Lexicon of the New Testament*. Peabody, Mass.: Hendrickson, 1995.

Spitta, Friedrich. "Die urchristlichen Traditionen über Ursprung und Sinn des Abendmahls." Pages 207-337 in *Zur Geschichte und Literatur des Urchristentums* 1. Göttingen, 1893.

Stambaugh, John. *The Ancient Roman City*. Baltimore: Johns Hopkins University Press, 1988.

Stark, Rodney. "Antioch as the Social Situation for Matthew's Gospel." Pages 189-210 in *Social History of the Matthean Community: Cross-Disciplinary Approaches*, edited by David L. Balch. Minneapolis: Fortress Press, 1991.

————. *The Rise of Christianity: A Sociologist Reconsiders History*. Princeton: Princeton University Press, 1996.

Stayer, James M., Werner O. Packull, and Klaus Deppermann. "From Monogenesis to Polygenesis: The Historical Discussion of Anabaptist Origins." *Mennonite Quarterly Review* 46 (April 1975): 83-121.

Ste. Croix, G. E. M. de. *The Class Struggle in the Ancient Greek World from the Archaic Age to the Arab Conquests*. Ithaca, N.Y.: Cornell University, 1981.

Stegemann, Hartmut. *The Library of Qumran: On the Essenes, Qumran, John the Baptist, and Jesus*. Grand Rapids: Eerdmans, 1998.

Stein, S. "The Influence of Symposia Literature on the Literary Form of the Pesah Haggadah." *Journal of Jewish Studies* 8 (1984): 379-94.

Steinman, A. *Die Apostelgeschichte*. Vol. 4 of *Die Heilige Schrift des Neuen Testamentes*. Bonn: Hanstein, 1934.

Stendahl, Krister. "The Scrolls and the New Testament: An Introduction and a Perspective." Pages 1-17 in *The Scrolls and the New Testament*, edited by Krister Stendahl. New York: Crossroad, 1992.

————, ed. *The Scrolls and the New Testament*. New York: Crossroad, 1992.

Sterling, Gregory. "'Athletes of Virtue': An Analysis of the Summaries in Acts." *Journal of Biblical Literature* 113, no. 4 (1994): 679-96.

Stoffer, Dale R., ed. *The Lord's Supper: Believers Church Perspectives*. Scottdale, Pa.: Herald Press, 1997.

Stokes, G. T. *The Acts of the Apostles*. The Expositor's Bible. New York: A. C. Armstrong & Son, 1903.

Strack, Herman L., and Paul Billerbeck. *Kommentar zum Neuen Testament aus Talmud und Midrasch*. 6 vols. Munich: Beck, 1922-1961.

Strange, James F. "First-Century Galilee from Archaeology and from the Texts." Pages 39-48 in *Archaeology and the Galilee*, edited by Douglas R. Edwards and C. Thomas McCollough. Atlanta: Scholars Press, 1997.

Swidler, Leonard. *Biblical Affirmations of Women.* Philadelphia: Westminster Press, 1979.

———. *Women in Judaism: The Status of Women in Formative Judaism.* Metuchen, N.J.: Scarecrow Press, 1976.

Talbert, Charles. *Literary Patterns, Theological Themes, and the Genre of Luke-Acts.* Society of Biblical Literature Monograph Series 20. Missoula, Mont.: Scholars Press, 1974.

Tannehill, Robert. *The Narrative Unity of Luke-Acts,* vol. 2. Minneapolis: Fortress Press, 1990.

Theissen, Gerd. *Sociology of Early Palestinian Christianity.* Translated by John Bowden. Philadelphia: Fortress Press, 1978.

Thurston, Bonnie Bowman. *The Widows: A Women's Ministry in the Early Church.* Minneapolis: Fortress Press, 1989.

Torjesen, Karen Jo. *When Women Were Priests: Women's Leadership in the Early Church and the Scandal of Their Subordination in the Rise of Christianity.* San Francisco: HarperSanFrancisco, 1993.

Troeltsch, Ernst. *The Social Teaching of the Christian Churches.* Louisville: Westminster/John Knox Press, 1992. Translated by Olive Wyon from *Die Soziallehren der christlichen Kirchen und Gruppen.* Tübingen: JCB Mohr (Paul Siebeck), 1912.

VanderKam, James C. *The Dead Sea Scrolls Today.* Grand Rapids: Eerdmans, 1994.

VanderKam, James C., and Peter Flint. *The Meaning of the Dead Sea Scrolls.* San Francisco: HarperSanFrancisco, 2002.

Vazakas, A. A. "Is Acts 1–15:35 a Literal Translation from an Aramaic Original?" *Journal of Biblical Literature* 37 (1918): 105-10.

Vermes, Geza. *The Dead Sea Scrolls: Qumran in Perspective.* Rev. ed. Philadelphia: Fortress Press, 1977.

———. *The Dead Sea Scrolls in English.* 4th ed. London and New York: Penguin Books, 1995.

Via, E. Jane. "Women, the Discipleship of Service, and the Early Christian Ritual Meal in the Gospel of Luke." *St. Luke's Journal of Theology* 29 (1985): 37-60.

Wallace-Hadrill, Andrew, ed. *Patronage in Ancient Society.* London and New York: Routledge, 1989.

Walpot, Peter. *True Surrender and Christian Community of Goods.* Bright, Ont.: Community Farm of the Brethren, 1962.

Weiss, Johannes. *Earliest Christianity: A History of the Period* A.D. *30-150,* vol. 1. Translated by Frederick C. Grant. Gloucester, Mass.: Peter Smith, 1970.

Wendland, Heinz-Dietrich. *Ethik des Neuen Testaments.* Göttingen: Vandenhoeck & Ruprecht, 1970.

Whalen, Teresa. *The Authentic Doctrine of the Eucharist.* Kansas City, Mo.: Sheed & Ward, 1993.

Williams, C. S. C. *A Commentary on the Acts of the Apostles.* Peabody, Mass.: Hendrickson, 1964, 1988.

Williams, George Huntston. *The Radical Reformation.* Philadelphia: Westminster Press, 1962.

Winn, Albert C. *Acts of the Apostles.* The Interpreter's Bible. Nashville: Abingdon Press, 1954.

Winter, Bruce W. "Acts and Food Shortages." Pages 59-78 in *The Book of Acts in Its Graeco-Roman Setting,* edited by David W. J. Gill and Conrad Gempf, vol. 2 of *The Book of Acts in Its First-Century Setting,* edited by Bruce W. Winter. Grand Rapids: Eerdmans, 1994.

Wire, Antoinette Clark. "Gender Roles in a Scribal Community." Pages 87-121 in *Social History of the Matthean Community: Cross-Disciplinary Approaches,* edited by David L. Balch. Minneapolis: Fortress Press, 1991.

Witherington, Ben, III. "'Making a Meal of It': The Lord's Supper in Its First-Century Social Setting." Pages 81-113 in *The Lord's Supper: Believers Church Perspectives,* ed. Dale R. Stoffer. Scottdale, Pa.: Herald Press, 1997.

Wright, N. T. *The New Testament and the People of God.* Minneapolis: Fortress Press, 1992.

Zeller, Eduard. *The Content and Origin of the Acts of the Apostles Critically Investigated.* Edinburgh: Williams & Norgate, 1875. Translated by Joseph Dare from *Die Apostelgeschichte nach ihrem Inhalt und Ursprung kritisch untersucht.* Berlin: Habel, 1854.

Index of Names and Subjects

Index of Scripture References

322